Labour, Unions and Politics under the North Star

International Studies in Social History

General Editor: Marcel van der Linden

Published under the auspices of the International Institute of Social History, Amsterdam, this series offers transnational perspectives on labor and working-class history. For a long time, labor historians have been working within national interpretive frameworks. But interest in studies contrasting different national and regional experiences and studying cross-border interactions has been increasing in recent years. This series is designed to act as a forum for these new approaches.

For a full volume listing, please see back matter.

Labour, Unions and Politics under the North Star

The Nordic Countries, 1700–2000

Edited by

Mary Hilson, Silke Neunsinger and Iben Vyff

berghahn
NEW YORK · OXFORD
www.berghahnbooks.com

Published in 2017 by
Berghahn Books
www.berghahnbooks.com

© 2017, 2019 Mary Hilson, Silke Neunsinger and Iben Vyff
First paperback edition published in 2019

Library of Congress Cataloging-in-Publication Data
A C.I.P. cataloging record is available from the Library of Congress

British Library Cataloguing in Publication Data
A catalogue record for this book is available from the British Library

ISBN 978-1-78533-496-2 hardback
ISBN 978-1-78920-081-2 paperback
ISBN 978-1-78533-497-9 ebook

This book is dedicated to the memory of Klaus Misgeld (1940–2015)

CONTENTS

ILLUSTRATIONS

TABLES AND MAPS

ACKNOWLEDGEMENTS

When Marcel van der Linden invited us to edit a volume on Scandinavian labour history, it was an offer that we could not refuse. We convinced him that Iceland should be included in this volume in order to add a truly Nordic perspective.

As editors of this book, we are indebted to a number of people and organizations for their support. Arbetarrörelsens arkiv och bibliotek in Sweden (ARAB) has supported this project from the start, not only economically but also in enabling us to meet and discuss the outline and content of this book. One of the early meetings took place at the International Institute of Social History in Amsterdam, which generously lent us an office. And in August 2013 many of the authors met at ARAB for a workshop to discuss the chapters. Many thanks to Håkan Blomqvist for his comments on some of the chapters during the workshop and to Ana Duran from ARAB, who organized all the practical details. We are also grateful to Lars Gogman for his work with the illustrations in this book and to Jonas Söderqvist for making the index. We would like to thank colleagues at ARAB; the Department of Scandinavian Studies, UCL, and the School of Culture and Society, Aarhus University, for providing a stimulating and supportive research environment during work on this book.

We are also grateful to Tapio Bergholm, Anette Eklund-Hansen, Martin Grass, Solveig Halvorsen, Knut Kjeldstadli, Pirjo Markkola and Klaus Misgeld for discussions about the content of this collection and especially the introduction.

Klaus Misgeld, former director of research at ARAB, passed away in October 2015 and never saw the final version of this book. From the beginning of his career he emphasized the importance of international perspectives, which also included a Nordic perspective on labour history. His own work and his ways of encouraging other scholars have been a great inspiration to us. Klaus's initiatives to bring together labour historians from the different Nordic countries and to establish and maintain networks has been hard work that has shown fruitful results. Amongst other things, he arranged the Nordic labour history conference in 2004 in Runö, Sweden. We dedicate this book to his memory.

Aarhus, Copenhagen and Stockholm, November 2016

ABBREVIATIONS

ABA	Arbejderbevægelsens Bibliotek og Arkiv (Denmark)
AMS	Arbetsmarknadsstyrelsen (labour market board, Sweden)
ARAB	Arbetarrörelsens Arkiv och Bibliotek (Sweden)
ARBARK	Arbeiderbevegelsens Arkiv og Bibliotek (Norway)
ASÍ	Alþýðusamband Íslands (Trade union confederation of Iceland)
Comintern	Communist (Third) International
CPSU	Communist Party of the Soviet Union
CSA	Centralförbundet för Socialt Arbete (National Association of Social Work, Sweden)
DfnA	De forenede norske Arbeidersamfund (The United Norwegian Workers' Society)
DIIS	Danish Institute for International Studies
DKP	Danmarks Kommunistiske Parti (Danish Communist party)
DNA	Det norske Arbeiderpartiet (Norwegian Labour Party)
ECCI	Executive Committee of the Comintern
ED	Kansallinen edistyspuolue (The National Progressive Party, Finland)
EKP	Eestimaa Kommunistlik Partei (Estonian Communist Party)
IALHI	International Association of Labour History Institutions
IFTU	International Federation of Trade Unions
ILO	International Labour Organization

ILS	International Lenin School
IPAC	International Propaganda and Action Committee of Transport Workers
ISH	International of Seaman and Harbour Workers
ITF	International Federation of Transport Workers
ITUCNW	International Trade Union Committee of Negro Workers
KOPA/BOPA	Kommunistiske/Borgerlige Partisaner (Denmark)
KPD	Kommunistische Partei Deutschlands (German Communist Party)
KFÍ	Kommúnistaflokkur Íslands (Icelandic Communist Party)
LO	Landsorganisationen i Danmark (Danish trade union confederation, earlier De samvirkende fagforbund)
LO	Landsorganisasjon i Norge (Norwegian trade union confederation, earlier Arbeidernes faglige Landsorganisasjon)
LO	Landsorganisationen (Swedish trade union confederation)
LSI	Labour and Socialist International
Metall	Metallindustriarbetareförbundet (Swedish national metalworkers' union)
MPS	Moscow Party School
NKP	Norges Kommunistiske Parti (Norwegian Communist party)
NKVD	People's Commissariat for Internal Affairs
OMS	Otdel mezhdunarodnoi svyazi (Liaison organisation of the Comintern)
PET	Politiets Efterretningstjeneste (Danish Security and Intelligence Service)
RILU	Red International of Labour Unions
SAF	Svenska Arbetsgivareföreningen (Swedish employers' federation)
SAJ	Suomen Ammattijärjestö (Finnish Federation of Trade Unions)

SAK	Statens arbetsmarknadskommission (Swedish labour market authority)
SAK	Suomen Ammattiliitojen Keskusjärjestö (The Central Organisation of Finnish Trade Unions)
SAMAK	Committee for Nordic labour movement cooperation
SAP	Sveriges Socialdemokratiska Arbetareparti (Swedish Social Democratic Party)
SDF	Socialdemokratisk Forbund (Danish Social Democratic Party)
SDP	Suomen Sosialidemokraattinen Puolue (Finnish Social Democratic Party)
SF	Socialistisk Folkeparti (Socialist People's Party, Denmark)
SFAH	Selskabet til Forskning i Arbejderbevægelsens Historie (Danish labour history society)
SFP	Svenska Folkpartiet (Swedish People's Party, Finland)
SKP	Sveriges Kommunistiska Parti (Swedish Communist Party)
SPD	Sozialdemokratische Partei Deutschlands (German Social Democratic party)
STK	Suomen Työnantajain Keskusliitto (Finnish Employers' federation)
TA	Työväen Arkisto (Labour archives, Finland)
WEB	Western European Bureau of the Comintern

Labour, Unions and Politics in the Nordic Countries, c. 1700–2000

Introduction

Mary Hilson, Silke Neunsinger, Iben Vyff
and Ragnheiður Kristjánsdóttir

The title of this book refers to Väinö Linna's trilogy *Täällä pohjantähden alla* ('Here under the North Star' 1959–62). An undisputed classic of Nordic literature – it was voted the most significant twentieth-century Finnish novel in a 1997 survey – the trilogy is, however, much less well known outside Finland, and an English translation appeared only in 2001–2003.[1] The translator, Richard Impola, described the first novel as an 'epic of work'; a story of how 'wilderness is turned into productive land' through the sheer bodily efforts of the main protagonist, Jussi.[2] Linna's ambitions were greater than this however, and the novels were set against the background of the immense social, political and economic changes of the period from the 1880s to the 1950s. Focusing on the lives of one tenant farming family and the village community in which they live, the trilogy takes the reader through the events of the 1905 revolution, the 1918 civil war and post-war reconciliation, up to the Winter and Continuity Wars of 1939–1944. It explores such themes as the tension between landowners and tenant farmers and the political struggles before and after independence and the civil war.

As a writer who gave the Finnish people a voice, a face and an historical significance – taking the everyday experiences of ordinary people as a point of departure – Linna's writing became very important for the identity of the Finnish people and the conception of history in post-war Finland.[3] Linna had no higher education and for several years after the turning point in his literary career, which came with the success of *Under the North Star*, he worked in a textile mill during the day and wrote during the night.[4] He is an example of a writer who wrote about the environment in which he was embedded. In the same vein, the Icelandic worker Tryggvi Emilsson (1902–1993) wrote a very well received and critically acclaimed autobiographical trilogy (*Fátækt fólk*, *Baráttan um brauðið* and *Fyrir sunnan*). Published in the 1970s, it follows Tryggvi from the farm where he was raised in poverty at the beginning of the twentieth century, to the growing town of Akureyri in the north of Iceland and eventually to Reykjavík where Tryggvi was active in working-class politics.[5]

Many of the themes described in these novels about the lives of working-class people are explored in the different contributions to this volume. Through the examples presented in this book, we seek to contribute to debates about a new global labour history that takes class, gender, ethnicity and race into account and that does not limit its narrative by national borders or confine it to the historical period of industrialization.[6] We have sought to include contributions representing all five Nordic countries and to cover the history of work and the history of workers' organizing. In the hope that this book might also stimulate further Nordic discussions on labour history and its future, we also seek to explore the implications of shared histories and the attempts to create transnational spaces.[7] The selection can never be representative in every sense and there are a number of issues that we do not address, including the history of everyday working-class life, the history of consumption, the history of working-class culture and – with the exception of the chapter on forestry workers – the history of certain occupations typical for the region, such as fisherman, sailors and agricultural workers.[8] These choices are influenced by available research and by trends in labour history outside the Nordic region. Moreover, although most of the contributions in this volume are written by historians and economic historians, it should also be noted that ethnologists, historians of ideas, feminist researchers, political scientists and sociologists have made important contributions to the field of labour history in the Nordic countries and that these in turn have created specific research traditions.

This introductory chapter presents an historical survey of the political history of the Nordic countries, focusing on their shared labour histories, which is intended to give the necessary context for the contributions in this volume. We have organized our summary in terms of five periods: 1) the 'classic' period of labour movement mobilization during the era of industrialization from 1860; 2) the reform or revolution debates during and after the First World War; 3) the Great Depression and the 1930s; 4) the period of social democratic hegemony after 1945; and 5) the period since the early 1970s. This is followed by a short account of the development of the oldest existing labour history archives in the world, since the availability of sources has structured the ways in which labour history has been written in the Nordic region. We then examine some of the most important historiographical currents in Nordic labour history and end with a short presentation of the contributions to this volume.

It should be noted that not only the level of interest in labour history but also the number of historians in general has varied between the Nordic countries. The content of what has been defined as labour history has of course varied in different contexts, but in the Nordic languages the term 'labour history' *(arbeiderhistorie; arbejderhistorie; arbetarhistoria; työväenhistoria; verkalýðssaga)* includes both the history of work and the history of the working classes and their institutions and organizations. Since the 1980s, labour historians have sometimes described labour history as being in decline, but this book shows rather the opposite.[9] One of the current challenges for the field is the need to broaden concepts of work to include free and unfree labour, paid and unpaid work. The broadening of concepts in this way can lead to more imprecise definitions, but exposing labour history to longer time frames and transnational perspectives can also make our results more reliable and help to deepen our analysis. Most of the chapters in this volume do indeed refer to the 'classic' period of labour history, namely the era of industrialization c.1870–c.1930, but we have also included contributions from earlier periods until the turn of the millennium.[10] Some of the chapters deal with specific countries or regions; others adopt a Nordic perspective, or seek to place the Nordic examples in a wider transnational context.

The history of Sweden has sometimes been presented and understood as synonymous with the history of social democracy. The political dominance of Sveriges Socialdemokratiska Arbetareparti (Social Democratic Party, SAP), which was in government 1932–76, cannot be denied, but this has also implied the marginalization of other political movements on the Left within the historiography, including, for example, the history of communism and its meaning for individuals and movements. In contrast, communism has been more thoroughly researched in the other Nordic countries.[11] Even if we want to understand Nordic labour history as the shared histories of the Nordic labour movements, we need to take the splits between political parties into account, as they have affected not only domestic and foreign politics but also relations to the institutions of international socialism.[12]

In addition to taking stock of the dominant directions in Nordic labour history, as well as its blind spots, we also want to focus on another common trend in labour history in the Nordic countries and in general. Despite the fact that a number of studies have been carried out on women and work and women in labour movement organizations, from most of the literature a particular worker emerges: white, male and employed in industry.[13] This dominant, albeit often implicit, understanding has resulted in an under-representation of specific groups of workers outside industry and for a long time has consolidated the importance of a division between productive and reproductive work. Feminist critique has pointed to the fact that productive work is not possible without reproductive work.[14] However, understandings of the spaces in which work takes place have changed in recent years, just as the boundaries of work and the nature of work itself has changed. Definitions of what is work, who is a worker and how workers and work are connected through local, national and global developments have challenged the focus on the national institutions of the labour movement and also the male industrial worker as the main character in this narrative. These issues are also relevant for historians, as the contributions to this volume by Malin Nilsson and Helle Stenum illustrate.[15] The figure of the worker has evolved in tandem with changes in the labour market and the political landscape, where, in echoes of the decade before the Second World War, different political parties now claim to represent the workers.[16]

Labour Histories of the Nordic Countries during Industrialization

Scholars have acknowledged the shared histories that have shaped the development of Norden as a distinctive 'historical region'.[17] These shared histories produced several common historical features that are relevant to our discussion of labour history, including the dominance of the Lutheran faith, the absence of feudalism or serfdom and traditions of local self-government within a strong and centralized state.[18] David Kirby distinguishes a number of 'Nordic' characteristics in the labour movements of northern Europe.[19] These include the absence of a reactionary land-owning class and a strong political culture of participation and representation, which meant that the mobilization of ordinary people in popular movements was tolerated. The emergence of the Nordic labour movements has often been understood within the context of the general mobilization of popular movements (*folkebevægelser, kansanliikkeet, folkebevegelser, folkrörelser, félagshreyfingar*) in the nineteenth century, including the free churches, temperance societies, adult education organizations and cooperative societies.[20]

An example of this can be seen in Iceland, where the first labour newspapers in Iceland predated the founding of a political party in 1916.[21] Published at the beginning of the twentieth century, these papers provided a forum for discussions concerning the social and political situation of the urban poor. Their publishers and contributors stood on the border between two worlds. On the one hand there was the old rural society, in which the urban poor were considered outcasts, a kind of cancerous disease. Clearly the labourers contributing to these newspapers felt that they were marginal, but wished that they could be of real use to their nation. But on the other hand, and alongside rural views and values, one may discern a still obscure idea of a modern society, where workers demand recognition as fully fledged members of the nation. This demand did not appear in the guise of Marxist ideas about the redefinition of power relations within society, but rather in an attempt to expand the definition of who really belonged to the nation, so that it also included workers. In the newspapers, an attempt is made to appropriate the characteristically positive image of the farmer and apply it to the worker. Another manifestation of this was the use of the term *alþýða* – meaning 'people' or 'the common people', equivalent to *folk* in the Scandinavian languages – to describe the workers' identity rather than *verkamaður*, 'worker', or *verkalýður*, 'proletariat'. In due course, when a political party and national organization of unions were founded in 1916, these features influenced the way in which the movement defined its objectives and role. The political discourse of the social democrats was, right from the beginning, embedded with claims that workers be recognized as a homogeneous group that not only played an important role in society, but were really the core of the nation and thus had a right to demand that the state secure them the possibility of leading a decent life. The name chosen for the party was Alþýðuflokkur (the party of the common people), not the labour or social democratic party as was common practice in Europe at the time.[22]

Kirby also notes – as have many other scholars – the distinctively rural character of the Nordic labour movements and the absence of a large urban, industrial working class.[23] Despite the long international depression, which lasted until about the mid 1890s, the Nordic economies grew rapidly after 1870. This was largely in response to international demand for the products of their primary and extractive industries: processed agricultural products such as butter and meat; fish; timber, pulp and paper; iron and metal products.[24] The largest individual sector was the household sector, but other industries such as textile production, shipbuilding and seafaring were also important. However, although an urban working class began to emerge in industrial centres like Tampere,

Bergen, Norrköping and the capitals, it was still outnumbered by the rural population until well into the twentieth century.[25] As Kirby writes, one of the remarkable features of the late nineteenth-century Nordic countries was that there was little or no fear of a mass degenerate and potentially revolutionary slum population comparable to that found in the large metropolises of countries such as Britain, France and Germany.[26] One possible reason for this was the relatively high rates of emigration from rural districts in Sweden and especially Norway, though it was lower in Denmark and Finland.[27]

Nonetheless, this did not preclude the possibility of labour market conflicts, which took place as a consequence of industrialization across the region, in industries such as timber, paper and pulp, mining and ore processing, hydroelectric power, engineering, electro chemicals and electrometallurgy. One particularly significant conflict was that between joiners (*snedkere*) and their employers in Denmark in 1899, which resulted in the so-called September Agreement between the national employers and trade union federations, which was to set the rules of labour market bargaining.[28] In Sweden there were conflicts in the engineering sector in 1903 and 1905 followed by a general strike in 1909, while in Norway there was a major conflict in the paper industry in 1907, but the same year also saw the first nationwide industrial agreement between workers and their employers in the metal industry.[29] Finland had symbolically important strikes by building workers in 1896 and at the Voikkaa paper mill in 1904, and Finnish workers participated in the general strike that took place across the Russian Empire in 1905, but these strikes were less significant in shaping Finnish industrial relations.[30] Iceland had no collective bargaining during the first half of the twentieth century and did not experience any general strike.[31]

Another peculiarly Nordic feature was the relatively large number of women responsible for earning their own income.[32] Among other reasons, this was because the Nordic countries lacked a large upper class that could afford to keep their daughters and wives at home, which led early on to high rates of women's labour market participation.[33] From the late nineteenth century, women started to organize women's unions and women's committees in political parties, using journals and events such as International Women's Day or congresses to exchange information across national boundaries. Finnish women were the first in Europe to gain suffrage in 1906 and in doing so attracted the attention of women campaigning for suffrage reform elsewhere.[34] The experiences of the first social democratic women elected to the Finnish Parliament in 1907, as well as those in Denmark after 1915, were important for women's mobilization in the Nordic countries and beyond, as were the experiences of the first female ministers, Miina Sillanpää in Finland and Nina Bang in Denmark. Clara Zetkin also played an important part in spreading information about women in the Nordic labour movements, through reports published in her journal *Die Gleichheit* and the exchange of socialist women's journals all over Europe.[35] The second international socialist women's conference was held in Copenhagen in 1910.[36] However, these international connections also created domestic problems regarding suffrage. According to the decisions of the international socialist women's congress held in Stuttgart in 1907, socialist women should only work together with organizations that demanded universal suffrage for men and women independent of income. For some years, for example, Swedish social democratic women were not able to form alliances with other women's organizations in Sweden due to this decision.[37]

The Nordic labour movements emerged against the background of democratization, but the achievement of political rights did not take place evenly across the region. As Nils Elvander noted, the Danish labour movement was a Nordic pioneer in its willingness to collaborate with the forces of bourgeois liberalism, following the new constitution of 1849, which gave most adult males the vote.[38] After the establishment of parliamentarianism in 1901, a faction broke away from the agrarian liberals to form a new party, Radikale Venstre (usually translated as Social Liberals), which collaborated with the social democrats.[39] In Norway, there was some electoral cooperation between Det Norske Arbeiderpartiet (the Norwegian Labour Party, DNA, founded 1887) and the liberal party Venstre during the 1890s, but this ceased after the introduction of universal male suffrage in 1898 and the end of the Swedish-Norwegian union in 1905, as Venstre moved to a more explicitly anti-socialist position.[40] The union crisis was also politically significant in Sweden, where leaders of the social democratic movement were imprisoned for their anti-nationalist propaganda.[41] In Sweden, the road to democracy was longer and more turbulent than in the rest of Scandinavia, though here too there was cooperation between social democrats and bourgeois liberals, especially at the local level.[42] In Finland, Sosialidemokraattinen puolue (the Social Democratic Party, SDP) benefited from the introduction of universal male and female suffrage in 1906 to become the most successful labour party in Europe, measured by its parliamentary seats, and despite its Kautskyist programme it was committed to parliamentary democracy.[43] The weakest of the Nordic social democratic parties, nationally as well as internationally, was the Icelandic one. Founded as late as 1916, at the same time as the trade union federation, it never gained momentum similar to that in the other Nordic countries. After the Second World War, and more or less throughout the twentieth century, the relatively strong Communist and later Socialist Party left the social democrats as the smallest of the four main political parties in Iceland.[44]

It is possible, therefore, to speak of a shared Nordic labour history from the very beginning of what has been regarded as the classical period of organizing. This can be attributed to the migration of workers within the Nordic region, to regional connections between workers' organizations and to common international influences, mainly from Germany. Martin Grass has divided so-called 'workers' Scandinavianism' *(arbetarskandinavism)* – a form of regional internationalism – into three phases: the first during the mobilization of workers, the second from the start of regular Scandinavian worker congresses in 1886 and the third from 1912, when the decision was made to establish a permanent collaboration committee.[45] We could also add a fourth with the foundation of SAMAK (the Nordic cooperation committee of the labour movement) in 1932, at a time when social democratic politicians were entering government.[46]

During the second half of the nineteenth century, many artisans travelled within the Nordic region as well as to Germany, and this network remained important even after the guilds were gone, at least until the beginning of the First World War.[47] More than a century before the construction of the Öresund Bridge, inter-Scandinavian labour markets were operating between Copenhagen and the Skåne region in southern Sweden, as well as between Bohuslän on the Swedish west coast and the south-eastern parts of Norway. Finnish apprentices working in various crafts and skilled occupations also travelled to the Scandinavian countries and beyond.[48] According to Bernt Schiller, an analysis of the collections of workers' memories at the Danish National Museum indicated that 41 per cent of the workers born between 1855 and 1890 had worked abroad at some point in their lives, which, although it might not be a representative sample, does indicate the mobility of workers at that time. Schiller also points out how the fear of foreign strike-breakers connected Scandinavian workers not only with each other but also to developments in Germany. He suggests that the Copenhagen hatmakers' union was originally founded in 1872 as a branch of a German union, while in turn Copenhagen workers helped to organize a cork-cutters' union in Malmö.[49] Women domestic workers also migrated to work within Scandinavia, the Netherlands and the United States.[50]

Cooperation between nascent labour movements was initially established through individual contacts. August Palm, traditionally regarded as the first Swedish socialist agitator, had been active in Germany and Denmark; influential in the early Norwegian labour movement were the Danish-born activists Marius Jantzen, Sophus Pihl, Carl Jeppesen and the Swede O.J. Ljungdahl.[51] Palm also travelled to the United States and agitated among Scandinavian immigrants there.[52] Icelandic workers encountered labour politics and socialism as migrant workers in Denmark or while working alongside Scandinavian workers in Iceland. The Icelandic labour pioneer Pétur G. Guðmundsson claimed to have first heard about labour politics from Norwegians working in the whaling industry in the eastern fjords. Reading whatever he could find about international labour and socialist politics, he went on to establish correspondence with influential leaders such as Hjalmar Branting in Sweden and August Bebel in Germany.[53] In Finland, too, first connections often depended on personal encounters. The Finnish furniture manufacturer Viktor Julius von Wright discovered the German labour movement while working in Nuremberg and Leipzig and later came into contact with Arbejderforeningen af 1860 (the worker's association of 1860) in Copenhagen, which inspired the foundation of a similar association in Helsinki.[54] Von Wright also wrote a report on the Norwegian and Swedish labour movements after a month long visit. In 1899 the leader of the Swedish Social Democratic party, Hjalmar Branting, attended the founding congress of Suomen Työväenpuolue (the Finnish Labour Party (the Finnish Labour Party, from 1903 the Finnish Social Democratic Party, SDP).[55]

Denmark was the Nordic representative at the First International and was the first country in the region to found a section of the International Workers' Association, in October 1871.[56] Variations in economic development in the Scandinavian countries led to different paces of organization. The economic recession of the 1870s hit Sweden and Norway more severely than it did Denmark and, according to Bernt Schiller, this temporarily halted developments until the 1880s.[57] A second phase in the development of Nordic labour cooperation can be discerned from the 1880s, when workers' Scandinavianism became more organized. This can be seen as part of what Ruth Hemstad has called an 'Indian summer' of transnational Nordic cooperation, which emerged following the defeat of pan-Scandinavianism in 1864, though it also reflects the broader tradition of internationalism within the labour movement.[58] Cooperation between different unions resulted in a Scandinavian labour congress in Gothenburg in 1886. The congress discussed trade union issues such as strikes but also the political role of trade unions. The idea was to create a common platform among the three Scandinavian labour movements, with a focus on union issues.[59]

Despite the fact that internationalism was generally understood as an expression of the sum of national units – inter-nationalism, as Kevin Callahan has described it for the Second International – early attempts at practical internationalism meant creating a transnational space in the

Scandinavian context.[60] Solveig Halvorsen has shown that for a short period of time the early labour congresses were in favour of organizing pan-Scandinavian unions. A resolution on this was first debated in 1886 and passed in 1890. Among the seven Scandinavian unions proposed were those for tanners, cork-cutters, basket makers, saddlers and upholsterers, stonemasons, seamen and stokers and tobacco workers. Most of these were short-lived but the saddlers and upholsterers' union survived until 1941.[61] The example of the Scandinavian stonemasons' union shows how strikes and solidarity with striking workers could be organized transnationally across the Scandinavian region.[62] Employers also began to move production to neighbouring countries, and as Grass notes, discussions of the 1912 cooperation committee were motivated partly by the experience of 'employers' Scandinavianism' across the region in the years 1909–1911.[63] However, the vision of pan-Scandinavian unions was never properly realized, as none of these unions could exist until they had representatives in each of the three Scandinavian countries. In 1897, therefore, the decision of the Scandinavian workers' congress was revised and it was decided that only national unions and federations should be formed. Soon after, national union federations were established: Denmark (De samvirkende fagforbund; from 1960 Landsorganisationen i Danmark, LO) and Sweden (Landsorganisationen, LO) in 1898 and Norway in 1899 (Arbeidernes faglige Landsorganisasjon i Norge, LO); Finland followed in 1907 (Suomen Ammattijärjestö, SAJ) and Iceland in 1916 (Alþýðusamband Íslands, ASÍ).[64]

The third phase of Nordic labour cooperation started during the 1912 Scandinavian workers' congress in Stockholm when a decision was made to establish a permanent committee for cooperation between the Nordic labour movements: Kommittén för skandinaviska arbetarrörelsens samarbete. Similarly to the workers' congresses, both unions and parties were represented in the committee. The committee gave recommendations that could be rejected or accepted by the national organizations and it worked like the other Internationals, although on a more limited regional level. Because of its political orientation, the leadership of the Finnish SDP, at that time dominated by Kautsky supporters, declined to participate in cooperation under such elaborate organizational forms.[65] The committee was criticized for being a meeting place for the leaders only and no longer representing the workers, while the Finnish representatives regarded it as a Scandinavian section of the Second International and stated that the interests of the Finnish movement lay elsewhere; for example, in maintaining contacts with the labour movement in Russia. Despite this, the Finnish movement stayed in touch with the committee.[66]

Between Reform and Revolution

The Nordic societies were profoundly shaken by the revolutionary currents of the early twentieth century. One of the central debates of Nordic labour history has been the need to explain variations in support for revolutionary politics across the region; in particular why there was apparently greater support for radicalism in Norway (where the majority of DNA voted to join the Comintern in 1919) and in Finland (where an attempted revolutionary coup d'état in January 1918 sparked a full blown civil war) than there was in either Denmark or Sweden. Similarly, until well into the twentieth century there were few indications that Iceland would be fertile ground for revolutionary politics. Most people seemed rather conservative and prudent in their outlook, and there was no history of contentious political struggles. The later strength of communism, imported to Iceland by students and intellectuals, has been explained in a recent study by its strong political identity as opposed to the weak political identity of the social democrats and in particular the party's efficient use of a combination of communist and nationalist discourses.[67]

As Einar Terjesen discusses in his contribution to this volume, one of the earliest and most influential interventions in the debate about Norwegian radicalism came in an article by the Norwegian social democrat and historian Edvard Bull, first published in 1922.[68] According to Bull, the radical left wing of the labour movement was strongest in Norway and relatively weak in Denmark, with Sweden adopting a middle path. These differences were attributable to three reasons: the suddenness and rapidity of Norwegian industrialization, compared to more gradual developments in Denmark and Sweden; the greater decentralization of the Norwegian labour movement and its failure to form coalitions with the liberal parties; and the influence of personalities: the Norwegian party was much more open to the theoretical influences of academics, compared to its more empirical Swedish and Danish counterparts.[69] Subsequent studies have refined and qualified Bull's thesis.[70] But most scholars have been at pains to emphasize the anomalous and atypical nature of the revolutionary outbursts in Norway and the other Scandinavian countries, which also explains why they ultimately failed to result in permanent revolution.[71]

Finland, which experienced a brief but violent civil war following the proclamation of revolution by the SDP in January 1918, must therefore be regarded as an anomaly in the Nordic context. The conflict and its aftermath were deeply traumatic and rarely discussed by academic historians before the 1960s, meaning that literary works of fiction had some impact on the historiography, notably those of Väinö Linna.[72] The reasons for the conflict must be understood in the context of the social and political turmoil following the Russian revolutions of 1917. Even so, the situation remained 'recognizably normal', in the words of one historian, until the late summer of 1917, with socialist and bourgeois politicians cooperating in the administration.[73] Following the rejection of its *valtalaki* – a proposal for independence based on parliamentary sovereignty – in the summer of 1917, the SDP accepted the provisional government's dissolution of Parliament and contested new parliamentary elections in October, but these resulted in a defeat for the party. Thereafter social order deteriorated rapidly, with the appearance of rival socialist and bourgeois paramilitary organizations. Rising social tensions were severely exacerbated by high unemployment and rapidly worsening food shortages. The situation was polarized still further by the Bolshevik seizure of power on 7 November 1917, which united the bourgeois parties behind a declaration of full independence. Meanwhile the SDP was rapidly losing control of its own ranks after it called off an attempted general strike in mid November and it proclaimed revolution in Helsinki on 26 January 1918, precipitating the civil war.

The difficulty for labour historians has been to explain why the SDP adopted a revolutionary position from late 1917. Although it was formally committed to a Kautskyist position and, like its Scandinavian sister parties, had based its ideology on the German Sozialdemokratische Partei Deutschlands' (SPD) Erfurt programme, the SDP was also prepared to collaborate with bourgeois groups to uphold Finnish autonomy and secure parliamentary reform.[74] 'The entire earlier history of the Finnish [workers'] movement spoke against organized revolutionary action', wrote the sociologist Risto Alapuro; 'it could not be created in a few months'.[75] What tipped the balance, according to Alapuro, was the rulers' loss of control over the forces of law and order after the Tsarist state collapsed. More recent research has complicated this picture further, drawing attention to the deepening social divisions emerging in Finland in the years before 1917 and the conflicts over land ownership in particular.[76] These cleavages were further exacerbated by the frustrations of the final years of autocracy and the rapid deterioration in the food supply during the war. The collapse of the Tsarist regime in 1917 unleashed enormous expectations that no political group was in a position to respond to. The SDP leadership struggled to keep control of the situation and use it – like their Swedish counterparts – to negotiate further political reforms, but the situation was becoming increasingly chaotic and dangerous, as both worker and bourgeois groups formed private militias. By the end of January 1918, the party had no choice but to launch a revolution for which it was extremely poorly prepared.[77] According to recent research, the violence that ensued – during the military conflict itself and the subsequent terror campaigns by both sides – cannot be dismissed simply as irrational acts or the deeds of rogue individuals, but was in many cases ideologically and strategically motivated.[78]

While Finland was the only Nordic country to experience a violent uprising during the revolutionary years 1917–1923, the potential for revolutionary unrest elsewhere in the region should not be overlooked. Despite being non-belligerents, all three Scandinavian countries were affected by the food shortages and price rises of the First World War, which led to mass hunger demonstrations in Sweden, especially during the spring of 1917.[79] There were further disturbances throughout 1917 and 1918, with riots in Copenhagen and Kristiania (Oslo) following the German revolution in November 1918.[80] In all three cases the social democratic leadership was able to channel this popular feeling into successful demands for constitutional and social reforms, even in Norway where a majority of DNA voted to join the Comintern.[81] Nor did the possibility of unrest cease after the establishment of parliamentary democracy; as Stefan Nyzell has shown, there were violent demonstrations in the city of Malmö during the autumn of 1926, in a dispute that originally stemmed from the use of strike-breaking labour. As Nyzell argues, the potential for violent conflict was never very far away throughout the 1920s, and even afterwards, in the Nordic countries as elsewhere in Europe.[82] Against this, Knut Kjeldstadli has pointed out that despite the threats of revolution only one person in Norway lost their life in a class-based political conflict, a fact he attributes to a 'pacificist political tradition' in Norway.[83]

Nordic Labour during the Interwar Period

The political divisions in the labour movement also affected Nordic and international cooperation. In 1917 labour representatives from the neutral Scandinavian countries planned an international socialist conference, together with their Dutch colleagues, but this never took place.[84] As a member of the Comintern from 1919, DNA ceased to participate in Nordic meetings, though the Norwegian LO continued to collaborate. Like the International Information Bureau of the Second International, Nordic labour movement cooperation remained a form of practical internationalism based on the exchange of information, though it differed in its inclusion of trade unions. After 1920 there were suggestions that collaboration should be based solely on contacts between the Nordic trade union confederations.[85] However, even the trade union confederations split in 1922 when the Norwegian LO left the so-called Amsterdam International, the social democratic International Federation of Trade Unions (IFTU), while the Swedish and the Danish trade union confederations remained members and the Finnish trade union confederation had never joined.[86]

With the exception of Norway and Iceland, communist parties split from the majority social democratic labour movement after 1917 and remained an influential political force in close contact with Moscow.[87] The majority of the labour movement remained committed to parliamentary socialism. Even in Norway, where DNA had joined the Comintern in 1919 and was regarded by many as a party committed to socialist revolution until the early 1930s, socialists were still prepared to cooperate with bourgeois parties to secure social reforms, among them the labour movement's long-standing goal of the eight hour day.[88] In Denmark and Sweden social democrats even participated in government, while in Norway DNA was particularly active in municipal reforms.

The stability of parliamentary democracy could not be taken for granted in the uncertain post-war world, however. Nordic societies in the 1920s remained fractured by the cleavages of worker and bourgeois, town and country, reflected in a fragmented political system that made it very difficult for any political party to form a stable government on its own.[89] The situation was in no way helped by the economic difficulties of the post-war period. Taken as a whole, the Nordic economies performed relatively strongly during the 1920s and 1930s, in comparison with elsewhere in Europe. The neutral countries were able to benefit from wartime demand, and manufacturing industry continued to expand, with high growth rates for Finland and Norway in particular.[90] Although the Scandinavian social democratic parties largely rejected nationalization as an economic strategy, they shared with the bourgeois parties a belief in the role of the state and its technocratic experts to plan the economy and to stimulate industrial development and modernization, and a tolerance of the concentration of capital as a means to business rationality and efficiency.[91]

Despite this, the region could not avoid the economic problems of the era. The initial post-war boom gave way to recession, not helped by the deflationary policies of governments determined to restore the gold standard.[92] The effects of this were particularly severe in Denmark and Norway, where there were also difficulties in the banking sector. But the great scourge of the period, in the Nordic region as in the rest of Europe, was unemployment.[93] This also had an impact on industrial relations, with employers able to profit from the weakened trade union movement to force reductions in wages. Throughout the 1920s there was labour unrest, and stimulated also by the intervention of the communist parties, social cleavages became more and more deeply entrenched. In some cases these were to lead to outbreaks of violence, most famously in Ådalen in northern Sweden in 1931, where military police sent to control large demonstrations fired into the crowd, killing five people.[94]

In the context of high unemployment, women's work and married women's work was under attack during the interwar years, in the Nordic countries as in other industrialized regions. Some regarded married women's work as a way for women to take men's jobs. This debate can also be analysed in terms of the shifting role of women in the labour market during the interwar years, when more women moved to new positions in the service sector at the same time as fewer women were willing to work as domestic servants and preferred to work in industry. As a consequence, domestic workers demanded the regulation of working hours and working conditions, but their demands were accepted only after the Second World War, when conditions had already changed in practice.[95] In Sweden this debate led to a large investigation on married women's right to work, which was also important for later International Labour Organization (ILO) investigations.[96] In an example of state feminism, well-known feminists formed a state committee of experts to investigate the conditions for women's work, revealing gender segregation in the labour market as well as women's comparatively large role in part-time work. Even today this characterizes women's position in the labour market despite comparatively high rates of labour force participation.[97] It was also during this time that the first attempts were made to make women's labour force participation easier in combination with motherhood and childcare. This debate, started by the Swedish social democrats Alva and Gunnar Myrdal, also initiated new ideas about day care and collective housing.[98]

Although urbanization was increasing fast during this period, the proportion of the population living in the countryside remained high and thus the social and political conflicts of the era also had a strongly rural dimension.[99] Some farmers had benefited from land reform, for example in Finland where, following nearly a decade of debate, legislation in October 1918 was passed allowing tenant farmers the right to purchase their land with the assistance of state loans.[100] Many of the region's farmers struggled, however, with rising debts, especially as the nineteenth-century solution to rural poverty – that is, emigration – had largely ceased to be an option.[101] This situation contributed to the consolidation, during the 1920s, of farmers' parties as a distinctive political interest.[102] Moreover, as in the rest of Europe, a further political development of the era was the rise of political groups willing to embrace explicitly anti-liberal and anti-democratic positions. The greatest threat was perhaps in Finland, where the populist right-wing Lapua movement started to take violent action against communists from 1929 and even made an unsuccessful attempt to stage a coup d'état in the small community of Mäntsälä in 1932.[103]

This also underlined the fact that the social democratic labour movement could not remain – if it had ever been – a party of the industrial working class only. In the era of universal suffrage it was quite clear that political success would be dependent on the mobilization of supporters in the countryside.[104] As Ingar Kaldal discusses in his contribution to this volume, the largest union in the Norwegian trade union federation was Skog- og Landarbeiderforbundet, representing forestry and agricultural workers, with over 30,000 members by 1940.[105] Perhaps one of the most remarkable features of the Nordic social democratic parties during this period, with the exception of Iceland, was the ease with which they were able to complete the transition from being parties of the industrial working class to the broader incarnation of 'people's parties' based on an appeal to the *folk*.[106]

Inter-Nordic contacts were intensified in 1932 when SAMAK was founded to coordinate the work of the labour movement committees formed by unions and parties. This meant that the leaders of the parties and the trade unions met regularly and SAMAK created a meeting place where they could speak very openly and off the record about their concerns.[107] After 1935, SAMAK also became a meeting place for the leaders of social democratic governments in the Nordic countries.[108] Mirja Österberg's chapter in this volume analyses an important theme of Nordic social democracy, namely the cooperation between social democrats and farmers' parties against the threats of the political Right.[109] Contacts in SAMAK were influential in stimulating a remarkable convergence in Nordic experiences during the 1930s, namely the negotiation of coalition agreements between the social democrats and the farmers' parties, which took place in all five Nordic countries. The Danes were first, in January 1933, followed by Sweden later that same year, with similar agreements in Iceland (1934), Norway (1935) and Finland (1937). The details of the agreements varied across the region, but in each case social democrats were able to agree to some support for agricultural subsidies in return for the farmers' support for social democratic welfare reforms.[110]

In Sweden the 1933 agreement also allowed the social democrats to introduce a countercyclical stimulation policy. Three years before Keynes published his *General Theory* this was certainly an innovative departure from the orthodox economic thinking of the time, though economic historians have cast doubt on how much it was able to influence Sweden's relatively swift recovery from the depression.[111] Perhaps the compromise was most remarkable in Finland, as it brought together two separate interests that less than a generation earlier had committed terrible atrocities against each other during the civil war.[112] The crisis agreements also went some way to resolving tensions in the labour market. In Denmark, the Kanslergade Agreement included a compromise on industrial relations, with the farmers agreeing to support a state-negotiated agreement to end the bitter round of strikes and lockouts.[113] This was followed by separate labour market agreements in Norway (Hovedavtalen 1935), Sweden (Saltsjöbadsavtalet 1938) and Finland (Tammikuun kihlaus, 1940), all of which were seen as milestones in the history of industrial relations.[114]

The interwar period also marked the high point in the development of the institutions of the labour movement as a culmination of the mobilization of the popular movements in the nineteenth century. Although the idea of a Nordic workers' culture never quite attracted the same fame as similar culture-building efforts in Austria's 'Red Vienna' or Germany, it was nonetheless significant.[115] Central to the movement were the 'people's halls' *(folkets hus; työväentalo; alþýðuhús)* where much of the labour movement's activities took place.[116] Although in the cities these could be elaborate demonstrations of proud working-class culture – for example in the areas around Norra Bantorget and Youngstorget in Stockholm and Oslo respectively, the workers' house and Hakaniemi square in Helsinki or Alþýðuhúsið by Arnarhóll in Reykjavík – in the rural districts they were more likely to be modest buildings, usually constructed by the workers themselves. During the 1920s and 1930s it became theoretically possible to live one's life in the embrace of the workers' movement: shopping at the cooperative store, benefiting from trade union insurance schemes, receiving education through the numerous study circles or workers' colleges in Denmark and participating in recreational activities through guest houses, sports clubs, choirs and the entertainments organized at the people's halls.[117] During the 1930s, women from the Nordic labour movements also started to meet regularly for so-called women's weeks and Nordic summer schools, which intensified their cooperation.[118]

The experiences of the Nordic countries during the Second World War created differences in attitudes and politics among the labour movements. Although DNA had rejoined the Nordic community in the early 1930s, cooperation between the movements was challenged, especially during the Second World War when solidarity and neutrality could not be practised in the same way due to the German occupation of Denmark and Norway and the fact that Finland fought on the German side against the USSR.[119] Sweden remained officially neutral, which in practice meant that the government did everything to avoid being drawn into the war, including tolerating the passage of German troops through Swedish territory to occupied Norway. These experiences had long-lasting effects on the foreign politics of the social democratic governments and their views on internationalism and international cooperation. One of the challenges was that international solidarity could hinder Nordic solidarity, or, as Klaus Misgeld has put it, the opposite was true and Nordic solidarity hindered international cooperation.[120] However, for a large part of this period the internationals were already largely defunct, as a result of the varying experiences of war.

From 1933 the Scandinavian countries received political refugees from the German-speaking regions, though after the occupation of Denmark and Norway this was confined to Sweden. Among these refugees were some of the future leaders of the German-speaking labour movements, including Willy Brandt, Herbert Wehner and Bruno Kreisky.[121] Although it is not possible to talk about large numbers, the experience of receiving anti-fascist refugees and the mistakes made during this period resulted in a much more open policy towards refugees after the Second World War.[122] Holger Weiss's chapter in this book analyses the early communist networks that were later also used to escape from persecution by the Nazi regime.[123]

Nordic Labour during the Period of Social Democratic Hegemony

The historiography of Nordic labour after 1945 distinguishes itself from most other parts of Europe in one important respect: it was written in the context of success or what Francis Sejersted has called the 'happy moment' of social democracy.[124] As Donald Sassoon has pointed out, the years immediately after the Second World War marked a high point for socialists in western Europe.[125] Stimulated by the spirit of collective sacrifice and equality of the war years, labour seemed poised on the threshold of a major victory, and this optimism was vindicated by election victories for labour parties in Sweden in 1944 and in Britain and Norway in the summer of 1945.[126] But in Britain, at least, the initial enthusiasm faded and Clement Attlee's reforming government was voted out of office in 1951. Only in Scandinavia were social democratic electoral successes sustained, so much so that it is justified to speak of social democratic hegemony in the post-war years.[127] In Sweden, the SAP had an almost unbroken run in government from 1932–1976; in Norway DNA was equally dominant in the two decades 1945–65.[128] Even in Denmark, where the social democrats never commanded a parliamentary majority and governed instead in coalition with other parties, they were rarely out of office. The thesis of social democratic hegemony holds less true for Finland and Iceland, where conservative and farming interests remained more dominant and where there was also still substantial support for communism within the labour movement.[129] These splits also hindered the development of centralized industrial relations, but Finland at least also shared some of the 'Nordic' characteristics of its neighbours, not least in its corporatist organization of interests.[130]

With the 1930s agreements, Sweden seemed to have abandoned the bad old days of poverty and conflict and entered a golden age of prosperity and stability. The industrial economy boomed in response to international demand for Swedish exports, and the result of this prosperity was the construction of the welfare state.[131] From the 1940s, the proportion of the population engaged in industrial work had surpassed that employed in agriculture, and Sweden was rapidly becoming a highly urbanized society.[132] These transitions were partly eased by the institutions of the state – in particular Arbetsmarknadsstyrelsen (labour market board, AMS), founded in 1948 – which assisted employees with moving jobs and homes, and introduced reforms including the three week summer holiday and the five day week.[133] Even so, and despite rapid depopulation of rural northern districts in particular, this was not enough to meet the rising demand for labour. With all formal obstacles removed, women entered paid work outside their homes to a larger degree than before, but there was still not public childcare. To begin with, most of the women worked in retail, production industries and in the public sector. At the end of the 1940s there was a discussion on how to meet demand for labour in industry and whether it should be through the recruitment of women, which would lead to the demand for public childcare, or migrant men.[134] Women were recruited to work in the public sector and Swedish employers actively recruited workers from southern Europe, as Johan Svanberg's contribution to this volume discusses.[135] During the 1960s, labour migration from Finland became significant, with several hundred thousand Finnish workers moving temporarily or permanently to work in industrial areas of Sweden such as Malmö, Gothenburg, Västerås or Eskilstuna.[136]

The industrial boom was not matched in the other Nordic countries to the same degree as it was in Sweden in the immediate post-war years.[137] In Denmark, the agricultural sector was still making a substantial contribution to Danish exports in 1950, though it was losing ground to industry.[138] In Norway, strongly regional patterns of development prevailed: in contrast to the centralizing impulses of the Swedish state, the Norwegian government invested in regional development, especially in the north of the country.[139] Nonetheless, in all the Nordic countries the trends were similar to that of the rest of Europe: the decline of agriculture, an increase in women's labour force participation, rising wages and productivity in industry, urbanization and rising consumption of new goods and services for the mass of the population.

There is, however, a danger of overstating the degree of social and political consensus that this generated.[140] Firstly, social democratic hegemony was never complete or unchallenged, even in Sweden. It is now widely acknowledged that social democrats were not the principal architects of the welfare state, but the inheritors of a longer tradition of tolerance for state intervention in welfare policy that dated from the late nineteenth century or even earlier.[141] Post-war welfare legislation was introduced through political compromises with the bourgeois parties, though such compromises were by no means a foregone conclusion, as the example of the Swedish supplementary pension reform – voted through the Riksdag by one vote in 1959 – demonstrates.[142] Nor was everyone a beneficiary of welfare reforms. As Klas Åmark has pointed out, social insurance in Sweden and Norway was conceived largely with the male, waged, industrial worker in mind. Many other groups remained unseen or were otherwise excluded: women engaged in unpaid work within the home; migrant workers and indigenous ethnic minority groups such as the Sami and Roma; farmers and agricultural workers; and those falling short of the hegemonic labour movement values of respectability, sobriety and diligence (*skötsamhet*).[143]

Moreover, although the so-called spirit of Saltsjöbaden seemed to prevail in Sweden and industrial conflicts were relatively infrequent, this was not true of the other Nordic countries. Iceland, Finland and Denmark continued to experience very high strike rates, even in comparison with other west European societies.[144] Social conflict erupted from the late 1960s as part of wider international currents. Like elsewhere, there were many different aspects of these protests: part youth rebellion, part post-materialist critique of post-war politics, part reaction to changing international circumstances.[145] But there were also some distinctively Nordic elements, not least in the relative mildness with which the authorities reacted to protests and demonstrations. The legacy of social democratic hegemony was influential here too: on the one hand, left-wing politics was part of the fabric of society, but on the other, the criticism of the conservative establishment was, by necessity, also directed against the social democratic leadership.[146] This was perhaps most marked in Sweden, where the truly shocking event of the era was not the 1968 student demonstrations, but a wildcat strike by workers at the state-owned iron ore mine in Kiruna, in the winter of 1969–70.[147] The miners' action was a direct criticism of the Stockholm-based social democratic leadership of the Swedish labour movement and as such a profound challenge to traditional hierarchies, at work and in trade unions. This triggered a new emphasis on industrial democracy in the Swedish labour movement, but radical plans for wage earner funds were never realized in full.[148]

International events were also important in 1968 in Scandinavia, with opposition to the Vietnam War one of the most symbolic issues.[149] In Norway, the 'New Left' was mobilized partly in opposition to Norway's membership of NATO and proposed entry to the European Community.[150] In Denmark, the international split in communism in 1956 led to the formation of Socialistisk Folkeparti (SF) in 1958, but the main challenge to the established party political system came instead from the populist Right, which gained ground on an anti-establishment, anti-tax platform in the so-called 'earthquake' elections of 1973.[151] In Sweden, the SAP was voted out of office in 1976 for the first time since 1932. But social democracy was also threatened in other ways. On the one hand, the legacy of the traditional popular movements that had been so important to the development of Scandinavian social democracy continued to be influential, perhaps in the distinctively 'puritan' character of the Nordic 1968 protests. But on the other hand, they also faced decline against the rise of newer organizations – based on issues such as environmentalism, feminism and international solidarity – that also broke with the organizational traditions associated with the popular movements by adopting more informal and less hierarchical styles and strategies.[152]

Nonetheless, although in retrospect the signs of a profound challenge to the Nordic social democratic model of high taxation and the redistributive welfare state were already present in the 1970s, the region still seemed to offer a favourable climate for labour. Trade union membership remained very high – partly due to the 'Ghent system', meaning that unemployment benefits were allocated through trade unions – and centralized collective bargaining arrangements prevailed in most industries.[153] With the exception of Iceland, the consensual corporatist system of making policy through negotiations between representatives of labour, industry and the government was more or less unchallenged.

The welfare state expanded during the 1970s, partly as a consequence of the incorporation of women into paid employment, and the consequent expansion of collective arrangements for childcare and other responsibilities previously associated with the family. Sweden was the first country to give fathers as well as mothers the right to paid parental leave. In 2006 80 per cent of mothers and 93 per cent of fathers with children under the age of seven were in gainful employment. However, one third of all women in gainful employment worked part-time, a percentage that had been decreasing.[154]

Challenges and Crisis: 1970s to the Present

The Nordic countries were all affected by the economic slowdown after 1970 and the ideological influences of neo-liberalism.[155] The timing of the late twentieth-century crisis varied across the Nordic region, however. The impact of the OPEC oil price rises in the early 1970s was greatest in Denmark, but somewhat less severe in Sweden, Norway and Finland.[156] Economic historians now agree that government actions in response to the 1970s difficulties failed adequately to address what in retrospect was a major structural shift: the decline of heavy industry, the outsourcing of production to lower wage economies overseas and the rise of the service sector.[157] Coupled with the results of a short-lived speculative boom in the 1980s, the consequence was a very severe recession in Sweden and Finland during the early 1990s.[158] From the 1990s Norway was shielded by its exploitation of North Sea oil reserves, which allowed for the rapid growth in national income and living standards. In 1973 Norwegian GDP per capita was still below the European average; by the first decade of the new millennium it was one of the richest countries in the world and frequently topped international surveys in measurements of its human development indicators.[159]

In Sweden, the early 1990s also marked a political, social and cultural watershed in that the crisis triggered a profound questioning of many aspects of twentieth-century development; in short, of what could be described as the social democratic legacy.[160] Despite the contemporary political rhetoric about the need to break with the past and reform – or even abandon – the Swedish or Nordic model, many scholars have concluded subsequently that the political impact of the crisis was less severe than it appeared, at least up until the mid 2000s. Although there were some attempts to reform welfare benefits, the fundamental premises of the welfare state remained intact, and unchallenged in political legitimacy.[161] In Finland and Sweden the recovery was based on rapid developments in the information, communication and technology sector, but in both cases this was as likely to involve older well-established companies as new start-ups, with Nokia and Ericsson as the outstanding examples.[162] In 2008 the Swedish business sector was still dominated by a small number of large family firms founded before 1914, even though many of these had shifted much of their operations away from Sweden overseas.[163]

One very profound change in the Nordic societies in the late twentieth and early twenty-first centuries has been the experience of mass immigration and the greatly increased ethnic diversity this has brought with it. The Nordic societies were never homogeneous societies, though perhaps it is fair to say that they did not experience the very significant ethnic and religious cleavages found in some other parts of Europe. Among historically significant minorities can be mentioned the Sami people of northern Finland, Norway and Sweden; Jewish communities, which grew following the late-nineteenth pogroms in eastern Europe; the Swedish speakers of Finland and the Finnish-speaking minorities in northern Sweden and Norway (Kvens); the Orthodox religious minority in Finland; the German-speaking minority in southern Jutland; and ethnic minority groups such as the Roma.[164] Until the post-war era, the Nordic countries were largely societies of emigration, and, as previously discussed, Finland remained so until the 1970s, as large numbers of citizens left to find industrial employment, mostly in Sweden. During the 1990s and after (earlier in Sweden) the composition of the Nordic populations changed enormously. Labour migration – mostly from southern Europe and also inter-Nordic migration from Finland – gave way in the 1990s to increased immigration of people from outside Europe, many arriving as refugees from conflict.[165] This became very significant again in 2015 with the arrival in Europe of hundreds of thousands of individuals fleeing conflicts in Syria, Afghanistan and elsewhere, and at the time of writing in early 2016, this seemed likely to have profound consequences for the Nordic passport union established in the 1950s. The introduction of border controls early in 2016 threatened to disrupt the common Swedish-Danish labour market that had emerged in the Öresund region between Copenhagen and Malmö in particular.[166]

Immigration has also had political consequences, provoking resistance from some who see ethnic diversity as a threat to social cohesion and national identity. This has – as in the rest of Europe – generally taken the form of new political parties espousing a right-wing populist brand of anti-immigration and 'welfare chauvinism', but more rarely it has also led to confrontations and even outbreaks of violence. Examples include the Mohammed cartoons controversy of 2005–6 in Denmark, the riots in parts of suburban Stockholm in the summer of 2013, and most horrifically, the Breivik massacre in Oslo in summer 2011.[167] The reputation of the Nordic societies for egalitarianism and tolerance has been challenged by the presence of ethnic 'others' and the responses of institutions and individuals towards this diversity.[168] The challenges seem to be most marked in the labour market, where instances of ethnic discrimination have been well documented.[169] Moreover, the tightening of controls in response to increased immigration, coupled with privatizations and subcontracting in the hotel and restaurant sector, construction, cleaning and in care work seems also to have led to the growth of the semi-formal or informal sectors of the economy and employment. [170] This is explored in Helle Stenum's contribution to this volume on Danish au pairs.[171] In this respect, too, the notion of Nordic exceptionalism seems to be increasingly difficult to sustain.

The Infrastructure of Labour History

Perhaps more than anywhere else in the world, the development of labour history in the Nordic countries is closely connected to the development of the labour history institutions. In the Nordic case, this means the development of national labour movement archives and libraries as well as the local social movement archives. The national labour movement archives are today among the largest non-governmental archives in the Nordic countries and their libraries are also regarded as being extremely valuable for research. The collections of these institutions have long structured the study of labour history, not only by making historical sources available and by the systematic acquisitions of literature and journals from all over the world, but also through the organization of seminars and conferences and the publication of their own books and journals.

The history of the Nordic labour archives is from the beginning an entangled history. Their developments are closely intertwined with each other and reflect the close connections between the Nordic labour movements. The Swedish Labour Movement Archives and Library (Arbetarrörelsens arkiv och bibliotek, ARAB) is the oldest existing institution of its kind in the world, founded in 1902. The establishment of the Norwegian equivalent (Arbeiderbevegelsens arkiv og bibliotek, ARBARK) was directly inspired by a visit of the Norwegian labour leaders to ARAB in 1904 or 1905.[172] The Danish Labour Library and Archives (Arbejderbevægelsens Bibliotek og Arkiv, ABA) and the Finnish Labour Archives (Työväen Arkisto/Arbetararkivet, TA) were both founded in 1909. It is important to note that these institutions were not established by professional historians, archivists or librarians but by the leaders of the movement, which shows how important they were considered to be. It is remarkable that the young labour movements were so concerned about documenting the history of their own organizations, especially during historical periods when they were more interested in revolution than tradition.[173] According to the statutes of the Swedish archives, the original intention was to collect material and make it available to write the necessary 'counter history' of the movement, including the work and success of the Scandinavian-American labour movement.[174] One of the reasons for the close cooperation was the Nordic labour congresses discussed above. During the 1907 Nordic labour congress, the delegates discussed the need for a Nordic information office similar to the Information Office of the Second International, with the ambition to collect statistics and to inform and educate the members of the Nordic labour movements. The labour press was not considered capable of fulfilling this task. The information office was never started, but what was left of this initiative became an agreement to start an archive in November 1908.[175]

The situation in Finland differed from that in Denmark, Sweden and Norway, due to the political history of the country. Here, the archives of the communist labour organizations are kept in a separate institution, the People's Archives (Kansanarkisto/Folkets arkiv) founded in 1945. Today, both archives share a common webportal, together with a number of museums with interests in labour history, including the Labour Museum Werstas in Tampere. The Labour Movement Library (Työväenliikkeen kirjasto) was founded as a joint initiative of the Labour and People's Archives and is today situated in the same building as TA.[176] The situation in Iceland was different again, as even today there is no comparable institution. The archives of ASÍ are held at the National Archives of Iceland. But the archives of the political parties – the social democrats, communists and socialists – have not yet been collected into one place and made available for public or academic use.

Today the Nordic archives collect the material of all parties from the left as well as material from the unions connected to the central trade union confederations, left-wing social movements and private individuals connected with the labour movement. In Norway, Denmark and Finland parts of the cooperative movement have also delivered material to the labour movement archives, while the Swedish cooperative movement started its own archives and library in 1927.[177] From the very beginning the labour archives also shared the aspiration to encourage workers to read about international socialism in books, journals and newspapers, and together with workers' education organizations, the archives were regarded as an educationally important tool for the movement until the beginning of the 1970s.[178] They were also important in the exchange of information across the Nordic region. Copies of publications were sent to all institutions and regular exchanges of information between the institutions continue today.[179]

The availability of sources and literature is important for the choice of research topics but also in influencing methodological approaches more generally. Early labour history was above all an organizational history of the movement, often produced in connection with anniversaries and undertaken within the labour movement itself. There was a revival of this type of organizational history in connection with the centenaries of many of the Nordic labour organizations from the 1980s. However, the Nordic labour history archives not only collected what was delivered to them by the main organizations, but also took their own initiatives to create sources. In 1949, under the leadership of Edvard Bull the younger, ARBARK planned a collection of interviews with ordinary workers, partly carried out by the Norwegian Folkmuseum (people's museum). A similar project was undertaken by Nordiska museet (the Nordic Museum) in Stockholm. Bull's initiative was an attempt to move the focus of labour history from the leaders to the ordinary people and bore fruit when this collection was used to write the first part of the Norwegian labour movement's history, published in 1985.[180] Parallel to this, in the 1940s, Swedish LO took the initiative for a history of the Swedish working class, which was exceptionally broad in terms of time frame and definition of the working class compared to what had existed before and what was to come. A whole volume was concerned with craftsmen since the middle ages, while the work also included an analysis of proto-industrialization, the history of agricultural workers and a cultural study of the working class.[181] In Finland, work began in 1960 under the auspices of Työväen Sivitysliitto/Arbetarnas Bildningsförbund (workers' educational union), initially to collect workers' memories of the 1918 civil war. These collections are now preserved in TA, covering many aspects of twentieth-century Finnish history.[182] In Denmark ordinary workers were interviewed about their time in school and their working lives. Nationalmuseet (National Museum of Denmark) was responsible for a collection on workers' and craftsmen's labour migration supported by the trade union movement, and workers' memories have been an important source for the history of everyday lives since the 1980s.[183]

Over time the labour archives have moved away from close relations to the labour movement to position themselves between the movement and academic institutions. With the exception of the Norwegian ARBARK, all the institutions have now moved from central locations in the 'red squares' of the capital cities, where they were close to unions and party offices. The number of staff has decreased and the archives have become modern documentation centres.[184] In the meantime, union confederations have established successful units for their own investigations, using academic research methods. Labour history itself has developed into an established field of academic research. The Norwegian archives' visitors book from 1910 shows that most of the visitors at that time were ordinary workers and leaders of the labour movement, whereas today most of the visitors are students, researchers and journalists from all over the world. In Sweden and Norway the archives were consciously positioned closer to academic research, with the requirement that the archive managers had to be qualified historians.[185] From the 1970s most visitors were academics, reflecting the growing interest in the period after the Second World War as a topic for academic historical research, though journalists have also become frequent visitors. Personal papers collected by the archives have become increasingly important for the studies of governments and political developments.[186]

In Denmark the new academic interest in labour history led to the establishment in 1970 of Selskabet til Forskning i Arbejderbevægelsens Historie (Association for research in the history of the labour movement, SFAH). Danish ABA chose not to become a research institution, so SFAH became responsible for publishing scholarly research in its journals, even though the board of the ABA, consisting of labour movement representatives, was initially sceptical.[187] As a result of this academic turn, unions and political organizations hired professional historians to write their history.[188] In 1974 the first Nordic labour history conference was held in Finland, coordinated by the archival institutions, and these conferences for academic researchers took place regularly until 2004. The tradition has recently been revived, and the fourteenth Nordic Labour History Conference took place in Reykjavík in November 2016.[189]

The upswing in academic labour history during the 1970s can also be seen in the foundation of labour history journals. In Sweden *Arkiv för studier i arbetarrörelsens historia* was started by a left-wing academic group in Lund in 1972.[190] Meanwhile *Arbetarhistoria* was first published as a newsletter by Swedish ARAB in 1977 but soon became the leading journal straddling the divide between academic and public history.[191] The Norwegian journal *Arbeiderhistorie* was founded in 1976 and became a yearbook from 1987. Between 1971 and 1994 the Danish SFAH published both *Årbog for arbejderbevægelsens historie* and the journal *Meddelelser om forskning i arbejderbevægelsens historie*, which changed its name to *Arbejderhistorie* in 1982. Finally, in Finland the journal *Työväen tutkimus* was first published in 1987 as a joint venture between the different archives and library. Since 1992 it has been published as a yearbook.[192] The Finnish society for labour history was founded in Tampere 1984. As its full name in Finnish (Työväen historian ja perinteen tutkimuksen seura) suggests, it had from the start the ambition to bring labour historians together with those working on folklore and ethnology, both professional and non-professional researchers. Its publications were also important in helping to disseminate knowledge about Finnish labour history outside Finland.[193]

The academic turn was also mirrored in the financial situation of the institutions. From the end of the 1960s the Swedish labour archives started to receive state funds to finance more academic expertise, just as in Norway and in Denmark from 1971. The Norwegian archives are still funded largely by the labour movement with around 30 per cent of their funding from the state, while ARAB receives 40 per cent of its funding from the state and the Finnish archives are funded between 70 and 80 per cent by the state. The Danish ABA was merged with Arbejdermuseet (workers' museum) in 2004 to reduce the running costs.

Historiographical Currents

Nordic labour history also needs to be understood against the background of broader historiographical currents and the larger framework of labour history in other parts of the northern transatlantic region. As a subfield its trajectory has much in common with the development of labour history in Germany, Britain and the United States. In many cases the starting point for the new labour history at the end of the 1960s and beginning of the 1970s was the work of British Marxist historians such as Eric Hobsbawm and E.P. Thompson, which resulted in a large number of dissertations at the end of the 1970s and the beginning of the 1980s.[194] As more students from working-class backgrounds entered higher education from the 1960s, this stimulated an interest in class formation as a field of study and research in all of the Nordic countries. And as elsewhere, the ebbs and flows of this academic field were also connected to interest in other so-called hyphenated histories such as women's history. Although labour history certainly existed before the end of the 1960s, Daniel Nyström has shown that earlier studies were seldom maintained in the historiographical writings of those who were part of the new labour history.[195] One of the first examples of this new labour history was the large research project on the history of social movements in Sweden, relating labour history to the general development of society.[196] In the following, we try to consider what – if anything – has been characteristically Nordic about Nordic labour history, shaped as it was by the shared institutional legacies discussed above and also by the tradition of Nordic labour cooperation discussed earlier in this introduction. At the same time, it is important not to overlook important differences between the Nordic countries, in this respect as in others.

Firstly, in contrast to Britain or the United States, for example, where labour history has often been dominated by a kind of pessimistic exceptionalism, Nordic labour history tended – until the 1980s at least – to be written in the context of success. The obvious exception here is Iceland. Despite considerable interest in the history of workers and labour politics and a number of specialized studies looking at political issues as well as local labour politics, Iceland has not produced a strong group

Illustration 0.1 Woman working in the fishing industry, Iceland. Arbetarrörelsens arkiv och bibliotek, Lantarbetaren. Unknown photographer.

of academic labour historians. As a result, the first extensive academic histories of the big labour unions – a couple of two-volume histories of the trade union confederation and the largest union of non-skilled workers, Dagsbrún – are a very recent addition to the historiography. These works, written in the vein of 'new labour history', looking at the social as well as the political side, were commissioned by the unions and had been planned for a couple of decades before publication.[197] One explanation for this lack of research is the smallness of the population and thus the academic community; another, the relatively weak position – in the Nordic context – of social democracy and the labour movement.

Elsewhere, Nordic labour history has been shaped by the success of the reformist social democratic wing of the labour movement. In Sweden, recent historiographical research has demonstrated the influence of the party's hegemony on the history of the Swedish labour movement.[198] Earlier histories such as Herbert Tingsten's study of the ideology of Swedish social democracy, or the popular movements project mentioned above, tended to emphasise the largely peaceful and consensual nature of popular politics.[199] This was challenged by a new generation of labour historians, who, radicalized by the 'New Left' of the 1960s and in many cases by a strong sense of their own working-class roots, insisted on the largely revolutionary nature of Nordic working-class consciousness in the years 1880–1920. Central to the more radical understanding of labour history, often strongly influenced by Marxism, was a focus on the politics of the class struggle. Class consciousness was forged through the shared experiences of political struggle over suffrage and workplace rights and through the conflicts over land and living conditions, but above all through work: the introduction of the factory system and the consequent loss of worker autonomy and skill. Research on working life, at least in Sweden, was from the early 1980s strongly influenced by Harry Braverman's study of the labour process, which was applied to studies of occupational groups such as printers, shipbuilders and forestry workers.[200] Such studies were also stimulated by the social and political context of the times in which they were written.[201] As we saw above, the economic difficulties of the early 1970s resulted in large-scale deindustrialization in Norway and Sweden. This was the trigger for several large popular history projects where laid-off workers studied the history of their former work place, often under the leadership of academics. Parallel to the History Workshop movement in the United Kingdom, for example, or *Geschichtswerkstätten* in Germany, Sven Lindqvist's 1978 book *Gräv där du står* ('Dig Where You Stand') on how to organize these kinds of projects was also published in the Swedish labour history journal. The book was later translated and became well known outside Sweden.[202]

Local history and history from below also became important during the first half of the 1970s, connected to the interest in microhistory as a new way of studying history in general. The foundation of local labour history archives had been on the table since the beginning, but a new initiative was taken during the 1960s when the Swedish ARAB acted as midwife for the Norwegian local social movement archives.[203] In the Norwegian case, regional politics became more important during the debate about membership in the European Union. A quick comparison of publications shows that local studies were much more common in Norway than for instance in Sweden during the 1970s. In contrast to Sweden, Norwegian studies focused much more on local developments and less on the centralized organizations of the labour movement.

During the 1990s and afterwards, the 'conflict perspective' in Nordic labour history became less prominent, as historians returned to earlier themes of consensus and compromise in the history of popular politics in the Nordic countries.[204] Again, this was influenced by contemporary political currents, in particular the decline of the social democratic parties that had dominated electoral politics for the previous half century, as well as world events such as the fall of the Soviet Union, the rise of neo-liberalism and debates about the 'end of history'. As formerly dominant Marxist perspectives were questioned, fewer studies were defined as labour history. At the same time, new theoretical insights were emerging. From the turn of the 1980s, power relations and power resources became an important part of theoretical models, borrowed from sociologists such as Walter Korpi.[205] The labour movement archives also played a role in the introduction of cultural studies approaches to labour history. Objects such as banners and emblems were made accessible at the archives, and several Nordic projects were started on the history of banners and labour movement art, for example.[206]

Given the international reputation of the Nordic countries for high levels of gender equality, it is perhaps not surprising that Nordic labour history has long been shaped by insights from first women's and later gender history. Many early studies in the evolving field of women's history owed their origins to labour history, especially in the history of women's work but also the history of politics concerned with women workers.[207] Yvonne Hirdman's history of the Swedish labour movement from the mid 1970s was the first to integrate women more systematically into this historiography.[208] Her theoretical work on the gender system, based on her research on the politics of women's work, became well known in the other Nordic countries.[209] Many of the pioneering works of women's and gender history were in fact first published in the Nordic labour history journals, surfing on the same wave of radicalization of society that inspired labour history in general.[210] Currently, a number of historians are or have been working on the history of labour and women's history in one or several Nordic countries.[211] Ulla Wikander's work on the gender segregation of work in the porcelain industry and on the prohibition of night work was path-breaking, not only within the Nordic countries but also beyond.[212] In Sweden it was scholars of women's history that initiated studies of the history of the welfare state, as a response to the contemporary sense of crisis in the Nordic welfare states during the 1990s and the growing interest in a broader history of politics concerning women and their family responsibilities.[213] Nonetheless, it is notable that today only a few women's and gender historians define themselves as labour historians, even though they work in the field of labour history. Part of the explanation is the development of gender history in the Nordic countries as a separate field, which also resulted in regular Nordic women's history meetings.

Another consequence of the relative success of the Nordic labour movements is the extent to which they have attracted international attention.[214] A bibliography on the foreign language literature on the Nordic labour movements, published by the four labour history archives in 1992, includes publications in English, French, German, Russian, Italian and Spanish.[215] The SAP's centenary history, the publication of which was funded by one of the largest Swedish research funds, was subsequently translated into English and Russian and has been used both as a source of information in research and public education.[216] International connections also shaped the development of the archive collections. Sweden received a number of political refugees who left their personal papers to the labour archives. For example, the SPD in exile left all its papers from the time of its exile in Prague in Stockholm, a deposit that was only discovered at the end of the 1960s and returned to the German archives. Other organizations in exile such as Polish Solidarność or the Workers' United Center of Chile had offices in Stockholm and some of their material is still kept by ARAB.[217]

Although it is probably fair to say there has been a decline in research on the labour history of the early twentieth century in recent years, those studies that have appeared have done much to broaden the subject. Several studies have emphasized the importance of alternative ideological currents beyond the reform or revolution dichotomy (such as anarcho-syndicalism) for particular groups of workers such as miners and quarrymen.[218] A rich tradition of local studies in labour history has continued to emphasize the diversity of labour politics across the region, while also noting the importance of transnational influences. Studies of other types of labour organization apart from political parties and trade unions, such as the workers' cooperative, for example, have also greatly enriched our knowledge of the Nordic labour movements.[219] Some trends were closely connected to the institutional framework of the labour movement, such as the historical studies of working life in Sweden from the late 1970s, referred to above. At the same time as the new Medbestämmandelagen (law on co-determination in the workplace from 1976) was adopted by the Swedish Parliament, the state invested in social science research on working life.[220] One emerging field was the growing interest in the history of the Nordic welfare states.[221] Another was the field of Cold War studies, which focused attention on the foreign politics of labour governments and biographies of leading politicians.

During the first decennium of the new millennium, under the influence of a general upswing in global labour history as well as a growing consciousness about the results of globalization, the field of labour history had a renaissance among academics. In all of the Nordic countries, the situation of migrant workers has come into focus, as well as different forms of international solidarity movements and the transnational and international activities of trade unions. In Sweden, many of these studies have taken place at history departments, in gender studies, sociology and political science. Many have been particularly concerned with what for some time has not been regarded as productive work and work that is invisible both in official records and in research, such as Gro Hagermann's large research project on the work of housewives in Norway.[222] Another example is the large gender and work project at Uppsala University.[223]

Contributions to this Volume

This book is organized around two themes: the history of work and trade unions and the history of labour politics and their organizations. Some of the contributions in this book revisit classic themes in Nordic labour history, while others present new fields of investigation. The first section on the history of work includes two chapters on industries characterized by high capital concentration in production, namely iron and wood, while the other two deal with work outside the traditional sites of investigation for labour historians, namely paid work at home.

The chapter by Göran Rydén and Chris Evans presents an entangled microhistory of ironmaking in Sweden during the eighteenth century. Although the role of Swedish iron in eighteenth-century Europe is well known, very little is known about the work process. Through a microhistorical study, Rydén and Evans connect workers producing bar iron in Uppland to the iron processing industry in England and the transatlantic slave trade and the work of slaves in parts of the British Empire. Previous attempts by labour historians to research earlier periods have often implied the application of modern concepts of work and society, leading to teleological explanations of the development of work in Sweden. By looking at the everyday life of workers – women as well as men – Rydén and Evans argue that it is possible to make comparisons of everyday life across time and space.

Similar to ironmaking, forestry was a typical occupation among workers in the Nordic countries and also a highly capital-intensive sector. The typical worker during the 1800s and early 1900s was not a factory or industrial worker but often a logger, and the history of work in this sector has long attracted the interest of labour historians. Ingar Kaldal's chapter not only adds to our knowledge of the everyday life of loggers in some Swedish and Norwegian regions, but also directs our attention to the importance of narratives about the life and work of loggers, which contributed to the construction of their identities as free men of the forest. Although the everyday life of loggers was very different to that of industrial workers or farmers, Kaldal also reminds us of the need to take stories about working life into consideration and how these have shaped individuals' outside work. Analysing more than 100 interviews with loggers, Kaldal shows how these stories remained important despite the fact that work in the forest underwent major changes since the 1950s.

Malin Nilsson's chapter on women in the Swedish home industry enters an entirely new field of labour history that has long remained underresearched in Sweden and elsewhere. Her chapter on industrial home work in the textile industry is based on more than 270 historical interviews with industrial homeworkers in Gothenburg. In contrast to earlier research on this group of workers outside Sweden, Nilsson shows that industrial production in the home was not limited to married women who had to earn an extra income to support their families. Instead, women in many different situations worked in this branch of production. None of them was described as a housewife or as a secondary breadwinner in the reports and articles on home-based production. Nilsson's study also reminds us of the high female labour market participation rates in Sweden compared to other parts of the northern transatlantic region. Female homeworkers formed a large group of workers during the early twentieth century, not only limited to the textile industry but also important in the metal trades. Nilsson's study also allows for future comparisons on a global scale and between different historical periods, as home-based production remains one of the largest sites of production in the global South.

Helle Stenum's chapter compares the working and living conditions of domestic workers at the turn of the twentieth century with Filipino au pair women working in Denmark in the early twenty-first century. With a few exceptions, domestic workers have only recently come into focus for historical research and have remained under-represented in the history of work. Stenum shows the many similarities between working conditions in domestic work over a period of more than 120 years. Despite improvements, the mobility of household workers is still tightly controlled through resident permits, which makes them an extremely vulnerable group. Despite attempts to professionalize and regulate this work, Stenum shows that even today domestic work is not regarded as ordinary wage work. Rather than wages, Filipino au pairs receive 'pocket money', which is subjected to tax regulations, and they do not require work permits but only residence permits. The chapter illustrates the necessity of studying working conditions in long-term perspectives and on a global scale.[224]

Knud Knudsen's chapter on Danish trade union history can be read as an attempt to build a bridge between the history of work and the history of trade unions. Knudsen argues that we need to focus on the ideology of work as well as the socio-economic aspects of work in order to find a new way of writing trade union history. Starting from a historiographical background, Knudsen suggests that Danish trade union history has either been a history from above, analysing the organizational history of trade unions and their relations to employers and the state, or a history from below, focusing on the workplace, working conditions and conflicts in the workplace. Knudsen argues that these hitherto incompatible perspectives can be reconciled if we combine the material approach of the 1970s with the cultural turn of the 1990s and use work as both a socio-economic and an ideological category of analysis. Using this approach, the chapter also shows the necessity of analysing the continuity and changes in work created through the 'second industrial revolution' and its consequences for the structures of organized labour.

Johan Svanberg's chapter is an example of a new trend in Nordic trade union history investigating the relationship between migrant workers and unions. Studying the processes by which migrant workers were recruited to the metal trades in Sweden, Svanberg's work is one of the few to use an industrial relations approach in labour history. The negotiations and agreements between Metall (the metalworkers' union), Verkstadsföreningen (the engineering employers' association) and the national labour market authority concerning the recruitment of foreign-born workers were the first compromises the labour market parties had to make directly after the Second World War and the first time the Saltsjöbaden Agreement was put into practice. It shows how employers, unions and the social democratic government were able to compromise in a gainful way.

The chapters by Sami Suodenjoki and Marko Tikka both focus on the political turmoil of early twentieth-century Finland, exploring questions about collective action and political strategy, rural workers, the land question and the links between socialism and nationalism in the Grand Duchy of Finland. According to Suodenjoki, previous research has overlooked the role of ordinary workers in the nationalist struggle for autonomy. Although Governor General Bobrikov's 'February Manifesto' of 1899 is often seen as a catalyst for nationalist mobilization in Finland, it was actually supported by many of the poorer rural classes, who looked to the tsar for assistance in their struggles for land reform. Focusing on the Häme district of south-western Finland, Suodenjoki shows that although the SDP tried to mobilize tenant farmers and rural labourers in support of suffrage reform, these groups adopted different tactics of protest, such as the spreading of rumours and the organization of mass petitions. He paints a portrait of early twentieth-century rural Häme as a deeply restless society and reminds us of the importance of long-established traditions of rural protest in the agrarian Nordic countries. The general strike of 1905 gave the SDP the opportunity to channel popular dissent into support for suffrage reform, and at the parliamentary elections in 1907 the party gained an overwhelming majority of votes among the tenant farmers and landless labourers.

Marko Tikka's chapter takes up the story of the General Strike of 1905, which took place across the whole of the Russian Empire. Tikka notes that the labour movement's role in the strike has been downplayed in Finnish historiography, which until recently interpreted it as part of the struggle to restore the autonomy of the Grand Duchy within Russia and thus as a milestone in a nationalist mobilization culminating in independence in 1917. For the labour movement, the strike was a moment that created 'not only political victories but also the opening of entirely new social concepts and possibilities', in Tikka's words. Although the initial outcome was a victory for the bourgeois constitutionalists, with the tsar's decision to restore the civil rights lost in the February Manifesto of 1899, only a year later the labour movement achieved its goal of a unicameral Parliament elected by universal male and female suffrage. As Tikka notes, this was an extremely important change in twentieth-century Finnish politics, which had lasting and significant repercussions. Unlike in Sweden, where the general strike tactic resulted in defeat and a lasting split in the labour movement, the 1905 strike in Finland strengthened social democracy and marginalized other traditions of political protest. The chapter also sheds some light on the geography of politics and protest in early twentieth-century Finland, demonstrating the importance of the railway as a means of political communication, for example, and the differences between centres of labour activity in Helsinki, Tampere and Pori.

Einar A. Terjesen's chapter takes a fresh look at one of the classic debates in Scandinavian labour history, namely the apparently greater support for radical politics in Norway than in Denmark and Sweden. Earlier research attributed this to the greater pace and social upheavals of Norwegian industrialization, whereas more recently Francis Sejersted argued that the relatively early democratization of Norway was more significant in marginalizing and thus radicalizing DNA. Terjesen rejects both these explanations. He argues that DNA's politics were less radical than has been claimed and indeed that the distinction between reformism and radicalism as consistent ideological positions is misleading. The Norwegian labour movement was not exceptional and like its Scandinavian and European counterparts it cooperated with liberals for democratic reform. More important than ideological differences were structural ones, namely the decentralized nature of the Norwegian labour movement, the strength of the peripheries and the absence of a strong leader like Hjalmar Branting in Sweden or Thorvald Stauning in Denmark.

As Mirja Österberg notes in her chapter, the Nordic cooperation committee of the labour movement, SAMAK, has been seen as significant in helping to draw the Norwegian labour movement into the social democratic fold from when it was established in 1932. Österberg examines in detail the SAMAK meetings of the 1930s, showing how the notion of a shared Nordic sphere was a resource that could be used by social democratic leaders in their domestic struggles against communism and fascism, while at the same time the aim was to present a united Nordic front in international organizations such as the Labour and Socialist International and the International Federation of Trade Unions. Moreover, Österberg shows that the Finnish delegates were not merely the passive observers of these developments, as has sometimes been assumed in previous research, but played an active role in negotiating a shared Nordic unity that overcame important differences in the parties' positions. Österberg's chapter demonstrates the interplay of the national, the regional (Nordic) and the broader international spheres in the history of labour politics in the Nordic region.

Finally, we have three chapters concerned with various aspects of the history of communism in the Nordic countries. While Weiss focuses on international communist networks, Ragnheiður Kristjánsdóttir considers the relations between communism and nationalism in all five Nordic countries during the first half of the twentieth century. While the Comintern was an important influence, for example through its Popular Front policy in operation 1935–1939, Ragnheiður Kristjánsdóttir reminds us that we should not overlook the importance of the domestic political context and the legacies of varying nationalist traditions in the region. In Denmark, Norway and Sweden, the social democratic majority in the labour movement was conspicuously successful in fusing its ideology with nationalist symbols and rhetoric during the 1930s, the best-known expression of which is Per Albin Hansson's concept of the *folkhem* or people's home. This left the minority communist parties politically marginalized and although they had begun to use national symbols by the 1940s they largely remained so after the war, especially in comparison to the success of social democracy. In Finland and Iceland the story was rather different, however. Kommúnistaflokkur Íslands (the Icelandic Communist Party, KFÍ) opposed what it saw as examples of 'bourgeois nationalism', such as preparations to celebrate the millennium of the Althing (Alþingi, the Icelandic Parliament), but at the same time could not ignore the force of nationalism altogether and attempted to construct its own alternative nationalist tradition. After the war, communism continued to attract political support in Iceland as a broader-based Socialist Party opposed to the American defence agreement and to NATO. The situation was more complicated in Finland, where the Communist Party was banned following the civil war and communists were largely regarded as outcasts, at least until 1944, but here too the Communist Party re-emerged as a broader social movement in the post-war period that was able to mobilize much greater popular support than in the Scandinavian countries. The chapter thus offers an important comparative perspective on explaining the different trajectories of Nordic politics in the twentieth century.

Holger Weiss's account of the northern European networks of the Comintern during the interwar period is an example of the importance of understanding Nordic labour history in a transnational and global context. Weiss focuses on the efforts of the Comintern to develop an underground communications network for the transmission of communist publications, funds and personnel between the Soviet Union and the rest of Europe. The Baltic Sea region was important in this network and especially so were the hubs established in the neutral Scandinavian states, where communists could operate more freely than elsewhere in Europe. The exception was Finland, where the Communist Party was illegal until 1944. After the collapse of the important Comintern centres in Hamburg and Berlin following the Nazi takeover in 1933, the activities of these cells were transferred to Copenhagen, though efforts to maintain a global communications network rapidly declined. Weiss's chapter also reminds us of an important occupational group found in all the Nordic countries, namely merchant seamen and the shore-based harbour trades (though regrettably this is beyond the scope of this book). Weiss shows how some of the most important sections of the Comintern's International of Seaman and Harbour Workers (ISH), established in 1930, were based in the Nordic ports and operated communist cells among Nordic seamen of different nationalities. Finally, in his discussion of the relocation of the network after 1933, Weiss also reminds us of the importance of the relative openness of the Scandinavian countries to political refugees, even before the Second World War.

In the third of our chapters on communism, Chris Holmsted Larsen adopts a biographical perspective to explore the links between Danmarks Kommunistiske Parti (the Danish Communist Party, DKP) and the Soviet Union during the Cold War period. His sources are the letters of the DKP member Otto Sand (1915–1984), who together with his family spent two years in the Soviet Union in 1958–1960 as a student of the Moscow Party School. Sand travelled to the Soviet Union during a period of post-1956 crisis in Danish communism, which resulted in the foundation of a new Socialist People's Party as a splinter of the DKP in 1959. As a loyal supporter of Khrushchev and a believer in the promise of communist utopia offered by the Soviet Union, Sand was willing to absorb the impressive spectacles presented by the Soviet hosts, but Larsen shows how the initial enthusiasm of the Danish students later turned to disillusion as they encountered what he calls 'the depressing realities of Soviet life'. These criticisms could not be expressed openly, but the private letters home to family members give us some idea of Sand's experiences. While much attention has been devoted to foreign interest in the Nordic countries as model societies, especially from the 1930s, Larsen's work reminds us also of the necessity to turn the gaze outwards and to explore how Nordic individuals and organizations drew inspiration from foreign political models.

Mary Hilson is Professor at the Department of History, School of Culture and Society, Aarhus University. Her research interests include Nordic and transnational social history, especially the history of the consumer cooperative movement in the Nordic countries and beyond.

Silke Neunsinger is Associate Professor in Economic History and Director of Research at the Labour Movement Archives and Library in Stockholm. She is currently leading the project 'Mind the gap! – An entangled history of economic history and the demand for equal pay'. She is also the editor of the Swedish labour history journal *Arbetarhistoria* and has published extensively on feminist and global labour history and methodology, especially comparative history and *histoire croisée*.

Iben Vyff gained her Ph.D. in history in 2008 and wrote her thesis on the Cold War in a cultural-historical perspective. Her recent research deals with modernity, identity, gender and everyday life in the twentieth century. Since 2008 she has been a member of the editorial board of *Arbejderhistorie*. From 2014 she has been curator of the municipal museums in Elsinore.

Ragnheiður Kristjánsdóttir is Senior Lecturer in History at the University of Iceland. She has written on nationalism, democracy and the politics of the Left. She is currently working on *A Concise History of Iceland* as well as a book on women and gender in Iceland in the twentieth century.

Notes

We are grateful to Tapio Bergholm, Anette Eklund-Hansen, Martin Grass, Knut Kjeldstadli, Pirjo Markkola and Klaus Misgeld for sharing their knowledge on different parts of Nordic labour history which has been of great help when writing this introduction.

1. V. Linna. 2001–2003. *Under the North Star; The Uprising; Reconciliation*, all trans. R. Impola, Beaverton: Aspasia Books. The trilogy or parts of it have been translated into Swedish and Danish among other languages.
2. R. Impola, translator's preface to *Under the North Star*, volume 1, v.
3. Linna's influence on the historiography of the Finnish civil war is discussed in R. Alapuro. 1988. *State and Revolution in Finland*, Berkeley: University of California Press, 203. See also chapter 7. On the significance of Linna's other famous work, *Tuntematon Sotilas* (1954) (*The Unknown Soldier*, 1957) and the film adaptations made in 1955 and 1985, see J. Sundholm. 2007. '"The Unknown Soldier": Film as a Founding Trauma and National Monument', in C. Mithander, J. Sundholm and M.H. Troy (eds), *Collective Traumas: Memories of War and Conflict in 20ᵗʰ-century Europe*, Brussels: Peter Lang, 111–41.
4. U. Marjomaa (ed.). 2000. *100 Faces from Finland: A Biographical Kaleidoscope*, Helsinki: Finnish Literature Society.
5. T. Emilsson. 1976–1979. *Fátækt folk; Baráttan um brauðið; Fyrir sunnan*, Reykjavík: Mál og menning. His work was nominated for the Nordic Literary Prize in 1978.
6. See for example M. van der Linden and J. Lucassen. 1999. *Prolegomena for a Global Labour History*, Amsterdam: International Institute of Social History, especially 8–12; M. van der Linden. 2008. *Workers of the World: Essays Toward a Global Labor History*, Leiden: Brill, especially ch. 2, 17–38. For a discussion about the future of transnational perspectives in labour history, including labour and empire as well as labour and migration see L. Fink. 2011. *Workers across the Americas: The Transnational Turn in Labor History*, New York: Oxford University Press. For a recent discussion of the definitions and yields of the global labour history approach see *International Labor and Working-Class History* 82 (2012), with contributions by Marcel van der Linden, Jürgen Kocka, Dorothy Sue Cobble and Prasannan Parthasarathi.
7. The terms Nordic and Scandinavian are often used interchangeably in English, but here we assume that the term Nordic refers to Denmark, Finland, Iceland, Norway and Sweden, while Scandinavian refers only to Denmark, Norway and Sweden. For a discussion of these terms see J. P. Árnason and B. Wittrock. 2012. 'Introduction', in J. P. Árnason and B. Wittrock (eds), *Nordic Paths to Modernity*, New York: Berghahn books,

21–23. Although Swedish, Norwegian and Danish are mutually intelligible, at least in the written form, this does not apply to Icelandic and Finnish. The use of Danish and Swedish in Iceland and Finland respectively is indicative of historical legacies and Finland remains officially a bilingual state with a Swedish-speaking minority. Today English often replaces the Scandinavian languages for discussions in the Nordic context.

8. On seamen see T. Nilsson. 2014. 'Fiktion, hierarki och havets hårda arbete: Skönlitteratur som källa till svensk maritim historia', *Historisk Tidskrift* 134(3), 462–98.

9. L. Edgren. 2011. 'Konflikt och samförstånd: Arbetarhistoria idag', in M. Olofsson (ed.), *Konflikt och samförstånd: Texter från arbetarhistoriska mötet i Landskrona i maj 2009*, Malmö: Skrifter från Centrum för Arbetarhistoria 4, 6. Edgren emphasizes that we cannot talk about a crisis, and in an earlier article examining current research at the different history departments in Sweden he showed that there is a growing younger generation of labour historians in Sweden: L. Edgren. 2007. 'Arbetarhistoriens marginaler: Några reflexioner angående svensk arbetarhistorisk forksning', in V. Lundberg (ed.), *Arbetarhistoria i brytningstid. Landskrona i maj 2005*, Malmö: Skrifter från Centrum för Arbetarhistoria 1, 30–47. Historian Lars Berggren has recently followed up Edgren's investigation. His results show that many themes that earlier would have been defined as labour history are now defined as gender history, history of capitalism, etc. According to his investigation labour history is still a vital part of Swedish historical research and the number of dissertations is still rather high. Thanks to Lars Berggren for sharing his investigation with us.

10. In contrast to developments during the last thirty years, earlier labour history was less limited in terms of time period. Studies of pre-industrial time and proto-industrialization were regarded as an integrated part of labour history. At the heart of the field of labour history, wrote Lars Edgren and Lars Olsson in 1989, was the agrarian revolution and the process of industrialization. L. Edgren and L. Olsson. 1989. 'Swedish Working-Class History', *International Labor and Working-Class History* 35, 70.

11. Å. Egge and S. Rybner (eds). 2015. *Red Star in the North: Communism in the Nordic Countries*, Stamsund: Orkana akademisk; Å. Sparring (ed.). 1966. *Kommunismen i Norden*, Stockholm: Albert Bonniers; A.F. Upton. 1973. *The Communist Parties of Scandinavia and Finland*, London: Weidenfeld and Nicholson.

12. See K. Misgeld. 1984. *Sozialdemokratie und Aussenpolitik in Schweden: Sozialistische Internationale, Europapolitik und die Deutschlandfrage 1945–1955*, Frankfurt/Main: Campus.

13. This is perhaps less true for Finland, where research on other groups, including female textile workers, male construction workers, male lumberjacks and male and female transport workers, has also been important.

14. E. van Nederveen Meerkerk, S. Neunsinger and D. Hoerder. 2015. 'Domestic Workers of the World: Histories of Domestic Work as Global Labor History', in D. Hoerder, E. van Nederveen Meerkerk and S. Neunsinger (eds), *Towards a Global History of Domestic and Caregiving Workers*, Leiden: Brill, 5–9.

15. See chapters 3 and 4.

16. On the efforts of the Swedish Moderaterna (conservatives) to brand themselves as the 'new workers' party' see N. Aylott and N. Bolin. 2007. 'Towards a Two-Party System? The Swedish Parliamentary Election of September 2006', *West European Politics* 30(3), 621–33. On the success of the right of centre parties in Finland (Kokoomus and Perussuomalaiset) in attracting working-class support, see D. Arter. 2011. 'Taking the Gilt off the Conservatives' Gingerbread: The April 2011 Finnish General Election', *West European Politics* 34(6), 1284–95.

17. Ø. Sørensen and B. Stråth (eds). 1997. *The Cultural Construction of Norden*, Oslo: Scandinavian University Press; N. Götz. 2003. 'Norden: Structures That Do Not Make a Region', *European Review of History* 10, 325–41; M. Hilson. 2008. *The Nordic Model: Scandinavia since 1945*, London: Reaktion, ch. 1; Árnason and Wittrock, 'Introduction'.

18. For example, Götz, 'Norden'.
19. D. Kirby. 2002. 'What Was "Nordic" about the Labour Movement in Europe's Northernmost Regions?', in P. Kettunen (ed.), *Lokalt och internationellt: Dimensioner den nordiska arbetarrörelsen och arbetarkulturen*, Tammerfors: Sällskapet för forskning i arbetarhistoria i Finland, 13–32.
20. For a comparative survey of the Nordic voluntary associations see H. Stenius. 2010. 'Nordic Associational Life in a European and an Inter-Nordic Perspective', in R. Alapuro and H. Stenius (eds), *Nordic Associations in a European Perspective*, Baden-Baden: Nomos Verlag, 29–86.
21. *Nýja Ísland* (Reykjavík, 1904–1906); *Alþýðublaðið* (Reykjavík, 1906–7) and *Dagsbrún* (Reykjavík, 1915–1919).
22. R. Kristjánsdóttir. 2008. *Nýtt fólk: Þjóðerni og íslensk vinstri stjórnmál 1901–1944*, Reykjavík: Háskólaútgáfan, 31–61. For a discussion of similar themes in Finland, see P. Haapala. 1994. 'Working Class in the Formation of Industrial Society: Methodological and Other Lessons from the Case of Finland', in K. Kjeldstadli, S. Myklebust and L. Thue (eds), *Formingen av industrisamfunnet i Norden fram til 1920*, Oslo: Pensumtjeneste, 104–17.
23. Kirby, 'What Was "Nordic"?', 15. On the rural nature of social conflict in early twentieth-century Finland see Haapala, 'Working Class'; also chapter 7.
24. Lennart Jörberg suggests growth rates (growth of GNP per annum in fixed prices) of 3.7 per cent in Denmark, 2.4 per cent in Norway, 3.4 per cent in Sweden and a rougher estimate of 2.3 per cent in Finland during the years 1870–1913. L. Jörberg. 1970. 'The Industrial Revolution in Scandinavia 1850–1914', volume IV, chapter 8 of C.M. Cipolla (ed.), *The Fontana Economic History of Europe*, trans. P.B. Austin, London: Fontana, 7–8. More recent research suggests slightly lower figures for GDP growth, with the exception of Finland, but confirms that GDP growth rates per capita were relatively high in the Nordic countries compared to some other parts of Europe, with Sweden the fastest growing European economy during the period 1870–1913. See A. Carreras and C. Josephson. 2010. 'Aggregate Growth, 1870–1914: Growing at the Production Frontier', in S. Broadberry and K.H. O'Rourke (eds), *The Cambridge Economic History of Modern Europe Volume 2: 1870 to the Present*, Cambridge: Cambridge University Press, 36, Table 2.2.
25. According to Jörberg, the percentage of the population living in urban areas in 1910 was as follows: Denmark 40%, Finland 15%, Norway 29% and Sweden 25%, while the percentage engaged in agriculture was as follows: Denmark 36% (1911), Finland 60%, Norway 43%, Sweden 49%. See Jörberg, 'The Industrial Revolution in Scandinavia', 16, 24–25. For Denmark these figures include fishing; for Norway and Sweden they also include forestry. As Carol Leonard and Jonas Ljungberg point out, however, levels of urbanization depend on how it is measured: they calculate that only 5.5 per cent of the Nordic population lived in settlements of 10,000 or more, but if the threshold is lowered to settlements of 5,000 inhabitants then between 10 and 25 per cent of the population could be considered urban. In other words, most Nordic towns were small. See C. Leonard and J. Ljungberg. 2010. 'Population and Living Standards, 1870–1914', in Broadberry and O'Rourke (eds), *The Cambridge Economic History of Modern Europe*, Cambridge: Cambridge University Press, 114.
26. Kirby, 'What was "Nordic"?', 16.
27. Emigration from Norway peaked in the early 1880s at over 1,000 emigrants annually per 100,000 population, the second highest rate in Europe after Ireland. See R. Gildea. 2003. *Barricades and Borders: Europe 1800–1914*, 3rd ed., Oxford: Oxford University Press, 281. Emigration from Iceland was also high in relation to population: see H.S. Kjartansson. 1980. 'Emigrant Fares and Emigration from Iceland to North America, 1874–1893', *Scandinavian Economic History Review* 28(1), 53–71. On relatively low rates of emigration from Finland, see A. Newby. 2014. '"Neither Do These Tenants or Their Children

Emigrate": Famine and Transatlantic Emigration from Finland in the Nineteenth Century', *Atlantic Studies* 11(3), 383–402.

28. L.K. Christensen et al. 2007. *Arbejdernes historie i Danmark 1800–2000*, København: SFAH, 78–81.

29. B. Schiller. 1987. 'Den skandinaviska arbetarrörelsens internationalism 1870–1914', *Arbetarhistoria* 42(2), 4. See also B. Schiller. 1967. *Storstrejken 1909: förhistoria och orsaker*, Göteborg: Elander; E. Bull. 1968. *Norsk fagbevegelse: Oversikt over fagorganisjonens historie*, 2nd ed., Oslo: Tiden Norsk Forlag, 113–20.

30. H. Stenius. 1987. *Frivilligt, jämlikt, samfällt: Föreningsväsendets utveckling i Finland fram till 1900-talets början med speciell hänsyn till massorganisationsprincipens genombrott*, Helsingfors: Skrifter utgivna av Svenska Litteratursällskapet i Finland, 327. On the 1905 strike in Finland see chapter 8. Tapio Bergholm writes that collective agreements were not widely adopted in Finland until the 1940s: T. Bergholm. 2002. 'Historieforskning och fackföreningsrörelse i Finland: Från organisationsbeskrivning till maktkamp, arbetskultur och arbetsvillkor', *Arbetarhistoria* 103–4 (3–4), 47.

31. S. Ísleifsson. 2013. *Saga Alþýðusambands Íslands* I, Reykjavík: Forlagið, 139–45.

32. K. Åmark. 2006. 'Women's Labour Force Participation in the Nordic Countries during the Twentieth Century', in N.F. Christiansen et al. (eds), *The Nordic Model of Welfare: A Historical Reappraisal*, Copenhagen: Museum Tusculanum Press, 299–333.

33. L. Sommestad. 1994. 'Privat eller offentlig välfärd? Ett genusprespektiv på välfärdsstatens historiska formering', *Historisk Tidskrift* 114(4), 611–29.

34. K. Hunt. 2007. 'Transnationalism in Practice: The Effect of Dora Montefiore's International Travel on Women's Politics in Britain before World War I', in P. Jonsson, S. Neunsinger and J. Sangster (eds), *Crossing Boundaries, Womens Organizing in Europe and the Americas, 1880s–1940s*, Uppsala: Uppsala Studies in Economic History, 73–94.

35. P. Jonsson and S. Neunsinger. 2012. *Gendered Money: Financial Organization in Women's Movements, 1880–1933*, New York: Berghahn, 202–3.

36. A.E. Hansen. 2010, 'De socialistiske kvinders internationale konference i København i 1910', *Arbejderhistorie* 2, 8–28.

37. Jonsson and Neunsinger, *Gendered Money*, 199.

38. N. Elvander. 1980. *Skandinavisk arbetarrörelse*, Sweden: Liber förlag, 33–34.

39. Elvander, *Skandinavisk arbetarrörelse*; K.J.V. Jespersen. 2011. *A History of Denmark*, trans. I. Hill and C. Wade, 2nd ed., Basingstoke: Palgrave Macmillan, 70–78; Christensen et al., *Arbejdernes historie i Danmark*, 114–16.

40. Elvander, *Skandinavisk arbetarrörelse*, 38; see also chapter 9.

41. K. Bosdotter (ed.). 2012. *Faror för staten av svåraste slag: politiska fångar på Långholmen 1880–1950*, Stockholm: Stockholmia; see also Schiller, 'Den skandinaviska arbetarrörelsens internationalism', 4. On the political context and impact of the union crisis in Sweden and Norway see also B. Stråth. 2005. *Union och demokrati. De förenade rikena Sverige-Norge 1814–1905*, Nora: Nya Doxa Förlag.

42. Elvander, *Skandinavisk arbetarrörelse*, 31.

43. D. Kirby. 1986. '"The Workers' Cause": Rank-and-File Attitudes and Opinions in the Finnish Social Democratic Party 1905–1918', *Past and Present* 111,132; Alapuro, *State and Revolution*, 150–1.

44. R. Kristjánsdóttir. 2012. 'For Equality or Against Foreign Oppression? The Politics of the Left in Iceland Leading Up to the Cold War', *Moving the Social* 48, 11–28.

45. Kommittén för skandinaviska arbetarrörelsens samarbete (Committee for the Cooperation of the Scandinavian Labour Movements). See M. Grass. 1987. 'Från arbetarkongress till samarbetskommitté: Om skandinaviska samarbetskommitténs bildande', *Arbetarhistoria* 42, 5–11.

46. Nordiska Samarbetskommittén. See also chapter 10; K. Blidberg. 1994. 'Ideologi och pragmatism. Samarbetet inom nordisk socialdemokratisk arbetarrörelse 1930–1955',

Den Jyske Historiker 69–70, 132–50. Nordic labour movement cooperation has continued into the twenty-first century: see the 'Sørmarka Declaration of the Nordic Workers' Congress, 11–12 November 2014, "We Build the Nordics"'. Retrieved 6 January 2016 from http://samak-nordicmodel.org/

47.   K. Kjeldstadli. 2016. 'Folkesosialisme. Stykke i tre satser', in R. Glenthøj (ed.), *Mellem brødre: Dansk-norsk samliv i 600 år*, København og Oslo: Gads forlag & SAP, 192–203.

48.   S. Halvorsen. 1988. 'Scandinavian Trade Unions in the 1890s, with Special Reference to the Scandinavian Stonemasons' Union', *Scandinavian Journal of History* 13(1), 3–21; E.K. Louhikko. 1946. *Vi gjorde revolution*, Helsingfors: Söderström.

49.   Schiller, 'Den skandinaviska arbetarrörelsens internationalism', 3.

50.   S. Sogner. 1998. 'Tjenestejenter til Holland', in *Vår barndoms have: årbok Vest-Agder fylkesmuseum*, Kristiansand, 22–35; S. Sogner and K. Telste. 2005. *Ut og søkje teneste: historia om tenestejentene*, Oslo: Det Norske Samlaget.

51.   Kjeldstadli, 'Folkesosialisme'.

52.   A. Palm. 1901. *Ögonblicksbilder från en resa till Amerika*, Stockholm: Författarnas Förlag. Contacts with Scandinavian migrants in the United States were also important later on; for example, the syndicalist Joe Hill and the Scandinavian workers' clubs in American cities like Boston and Chicago were important for the labour movement in Norway and Sweden. See also D. Hoerder. 1987. *The Immigrant Labor Press in North America, 1840s–1970s. Vol. 1, Migrants from Northern Europe*, New York: Greenwood; and D. Hoerder. 1984. *Essays on the Scandinavian-North American Radical Press 1880s–1930s*, Bremen: Bremen University.

53.   G. Gröndal. 2003. *Fólk í fjötrum: Baráttusaga íslenskrar alþýðu*, Reykjavík: JPV Útgafa, 136–38.

54.   E. Lahtinen. 1988. 'Finnish Participation in Co-operation within the Nordic Labour Movement, 1880–1918', *Scandinavian Journal of History* 13(1), 23. On contacts between the Finnish and Swedish labour movement see S. Hentilä. 1980. *Veljeyttä yli Pohjanlahden: Suomen ja Ruotsin työväenliikkeen kosketuskohtia suuresta Sundsvallin lakosta Suomen kansalaissotaan*, Helsinki: Gaudeamus. According to David Kirby, subsequent research has downplayed the role of von Wright in the early Finnish labour movement, noting instead the influence of Fennoman nationalism and the popular movements tradition: D. Kirby. 1990. 'Finland', in M. van der Linden and J. Rojahn (eds), *The Formation of Labour Movements 1870–1914: An International Perspective*, vol. 2, Leiden: E.J Brill, 524.

55.   J. von Schoultz. 1924. *Bidrag till belysande av Finlands socialdemokratiska partis historia*, Helsingfors: Söderström, 135; H. Soikkanen. 1961. 'Sosialismin tulo Suomeen: Ensimmäisiin yksikamarisen eduskunnan vaaleihin asti', Ph.D. dissertation, Turku: Turun yliopisto, 69. Von Schoultz writes that the DNA's leader Ludvig Meyer was also invited but did not attend.

56.   G. Callesen. 1990. 'Denmark', in M. van der Linden and J. Rojahn (eds), *The Formation of Labour Movements 1870–1914*, vol. 1, Leiden: E.J. Brill, 135–6.

57.   Schiller, 'Den skandinaviska arbetarrörelsens internationalism'.

58.   R. Hemstad. 2008. *Fra Indian Summer til nordisk vinter: Skandinavisk samarbeid, skandinavisme og unionsoppløsningen*, Oslo: Akademisk publisering; see also N. Götz, H. Haggrén and M. Hilson. 2016. 'Nordic Cooperation in the Voluntary Sector', in J. Strang (ed.), *Nordic Cooperation: A European Region in Transition*, London: Routledge, 49–68. Martin Grass suggests the establishment of the 1912 committee, for example, was partly shaped by contemporary developments in the Second International. Grass, 'Från arbetarkongress till samarbetskommitté', 5–11.

59.   M. Grass. 1974. 'Arbetarskandinavism 1912–1920: Kommittén för skandinaviska arbetarrörelsens samarbete, några aspekter', *Årbog for arbejderbevægelsens historie* 4, 55–88. No

Finnish representatives took part, for, as Esa Lahtinen has pointed out, there were no trade unions in the Grand Duchy before 1887–8: see Lahtinen, 'Finnish Participation', 24.

60. K. Callahan. 2000. '"Performing Inter-nationalism" in Stuttgart in 1907: French and German Socialist Nationalism and the Political Culture of an International Socialist Congress', *International Review of Social History* 45, 51–87. Henrik Stenius has described this as the 'Olympic Games principle' in internationalism.

61. Halvorsen, 'Scandinavian Trade Unions', 3–4.

62. See also Kjeldstadli, 'Folkesosialisme'.

63. Halvorsen, 'Scandinavian Trade Unions', 7; Grass, 'Från arbetarkongress till samarbetskommitté', 8.

64. Halvorsen, 'Scandinavian Trade Unions', 3; Grass, 'Arbetarskandinavism 1912–1920', 56; T. Bergholm. 2003. *A Short History of SAK*, Helsinki: SAK, 5–12. The Finnish Federation of Trade Unions was re-organized in 1930 as Suomen Ammattiyhdistysten Keskusliitto, SAK, following a period of trade union persecution under anti-communist laws. See Bergholm, *A Short History of SAK*, 26–27.

65. For the influence of Kautsky on the early Finnish labour movement see H. Soikkanen. 1978. 'Revisionism, Reformism and the Finnish Labour Movement before the First World War', *Scandinavian Journal of History* 3, 347–60.

66. Grass, 'Arbetarskandinavism 1912–1920', 57ff; E. Lahtinen. 1987. 'Finländarna i det nordiska samarbetet 1880–1918', *Arbetarhistoria* 42(2), 22.

67. Kristjánsdóttir, *Nýtt fólk*. See also chapter 11.

68. See chapter 9. E. Bull. 1976. 'Arbeiderbevægelsens stilling i de tre nordiske land 1914–1920', *Tidsskrift for arbeiderbevegelsens historie* 1, 3–28. First published in German in 1922; also published in Swedish (1979) as 'Arbetarrörelsens utveckling i de tre nordiska länderna, 1914–1920', *Arkiv för studier i arbetarrörelsens historia* 15/16, 62–80.

69. Bull, 'Arbeiderbevægelsens stilling'. For further discussion of Bull's thesis, see K. Kjeldstadli. 2002. 'Noen vitenskapsteoretiske spørsmål slik de framtrer i Edvard Bull: "Arbeiderbevægelsens stilling i de nordiske land 1914–1920"', in *Historie, kritikk og politikk: Festskrift til Per Maurseth på 70-års dagen 7. juni 2002*, Trondheim: Skrifter fra Historisk tidsskrift i Trondheim, 321–36.

70. Walter Galenson drew on Bull's work to develop a more general theory about the relationship between the nature of the industrialization process and variations in the growth, structure and ideology of the workers' movement. On Norway, he wrote that, 'the explosive industrialisation of the country, recruitment of the industrial workers from small farms without previous experience in steady employment, and the poor working and living conditions they found in the hastily constructed industrial towns, all contributed to the formation of an extreme radical ideology, matched by few others in Europe'. W. Galenson. 1952. *Comparative Labor Movements*, New York: Prentice-Hall, 149; see also Elvander, *Skandinavisk arbetarrörelse*, 48–49. For a critique of the so-called Bull-Galenson thesis see F. Mikkelsen. 1988. 'Fra proletarisering til klassesamfund: Industrialisering, urbanisering og fremvæksten af en arbejderklasse og arbejderbevægelse i Skandinavien ca 1750–1900', *Arbejderhistorie* 30, 2–20. See also N.F. Christiansen. 1995. 'Arbejderklasserne i de nordiske lande før 1920 – et forsøg på komparation', *Arbejderhistorie* 3, 14–21.

71. On the 'breakthrough of reformism' debate in Sweden, see S. Hentilä. 1978. 'The Origins of the Folkhem Ideology in Swedish Social Democracy', *Scandinavian Journal of History* 3, 323–45; L. Gröning. 1988. *Vägen till makten. SAP:s organisation och dess betydelse för den politiska verksamheten 1900–1933*, Uppsala: Acta Universitatis Upsaliensia; Edgren and Olsson, 'Swedish Working-Class History', 74; B. Schüllerqvist. 1992. *Från kosackval till kohandel: SAP:s väg till makten 1928–33*, Stockholm: Tiden. On Norway see chapter 9.

72. Alapuro, *State and Revolution*, 170.

73. A.F. Upton. 1981. *The Finnish Revolution 1917–1918*, Minneapolis: University of Minnesota Press, 102. The following summary draws on this work; also on D. Kirby.

2006. *A Concise History of Finland*, Cambridge: Cambridge University Press; J. Lavery. 2006. *The History of Finland*, Westport, Connecticut: Greenwood Press.

74. On the influence of Kautskyism on the Finnish labour movement see Soikkanen, 'Revisionism, Reformism'.

75. Alapuro, *State and Revolution*, 170. A similar point is made by D. Kirby. 1974. 'Stockholm-Petrograd-Berlin: International Social Democracy and Finnish Independence, 1917', *Slavonic and East European Review* 52(126), 63.

76. See for example P. Haapala and M. Tikka. 2012. 'Revolution, Civil War and Terror in Finland in 1918', in R. Gerwarth and J. Horne (eds), *War in Peace: Paramilitary Violence in Europe after the Great War*, Oxford: Oxford University Press; J. Siltala. 2015. 'Dissolution and Reintegration in Finland, 1914–1932: How Did a Disarmed Country Become Absorbed into Brutalization?', *Journal of Baltic Studies* 46(1), 11–33. See also chapters 7 and 8.

77. Alapuro, *State and Nation*. Henrik Stenius has also emphasized the culture of obedience and conformity in Finland with its tradition of strong popular movements. This explains why the civil war was so violent: when civil order broke down citizens had very little experience of how to communicate and to resolve conflict; to deal with contingency in short. H. Stenius. 2012. 'Paradoxes of the Finnish Political Culture', in J.P. Árnason and B. Wittrock (eds), *Nordic Paths to Modernity*, New York: Berghahn Books, 207–28; see also Stenius, *Frivilligt, jämlikt, samfällt*, 336–44.

78. Siltala, 'Dissolution and Reintegration', 15; Haapala and Tikka, 'Revolution, Civil War and Terror', 79–83. Based on the research of Marko Tikka and others, Siltala reports a total of 36,640 deaths as a result of the conflict in the years 1918–1922: 27,038 on the Red side and 5179 on the White side. Siltala, 'Dissolution and Reintegration', 18.

79. On hunger demonstrations in Sweden see C.G. Andræ. 1998. *Revolt eller reform: Sverige inför revolutionerna i Europa 1917–1918*, Stockholm: Carlsson; K. Östberg. 1997. *Efter rösträtten: kvinnors utrymme efter det demokratiska genombrottet*, Eslöv: B Östlings bok-förl. Symposion.

80. Carl-Göran Andræ has suggested that there was more revolutionary potential in Denmark and Sweden in 1917–18 than there was in Norway: Andræ, *Revolt eller reform*, 302–13; also F. Sejersted. 2005. *Socialdemokratins tidsålder: Sverige och Norge under 1900-talet*, Nora: Bokförlaget Nya Doxa, 156.

81. K. Kjeldstadli. 1994. *Et splittet samfunn, 1905–1935*, vol. 10 of K. Helle (ed.), *Aschehougs Norgeshistorie*, Oslo: Aschehoug, 114–15.

82. S. Nyzell. 2010. *'Striden ägde rum i Malmö': Möllevångskravallerna 1926: En studie av politiskt våld i mellankrigstidens Sverige*, Malmö: Malmö högskola. See also *Arbetarhistoria* 138–39 (2011): special issue 'A Hard Day's Fight: Strejker och sociala konflikter'; J. Hamark. 2014. *Ports, Dock Workers and Labour Market Conflicts*, Gothenburg: Gothenburg Studies in Economic History, 131–65. For a discussion of recent work on 'contentious politics' in Scandinavia, see A.B. Pinto, M. Ericsson and S. Nyzell. 2015. 'Contentious Politics Studies: Forskningsfältet social och politisk confrontation på frammarsch i Skandinavien', *Scandia* 81(1), 93–110; see also M. Kaihovirta. 2015. 'Oroliga inför framtiden: En studie av folkligt politiskt agerande bland bruksarbetarna i Billnäs ca 1900–1920', Ph.D. thesis, Åbo Akademi. Retrieved 6 January 2016 from https://www.doria.fi/handle/10024/113083

83. Kjeldstadli, *Et splittet samfunn*, 91.

84. M. Grass. 1975. *Friedensaktivität und Neutralität: die skandinavische Sozialdemokratie und die neutrale Zusammenarbeit im Krieg, August 1914 bis Februar 1917*, Bonn-Bad Godeberg: Verlag Neue Gesellschaft. The minutes of these meetings are available online at http://www.socialhistoryportal.org/stockholm1917, retrieved 24 February 2015. See also D. Kirby. 1986. *War, Peace and Revolution: International Socialism at the Crossroads 1914–1918*, Aldershot: Gower.

85. Grass, 'Arbetarskandinavism 1912–1920', 63.
86. M. Lähteenmäki. 1987. 'Orientering mot Norden 1919–1939', *Arbetarhistoria* 42(2), 23–24; G. van Goethem. 2006. *The Amsterdam International: The World of the International Federation of Trade Unions (IFTU), 1913–1945*, Aldershot: Ashgate.
87. On communism see chapters 11, 12 and 13.
88. Kjeldstadli, *Et splittet samfunn*, 114; D. Redvaldsen. 2011. *The Labour Party in Britain and Norway: Elections and the Pursuit of Power between the World Wars*. London: I.B. Tauris, 27; see also chapter 9.
89. S. Hadenius, H. Wieslander and B. Molin. 1969 [1967]. *Sverige efter 1900: En modern politisk historia*, Stockholm: Bokförlaget Aldus/Bonniers, 97–99.
90. D.H. Aldcroft. 1989. *The European Economy 1914–1980*, London: Routledge, 22, 53. Charles Feinstein et al. give average growth rates as follows: 1913–1929: Denmark 2.7%, Finland 2.4%, Norway 2.9% and Sweden 1.9%. 1929–1938: Denmark 2.2%, Finland 3.9%, Norway 3.1%, Sweden 2.6%. C. Feinstein, P. Temin and G. Toniolo. 1997. *The European Economy Between the Wars*, Oxford: Oxford University Press, 13.
91. F. Sejersted. 2011. *The Age of Social Democracy: Norway and Sweden in the Twentieth Century*, trans. R. Daly, edited M.B. Adams, Princeton: Princeton University Press, 45.
92. Feinstein et al., *The European Economy*, 45–46.
93. E. Hobsbawm. 1994. *Age of Extremes: The Short Twentieth Century 1914–1991*, London: Michael Joseph, 92–96. Estimations of unemployment rates vary considerably; for a discussion see O.H.Gryten. 1995. 'The Scale of Norwegian Interwar Unemployment in International Perspective', *Scandinavian Economic History Review* 43(2), 226–50. Gryten suggests average unemployment rates of 9.7 per cent (Denmark), 2.9 per cent (Finland), 7.4 per cent (Norway) and 6.2 per cent (Sweden) for the years 1920–1938. These are considerably lower than the 'official' unemployment figures but compare with average rates of 6.4 per cent in Germany, 10 per cent in the United Kingdom and 9.5 per cent in the United States for the same period. Unemployment rates in particular industries were at times considerably higher.
94. Sejersted, *The Age of Social Democracy*, 156–57. On the impact and subsequent interpretations of the events in Ådalen, see R. Johansson. 2002. 'Bilden av Ådalshändelserna 1931: 70 år av kamp om historien', *Historisk Tidskrift* 122(2), 243–70.
95. S. Neunsinger. 2015. 'From Servitude to Domestic Service: The Role of International Bodies, States and Elites for Changing Conditions in Domestic Work Between the 19th and 20th Centuries. An Introduction', in D. Hoerder, E. van Nederveen Meerkerk and S. Neunsinger, *Towards a Global History of Domestic and Caregiving Workers*, 392.
96. S. Neunsinger. 2001. *Die Arbeit der Frauen – die Krise der Männer: Die Erwerbstätigkeit verheirateter Frauen in Deutschland und Schweden 1919–1939*, Uppsala: Studia historica Upsaliensia, 198.
97. R. Frangeur. 1998. *Yrkeskvinna eller makens tjänarinna? Striden om yrkesrätten för gifta kvinnor i mellankrigstidens Sverige*, Lund: Arkiv; Neunsinger, *Die Arbeit der Frauen*.
98. A. Myrdal and G. Myrdal. 1934. *Kris i befolkningsfrågan*, Stockholm: Bonnier; Y. Hirdman. 1989. *Att lägga livet till rätta: studier i svensk folkhemspolitik*, Stockholm: Carlsson.
99. By 1940, 47.7 per cent of the Danish population lived in urban areas, compared to 28.6 per cent in Norway and 37.4 per cent in Sweden. Elvander, *Skandinavisk arbetarrörelse*, 58–59.
100. P. Markkola and A.-C. Östman. 2012. 'Torparfrågan tillspetsas. Frigörelse, oberoende och arbete – 1918 års torparlagstiftning ur mansperspektiv', *Historisk Tidskrift för Finland* 97(1), 17–41. Over 50,000 tenant farmers benefited, but former members of the red guards were excluded.
101. H. Meinander. 2012. *Republiken Finland: igår och idag*, Helsingfors: Schildts & Söderströms, 59–60. According to Hans Fredrik Dahl, by 1930 one tenth of Norwegian

farmers were threatened with bankruptcy. H.F. Dahl. 1971. *Norge mellom krigene: Det norske samfunnet i krise og konflikt 1918–1940*, Oslo: Pax Forlag, 86.
102. On the Nordic farmers' parties see D. Arter (ed.). 2003. *From Farmyard to City Square? The Electoral Adaptation of the Nordic Agrarian Parties*, Aldershot: Ashgate.
103. See Kirby, *A Concise History of Finland*, 174–80. On right-wing movements in interwar Scandinavia more generally see U. Lindström. 1985. *Fascism in Scandinavia 1920–1940*, Stockholm: Almqvist & Wiksell.
104. Elvander, *Skandinavisk arbetarrörelse*, 58–61. On the efforts of DNA to appeal to rural voters in the 1930s see Redvaldsen, *The Labour Party*, 36–38.
105. See chapter 2.
106. G. Esping-Andersen. 1985. *Politics Against Markets: The Social Democratic Road to Power*, Princeton: University Press, 314–19.
107. Kersti Blidberg has analysed the split in the Nordic social democratic cooperation in relation to the Labour and Socialist International between 1931 and 1945 and considers some of the consequences of this for the foreign policies of the Nordic governments. See K. Blidberg. 1984. *Splittrad gemenskap: kontakter och samarbete inom nordisk socialdemokratisk arbetarrörelse 1931–1945*, Stockholm: Almqvist & Wiksell International.
108. Grass, 'Arbetarskandinavism 1912–1920', 64.
109. See chapter 10.
110. For further discussion of the crisis agreements see chapter 10.
111. For a discussion of Sweden's recovery from the Great Depression see L. Magnusson. 2000. *An Economic History of Sweden*, London: Routledge, 194–99.
112. See T. Soikkanen. 1984. *Kansallinen eheytymien – myytti vai todellisuus? Ulko- ja sisäpolitiikan linjat ja vuorovaikutus Suomessa vuosina 1933–1939*, Porvoo: WSOY; H. Soikkanen.1987. *Kohti kansanvaltaa 2: 1937–1944*, Joensuu: Suomen Sosialidemokraattinen Puolue, 13–107. We are grateful to Tapio Bergholm for these references.
113. Elvander, *Skandinavisk arbetarrörelse*, 69–70; Christensen et al., *Arbejdernes historie i Danmark 1800–2000*.
114. Sejersted, *The Age of Social Democracy*, 158; Bergholm, *A Short History of SAK*, 31.
115. On workers' culture: G. Eley. 2002. *Forging Democracy: The History of the Left in Europe, 1850–2000*, Oxford: Oxford University Press, 210–15.
116. M. Ståhl. 2005. *Möten och människor i Folkets hus och Folkets park*, Stockholm: Atlas; L. Karlsson. 2009. *Arbetarrörelsen, Folkets Hus och offentligheten i Bromölla 1905–1960*, Växjö: Växjö University Press.
117. E.S. Einhorn and J. Logue. 2003. *Modern Welfare States: Scandinavian Politics and Policy in the Global Age*, 2nd edn.,Westport, Conn: Praeger, 103; A. Laubjerg. 2006. *Den store bølge: erindringsbilleder fra storkøbenhavnske industriarbejdspladser*, Rødovre: Forlaget Sohn; N. Helge, H. Grelle and J.I. Sørensen. 2005. *Velkommen i forsamlingsbygningen: Historien om arbejdernes forenings- og forsamlingsbygning i Rømersgade 1879–1983*, København: Arbejdermuseet. On cooperation as part of the labour movement see H. Grelle. 2012. *Det kooperative alternative: Arbejderkooperationen i Danmark 1852–2012*, København: Arbejdermuseet, and the special themed issue of *Arbejderhistorie* 4 (2003). Although this type of workers' culture also flourished in Finland, especially in the period before the First World War, David Kirby suggests that it was undermined in the difficult aftermath of the civil war, when the labour movement was severely demoralized and the workers' halls in some districts became associated with drunkenness and rowdy behaviour. The cooperative movement provides an example of continuity, however. See D. Kirby. 1988. 'New Wine in Old Vessels? The Finnish Socialist Workers' Party, 1919–1923', *The Slavonic and East European Review* 66(3), 434–37.
118. Y. Waldemarson. 1998. *Mjukt till formen – hårt till innehållet: LOs kvinnoråd 1947–1967*, Stockholm: Atlas.

119. On Finland and Nordic cooperation in the post-war period, see M. Majander. 1997. 'Tillbaka till den nordiska gemenskapen: De finska socialdemokraterna och Norden 1944–1948', *Historisk Tidskrift för Finland* 82(1), 45–76.

120. K. Misgeld. 1985. 'Arbetarrörelsens samarbete i Norden 1931–1945', *Historisk Tidskrift* 84(4), 474–81.

121. K. Misgeld. 1976. *Die "Internationale Gruppe demokratischer Sozialisten" in Stockholm 1942–1945: Zur sozialistischen Friedensdiskussion während des Zweiten Weltkrieges*, Uppsala: Studia historica upsaliensia; H. Müssener. 1974. *Exil in Schweden: Politische und kulturelle Emigration nach 1933*, München: C Hanser; E. Lorenz. 1992. *Exil in Norwegen. Lebensbedingungen und Arbeit deutschsprachiger Flüchtlinge 1933–1943*, Baden-Baden: Nomos.

122. K.-J. Lorenzen-Schmidt and H.U. Petersen. 1991. *Hitlerflüchtlinge im Norden: Asyl und politisches Exil: 1933–1945*, Kiel: Neuer Malik-Vlg; Lorenz, *Exil in Norwegen*; E. Lorenz, K. Misgeld, H. Müssener and H.U. Petersen (eds). 1998. *Ein sehr trübes Kapitel?: Hitlerflüchtlinge im nordeuropäischen Exil 1933 bis 1950*, Hamburg: Ergebnisse-Verl.; F. Meyer. 2001. *"Dansken, svensken og nordmannen-": skandinaviske habitusforskjeller sett i lys av kulturmøtet med tyske flyktinger: en komparativ studie*, Oslo: Unipub. M. Byström. 2006. *En broder, gäst och parasit: uppfattningar och föreställningar om utlänningar, flyktingar och flyktingpolitik i svensk offentlig debatt 1942–1947*, Stockholm: Acta Universitatis Stockholmiensis; M. Byström and P. Frohnert (eds). 2013. *Reaching a State of Hope: Refugees, Immigrants and the Swedish Welfare State, 1930–2000*, Lund: Nordic Academic Press.

123. See chapter 12; also D. Nelles. 2001. 'Der Widerstand der Internationalen Transportarbeiter Föderation (ITF) gegen Nationalsozialismus und Faschismus in Deutschland und Schweden', in A. Graf (ed.), *Anarchisten gegen Hitler. Anarchisten, Anarcho-Syndikalisten, Rätekommunisten in Widerstand und Exil*, Berlin: Lukas, 114–55.

124. Sejersted, *Socialdemokratins tidsålder*, 290; Sejersted, *The Age of Social Democracy*, 207, 265–66.

125. D. Sassoon. 1996. *One Hundred Years of Socialism: The West European Left in the Twentieth Century*, New York: The New Press, 117–18.

126. In Denmark the Social Democratic Party lost votes and seats to the communists, due to their participation in the wartime government that had until 1943 collaborated with the Nazi occupiers: Sassoon, *One Hundred Years*, 119–20. On the so-called 'future election' *(framtidsvalet)* in Sweden in 1944, see P. Esaiasson. 1990. *Svenska valkampanjer 1866–1988*, Stockholm: Allmänna Förlaget, 165–68.

127. Hilson, *The Nordic Model*, 41–46.

128. For a comparison of post-war social democracy in Norway and Sweden see Sejersted, *The Age of Social Democracy*, 207, ch. 10 passim especially pp. 289–93. For information on election results and governments in all the Nordic countries see Einhorn and Logue, *Modern Welfare States*, 353–75.

129. D. Arter. 1999. *Scandinavian Politics Today*, Manchester: Manchester University Press, 79–89.

130. T. Bergholm. 2009. 'The Making of the Finnish Model', *Scandinavian Journal of History* 34(1), 29–48.

131. Sejersted, *The Age of Social Democracy*, 211, 216–18; Hilson, *The Nordic Model*, 68–70.

132. Elvander, *Skandinavisk arbetarrörelse*, 59.

133. H. Sjögren. 2008. 'Welfare Capitalism: The Swedish Economy, 1850–2005', in S. Fellman et al., (eds), *Creating Nordic Capitalism: The Business History of a Competitive Periphery*, Basingstoke: Palgrave Macmillan, 45–46; Sejersted, *The Age of Social Democracy*, 221–23.

134. A. Göransson. 2006. 'Från hushåll och släkt till markand och stat!', in S. Hedenborg and M. Morell (eds), *Sverige – En social och ekonomisk historia*, Lund: Studentlitteratur, 251.

135. See chapter 6.

136. There was a significant spike in Finnish emigration to Sweden in 1950 and 1951 (see also chapter 6) and emigration grew again from 1964. In the peak year, 1970, over 40,000 Finns moved to Sweden, so many that the overall population of Finland declined. Overall, more than half a million Finns moved to Sweden during the period 1945–1990, though when return migration is also taken into account the figure for net migration is just over 250,000. According to Henrik Meinander, if unregistered migration is also taken into account there may have been as many as 800,000 Finns who worked in Sweden at some point during the post-war period. See figures from Institute of Migration available at http://www.migrationinstitute.fi/fi/tietopalvelut/tilastot#quickset-fi_tietopalvelut_ti-lastot=1, retrieved 19 March 2015; Meinander, *Republiken Finland*, 361–65.

137. For a discussion of the decline of agriculture in Sweden, see M. Morell, 'Agriculture in Industrial Society 1870–1945', in J. Myrdal and M. Morell (eds). 2011. *The Agrarian History of Sweden from 4000 BC to AD 2000*, Lund: Nordic Academic Press, 179–81. The proportion of the Finnish population employed in agriculture, forestry and fishing in 1950 was still relatively high at 45.9 per cent: see D. Arter. 2003. 'The Finnish Centre Party: A Case of Successful Transformation?' in Arter, *From Farmyard to City Square?*, 66.

138. M.J. Iversen and S. Andersen, 'Co-operative Liberalism: Denmark from 1857 to 2007', in Fellman et al. (eds), *Creating Nordic Capitalism*, 306.

139. Sejersted, *Socialdemokratins tidsålder*, 247.

140. Sejersted notes the 'peculiar mixture of consensus and will to cooperate, on the one hand, and of fear and ideological oppositions, on the other', in Sweden and Norway after 1945. See Sejersted, *The Age of Social Democracy*, 289 and ch. 10 passim.

141. For a summary, see Hilson, *The Nordic Model*, 96–102.

142. U. Lundberg. 2003. *Juvelen i kronan: Socialdemokraterna och den allmänna pensionen*, Stockholm: Hjalmarson & Högberg; For the politics of the pension reform see L. Lewin. 1988. *Ideology and Strategy: A Century of Swedish Politics*, Cambridge: Cambridge University Press, ch. 7.

143. K. Åmark. 2005. *Hundra år av välfärdspolitik: Välfärdsstatens framväxt i Norge och Sverige*, Umeå: Boréa, 267; see also Bergholm, 'The Making of the Finnish Model', 31.

144. T. Bergholm and P. Jonker-Hoffrén. 2012. 'Farewell to Communist Strike Hypothesis: The Diversity of Striking in Finland between 1971 and 1990', in S. van der Velden et al. (eds), *Strikes and Social Conflicts: Towards a Global History*, Lisbon: International Association for Strikes and Social Conflict, 401–13. Retrieved 24 March 2015 from http://www.ilera-directory.org/15thworldcongress/files/papers/Track_4/Poster/CS1W_12_BERGHOLM.pdf; G. Jónsson. 2014. 'Iceland and the Nordic Model of Consensus Democracy', *Scandinavian Journal of History* 39(4), 514–15; Elvander, *Skandinavisk arbetarrörelse*, 152–53.

145. T.E. Jørgensen. 2008. 'The Scandinavian 1968 in a European Perspective', *Scandinavian Journal of History* 33(4), 326–38; for a summary see also T. Judt. 2005. *Postwar: A History of Europe since 1945*, London: William Heinemann, ch. 12.

146. Jørgensen, 'The Scandinavian 1968'; see also other contributions to the special themed issue of *Scandinavian Journal of History* 33(4) (2008).

147. L. Ekdahl. 2011. 'Makten och människovärdet. Gruvstrejken 1969 som samhällskritik', *Arbetarhistoria* 138–39, 12–17; E. Schmitz. 2011. '"Kan de strejka i Norge kan väl vi också". ASAB-städerskornas strejker under 1974 och 1975', *Arbetarhistoria* 138–39, 18–26.

148. On wage earner funds see L. Ekdahl (ed.). 2002. *Löntagarfondsfrågan: en missad möjlighet?*, Huddinge: Samtidshistoriska institutet, Södertörns högskola; L. Ekdahl. 2001. *Mot en tredje väg: en biografi över Rudolf Meidner. Vol 1: Tysk flykting och svensk modell*, Lund: Arkiv; L. Ekdahl. 2005. *Vol 2: Facklig expert och demokratisk socialist*, Lund: Arkiv; I. Viktorov. 2006. *Fordismens kris och löntagarfonder i Sverige*, Stockholm: Acta Universitatis Stockholmiensis; C. Lundh. 2002. *Spelets regler: institutioner och lönebildning*

på den svenska arbetsmarknaden 1850–2000, Stockholm: SNS förlag; G.M. Olsen. 1992. *The Struggle for Economic Democracy in Sweden*, Aldershot: Avebury.

149. K. Östberg. 2008. 'Sweden and the long "1968": Break or continuity?', *Scandinavian Journal of History* 33(4), 339–52.

150. T.E. Førlund. 2008. '"1968" in Norway: Piecemeal, Peaceful and Postmodern', *Scandinavian Journal of History* 33(4), 382–94.

151. On the 'earthquake elections' and the changing party system see Arter, *Scandinavian Politics Today*, ch. 5; Hilson, *The Nordic Model*, 46–52.

152. Jørgensen, 'The Scandinavian 1968'.

153. According to Anders Kjellberg, Sweden, Finland and Denmark topped international rankings for union membership as a percentage of wage earners in 1980 (78%, 67% and 75% of wage earners respectively), and union membership continued to rise in Sweden and especially Finland throughout the 1980s. In Norway rates were slightly lower, 57% in 1980. Swedish trade union membership peaked at 86% of wage earners in 1986–87. A. Kjellberg. 2001. *Fackliga organisationer och medlemmar i dagens Sverige*, 2nd edn., Lund: Arkiv, 25, 27.

154. Göransson, 'Från hushåll och släkt', 253.

155. For a summary see N. Crafts and G. Toniolo. 2010. 'Aggregate Growth, 1950–2000', in S. Broadberry and K.H. O'Rourke (eds), *The Cambridge Economic History of Modern Europe. Volume 2: 1870 to the Present*, Cambridge: Cambridge University Press, 315–23.

156. For a summary see Hilson, *The Nordic Model*, 76–84.

157. See L. Schön. 2000. *En modern svensk ekonomisk historia: Tillväxt och omvandling under två sekel*, Stockholm: SNS Förlag, 469–77.

158. S. Honkapohja and E. Koskela. 2001. 'The Economic Crisis of the 1990s in Finland', in J. Kalela et al. (eds), *Down from the Heavens, Up from the Ashes: The Finnish Economic Crisis of the 1990s in the Light of Economic and Social Research*, Helsinki: Valtion Taloudellinen Tutkimuskeskus, 52–101; Schön, *En modern svensk ekonomisk historia*, 503–8.

159. M.J. Iversen and L. Thue. 2008. 'Creating Nordic Capitalism – The Business History of a Comparative Periphery', in Fellman et al., (eds), *Creating Nordic Capitalism*, 10; see also K. Halvorsen and S. Stjernø. 2008. *Work, Oil and Welfare: The Welfare State in Norway*, Oslo: Universitetsforlaget.

160. On the early 1990s as watershed see J. Andersson and M. Hilson. 2009. 'Images of Sweden and the Nordic Countries', *Scandinavian Journal of History* 34(4), 219–28.

161. V. Timonen. 2003. *Restructuring the Welfare State: Globalization and Social Policy Reform in Finland and Sweden*, Cheltenham: Edward Elgar, 183–86; for a summary see Hilson, *The Nordic Model*, 110–11.

162. Schön, *En modern svensk ekonomisk history*, 512–13; Hilson, *The Nordic Model*, 83.

163. Sjögren, 'Welfare capitalism', 61.

164. See Hilson, *The Nordic Model*, 150–55; G. Brochmann and K. Kjeldstadli. 2008. *A History of Immigration: The Case of Norway 900–2000*, Oslo: Universitetsforlaget, 133–40; see also I. Svanberg and M. Tydén. 1992. *Tusen år av invandring: en svensk kulturhistoria*, Stockholm: Gidlunds.

165. Hilson, *The Nordic Model*, 155–60.

166. '150 vakter ska stoppa flyktingar utan id-handlingar', *Dagens Nyheter*, 3 January 2016; 'Gränskontroller – så funkar det', *Aftonbladet*, 4 January 2016; 'Så fungerar id- och gränskontroller', Sveriges Radio, 5 February 2016; C.L. Kristiansen, 'Klar... parat... grænsekontrol', *Politiken*, 4 January 2016; J.A. Bjørnager et al., 'Bommen går ned for borgmestres drøm om en samlet Øresundsregion', *Berlingske*, 4 January 2016; 'Border controls threaten co-operation', retrieved 27 April 2016 from http://www.norden.org/en/news-and-events/news/border-controls-threaten-co-operation

167. For the populist Right in the Nordic countries see A.-C. Jungar and A.R. Jupskås. 2014. 'Populist Radical Right Parties in the Nordic Region: A New and Distinct Party Family?', *Scandinavian Political Studies* 37(3), 215–38.

168. A. Pred. 1998. 'Memory and the Cultural Reworking of Crisis: Racisms and the Current Moment of Danger in Sweden, or Wanting It Like Before', *Environment and Planning D: Society and Space* 16, 647.

169. For a summary see Hilson, *The Nordic Model*, 171–72.

170. A. Thörnquist. 2013. *False (Bogus) Self-Employment in East-West Labour Migration: Recent Trends in the Swedish Construction and Road Haulage Industries*, Norrköping: REMESO; A. Thörnquist. 2015. *East-West Labour Migration and the Swedish Cleaning Industry: A Matter of Immigrant Competition?*, Norrköping: REMESO; A. Thörnquist and Å.-K. Engstrand (eds). 2011. *Precarious Employment in Perspective: Old and New Challenges to Working Conditions in Sweden*, Bruxelles and New York: P.I.E. Peter Lang; A. Gavanas. 2010. *Who Cleans the Welfare State? Migration, Informalization, Social Exclusion and Domestic Services in Stockholm*, Stockholm: Institute for Futures Studies; A. Gavanas and C. Calleman (eds). 2013. *Rena hem på smutsiga villkor?: hushållstjänster, migration och globalisering*, Göteborg; Stockholm: Makadam.

171. See chapter 4.

172. K.E. Eriksen, S. Halvorsen and E.A. Terjesen, 'Arbeiderbevegelsens arkiv og bibliotek gjennom 100 år', *Arbeiderhistorie Årbok for arbeiderbevegelsens arkiv og bibliotek*, 12. See also M. Grass. 1992–93 'Arbetarrörelsens arkiv och bibliotek – i Sverige, i Norden, i Europa. ARAB förebilden', *Arbetarhistoria* 63–65, 54–58; T. Bergh. 1992–93. 'Nordiskt samarbete från norsk horisont', *Arbetarhistoria* 63–65, 59–62. The acronyms are a recent invention and became official only at the end of the 1990s.

173. Eriksen, Halvorsen and Terjesen, 'Arbeiderbevegelsens arkiv', 9–10.

174. We are grateful to Martin Grass for bringing this to our knowledge.

175. Grass, 'Från arbetarkongress till samarbetskommitté'. This is also the period when a number of Nordic trade secretariats were started such as the Scandinavian Transport Workers' Federation or the Nordic textile workers' union. These remain an under-researched area of Nordic labour history; see however A. Uhlén. 1957. *Skandinaviska transportarbetarefederationen 1907–1957: historik*, Helsingborg: Skandinaviska transportarbetarefederationen; K.E. Persson and C. Högmark. 1995. *Nordiska beklädnadsarbetareunioner 1897–1993*, Stockholm: Nordiska industriarbetarefederationen.

176. Työväen Arkisto, 'Työväen Arkisto: Eilistä ja nykypäivää', retrieved 13 January 2016 from http://www.tyark.fi/meolemme.htm; other information retrieved 13 January 2016 from http://www.arjenhistoria.fi/; http://www.kansanarkisto.fi/; http://www.tyovaenperinne.fi/?page_id=10; see also E. Lahtinen. 1992–93. 'Från förråd till arkiv i Helsingfors', *Arbetarhistoria* 63–65, 63–65.

177. M. Hagström. 2002. *KF Bibliotek – 75 år i konsumentkooperationens tjänst*, Stockholm: KF Bibliotek, retrieved 27 April 2016 from www.mersmak.kf.se/upload/KFBibliotek75_jubelskrift.pdf. In Denmark and Finland the cooperative movement developed separate institutions for cooperative societies associated with farmers and workers respectively. In Finland, the Labour Archives hold material from the so-called 'progressive' cooperatives and their central organizations KK and OTK, while in Denmark the Labour Archives hold material from Det kooperative Fællesforbund and related societies. See H. Grelle. 2012. *Det kooperative alternative: Arbejderkooperationen i Danmark 1852–2012*, København: Arbejdermuseet.

178. Eriksen, Halvorsen and Terjesen, 'Arbeiderbevegelsens arkiv', 25.

179. M. Grass and H. Larsson. 2002. *Labour's Memory: The Labour Movement Archives and Library, 1902–2002*, Stockholm: Arbetarrörelsens arkiv och bibliotek, 17–18.

180. Eriksen, Halvorsen and Terjesen, 'Arbeiderbevegelsens arkiv', 29ff.

Introduction 53

181. L. Edgren and L. Olsson. 1991. 'Arbetare och arbetsliv: Svensk arbetarhistorisk forskning', in K. Misgeld and K. Åmark (eds), *Arbetsliv och arbetarrörelse: Modern historiskning i Sverige*, Stockholm: Arbetarrörelsens arkiv och bibliotek, 7.

182. Information retrieved 23 March 2016 from http://www.tyark.fi/muistitieto.htm.

183. H. Grelle, '100 år med bøger og arkivalier', in H. Abildgaard and H. Grelle (eds). 2008. *Årbog 2008*, København: Arbejdermuseet and Arbejderbevægelsens Bibliotek og Arkiv, 15; M. Rostgaard and A.E. Hansen. 1992. 'Signalement af forskningen i arbejdslivets historie i Danmark', *Årbog for arbejderbevægelsens historie* 22, 15–33. We are grateful to Knud Knudsen for this reference.

184. Eriksen, Halvorsen and Terjesen, 'Arbeiderbevegelsens arkiv'.

185. Eriksen, Halvorsen and Terjesen, 'Arbeiderbevegelsens arkiv', 33; Grass and Larsson, *Labour's Memory*, 28.

186. Eriksen, Halvorsen and Terjesen, 'Arbeiderbevegelsens arkiv', 41. For example, the extensive personal archives of Gunnar and Alva Myrdal and of Olof Palme in Stockholm have attracted researchers both in and outside Sweden for many years.

187. Information on the journals is taken from the website of SFAH: see http://sfah.dk/om-sfah/, retrieved 15 March 2015. For a short history see V.O. Nielsen. 1990. 'SFAHs historie – baggrund, start og udvikling', in N.O.H. Jensen et al., *Fremad, ad nye veje: bidrag til diskussionen om arbejderhistorien i 1990'erne*, København: SFAH, 215–30.

188. For example, all the centenary histories of the trade union confederations were produced by academics. These included the history of Swedish LO, initated through a research project led by Lars Magnusson, which resulted in ten volumes. For the Norwegian LO's history see F. Olstad. 2009. *Med knyttet neve: LO:s historie 1899–1935*, Oslo: Pax; I. Bjørnhaug. 2009. *Medlemsmakt og samfunnsansvar: LO:s historie, 1935–1969*, Oslo: Pax, 2009; T. Bergh. 2009. *Kollektiv fornuft: LO:s historie, 1969–2009*, Oslo: Pax. For the history of the Danish LO see H. Tjørnehøj. 1998. *Fremad og atter fremad ... LO:s historie 1871–1960*, vol. 1, København: LO; H. Grelle (ed.). 1998. *I takt med tiden: LO:s historie 1960–1997*, vol. 2, København: LO. For Iceland see S. Ísleifsson, *Saga Alþýðusambands Íslands*, Reykjavík: Forlagið. For SAK in Finland see P. Ala-Kapee and M. Valkonen. 1982. *Yhdessä elämä turvalliseksi. SAK:laisen ammattiyhdistysliikkeen kehitys vuoteen 1930*, Helsinki: SAK; M. Valkonen. 1987. *Yhdessä elämä turvalliseksi: Suomen Ammattiyhdistysten Keskusliitto 1930–1947*, Helsinki: SAK; T. Bergholm. 2005. *Sopimusyhteiskunnan synty I: Työehtosopimusten läpimurrosta yleislakkoon. SAK 1944–1956*, Keuruu: Otava; T. Bergholm. 2007. *Sopimusyhteiskunnan synty II: Hajaannuksesta tulopolitiikkaan. SAK 1956–1969*, Keuruu: Otava; T. Bergholm. 2012. *Kohti tasa-arvoa: Tulopolitiikan aika I. SAK 1969–1977*, Keuruu: Otava.

189. Eriksen, Halvorsen and Terjesen, 'Arbeiderbevegelsens arkiv', 43. On the Reykjavík conference see http://www.nordiclabourhistory.org/, retrieved 26 April 2016.

190. Website of journal *Arkiv*: http://www.tidskriftenarkiv.se/index.php/hem, retrieved 15 March 2015. It ceased to publish for a few years in 2009 but started publication again from 2013, now with the title *Arkiv: Tidskrift för samhällsanalys* (Archive: Journal for Social Analysis).

191. Website of *Arbetarhistoria*: www.arbetarhistoria.se, retrieved 15 March 2015.

192. Website of *Työväentutkimus*: http://www.tyovaenperinne.fi/tyovaentutkimus/, retrieved 16 March 2015. The journal is produced through the cooperation of a number of institutions, including the Labour Archives and Library, the People's Archives, the Society for Labour History Research and two museums: the Lenin Museum and the Labour Museum Werstas, both in Tampere.

193. Website of the Finnish Society for Labour History: http://www.thpts.fi/mika-thpts/about-the-fslh/, retrieved 16 March 2015. The full name of the society is Työväen historian ja perinteen tutkimuksen seura (Society for the study of labour history and traditions). On the society and the development of labour history in Finland see P. Markkola. 2013.

'The Nordic and Gendering Dimensions of Labour History in Finland', in H. Haggrén, J. Rainio-Niemi and J. Vauhkonen (eds), *Multi-Layered Historicity of the Present: Approaches to Social Science History*, Helsinki: Department of Political and Economic Studies, 33–46.

194. K. Åmark. 2002. 'Arbete, arbetarrörelse och arbetarkultur. Skandinavisk historisk forskning', *Arbetarhistoria* 103–4(3–4), 7.

195. D. Nyström. 2015. *Innan forskningen blev radikal: En historiografisk studie av arbetarhistoria och kvinnohistoria*, Malmö: Universus Academic Press.

196. S. Lundkvist. 1977. *Folkrörelserna i det svenska samhället 1850–1920*, Uppsala: Uppsala universitet.

197. Ísleifsson, *Saga Alþýðusambands Íslands*; Þ. Friðriksson. 2007. *Við brún nýs dags: Saga verkamannafélagsins Dagsbrúnar 1906–1930*, Reykjavík: Efling, stéttarfélag and Sagnfræðistofnun Háskóla Íslands; Þ. Friðriksson. 2012. *Dagar vinnu og vona: Saga verkamannafélagsins Dagsbrúnar í kreppu og köldu stríði*, Reykjavík: Efling, stéttarfélag and Sagnfræðistofnun Háskóla Íslands.

198. Å. Linderborg. 2001. *Socialdemokraterna skriver historia: Historieskrivning som ideologisk maktresurs 1892–2000*, Stockholm: Atlas.

199. H. Tingsten. 1941. *Den svenska socialdemokratins idéutveckling*, Stockholm: Tidens förlag.

200. For the influence of Braverman in Swedish labour history, see L. Olsson. 1980. *Då barn var lönsamma: om arbetsdelning, barnarbete och teknologiska förändringar i några svenska industrier under 1800- och början av 1900-talet*, Stockholm: Tiden; L. Ekdahl. 1983. *Arbete mot kapital: typografer och ny teknik – studier av Stockholms tryckeriindustri under det industriella genombrottet*, Lund: Arkiv; L. Olsson. 1986. *Gamla typer och nya produktionsförhållanden: om rationalisering och medbestämmande, åldrande och solidaritet bland typografer i Sverige från slutet av 1800-talet till omkring 1960*, Lund: Lucifer; U. Wikander. 1988. *Kvinnors och mäns arbeten: Gustavsberg 1880–1980: genusarbetsdelning och arbetets degradering vid en porslinsfabrik*, Lund: Arkiv; M. Isacson. 1990. *Verkstadsindustrins arbetsmiljö: Hedemora verkstäder under 1900-talet*, Lund: Arkiv; A.O. Johansson. 1990. *Arbetarrörelsen och taylorismen: Olofström 1895–1925: en studie av verkstadsindustrin och arbetets organisering*, Lund: Arkiv. For summaries see S.O. Karlsson. 1988. *När industriarbetaren blev historia: studier i svensk arbetarhistoria 1965–1995*, Lund: Studentlitteratur, 170–71; Edgren and Olsson, 'Swedish Working-Class History', 75. For a discussion of the history of working life in Norway, see K. Kjeldstadli. 2015. 'En ny arbeidslivets historie?', in *Myndighet og medborgarskap: Festskrift til Gro Hagemann på 70-årsdagen 3. september 2015*, Oslo: Novus Forlag, 281–92.

201. According to Tapio Bergholm labour history was strongly politicized in Finland, but from the 1980s this was replaced by a greater focus on work and working life. See Bergholm, 'Historieforskning och fackföreningsrörelse i Finland', 45–50.

202. S. Lindqvist. 1978. *Gräv där du står: Hur man utforskar ett job*, Stockholm: Bonniers. Lindqvist presented his approach to an international audience during the eleventh International Association of Labour History Institutions (IALHI) conference in Stockholm in September 1980: see S. Lindqvist. 1980. 'Dig Where You Stand', in *Meddelande från Arbetarrörelsens arkiv och bibliotek* 16, 42–47; also S. Lindqvist et al. 1978. *Grav hvor du står: Håndbog i at udforske et arbejde*, København: Forlaget SOC. For the German translation by Manfred Dammeyer see *Grabe wo du stehst: Handbuch zur Erforschung der eigenen Geschichte* (Bonn: Dietz, 1989). In 1985 *Arbetarhistoria* published a special issue, 'Grävboken: ett stöd för grävare inom arbetarrörelsen', *Arbetarhistoria* 34(2). Writing in *History Workshop Journal* in 1978, Paul Thompson reported on the established tradition of history from below in the Scandinavian countries (and Poland) and lamented that it was not more widely known in the United Kingdom: P. Thompson. 1978. 'Life Histories in Poland and Scandinavia', *History Workshop Journal* 6, 208–10. The history workshop

movement also inspired similar attempts to organize history from below in Finland: see Markkola, 'The Nordic and Gendering Dimensions', 41.

203. Eriksen, Halvorsen and Terjesen, 'Arbeiderbevegelsens arkiv', 38–40.

204. For a summary of the debate see Nyzell, *'Striden ägde rum i Malmö'*, ch. 17; also the introduction to L. Edgren and M. Olofsson (eds). 2009. *Political Outsiders in Swedish History, 1848–1932*, Newcastle upon Tyne: Cambridge Scholars Publishing, esp. 1–3.

205. K. Åmark. 1989. *Maktkamp i byggbransch: avtalsrörelser och konflikter i byggbranschen 1914–1920*, Lund: Arkiv; E.A. Terjesen. 2012. 'Partsforholdet i arbeidslivet. Kompromiss, allianse, samarbeid eller kamp?', *Arbeiderhistorie*, 11–37.

206. M. Ståhl. 1999. *Vår fana röd till färgen: fanor som medium för visuell kommunikation under arbetarrörelsens genombrottstid i Sverige fram till 1890*, Linköping: Tema, Univ.; on labour movement banners see also chapters by Margareta Ståhl, Pirjo Kaihovaara and Katri Kaunisto, and Lill-Ann Jensen in Kettunen (ed.), *Lokalt och internationellt*; M. Ståhl. 2008. *Vår röda fana!*, Stockholm: IF Metall; K. Bosdotter and M. Isacson (eds). 2009. *Fram träder arbetaren: arbetarkonst och industrisamhällets bilder i Norden*, Stockholm: Arbetarnas bildningsförbund. In Denmark Henning Grelle published *Under de røde faner: en historie om arbejderbevægelsen*, København: Fremad, 1984, on the occasion of ABA's 75th anniversary.

207. See, for example, Gunnar Qvist's pioneering study of women in the Swedish Trade union confederation: G. Qvist. 1974. *Statistik och politik: Landsorganisationen och kvinnorna på arbetsmarknaden*, Stockholm: Prisma.

208. Y. Hirdman. 1979. *Vi bygger landet: den svenska arbetarrörelsens historia från Per Götrek till Olof Palme*, Solna: Pogo Press; also Y. Hirdman. 1992. *Den socialistiska hemmafrun och andra kvinnohistorier*, Stockholm: Carlsson.

209. Y. Hirdman, *Genus: om det stabilas föränderliga former*, Malmö: Liber.

210. See for example the special issue of *Arbetarhistoria* 44–45 (1987: 4–1988: 1).

211. D. Blazevic. 2015. *Jakten på et fagfelt: den skandinaviske kvinne- og kjønnshistoriens fremvekst i skjæringsfeltet mellom historieforskning og kvinne- og kjønnsforskning*, Bergen: Universitetet i Bergen; Nyström, *Innan forskningen blev radikal*; U. Manns. 2011. 'Historico-political Strategies of Scandinavian Feminist Movements: Preliminary Perspectives of a Research Project', in J. Mittag, B. Unfried and E. Himmelstoss (eds), *Arbeiter- und soziale Bewegungen in der öffentlichen Erinnerung: Eine globale Perspektive*, Berlin: Akademische Verlagsanstalt, 219–30.

212. U. Wikander. 1989. 'Periodisering av kapitalismen - med kvinnor', *Arbetarhistoria* 51, 7–11; U. Wikander. 1999. *Kvinnoarbete i Europa 1789–1950: genus, makt och arbetsdelning*, Stockholm: Atlas; S. Hedenborg and U. Wikander. 2003. *Makt och försörjning*, Lund: Studentlitteratur; U. Wikander. 2006. *Feminism, familj och medborgarskap: debatter på internationella kongresser om nattarbetsförbud för kvinnor 1889–1919*, Göteborg: Makadam.

213. K. Åmark. 1991. 'Den svenska modellen: Arbetarnas fackföreningsrörelse och samverkan på svensk arbetsmarknad', in K. Misgeld and K. Åmark (eds), *Arbetsliv och arbetarrörelse: Modern historisk forskning i Sverige*, Stockholm: Arbetarrörelsens arkiv och bibliotek, 27–42.

214. Among examples of foreign interest, specifically in Nordic social democracy and the labour movement, see M. Childs. 1938. 'How the Scandinavians Do It: Three Countries Where Labor Rules Democratically', *Harper's Monthly Magazine* 177, 400–11; P. Anderson. 1961. 'Sweden: Mr Crosland's Dreamland', *New Left Review* 7 (January/February). See also G. O'Hara. 2008. 'Applied Socialism of a Fairly Moderate Kind', *Scandinavian Journal of History* 33(1), 1–25, which discusses British interest in Scandinavian policy during the post-war era and A. Scott. 2006. 'Social Democracy in Northern Europe: Its Relevance for Australia', *Australian Review of Public Affairs* 7(1), 1–17, which focuses on the 1986 Australian trade union report on Scandinavia, *Australia Reconstructed*.

215. The selection of publications was based on the available literature at these four labour history institutes. M.B. Hansen and G. Callesen (eds). 1992. *Foreign Language Literature on the Nordic Labour Movements. Fremdsprachige Literatur über die nordischen Arbeiterbewegungen*, vol. 7, ABAs bibliografiske serie, København: Arbejderbevægelsens Bibliotek og Arkiv. Cooperation outside the Nordic countries illustrates this as well as the overview on the historiography of Swedish labour history published in 1990 by the then Institut zur Erforschung der europäischen Arbeiterbewegungen at Ruhr Universität Bochum in cooperation with ARAB: H. Grebing, K. Misgeld and K. Åmark (eds). 1990. *Forschung über die Arbeiterbewegung in Schweden*, vol. 10, Mitteilungsblatt des Instituts zur Erforschung der europäischen Arbeiterbewegung, Ruhr Universität Bochum. The overview was translated into Swedish the following year: K. Misgeld and K. Åmark (eds). 1991. *Arbetsliv och arbetarrörelse: Modern historisk forskning i Sverige*, Stockholm: Uppsatser utgivna av Arbetarrörelsens arkiv och bibliotek.
216. In contrast to the thematic organization of the centenary anniversary publications of some of the Swedish labour movement organizations, publications in the other Nordic countries were organized chronologically.
217. M. Grass, G. Litzell and K. Misgeld (eds). 2002. *The World in the Basement: International Material in Archives and Collections*, Stockholm: Labour Movement Archives and Library.
218. See, for example, E. Blomberg. 1995. *Män i mörker. Arbetsgivare, reformister och syndikalister: Politik och identitet i svensk gruvindustri 1910–1940*, Stockholm: Almquist & Wiksell International; L.K. Persson. 1984. *Arbete, politik, arbetarrörelse: En studie av stenindustrins Bohuslän 1860–1910*, Göteborg: Meddelanden från Historiska Institutionen i Göteborg; B. Henningson. 1996–97, 'Humanism, anarchism och socialism: Varför splittrades det socialdemokratiska vänsterpartiet?', *Arbetarhistoria* 80–81, 25–36; Kirby, 'New Wine in Old Vessels?', 439–442.
219. Grelle, *Det kooperative alternativ*; E. Lange (ed.). 2006. *Organisert kjøpekraft: Forbrukersamvirkets historie i Norge*, Oslo: Pax forlag.
220. The Institute of Working Life was established to follow up on new legislation and employed about 400 researchers, among them a number of historians. It was closed down in 2007 by the conservative Swedish government. See Åmark, 'Den svenska modellen'.
221. Among other projects can be mentioned the Nordic Centre of Excellence NordWel: 'The Nordic Welfare States: Historical Foundations and Future Challenges', 2007–2012, retrieved 13 January 2016 from http://blogs.helsinki.fi/nord-wel/.
222. G. Hagemann and H. Roll-Hansen (eds). 2005. *Twentieth-Century Housewives: Meanings and Implications of Unpaid Work*, Oslo: Oslo Academic Press.
223. See http://gaw.hist.uu.se/, retrieved 29 January 2016.
224. Hoerder, van Nederveen Meerkerk and Neunsinger, *Towards a Global History of Domestic and Caregiving Workers*.

References

Ala-Kapee, P. and M. Valkonen. 1982. *Yhdessä elämä turvalliseksi. SAK: laisen ammattiyhdistysliikkeen kehitys vuoteen 1930*, Helsinki: SAK.

Alapuro, R. 1988. *State and Revolution in Finland*, Berkeley: University of California Press.

Aldcroft, D.H. 1989. *The European Economy 1914–1980*, London: Routledge.

Åmark, K. 1989. *Maktkamp i byggbransch: avtalsrörelser och konflikter i byggbranschen 1914–1920*, Lund: Arkiv.

_____. 'Den svenska modellen: Arbetarnas fackföreningsrörelse och samverkan på svensk arbetsmarknad', in K. Misgeld and K. Åmark (eds), *Arbetsliv och arbetarrörelse: Modern historisk forskning i Sverige*, Stockholm: Arbetarrörelsens arkiv och bibliotek, 1991, 27–42.

_____. 2002. 'Arbete, arbetarrörelse och arbetarkultur: Skandinavisk historisk forskning', *Arbetarhistoria* 103–4(3–4), 4–12.

_____. 2005. *Hundra år av välfärdspolitik: Välfärdsstatens framväxt i Norge och Sverige*, Umeå: Boréa.

_____. 'Women's Labour Force Participation in the Nordic Countries during the Twentieth Century', in N.F. Christiansen et al. (eds), *The Nordic Model of Welfare: A Historical Reappraisal*, Copenhagen: Museum Tusculanum Press, 2006, 299–333.

Anderson, P. 1961. 'Sweden: Mr Crosland's Dreamland', *New Left Review* 7.

Andersson, J. and M. Hilson. 2009. 'Images of Sweden and the Nordic Countries', *Scandinavian Journal of History* 34(4), 219–28.

Andræ, C.G. 1998. *Revolt eller reform: Sverige inför revolutionerna i Europa 1917–1918*, Stockholm: Carlsson.

Árnason, J.P. and B. Wittrock. 'Introduction', in J.P. Árnason and B. Wittrock (eds), *Nordic Paths to Modernity*, New York: Berghahn Books, 2012, 1–23.

Arter, D. 1999. *Scandinavian Politics Today*, Manchester: Manchester University Press.

_____. 2011. 'Taking the Gilt off the Conservatives' Gingerbread: The April 2011 Finnish General Election', *West European Politics* 34(6), 1284–95.

Arter, D. (ed.). 2003. *From Farmyard to City Square? The Electoral Adaptation of the Nordic Agrarian Parties*, Aldershot: Ashgate.

Aylott, N. and N. Bolin. 2007. 'Towards a Two-Party System? The Swedish Parliamentary Election of September 2006', *West European Politics* 30(3), 621–33.

Berend, I. 2013. *An Economic History of Nineteenth-Century Europe: Diversity and Industrialization*, Cambridge: Cambridge University Press.

Bergh, T. 1992–93. 'Nordiskt samarbete från norsk horisont', *Arbetarhistoria* 63–65, 59–62.

_____. 2009. *Kollektiv fornuft: LO:s historie, 1969–2009*, Oslo: Pax.

Bergholm, T. 2002. 'Historieforskning och fackföreningsrörelse i Finland: Från organisationsbeskrivning till maktkamp, arbetskultur och arbetsvillkor', *Arbetarhistoria* 103–4(3–4), 45–50.

_____. 2003. *A Short History of SAK*, Helsinki: SAK.

_____. 2005. *Sopimusyhteiskunnan synty I: Työehtosopimusten läpimurrosta yleislakkoon. SAK 1944–1956*, Keuruu: Otava.

_____. 2007. *Sopimusyhteiskunnan synty II: Hajaannuksesta tulopolitiikkaan. SAK 1956–1969*, Keuruu: Otava.

_____. 2009. 'The Making of the Finnish Model', *Scandinavian Journal of History* 34(1), 29–48.

_____. 2012. *Kohti tasa-arvoa: Tulopolitiikan aika I. SAK 1969–1977*, Keuruu: Otava.

Bergholm, T. and P. Jonker-Hoffrén. 'Farewell to Communist Strike Hypothesis: The Diversity of Striking in Finland between 1971 and 1990', in S. van der

Velden et al. (eds), *Strikes and Social Conflicts: Towards a Global History*, Lisbon: International Association for Strikes and Social Conflict, 2012, 401–13. Retrieved 24 March 2015 from http://www.ilera-directory.org/15thworldcongress/files/papers/Track_4/Poster/CS1W_12_BERGHOLM.pdf

Bjørnhaug, I. 2009. *Medlemsmakt og samfunnsansvar: LO:s historie, 1935–1969*, Oslo: Pax.

Blazevic, D. 2015. *Jakten på et fagfelt: den skandinaviske kvinne- og kjønnshistoriens fremvekst i skjæringsfeltet mellom historieforskning og kvinne- og kjønnsforskning*, Bergen: Universitetet i Bergen.

Blidberg, K. 1984. *Splittrad gemenskap: kontakter och samarbete inom nordisk socialdemokratisk arbetarrörelse 1931–1945*, Stockholm: Almqvist & Wiksell International.

———. 1994. 'Ideologi och pragmatism: Samarbetet inom nordisk socialdemokratisk arbetarrörelse 1930–1955', *Den Jyske Historiker* 69–70, 132–50.

Blomberg, E. 1995. *Män i mörker. Arbetsgivare, reformister och syndikalister: Politik och identitet i svensk gruvindustri 1910–1940*, Stockholm: Almquist & Wiksell International.

Bosdotter, K. (ed.). 2012. *Faror för staten av svåraste slag: politiska fångar på Långholmen 1880–1950*, Stockholm: Stockholmia.

Bosdotter, K. and M. Isacson (eds). 2009. *Fram träder arbetaren: arbetarkonst och industrisamhällets bilder i Norden*, Stockholm: Arbetarnas bildningsförbund.

Brochmann, G. and K. Kjeldstadli. 2008. *A History of Immigration: The Case of Norway 900–2000*, Oslo: Universitetsforlaget.

Bull, E. 1968. *Norsk fagbevegelse: Oversikt over fagorganisjonens historie*, Oslo: Tiden Norsk Forlag.

———. 1976. 'Arbeiderbevægelsens stilling i de tre nordiske land 1914–1920', *Tidsskrift for arbeiderbevegelsens historie* 1, 3–28.

———. 1979. 'Arbetarrörelsens utveckling i de tre nordiska länderna, 1914–1920', *Arkiv för studier i arbetarrörelsens historia* 15/16, 62–80.

Byström, M. 2006. *En broder, gäst och parasit: uppfattningar och föreställningar om utlänningar, flyktingar och flyktingpolitik i svensk offentlig debatt 1942–1947*, Stockholm: Acta Universitatis Stockholmiensis.

Byström, M. and P. Frohnert (eds). 2013. *Reaching a State of Hope: Refugees, Immigrants and the Swedish Welfare State, 1930–2000*, Lund: Nordic Academic Press.

Callahan, K. 2000. '"Performing Inter-nationalism" in Stuttgart in 1907: French and German Socialist Nationalism and the Political Culture of an International Socialist Congress', *International Review of Social History* 45, 51–87.

Callesen, G. 'Denmark', in M. van der Linden and J. Rojahn (eds), *The Formation of Labour Movements 1870–1914: An International Perspective*, Leiden: Brill, 1990, 131–60.

Carreras, A. and C. Josephson. 'Aggregate Growth, 1870–1914: Growing at the Production Frontier', in S. Broadberry and K.H. O'Rourke (eds), *The Cambridge Economic History of Modern Europe Volume 2: 1870 to the Present*, Cambridge: Cambridge University Press, 2010, 30–58.

Childs, M. 1938. 'How the Scandinavians Do It: Three Countries Where Labor Rules Democratically', *Harper's Monthly Magazine* 177, 400–11.

Christensen, L.K. et al. 2007. *Arbejdernes historie i Danmark 1800–2000*, København: SFAH.

Christiansen, N.F. 1995. 'Arbejderklasserne i de nordiske lande før 1920 – et forsøg på komparation', *Arbejderhistorie* 3, 14–21.

Crafts, N. and G. Toniolo. 'Aggregate Growth, 1950–2000', in S. Broadberry and K.H. O'Rourke (eds), *The Cambridge Economic History of Modern Europe. Volume 2: 1870 to the Present*, Cambridge: Cambridge University Press, 2010, 296–332.

Dahl, H.F. 1971. *Norge mellom krigene: Det norske samfunnet i krise og konflikt 1918–1940*, Oslo: Pax Forlag.

Edgren, L. 'Arbetarhistoriens marginaler: Några reflexioner angående svensk arbetarhistorisk forksning', in V. Lundberg (ed.), *Arbetarhistoria i brytningstid: Landskrona i maj 2005*, Malmö: Skrifter från Centrum för Arbetarhistoria 1, 2007, 30–47.

———. 'Konflikt och samförstånd: Arbetarhistoria idag', in M. Olofsson (ed.), *Konflikt och samförstånd: Texter från arbetarhistoriska mötet i Landskrona i maj 2009*, Malmö: Skrifter från Centrum för Arbetarhistoria 4, 2011, 6–10.

Edgren, L. and M. Olofsson (eds). 2009. *Political Outsiders in Swedish History, 1848–1932*, Newcastle upon Tyne: Cambridge Scholars Publishing.

Edgren, L. and L. Olsson. 1989. 'Swedish Working-Class History', *International Labor and Working-Class History* 35, 69–80.

———. 'Arbetare och arbetsliv: Svensk arbetarhistorisk forskning', in K. Misgeld and K. Åmark (eds), *Arbetsliv och arbetarrörelse: Modern historisk forskning i Sverige*, Stockholm: Arbetarrörelsens arkiv och bibliotek, 1991, 7–26.

Egge, Å. and S. Rybner (eds). 2015. *Red Star in the North: Communism in the Nordic Countries*, Stamsund: Orkana akademisk.

Einhorn, E.S. and J. Logue. 2003. *Modern Welfare States: Scandinavian Politics and Policy in the Global Age*, Westport, Conn: Praeger.

Ekdahl, L. 1983. *Arbete mot kapital: typografer och ny teknik - studier av Stockholms tryckeriindustri under det industriella genombrottet*, Lund: Arkiv.

———. 2001. *Mot en tredje väg: en biografi över Rudolf Meidner, Vol 1: Tysk flykting och svensk modell*, Lund: Arkiv.

———. 2005. *Vol 2: Facklig expert och demokratisk socialist*, Lund: Arkiv.

———. 2011. 'Makten och människovärdet: Gruvstrejken 1969 som samhällskritik', *Arbetarhistoria* 138–39, 12–17.

Ekdahl, L. (ed.). 2002. *Löntagarfondsfrågan: en missad möjlighet*, Huddinge: Samtidshistoriska institutet, Södertörns högskola.

Eley, G. 2002. *Forging Democracy: The History of the Left in Europe, 1850–2000*, Oxford: Oxford University Press.

Elvander, N. 1980. *Skandinavisk arbetarrörelse*, Stockholm: Liber förlag.

Emilsson, T. 1976–1979. *Fátækt folk; Baráttan um brauðið; Fyrir sunnan*, Reykjavík: Mál og menning.

Eriksen, K.E., S. Halvorsen and E.A. Terjesen. 2008. 'Arbeiderbevegelsens arkiv og bibliotek gjennom 100 år', *Arbeiderhistorie Årbok for arbeiderbevegelsens arkiv og bibliotek*, 7–69.

Esaiasson, P. 1990. *Svenska valkampanjer 1866–1988*, Stockholm: Allmänna Förlaget.

Esping-Andersen, G. 1985. *Politics Against Markets: The Social Democratic Road to Power*, Princeton: Princeton University Press.

Feinstein, C., P. Temin and G. Toniolo. 1997. *The European Economy Between the Wars*, Oxford: Oxford University Press.

Fink, L. 2011. *Workers across the Americas. The Transnational Turn in Labor History*, New York: Oxford University Press.

Frangeur, R. 1998. *Yrkeskvinna eller makens tjänarinna? Striden om yrkesrätten för gifta kvinnor i mellankrigstidens Sverige*, Lund: Arkiv.

Friðriksson, Þ. 2007. *Við brún nýs dags: Saga verkamannafélagsins Dagsbrúnar 1906–1930*, Reykjavík: Efling, stéttarfélag and Sagnfræðistofnun Háskóla Íslands.

———. 2012. *Dagar vinnu og vona: Saga verkamannafélagsins Dagsbrúnar í kreppu og köldu stríði*, Reykjavík: Efling, stéttarfélag and Sagnfræðistofnun Háskóla Íslands.

Førlund, T.E. 2008. '"1968" in Norway: Piecemeal, Peaceful and Postmodern', *Scandinavian Journal of History* 33(4), 382–94.

Galenson, W. 1952. *Comparative Labor Movements*, New York: Prentice-Hall.

Gavanas, A. 2010. *Who Cleans the Welfare State? Migration, Informalization, Social Exclusion and Domestic Services in Stockholm*, Stockholm: Institute for Futures Studies.

Gavanas, A. and C. Calleman (eds). 2013. *Rena hem på smutsiga villkor? Hushållstjänster, migration och globalisering*, Göteborg and Stockholm: Makadam.

Gildea, R. 2003. *Barricades and Borders: Europe 1800–1914*, Oxford: Oxford University Press.

Grass, M. 1974. 'Arbetarskandinavism 1912–1920: Kommittén för skandinaviska arbetarrörelsens samarbete, några aspekter', *Årbog for arbejderbevægelsens historie* 4, 55–88.

———. 1975. *Friedensaktivität und Neutralität: Die skandinavische Sozialdemokratie und die neutrale Zusammenarbeit im Krieg, August 1914 bis Februar 1917*, Bonn-Bad Godeberg: Verlag Neue Gesellschaft.

———. 1987. 'Från arbetarkongress till samarbetskommitté: Om skandinaviska samarbetskommitténs bildande', *Arbetarhistoria* 42(2), 5–11.

———. 1992–93. 'Arbetarrörelsens arkiv och bibliotek – i Sverige, i Norden, i Europa. ARAB förebilden', *Arbetarhistoria* 63–65, 54–58.

Grass, M. and H. Larsson. 2002. *Labour's Memory: The Labour Movement Archives and Library, 1902–2002*, Stockholm: Arbetarrörelsens arkiv och bibliotek.

Grass, M., G. Litzell and K. Misgeld (eds). 2002. *The World in the Basement: International Material in Archives and Collections*, Stockholm: Labour Movement Archives and Library.

Grebing, H., K. Misgeld and K. Åmark (eds). 1990. *Forschung über die Arbeiterbewegung in Schweden*, Mitteilungsblatt des Instituts zur Erforschung der europäischen Arbeiterbewegung Ruhr Universität Bochum, vol 10, Bochum: Institut zur Erforschung der europäischen Arbeiterbewegung Ruhr Universität Bochum.

Grelle, H. 1984. *Under de røde faner: en historie om arbejderbevægelsen*, København: Fremad.

_____. '100 år med bøger og arkivalier', in H. Abildgaard and H. Grelle (eds), *Årbog 2008*, København: Arbejdermuseet and Arbejderbevægelsens Bibliotek og Arkiv, 2008, 6–22.

_____. 2012. *Det kooperative alternativ: Arbejderkooperationen i Danmark 1852–2012*, København: Arbejdermuseet.

Grelle, H. (ed.). 1998. *I takt med tiden: LO:s historie 1960–1997*, København: LO.

Gryten, O.H. 1995. 'The Scale of Norwegian Interwar Unemployment in International Perspective', *Scandinavian Economic History Review* 43(2), 226–50.

Gröndal, G. 2003. *Fólk í fjötrum: Baráttusaga íslenskrar alþýðu*, Reykjavík: JPV Útgafa.

Gröning, L. 1988. *Vägen till makten: SAP:s organisation och dess betydelse för den politiska verksamheten 1900–1933*, Uppsala: Acta Universitatis Upsaliensia.

'Grävboken: ett stöd för grävare inom arbetarrörelsen'. 1985. *Arbetarhistoria* 34(2).

Göransson, A. 'Från hushåll och släkt till markand och stat!', in S. Hedenborg and M. Morell (eds), *Sverige: En social och ekonomisk historia*, Lund: Studentlitteratur, 2006, 231–61.

Götz, N. 2003. 'Norden: Structures That Do Not Make a Region', *European Review of History* 10, 325–41.

Götz, N., H. Haggrén and M. Hilson. 'Nordic Cooperation in the Voluntary Sector', in J. Strang (ed.), *Nordic Cooperation: A European Region in Transition*, London: Routledge, 2016, 49–68.

Haapala, P. 'Working Class in the Formation of Industrial Society: Methodological and Other Lessons from the Case of Finland', in K. Kjeldstadli, S. Myklebust and L. Thue (eds), *Formingen av industrisamfunnet i Norden fram til 1920*, Oslo: Pensumtjeneste, 1994, 104–17.

Haapala, P. and M. Tikka. 'Revolution, Civil War and Terror in Finland in 1918', in R. Gerwarth and J. Horne (eds), *War in Peace: Paramilitary Violence in Europe after the Great War*, Oxford: Oxford University Press, DOI:10.1093/acprof:o so/9780199654918.003.0005.

Hadenius, S., H. Wieslander and B. Molin. 1969 [1967]. *Sverige efter 1900: En modern politisk historia*, Stockholm: Bokförlaget Aldus/Bonniers.

Hagemann, G. and H. Roll-Hansen (eds). 2005. *Twentieth-Century Housewives: Meanings and Implications of Unpaid Work*, Oslo: Oslo Academic Press.

Hagström, M. 2002. *KF Bibliotek – 75 år i konsumentkooperationens tjänst*, Stockholm: KF Bibliotek. Retrieved 27 April 2016 from www.mersmak.kf.se/ upload/KFBibliotek75_jubelskrift.pdf.

Halvorsen, K. and S. Stjernø. 2008. *Work, Oil and Welfare: The Welfare State in Norway*, Oslo: Universitetsforlaget.

Halvorsen, S. 1988. 'Scandinavian Trade Unions in the 1890s, with Special Reference to the Scandinavian Stonemasons' Union', *Scandinavian Journal of History* 13(1), 3–21.

Hamark, J. 2014. *Ports, Dock Workers and Labour Market Conflicts*, Gothenburg: Gothenburg Studies in Economic History.

Hansen, A.E. 2010. 'De socialistiske kvinders internationale konference i København i 1910', *Arbejderhistorie* 2, 8–28.

Hansen, M.B. and G. Callesen (eds). 1992. *Foreign Language Literature on the Nordic Labour Movements. Fremdsprachige Literatur über die nordischen Arbeiterbewegungen*, ABAs bibliografiske serie, København: Arbejderbevægelsens Bibliotek og Arkiv.

Hedenborg, S. and U. Wikander. 2003. *Makt och försörjning*, Lund: Studentlitteratur.

Helge, N., H. Grelle and J.I. Sørensen. 2005. *Velkommen i forsamlingsbygningen: Historien om arbejdernes forenings- og forsamlingsbygning i Rømersgade 1879–1983*, København: Arbejdermuseet.

Hemstad, R. 2008. *Fra Indian Summer til nordisk vinter: Skandinavisk samarbeid, skandinavisme og unionsoppløsningen*, Oslo: Akademisk publisering.

Henningson, B. 1996–97. 'Humanism, anarchism och socialism: Varför splittrades det socialdemokratiska vänsterpartiet?', *Arbetarhistoria* 80–81, 25–36.

Hentilä, S. 1978. 'The Origins of the Folkhem Ideology in Swedish Social Democracy', *Scandinavian Journal of History* 3, 323–45.

———. 1980. *Veljeyttä yli Pohjanlahden: Suomen ja Ruotsin työväenliikkeen kosketuskohtia suuresta Sundsvallin lakosta Suomen kansalaissotaan*, Helsinki: Gaudeamus.

Hilson, M. 2008. *The Nordic Model: Scandinavia since 1945*, London: Reaktion.

Hirdman, Y. 1979. *Vi bygger landet: den svenska arbetarrörelsens historia från Per Götrek till Olof Palme*, Solna: Pogo Press.

———. 1989. *Att lägga livet till rätta: studier i svensk folkhemspolitik*, Stockholm: Carlsson.

———. 1992. *Den socialistiska hemmafrun och andra kvinnohistorier*, Stockholm: Carlsson.

———. 2001. *Genus: om det stabilas föränderliga former*, Malmö: Liber.

Hobsbawm, E. 1994. *Age of Extremes: The Short Twentieth Century 1914–1991*, London: Michael Joseph.

Hoerder, D. 1984. *Essays on the Scandinavian-North American Radical Press 1880s–1930s*, Bremen: Bremen University.

———. 1987. *The Immigrant Labor Press in North America, 1840s–1970s. Vol. 1: Migrants from Northern Europe*, New York: Greenwood.

Hoerder, D., E. van Nederveen Meerkerk and S. Neunsinger (eds). 2015. *Towards a Global History of Domestic and Caregiving Workers*, Leiden: Brill.

Honkapohja, S. and E. Koskela. 'The Economic Crisis of the 1990s in Finland', in J. Kalela et al. (eds), *Down from the Heavens, Up from the Ashes: The Finnish Economic Crisis of the 1990s in the Light of Economic and Social Research*, Helsinki: Valtion Taloudellinen Tutkimuskeskus, 2001, 52–101.

Hunt, K. 'Transnationalism in Practice: The Effect of Dora Montefiore's International Travel on Women's Politics in Britain before World War I', in P. Jonsson, S. Neunsinger and J. Sangster (eds), *Crossing Boundaries: Women's Organizing in Europe and the Americas, 1880s–1940s*, Uppsala: Uppsala Studies in Economic History, 2007, 73–94.

Isacson, M. 1990. *Verkstadsindustrins arbetsmiljö: Hedemora verkstäder under 1900-talet*, Lund: Arkiv.

Ísleifsson, S. 2013. *Saga Alþýðusambands Íslands* I, Reykjavík: Forlagið.

Iversen, M.J. and S. Andersen. 'Co-operative Liberalism: Denmark from 1857 to 2007', in S. Fellman et al. (eds), *Creating Nordic Capitalism: The Business*

History of a Competitive Periphery, Basingstoke: Palgrave Macmillan, 2008, 265–334.

Iversen, M.J. and L. Thue. 'Creating Nordic Capitalism: The Business History of a Comparative Periphery', in S. Fellman et al. (eds), *Creating Nordic Capitalism: The Business History of a Competitive Periphery*, Basingstoke: Palgrave Macmillan, 2008, 1–19.

Jespersen, K.J.V. 2011. *A History of Denmark*, trans. I. Hill and C. Wade, Basingstoke: Palgrave Macmillan.

Johansson, A.O. 1990. *Arbetarrörelsen och taylorismen: Olofström 1895–1925: en studie av verkstadsindustrin och arbetets organisering*, Lund: Arkiv.

Johansson, R. 2002. 'Bilden av Ådalshändelserna 1931: 70 år av kamp om historien', *Historisk Tidskrift* 122(2), 243–70.

Jónsson, G. 2014. 'Iceland and the Nordic Model of Consensus Democracy', *Scandinavian Journal of History* 39(4), 510–28.

Jonsson, P. and S. Neunsinger. 2012. *Gendered Money: Financial Organization in Women's Movements, 1880–1933*, New York: Berghahn Books.

Jörberg, L. 'The Industrial Revolution in Scandinavia 1850–1914', trans. P. Britten Austin, Volume IV, chapter 8 of C.M. Cipolla (ed.), *The Fontana Economic History of Europe*, London: Fontana, 1970.

Jørgensen, T.E. 2008. 'The Scandinavian 1968 in a European Perspective', *Scandinavian Journal of History* 33(4), 326–38.

Judt, T. 2005. *Postwar: A History of Europe since 1945*, London: William Heinemann.

Jungar, A.-C. and A.R. Jupskås. 2014. 'Populist Radical Right Parties in the Nordic Region: A New and Distinct Party Family?', *Scandinavian Political Studies* 37(3), 215–38.

Kaihovirta, M. 2015. 'Oroliga inför framtiden: En studie av folkligt politiskt agerande bland bruksarbetarna i Billnäs ca 1900–1920', Ph.D. thesis, Åbo Akademi. Retrieved 6 January 2016 from https://www.doria.fi/handle/10024/113083

Karlsson, L. 2009. *Arbetarrörelsen, Folkets Hus och offentligheten i Bromölla 1905–1960*, Växjö: Växjö University Press.

Karlsson, S.O. 1998. *När industriarbetaren blev historia: studier i svensk arbetarhistoria 1965–1995*, Lund: Studentlitteratur.

Kirby, D. 1974. 'Stockholm-Petrograd-Berlin: International Social Democracy and Finnish Independence, 1917', *Slavonic and East European Review* 52(126), 63–84.

———. 1986. '"The Workers' Cause": Rank-and-File Attitudes and Opinions in the Finnish Social Democratic Party 1905–1918', *Past and Present* 111, 130–64.

———. 1986. *War, Peace and Revolution: International Socialism at the Crossroads 1914–1918*, Aldershot: Gower.

———. 1988. 'New Wine in Old Vessels? The Finnish Socialist Workers' Party, 1919–1923', *The Slavonic and East European Review* 66(3), 426–45.

———. 'Finland', in M. van der Linden and J. Rojahn (eds), *The Formation of Labour Movements 1870–1914: An International Perspective*, Leiden: E.J. Brill, 1990, 523–40.

———. 'What Was "Nordic" about the Labour Movement in Europe's Northernmost Regions?', in P. Kettunen, (ed.), *Lokalt och internationellt: Dimensioner i den nordiska arbetarrörelsen och arbetarkulturen*, Tammerfors: Sällskapet för forskning i arbetarhistoria i Finland, 2002, 13–32.

———. 2006. *A Concise History of Finland*, Cambridge: Cambridge University Press.

Kjartansson, H.S. 1980. 'Emigrant Fares and Emigration from Iceland to North America, 1874–1893', *Scandinavian Economic History Review* 28(1), 53–71.

Kjeldstadli, K. 1994. *Et splittet samfunn, 1905–1935*, Oslo: Aschehoug.

———. 'Noen vitenskapsteoretiske spørsmål slik de framtrer i Edvard Bull: "Arbeiderbevægelsens stilling i de nordiske land 1914–1920"', in *Historie, kritikk og politikk. Festskrift til Per Maurseth på 70-års dagen 7. juni 2002*, Trondheim: Skrifter fra Historisk tidsskrift i Trondheim, 2002, 321–36.

———. 'En ny arbeidslivets historie?', in *Myndighet og medborgarskap. Festskrift til Gro Hagemann på 70-årsdagen 3. september 2015*, Oslo: Novus Forlag, 2015, 281–92.

———. 'Folkesosialisme. Stykke i tre satser', in R. Glenthøj (ed.), *Mellem brødre: Dansk-norsk samliv i 600 år*, København og Oslo: Gads forlag & SAP, 2016, 192–203.

Kjellberg, A. 2001. *Fackliga organisationer och medlemmar i dagens Sverige*, Lund: Arkiv.

Kristjánsdóttir, R. 2008. *Nýtt fólk: Þjóðerni og íslensk vinstri stjórnmál 1901–1944*, Reykjavík: Háskólaútgáfan, 31–61.

———. 2012. 'For Equality or Against Foreign Oppression? The Politics of the Left in Iceland Leading up to the Cold War', *Moving the Social* 48, 11–28.

Lähteenmäki, M. 1987. 'Orientering mot Norden 1919–1939', *Arbetarhistoria* 42(2), 23–24.

Lahtinen, E. 1987. 'Finländarna i det nordiska samarbetet 1880–1918', *Arbetarhistoria* 42(2), 20–23.

———. 1988. 'Finnish Participation in Co-operation within the Nordic Labour Movement, 1880–1918', *Scandinavian Journal of History* 13(1), 23–28.

———. 1992–93. 'Från förråd till arkiv i Helsingfors', *Arbetarhistoria* 63–65, 63–65.

Lange, E. (ed.). 2006. *Organisert kjøpekraft: Forbrukersamvirkets historie i Norge*, Oslo: Pax forlag.

Laubjerg, A. 2006. *Den store bølge: erindringsbilleder fra storkøbenhavnske industriarbejdspladser*, Rødovre: Forlaget Sohn.

Lavery, J. 2006. *The History of Finland*, Westport, Connecticut: Greenwood Press.

Leonard, C. and J. Ljungberg. 'Population and Living Standards, 1870–1914', in S. Broadberry and K.H. O'Rourke (eds), *The Cambridge Economic History of Modern Europe*, Cambridge: Cambridge University Press, 108–129.

Linderborg, Å. 2001. *Socialdemokraterna skriver historia: Historieskrivning som ideologisk maktresurs 1892–2000*, Stockholm: Atlas.

Lindqvist, S. 1978. *Gräv där du står: Hur man utforskar ett job*, Stockholm: Bonniers.

———. 1980. 'Dig Where You Stand', *Meddelande från Arbetarrörelsens arkiv och bibliotek* 16, 42–47.

———. 1989. *Grabe wo du stehst: Handbuch zur Erforschung der eigenen Geschichte*, trans. M. Dammeyer, Bonn: Dietz.

Lindqvist, S., et al. 1978. *Grav hvor du står: Håndbog i at udforske et arbejde*, København: Forlaget SOC.

Lindström, U. 1985. *Fascism in Scandinavia 1920–1940*, Stockholm: Almqvist & Wiksell.

Linna, V. 2001–2003. *Under the North Star; The Uprising; Reconciliation*, trans. R. Impola, Beaverton: Aspasia Books.

Lorenz, E. 1992. *Exil in Norwegen: Lebensbedingungen und Arbeit deutschsprachiger Flüchtlinge 1933–1943*, Baden-Baden: Nomos.

Lorenz, E., K. Misgeld, H. Müssener and H.U. Petersen (eds).1998. *Ein sehr trübes Kapitel?: Hitlerflüchtlinge im nordeuropäischen Exil 1933 bis 1950*, Hamburg: Ergebnisse-Verl.

Lorenzen-Schmidt, K.-J. and H.U. Petersen. 1991. *Hitlerflüchtlinge im Norden: Asyl und politisches Exil: 1933–1945*, Kiel: Neuer Malik-Vlg.

Louhikko, E.K. 1946. *Vi gjorde revolution*, Helsingfors: Söderström.

Lundberg, U. 2003. *Juvelen i kronan: Socialdemokraterna och den allmänna pensionen*, Stockholm: Hjalmarson & Högberg.

Lundh, C. 2002. *Spelets regler: institutioner och lönebildning på den svenska arbetsmarknaden 1850–2000*, Stockholm: SNS förlag.

Lundkvist, S. 1977. *Folkrörelserna i det svenska samhället 1850–1920*, Uppsala: Uppsala universitet.

Magnusson, L. 2000. *An Economic History of Sweden*, London: Routledge.

Majander, M. 1997. 'Tillbaka till den nordiska gemenskapen. De finska socialdemokraterna och Norden 1944–1948', *Historisk Tidskrift för Finland* 82(1), 45–76.

Manns, U. 'Historico-Political Strategies of Scandinavian Feminist Movements: Preliminary Perspectives of a Research Project', in J. Mittag, B. Unfried and E. Himmelstoss (eds), *Arbeiter- und soziale Bewegungen in der öffentlichen Erinnerung: Eine globale Perspektive*, Berlin: Akademische Verlagsanstalt, 2011, 219–30.

Marjomaa, U. (ed.). 2000. *100 Faces from Finland: A Biographical Kaleidoscope*, Helsinki: Finnish Literature Society.

Markkola, P. 'The Nordic and Gendering Dimensions of Labour History in Finland', in H. Haggrén, J. Rainio-Niemi and J. Vauhkonen (eds), *Multi-Layered Historicity of the Present: Approaches to Social Science History*, Helsinki: Department of Political and Economic Studies, 2013, 33–46.

Markkola, P. and A.-C. Östman. 2012. 'Torparfrågan tillspetsas: Frigörelse, oberoende och arbete – 1918 års torparlagstiftning ur mansperspektiv', *Historisk Tidskrift för Finland* 97(1), 17–41.

Meinander, H. 2012. *Republiken Finland: igår och idag*, Helsingfors: Schildts & Söderströms.

Meyer, F. 2001. *"Dansken, svensken og nordmannen": skandinaviske habitusforskjeller sett i lys av kulturmøtet med tyske flyktinger: en komparativ studie*, Oslo: Unipub.

Mikkelsen, F. 1988. 'Fra proletarisering til klassesamfund: Industrialisering, urbanisering og fremvæksten af en arbejderklasse og arbejderbevægelse i Skandinavien ca 1750–1900', *Arbejderhistorie* 30, 2–20.

Misgeld, K. 1976. *Die "Internationale Gruppe demokratischer Sozialisten" in Stockholm 1942–1945: Zur sozialistischen Friedensdiskussion während des Zweiten Weltkrieges*, Uppsala: Studia historica upsaliensia.

———. 1984. *Sozialdemokratie und Aussenpolitik in Schweden. Sozialistische Internationale, Europapolitik und die Deutschlandfrage 1945–1955*, Frankfurt/ Main: Campus.

———. 1985. 'Arbetarrörelsens samarbete i Norden 1931–1945', *Historisk Tidskrift* 84(4), 474–81.

Misgeld, K. and K. Åmark (eds). 1991. *Arbetsliv och arbetarrörelse: Modern historisk forskning i Sverige*, Stockholm: Uppsatser utgivna av Arbetarrörelsens arkiv och bibliotek.

Morell, M. 'Agriculture in Industrial Society 1870–1945', in J. Myrdal and M. Morell (eds), *The Agrarian History of Sweden from 4000 BC to AD 2000*, Lund: Nordic Academic Press, 2011, 165–213.

Müssener, H. 1974. *Exil in Schweden: Politische und kulturelle Emigration nach 1933*, München: C Hanser.

Myrdal, A. and G. Myrdal. 1934. *Kris i befolkningsfrågan*, Stockholm: Bonnier.

Nelles, D. 'Der Widerstand der Internationalen Transportarbeiter Föderation (ITF) gegen Nationalsozialismus und Faschismus in Deutschland und Schweden', in A. Graf (ed.), *Anarchisten gegen Hitler: Anarchisten, Anarcho-Syndikalisten, Rätekommunisten in Widerstand und Exil*, Berlin: Lukas, 2001, 114–55.

Neunsinger, S. 2001. *Die Arbeit der Frauen - die Krise der Männer: Die Erwerbstätigkeit verheirateter Frauen in Deutschland und Schweden 1919–1939*, Uppsala: Studia historica Upsaliensia, 198.

———. 'From Servitude to Domestic Service: The Role of International Bodies, States and Elites for Changing Conditions in Domestic Work Between the 19th and 20th Centuries. An Introduction', in D. Hoerder, E. van Nederveen Meerkerk and S. Neunsinger (eds), *Towards a Global History of Domestic and Caregiving Workers*, Leiden: Brill, 2015, 389–99.

Newby, A. 2014. '"Neither Do These Tenants or Their Children Emigrate": Famine and Transatlantic Emigration from Finland in the Nineteenth Century', *Atlantic Studies* 11(3), 383–402.

Nielsen, V.O. 'SFAHs historie – baggrund, start og udvikling', in N.O.H. Jensen et al., *Fremad, ad nye veje: bidrag til diskussionen om arbejderhistorien i 1990'erne*, København: SFAH, 1990, 215–30.

Nilsson, T. 2014. 'Fiktion, hierarki och havets hårda arbete: Skönlitteratur som källa till svensk maritim historia', *Historisk Tidskrift* 134(3), 462–98.

Nordic Centre of Excellence NordWel: 'The Nordic Welfare States: Historical Foundations and Future Challenges', 2007–2012. Retrieved 13 January 2016 from http://blogs.helsinki.fi/nord-wel/

Nyström, D. 2015. *Innan forskningen blev radikal: en historiografisk studie av arbetarhistoria och kvinnohistoria*, Malmö: Universus Academic Press.

Nyzell, S. 2010. *'Striden ägde rum i Malmö'. Möllevångskravallerna 1926: En studie av politiskt våld i mellankrigstidens Sverige*, Malmö: Malmö högskola.

O'Hara, G. 2008. 'Applied Socialism of a Fairly Moderate Kind', *Scandinavian Journal of History* 33(1), 1–25.

Olsen, G.M. 1992. *The Struggle for Economic Democracy in Sweden*, Aldershot: Avebury.

Olsson, L. 1980. *Då barn var lönsamma: om arbetsdelning, barnarbete och teknologis-ka förändringar i några svenska industrier under 1800- och början av 1900-talet*, Stockholm: Tiden.

———. 1986. *Gamla typer och nya produktionsförhållanden: om rationalisering och medbestämmande, åldrande och solidaritet bland typografer i Sverige från slutet av 1800-talet till omkring 1960*, Lund: Lucifer.

Olstad, F. 2009. *Med knyttet neve: LO:s historie 1899–1935*, Oslo: Pax.

Östberg, K. 1997. *Efter rösträtten: kvinnors utrymme efter det demokratiska genom-brottet*, Eslöv: B Östlings bokförl. Symposion.

———. 2008. 'Sweden and the Long "1968": Break or Continuity?', *Scandinavian Journal of History* 33(4), 339–52.

Palm, A. 1901. *Ögonblicksbilder från en resa till Amerika*, Stockholm: Författarnas Förlag.

Persson, K.E. and C. Högmark. 1995. *Nordiska beklädnadsarbetareunioner 1897–1993*, Stockholm: Nordiska industriarbetarefederationen.

Persson, L.K. 1984. *Arbete, politik, arbetarrörelse: En studie av stenindustrins Bohuslän 1860–1910*, Göteborg: Meddelanden från Historiska Institutionen i Göteborg.

Pinto, A.B., M. Ericsson and S. Nyzell. 2015. 'Contentious Politics Studies: Forskningsfältet social och politisk confrontation på frammarsch i Skandinavien', *Scandia* 81(1), 93–110.

Pred, A. 1998. 'Memory and the Cultural Reworking of Crisis: Racisms and the Current Moment of Danger in Sweden, or Wanting It Like Before', *Environment and Planning D: Society and Space* 16, 635–64.

Qvist, G. 1974. *Statistik och politik: Landsorganisationen och kvinnorna på arbets-marknaden*, Stockholm: Prisma.

Redvaldsen, D. 2011. *The Labour Party in Britain and Norway: Elections and the Pursuit of Power between the World Wars*, London: I.B. Tauris.

Rostgaard, M. and A.E. Hansen. 1992. 'Signalement af forskningen i arbejdslivets historie i Danmark', *Årbog for arbejderbevægelsens historie* 22, 15–33.

SAMAK. 'Sørmarka Declaration of the Nordic Workers' Congress, 11–12 November 2014, "We Build the Nordics"'. Retrieved 6 January 2016 from http://samak-nordicmodel.org/

Sassoon, D. 1996. *One Hundred Years of Socialism: The West European Left in the Twentieth Century*, New York: The New Press.

Schiller, B. 1967. *Storstrejken 1909: förhistoria och orsaker*, Göteborg: Elander.

———. 1987. 'Den skandinaviska arbetarrörelsens internationalism 1870–1914', *Arbetarhistoria* 42(2), 3–4.

Schmitz, E. 2011. '"Kan de strejka i Norge kan väl vi också". ASAB-städerskornas strejker under 1974 och 1975', *Arbetarhistoria* 138–39, 18–26.

Schüllerqvist, B. 1992. *Från kosackval till kohandel: SAP:s väg till makten 1928–33*, Stockholm: Tiden.

Schön, L. 2000. *En modern svensk ekonomisk historia: Tillväxt och omvandling under två sekel*, Stockholm: SNS Förlag.

Scott, A. 2006. 'Social Democracy in Northern Europe: Its Relevance for Australia', *Australian Review of Public Affairs* 7(1), 1–17.

Sejersted, F. 2005. *Socialdemokratins tidsålder: Sverige och Norge under 1900-talet*, Nora: Bokförlaget Nya Doxa.

———. 2011. *The Age of Social Democracy: Norway and Sweden in the Twentieth Century*, trans. R. Daly, edited M.B. Adams, Princeton: Princeton University Press.

Siltala, J. 2015. 'Dissolution and Reintegration in Finland, 1914–1932: How Did a Disarmed Country Become Absorbed into Brutalization?', *Journal of Baltic Studies* 46(1), 11–33.

Sjögren, H. 'Welfare Capitalism: The Swedish Economy, 1850–2005', in S. Fellman et al. (eds), *Creating Nordic Capitalism: The Business History of a Competitive Periphery*, Basingstoke: Palgrave Macmillan, 2008, 22–74.

Sogner, S. 'Tjenestejenter til Holland', in *Vår barndoms have: årbok Vest-Agder fylkesmuseum*, Kristiansand: Vest-Agder fylkesmuseum, 1998, 22–35.

Sogner, S. and K. Telste. 2005. *Ut og søkje teneste: historia om tenestejentene*, Oslo: Det Norske Samlaget.

Soikkanen, H. 1961. 'Sosialismin tulo Suomeen: Ensimmäisiin yksikamarisen eduskunnan vaaleihin asti', Ph.D. dissertation, Turku: Turun yliopisto.

———. 1978. 'Revisionism, Reformism and the Finnish Labour Movement before the First World War', *Scandinavian Journal of History* 3, 347–60.

———. 1987. *Kohti kansanvaltaa 2: 1937–1944*, Joensuu: Suomen Sosialidemokraattinen Puolue.

Soikkanen, T. 1984. *Kansallinen eheytymien – myytti vai todellisuus? Ulko- ja sisäpolitiikan linjat ja vuorovaikutus Suomessa vuosina 1933–1939*, Porvoo: WSOY.

Sommestad, L. 1994. 'Privat eller offentlig välfärd? Ett genusperspektiv på välfärdsstatens historiska formering', *Historisk Tidskrift* 114(4), 611–29.

Sørensen, Ø. and B. Stråth (eds). 1997. *The Cultural Construction of Norden*, Oslo: Scandinavian Academic Press.

Sparring, Å. (ed.). 1966. *Kommunismen i Norden*, Stockholm: Albert Bonniers.

Ståhl, M. 1999. *Vår fana röd till färgen: fanor som medium för visuell kommunikation under arbetarrörelsens genombrottstid i Sverige fram till 1890*, Linköping: Tema, Univ.

———. 2005. *Möten och människor i Folkets hus och Folkets park*, Stockholm: Atlas.

———. 2008. *Vår röda fana!*, Stockholm: IF Metall.

Stenius, H. 1987. *Frivilligt, jämlikt, samfällt. Föreningsväsendets utveckling i Finland fram till 1900-talets början med speciell hänsyn till massorganisationsprincipens genombrott*, Helsingfors: Skrifter utgivna av Svenska Litteratursällskapet i Finland.

———. 'Nordic Associational Life in a European and an Inter-Nordic Perspective', in R. Alapuro and H. Stenius (eds), *Nordic Associations in a European Perspective*, Baden-Baden: Nomos Verlag, 2010, 29–86.

———. 'Paradoxes of the Finnish Political Culture', in J.P. Árnason and B. Wittrock (eds), *Nordic Paths to Modernity*, New York: Berghahn Books, 2012, 207–28.

Stråth, B. 2005. *Union och demokrati: De förenade rikena Sverige-Norge 1814–1905*, Nora: Nya Doxa Förlag.

Sundholm, J. '"The Unknown Soldier": Film as a Founding Trauma and National Monument', in C. Mithander, J. Sundholm and M. Holmgren Troy (eds),

Collective Traumas: Memories of War and Conflict in 20ᵗʰ-Century Europe, Brussels: Peter Lang, 2007, 111–41.

Svanberg, I. and M. Tydén. 1992. *Tusen år av invandring: en svensk kulturhistoria*, Stockholm: Gidlunds.

Terjesen, E.A. 2012. 'Partsforholdet i arbeidslivet: Kompromiss, allianse, samarbeid eller kamp?', *Arbeiderhistorie*, 11–37.

Thompson, P. 1978. 'Life Histories in Poland and Scandinavia', *History Workshop Journal* 6, 208–10.

Thörnquist, A. 2013. *False (Bogus) Self-Employment in East-West Labour Migration: Recent Trends in the Swedish Construction and Road Haulage Industries*, Norrköping: Remeso.

———. 2015. *East-West Labour Migration and the Swedish Cleaning Industry: A Matter of Immigrant Competition?*, Norrköping: REMESO.

Thörnquist, A. and Å.-K. Engstrand (eds). 2011. *Precarious Employment in Perspective: Old and New Challenges to Working Conditions in Sweden*, Bruxelles and New York: P.I.E. Peter Lang.

Timonen, V. 2003. *Restructuring the Welfare State: Globalization and Social Policy Reform in Finland and Sweden*, Cheltenham: Edward Elgar.

Tingsten, H. 1941. *Den svenska socialdemokratins idéutveckling*, Stockholm: Tidens förlag.

Tjørnehøj, H. 1998. *Fremad og atter fremad ... LO:s historie 1871–1960*, København: LO.

Työväen Arkisto. 'Työväen Arkisto: Eilistä ja nykypäivää'. Retrieved 13 January 2016 from http://www.tyark.fi/meolemme.htm.

Uhlén, A. 1957. *Skandinaviska transportarbetarefederationen 1907–1957: Historik*, Helsingborg: Skandinaviska transportarbetarefederationen.

Upton, A.F. 1973. *The Communist Parties of Scandinavia and Finland*, London: Weidenfeld and Nicolson.

———. 1981. *The Finnish Revolution 1917–1918*, Minneapolis: University of Minnesota Press.

Valkonen, M. 1987. *Yhdessä elämä turvalliseksi: Suomen Ammattiyhdistysten Keskusliitto 1930–1947*, Helsinki: SAK.

van der Linden, M. 2008. *Workers of the World: Essays Toward a Global Labor History*, Leiden: Brill.

van der Linden, M. and J. Lucassen. 1999. *Prolegomena for a Global Labour History*, Amsterdam: International Institute of Social History.

van Goethem, G. 2006. *The Amsterdam International: The World of the International Federation of Trade Unions (IFTU), 1913–1945*, Aldershot: Ashgate.

van Nederveen Meerkerk, E., S. Neunsinger and D. Hoerder. 'Domestic Workers of the World: Histories of Domestic Work as Global Labor History', in D. Hoerder, E. van Nederveen Meerkerk and S. Neunsinger (eds), *Towards a Global History of Domestic and Caregiving Workers*, Leiden: Brill, 2015, 1–24.

Viktorov, I. 2006. *Fordismens kris och löntagarfonder i Sverige*, Stockholm: Acta Universitatis Stockholmiensis.

von Schoultz, J. 1924. *Bidrag till belysande av Finlands socialdemokratiska partis historia*, Helsingfors: Söderström.

Waldemarson, Y. 1998. *Mjukt till formen - hårt till innehållet: LOs kvinnoråd 1947–1967*, Stockholm: Atlas.

Wikander, U. 1988. *Kvinnors och mäns arbeten: Gustavsberg 1880–1980: genusarbetsdelning och arbetets degradering vid en porslinsfabrik*, Lund: Arkiv.

――――. 1989. 'Periodisering av kapitalismen – med kvinnor', *Arbetarhistoria* 51, 7–11.

――――. 1999. *Kvinnoarbete i Europa 1789–1950: genus, makt och arbetsdelning*, Stockholm: Atlas.

――――. 2006. *Feminism, familj och medborgarskap: debatter på internationella kongresser om nattarbetsförbud för kvinnor 1889–1919*, Göteborg: Makadam.

CHAPTER 1

CONNECTING LABOUR
Organizing Swedish Ironmaking in an Atlantic Context

Göran Rydén and Chris Evans

Stepping Through the Gates at Leufsta Bruk

On the last day of June 1753, Christer Berch, the future professor of economics at Uppsala University, arrived at Leufsta *bruk*,[1] one of the largest ironmaking sites in Sweden. He stepped through the gates and arrived in a distinctively urban place in the midst of the rural county of Uppland. Leufsta did not enjoy the formal status of a town, but it was still quite different to its surroundings. Berch had taken some time off from his university studies and, together with his younger brother, set off for a tour of his native county; he wanted to enjoy 'the sweet pleasures of summer', as well as improve his knowledge about his 'Fatherland'. Countryside walking might have been a part of the former, but the latter was achieved by visiting ironmaking sites; bar iron was of prime importance to Sweden as its major export commodity. However, on arrival at Leufsta, the brothers might have been a bit disappointed. It was a Saturday and they entered a silent place, at least for a couple of hours, until the inhabitants started to drink beer; no furnace was in blast and the forges lay idle.[2]

The aim of this chapter is to tell the story of work at one of eighteenth-century Sweden's most important places for bar iron making, Leufsta bruk. It will centre on what took place at the forges, in the manly workplaces at the very centre of the communities, but also discuss what took place in other areas of the bruk, including women's work. Labour history (at least its Scandinavian guise) has been devoted to unveiling hidden aspects of work and labour within modern society. When labour historians have made excursions into early modern terrain they have all too often taken with them concepts and theoretical preconceptions born of modernity. The danger of teleology in such a procedure is plain. A focus on concrete everyday practices, however, can help us avoid treating early modern work as a mere precursor of modernity and thus afford us a better way to make comparisons across time. However, such an ambitious undertaking cannot be accomplished here. Before that can be done, much more work is needed on daily practice in the modern era, let alone the early modern, for if we leave to one side research undertaken within the project 'Det svenska arbetets history' in the 1980s, modern labour historians have shown relatively little interest in the 'everyday'.[3] For now, we will merely point towards the possibility of connections and comparisons over time; this chapter will first and foremost tell a story about work at eighteenth-century Leufsta.[4]

This chapter has been written with a microhistorical ambition, with a starting point that the 'micro' in microhistory is more than writing about what is 'small'. It should rather be about reaching 'generalizations without filtering out individuals and situations'; it requires from historians a 'return' to 'moments, situations', persons and places where history was made. It is only from a perspective of the 'micro' that we can view life in its full complexity, and also expose differences from the grander explanatory models we have used for a long time.[5] Giovanni Levi stressed that microhistory should foremost be seen as a 'practice' and not a theoretical undertaking; the historian's 'practice' should aim at unveiling the 'practice' of the people of the past and Levi's approach can be viewed as a 'double-edged practice'.[6]

Recent years have seen a rebirth of an interest in microhistory, often as an integrated part of writing global history; important studies have attempted to merge micro studies with analyses stretching around the globe.[7] Emma Rothschild's *The Inner Life of Empires*, from 2011, is a good example of this. The very title of her book might be read as an intricate way of combining two levels of analysis; the object of this penetrating study, the Johnstones, a Scottish family of imperial activists and travellers, might be viewed as an 'empire' in itself. For Rothschild, as for most global historians, connections are key, but she refuses to privilege the major imperial connections that spanned the globe above the micro-connections that linked family members. Nor does she distinguish between the material life of the Johnstones and the interior life of the mind. She deals with a world in which the conceptual language needed to make such distinctions was absent: 'the idea of race was indistinct ... [as were] the ideas of empire, or law, or economic life'. Only by delving into the microhistory of the Johnstones can 'a new way of thinking about one of the oldest historical inquiries ... the history of the inner life' be pursued. It is at such a micro level, Rothschild suggests, that the emergence of new languages of social understanding can be traced in the eighteenth century.[8]

Seen from a rather shallow definition of historical practice, this text begins with just one community, but by investigating work in a local setting during the early modern period we aim to reveal something more. Work is an essential aspect of human existence, and work has played an important role in most theories of human development. Yet we know very little about it. This statement could be downscaled, and we could start from a Swedish perspective: it is known that the making of bar iron was an important aspect of Swedish eighteenth-century development, yet hardly anything is known about the actual work that made this production a reality. We have a somewhat artificial knowledge about the bruk, but mainly the bruk as an enterprise or as a technological arena. However, it was the men and women of places like Leufsta that actually made the bars, and their work is almost unknown. Our ambition is to begin with the concrete work done by the people at the bruk, but to link that with the work of other people in other places. Global history as a practice has had connections as one of its distinguishing features, and many studies have been published stressing how people and places around the world were linked. Few, however, have linked workers to workers.[9]

Work at Leufsta Bruk

In the early hours of Monday morning the bruk took on a different character, and the Berch brothers woke in a totally different soundscape. The whole community was now on its feet. In many ways this morning experience was much closer to the true character of Leufsta, or, for that matter, the character of any other bruk in Sweden. Leufsta was a place made for production and work. Having said that, Leufsta extended far beyond the quasi-urban community the Berch brothers had entered that Saturday, for early modern ironmaking was more than an urban craft; it transgressed the rural-urban distinction. A bruk was both a large landed estate and an industrial community, and although the imposing gate through which the Berch brothers had walked marked the beginning of

Leufsta as an industrial settlement, they had entered Leufsta territory long before that.[10]

Leufsta bruk has a long history. Founded by peasants in the sixteenth century and then taken over by the Crown, Leufsta had a 'new beginning' in the following century when the Dutch merchant Louis De Geer acquired control of it. From the 1620s he took charge of the development of the iron industry in Uppland, centred as it was around the rich Dannemora mine; De Geer also acquired Österby and Gimo bruk. In the eighteenth century, the De Geer family still owned Leufsta, but were in the midst of expanding their interests. They purchased other bruk in the county and came to control the majority of shares in Dannemora. In 1740, when the twenty-year-old Charles De Geer took possession of his estate, Leufsta bruk was a very large ironmaking estate, possibly the largest in Sweden, consisting of huge tracts of land, blast furnaces at Tobo, Hillebola, Åkerby and Carlholm and forges at Åkerby and Leufsta. Within the gates through which Berch passed was a blast furnace and four forges. Iron ore from Dannemora and charcoal made by tenants on the estate were carted to the furnace where pig iron was made. This crude iron was then distributed among the forges along with yet more charcoal. It was an intricate and complicated structure.[11]

It is very difficult to give an accurate measure of how large Leufsta bruk really was in the time of Charles De Geer. For a start, it was constantly changing, with smaller estates being bought, sold or bartered. In addition, the De Geer family owned other 'non-Leufsta' estates in the county and sometimes managed everything as a single unit. However, by viewing the output of bar iron from Uppland as a whole, it is clear that the De Geers' share of the total was as much as 75 per cent at its peak in the 1740s. From a source from 1739 we know that the estate included 246 farmsteads in thirteen different parishes, inhabited by 326 male peasants and crofters,[12] along with their wives and servants – a total of 716 adults. The same source says that 344 inhabitants over the age of fifteen lived within the gates of the ironmaking community that Berch was to visit some fourteen years later.[13]

In 1748 there were about twenty bruk in the county of Uppland and together they produced about 6,000 tons of bar iron. All of these works used the so-called Walloon forging method and they produced the most sought-after iron in Europe at the time, Öregrund iron.[14] However, this was only a fraction of the total volume of iron produced in Sweden at the time. At mid century, slightly more than 400 bruk made approximately 50,000 tons of iron. All bruk outside Uppland used another forging technique, the German method. Most of these works were located in the Bergslagen region of central Sweden, but ironmaking was scattered around many other parts of Sweden as well. Georg Haggrén has talked about the works outside central Sweden as 'provincial bruk', and he has highlighted bruk along the Gulf of Bothnia, in southern Finland and in the county of Småland.[15]

When the Berch brothers woke up in the early hours of 2 July 1753, it was the movement of women around the bruk that caught their eye. The large population of the place needed grain and other provisions for its subsistence, Berch noted in his diary, and these were supplied from two old warehouses on a monthly basis: 'The Bruk's-people always take out their supplies the first day of each month'. From the accounts we can sense the size of the operation that Monday morning, with 592 barrels of rye and 343 barrels of malt being dispensed, along with smaller volumes of tobacco, barley, hops and tallow. People were also provided with salt, herring, salted salmon, butter and fresh fish. They could pick up cloth and other textiles from another warehouse. Berch's description gives us an opportunity to sense what happened at Leufsta that very morning. The staff at the bruk's office had been busy since two o'clock in the morning, signing chits for the amount each household was allowed to take from the stores. From a description in 1739 we know that a treasurer at the office was in charge of the warehouses, helped by an office boy. On delivery days, other clerks and workers probably assisted. As soon as the work in the office was done, it was the women's turn to work. Berch noted that 'this was the task for the women, when the men were at work', and he was particularly impressed by the small wagons with which the women carted their provisions from the warehouses to the sheds attached to their dwellings, and the intensity of this activity: 'they crawled like ants, to and fro, and the streets were filled with wagons'.[16]

According to Berch, the women's work that Monday morning was related to men's work in two ways. On the one hand, the supplies the women got at the warehouses were related to the wage earned by the men, and paid work was thus connected to unpaid work; on the other, Berch stated that the women carted supplies while 'the men were at work', indicating that Leufsta bruk was a place where everybody worked. These two features of Leufsta – the ubiquity of labour and the interconnectedness of its different facets – are present in other sources as well. The manager in charge during Charles De Geer's adolescence in the 1730s, *Directeur* Eric Touscher, made that clear in an instruction booklet he penned for his master. Chapter 7, on 'Daily tasks', described how a bell divided the day into different segments of labour and rest; work began at five in the morning and ended at seven o'clock in the evening. Two hour-long breaks for meals were given. Touscher also mentioned that he had one of his clerks walking around the place to see that 'work was done with fidelity'.[17]

With respect to interconnectedness, it was not just that men's work was tied to women's, but that there were connections between different parts of the bruk. The most important of these were the links that led from the mine, via the blast furnaces, to the forges, but other workshops were also attached to this commodity chain: a wheelwright's shop, a smithy, even a shoemaker's workshop, where shoes for the people of Leufsta were made or repaired. At the very centre of this structure was the bar iron making in the forges, something that was not missed by Berch. It was the only work he described in detail, and from the way it was introduced one can assume that he had longed to see it: 'Here could we for the first time see Walloon forging'.[18]

Leufsta was, thus, a very large bruk; it contained four forges, when two would have been standard. As Berch stated, the Walloon forging method was used instead of the more common German method. The former had a larger forge crew and a more intricate division of labour. Most of the forges in the county of Uppland made bar iron according to the Walloon method. This was an inheritance from the previous century, when Dutch merchants like Louis De Geer had brought not only capital and mercantile expertise to the region, but also skilled workers from Wallonia. About 1,000 such migrants arrived in Sweden in the mid seventeenth century, and they were armed with skills and technologies not previously common in Sweden. Walloon forging was the most important of these, and it remained in use well into the twentieth century at bruk in the county of Uppland.[19] The iron made by the descendants of these migrant forgemen was sometimes called Walloon iron, and the places where it was made are still called *Vallonbruk*. As Christer Berch observed, when the 'Walloon' forgemen marched to their forges at six o'clock on Sunday evening, they wore distinctive garb: 'The forgemen arrive then in their long white clean shirts, with the leather apron in front'.[20]

There are no clues in Berch's description as to which of the four forges he visited during his stay at Leufsta in those early days of July 1753, but one can probably rule out the upper and lower forges at the edge of the bruk. A more likely choice is one of the remaining two, *Spikhammaren* or *Storhammaren*, as they were placed at the very centre of Leufsta, next to each other, where the stream ran out of the largest pond. He might have looked in at both, but he would certainly not have missed the opportunity to enter Storhammaren, perhaps the most prestigious of all workplaces within the Swedish iron industry.[21] If he did so, then one of the forgemen walking towards the forge that evening, with his 'leather apron in front', was the master finer Raphael Pousett, a thirty-six year old of Walloon descent. He was the leading worker in this forge and together with one of the two finer apprentices he began by setting the fire in the finery. Then they 'released the bellows', and put the pig iron in the hearth 'to be melted on charcoal'. As soon as a sufficient quantity of iron had melted and gathered at the bottom of the hearth they extracted it with a pair of tongs, brought it to the water-powered hammer, and formed it into 'the shape of a brick'. This piece of iron, called an anchony, was then left on the forge floor. By this time the two finers had been joined in the forge by three other workers, a master hammerman, his hand and a charcoal-hauling *goudjar*. It was the task of the two hammermen to pick up the anchony and place it in another hearth, the chafery, where it was reheated. When hot enough, this piece of iron was drawn out into a bar under the water-powered hammer.[22]

This first bar of the week took less than an hour to make, but it was the first of many, as the process was to be repeated many times over a long working week. The five forgemen made another six bars before being replaced by another five forgemen. They had then performed their first 'Tourneij' (that is, their first shift of about four hours) and were given a break for an equally long period. Berch noted 'when each has done his work, in its time and Tourneij, he steps down, and new people come in and continue work. The forgeman goes home sweaty, first to eat then to sleep, until the time he is to return'. (Hidden behind this description is another of these links between paid and unpaid work; food was prepared by the women at home.) The new arrivals at the forge were a finer's hand and a second apprentice at the finery and another hammermen's hand, a helper and a second goudjar at the chafery. Together these ten men kept the forge running around the clock, until the following Saturday morning, when their weekly make was weighed. When that was done the forgemen turned to drinking beer.[23]

One striking feature of the forge crew at Storhammaren was the prevalence of Walloon names; eight of the ten forgemen were of Walloon descent. Walloon dominance was even more pronounced at the three other forges; out of more than forty forgemen at Leufsta in 1753 only four bore distinctively Swedish names. One could also add that one of them, the finer's hand Antoine Holm, would take the Walloon-descended Caisa Pousett as his wife the following year. The organization of bar iron production at Leufsta in the mid eighteenth century was totally dominated by heirs to the migrants from the Low Countries, who had arrived in Uppland a century before. Tradition was thus of the utmost importance in making bar iron at Leufsta, but as the table reveals there was no clear ladder of promotion at work. Had there been, one would have assumed that the masters would have been older than the hands and that the hands would in turn have been older than the apprentices. This was clearly not so at the finery, as the two main forgemen were younger than the apprentices. The structure at the chafery, on the other hand, was closer to that of a more 'normal' hierarchy; the master hammerman was the oldest within the whole crew, with the hands being younger, but with the helper as the second oldest member.

Another unusual feature of the forge crew at Storhammaren in that first week of July 1753 was that it had very recently been reconfigured. The bookkeeping year of Swedish ironmaking in the early modern period began on 1 November and that was the normal time to change the members of the crews in the forges, unless death or illness called for urgent action. Some emergency must have arisen before midsummer that year, as two members of the crew from Storhammaren were replaced by two from the Upper Forge, so the team Berch saw making the bars at the chafery had only been working together for a couple of weeks. The change may have been connected with a gradual generational shift at this most prestigious workplace: the new master hammerman, Jacob Bouveng, had one of his sons with him as a kind of extra assistant. The year after, two of Bouveng's sons had been installed in the forge, replacing old Eric Jägare and Antoine Holm.

The sources used so far – the notebooks of Christer Berch and Eric Touscher, and the estate account books – have given glimpses of working life at Leufsta. The interconnected nature of production at the bruk has been made plain: the different phases of making iron (the mine, the

Table 1.1 The forge crew at Storhammaren in July 1753

Master finer:	Raphael Pousett	36 years
Master hammerman:	Jacob Bouveng	53 years
Finer's hand:	Antoine Holm	27 years
Hammerman's hand:	André Bonivier	40 years
Hammerman's hand:	Raphael Pousett	32 years
Apprentice finer:	Michel Gilliam	39 years
Apprentice finer:	Charl Martinell	30 years
Helper:	Eric Jägare	51 years
Goudjar:	Henrich Bonivier	23 years
Goudjar:	Petter Bonivier	26 years

Source: Leufsta Bruksarkiv, Leufsta, vol. Bruksbok 1753, vol. 196

forest, the furnace, the forge, etc.) have been outlined, the interrelationship between men's paid work and the unpaid work of the women has been touched upon, and the role of specialized auxiliary workers (carpenters, day labourers, masons, shoemakers, etc.) in the reproduction of daily life has been sketched. Yet it is difficult to penetrate deeper into these hidden worlds of work at eighteenth-century Leufsta, to delve into the actual tasks performed by individual workers. Only on rare occasions do the sources allow for a deeper understanding of tasks, and examination of the use of tools or the nature of collaboration amongst workers. One such occasion did arise in the mid 1770s when an employee of Bergscollegium (The Board of Mines), Salomon von Stockenström, travelled around the Uppland bruk, inspecting forges and taking notes on matters that might affect the quality of Swedish bar iron. He did not visit Leufsta, but he witnessed Walloon forging at neighbouring works, such as Forsmark, Gimo, Harg and Strömsberg. He began by noting how forgemen built their hearths and how they made weekly adjustments to them, but most of his attention was devoted to the successive phases of Walloon forging. In von Stockenström's account, the forgemen arrived at the finery somewhat earlier than they did in Berch's account (preheating the hearth was essential if pig iron was to be effectively melted). He then went on to study the division of labour between the finery workers. There were, von Stockenström reckoned, three distinct phases of making an anchony, each with its own pattern of work. At first the apprentice was alone at the hearth, where he was in charge of melting the pig iron. With the help of a mandrel he was to expose the iron to the air blast from the bellows, to make sure that everything was properly melted. Then, as von Stockenström phrased it, the master 'appeared at the hearth' and the second phase commenced, which included a reduction of the heat in the hearth by splashing water onto the coals. The two men made sure that no iron was stuck at the bottom of the hearth, and cleaned it from charcoal. Then the apprentice withdrew, leaving the master to perform the last task – that of forming the anchony. This was the skilled task that marked out a master finer. He had to make sure that all the iron in the hearth was evenly refined, and he once again exposed the semi-melted iron to the air from the bellows, using the mandrel to lever the iron up into the oxidising blast.[24]

Von Stockenström, having described the interplay between the apprentice and the master at the finery, did not elaborate on the fate of the anchony. Eric Touscher, writing in 1739, did just this however, pointing towards an uneasy relationship between the finery crew and the hammer crew. The brick-shaped anchony was left on the forge floor for the hammermen to pick up and therein lies the problem. The finers were in the habit of making larger anchonies than they were supposed to, as producing heavier pieces of iron either increased output and therefore their wages or reduced their working hours. However, there was no such advantage for the hammermen, as larger anchonies were more difficult to shape into bars. What was good for the finers was not so welcome to the hammermen.[25]

Whether they were happy with one another's work or not, both finers and hammermen stopped work on Saturday afternoon. The finers quit once they had made their last anchony and the hammerman followed suit once that anchony had been drawn out into a bar. The waterwheel that drove the bellows was stopped and the fire in the two hearths was allowed to burn out. This was the moment that Christer Berch and his brother arrived at the bruk, when the forges were silent and the weekly output totted up. They found the forgemen lounging in a small meadow, close to the garden belonging to the manor house, drinking the ale the owner had given the workers for midsummer.

The following Monday morning, work commenced again, and one important task was to cart the iron bars to the coast for further shipment to Stockholm. In 1753 the iron went to Ängskär, a fairly new wharf on the Baltic coast, 20 kilometres distant down a newly straightened road from the bruk. Ängskär was an integral part of the larger entity that was Leufsta bruk, as much as the blast furnaces at Tobo and Hillebola or the charcoal-producing farmsteads inhabited by the leaseholders. In 1749 this was home to only four households, headed by two clerks, one ship's master and one day labourer. However, Ängskär was being developed to replace the old wharf at Löten, a process completed in 1758 when the new stone-built warehouse was taken into use. In 1749 Löten was a thriving community with almost fifty households, headed by sailors, clerks, day labourers and iron guards, with a total population of about 200 people. By the early 1750s, however, most of the shipping business had shifted to Ängskär, and workers from Löten had to go there too. The Leufsta estate also owned the ships that would carry the iron bars to Stockholm. In 1740 the bruk possessed three ships, which made more than twenty sailings between Ängskär and Stockholm over the course of the summer shipping season. On their return voyages from Stockholm these ships were loaded with the supplies needed by the 'Bruk's-people' at Leufsta and all the other places attached to the bruk, and one can assume that many of the barrels of grain carted by the women at Leufsta that Monday morning had passed through Ängskär en route to the warehouses in Leufsta.[26]

The Wider World

We have, at the moment, no sources that can tell us what the forgemen at Leufsta, or any of the other inhabitants, thought about their work and toil. We know little of their inner lives but we can say quite a lot about their material existence. We know that they spent most of their waking hours at work, either making iron or supporting its production. We can also do one more thing: we can connect their toil with that of others at different places around the globe. We can write a microhistory from a global perspective, at least if we remain attached to the material aspects of life.

On 27 July 1754, about a year after the Berch brothers' visit to Leufsta, the Swedish traveller Reinhold Angerstein left London to travel to the north east of England. Some weeks later he arrived in Newcastle and spent a lot of time inspecting coal mines and industrial sites in the area. He also picked up the trail of the iron made at Leufsta the previous year. After arriving at Stockholm, the bars made by master finer Raphael Pousett and his fellow forgemen passed from the hands of Charles De Geer into

Illustration 1.1 Interior of the forge at Lövsta, Uppland, 1787. Oil painting by Pehr Hilleström. Jernkontoret.

those of Stockholm merchants like Jacob Graver and John Jennings, who were responsible for exporting the iron.[27] Most Swedish bar iron went to the British market in the eighteenth century. Up to the 1720s, however, bar iron from Uppland, known as Walloon iron or 'Orground' (after the historic port of Öregrund), cleaved to an older pattern and remained tied to the Dutch market. That changed very quickly after 1720. For one thing, the British navy began to insist on 'Orground' for anchors and other naval wares; but more importantly, England's nascent steel industry depended upon iron made from the ore of the Dannemora mine. Leufsta iron, along with material from the neighbouring bruk at Åkerby, Österby and Gimo, rose in price as it became the premium raw material for steel makers in Sheffield, Birmingham and the north east.

Metal manufacturing sites were, of course, of intense interest to Angerstein, and he devoted a lot of time to visiting 'Mr Crowley's works' at Teams, Swalwell and Winlaton. These were exceptionally large units at which a very wide variety of metal wares were manufactured. At Swalwell the Swedish traveller saw a forge for making bar iron, along with a slitting mill, steel furnaces and numerous mills and workshops. There was another forge at Winlaton, along with a slitting mill and workshops, and at Teams a hammer at which steel was drawn down to bars. Although these works had the capacity to make their own bar iron, the consumption of iron in the workshops was such that imported iron from Sweden and Russia was needed as well. Indeed, about 2,000 tons of iron from the Baltic was consumed annually. Angerstein noted that the majority of the iron used in the steel furnaces came from Uppland, and that Leufsta bars were among the most sought after.[28]

Domestically made iron – imported iron and steel made locally from imported iron – was forged, rolled, or slit at the Crowley works, and then put into the hands of a regiment of skilled artisans and transformed into an assortment of metal wares. There were workshops and forges for frying pans, shovels, anchors, screws, bolts, harpoons, pokers, saws, hinges, rivets and nails. Many of the workshops were devoted to making goods specifically for the New World colonies. 'Three kinds of hoes are made', Angerstein learned at Swalwell, 'which are shipped to America and used there at the tobacco and sugar plantations'. There were twenty-two workshops dedicated to the making of hoes at Swalwell, each occupied by three workers, and twenty-six more at Winlaton. The hoe makers hammered out bar iron into the proper shape and then forged a steel edge, prepared by specialized workers in another shop, into place. The roughly finished hoe was then ground sharp by other workers at a grinding mill.[29]

From a Swedish perspective, the elaborate division of labour at the Crowley factories can be seen as an extension of the cooperative pattern of labour we have seen at Leufsta. Indeed, the work done at Leufsta can be seen as the starting point for a productive skein that spanned the North Sea and which would, in due course, extend across the Atlantic. Machetes made in the north east of England, edged with steel that originated in ore from Dannemora and the Uppland forges, were used to cut down cane in the Caribbean and produce the sugar that would sweeten the coffee drunk in European salons. Axes from Swalwell were used in Honduran logging camps to fell mahogany trees, the wood of which found its way to the workshops of cabinetmakers in colonial centres like Newport, Rhode Island. There, tropical hardwoods were sawn, chiselled and planed using steel-edged tools whose ferrous content could also be traced back to Uppland. Each of these locations had microhistories to narrate: the bruk, with its intimate connection between industrial and household labour, or the remote logging camps that occupied a netherworld that fell outside both the English Caribbean and the Spanish Empire. In each, new social identities were generated. The craftsmen of Rhode Island, for example, developed a creolised rococo style that combined European patterns and New World materials. Such a development drew upon global commodity flows, but it was articulated at a local level by family loyalties (which governed the taking of apprentices), patterns of inheritance (which facilitated the acquisition of tools), the giving of credit (which enabled materials to be purchased) and the negotiation of subcontracting arrangements (which affected how knowledge was shared amongst skilled workers). The creation of a single piece of furniture calls for a microhistory with many different threads. Such a microhistory is of necessity rooted in a particular spot; the narrative is driven, however, by interconnected patterns of labour that stretch over long distances. The rasp of a plane as it shaved wood in a Newport workshop echoed distantly the thump of the forge hammers at Leufsta. They were part of a single labour process that had both micro and macro dimensions.

A Global Labour History for the Early Modern Period

Labour history has traditionally concerned itself with the modern era – with the institutional landscape of working-class movements and more recently with the practices of working life. It has, however, to a large extent, neglected most aspects of work and waged labour before the advent of modernity. Labour history was also, for many decades, a field devoted to the development of the Western world. Globalization has put paid to that, with increasing attention now being given to 'subaltern' labour, both as a subject area in its own right and as an integrated part of a transnational history of labour. The study of early modern labour remains underdeveloped, however, both conceptually and as an archival practice.

We have suggested that one response to this problem should be the use of microhistorical techniques. A practice-oriented approach that focuses on the quotidian; the material can help us reconstruct working life in the early modern era and – if used sensitively – unveil 'thought worlds' as well as the world of work. We can speak, then, of labour history without reference to the imposing organizational features that came later – trade unions, cooperative movements and workers' parties – that structured labour history in its early days as a discipline. For this to happen though, the microhistorical cannot be equated with the parochial. Every working arena in the early modern world was part of an interconnected chain. Industrial work, in particular, was always enmeshed in transnational link-ages. Microhistorical study, if it is to be effective, should therefore never be restricted to one locality. It should always demonstrate an awareness of the global setting for each instance of the microcosmic. Labour in the modern world has often been moulded by the nation state, and the history of labour has all too often been viewed through a national lens. Conditions in the early modern world were different, and scholars study-ing periods preceding modernity can take advantage of that and produce analyses that are close-grained and respectful of local context but that skip across national boundaries.

Göran Rydén is Professor of Economic History at the Institute for Housing and Urban Research, Uppsala University. His research in-terests include the forming and creation of modern society in Sweden and Europe as well as on a more global scale, the Enlightenment and urbanization and the Swedish and European iron industry. With Chris Evans he is currently leading the project 'Places for making, places for taking: metals in the global world, 1630–1820'. His publications in-clude *Sweden in the Eighteenth-Century World: Provincial Cosmopolitans* (2013) and with Leos Müller and Holger Weiss, *Global historia från periferin. Norden 1600–1850* (2009).

Chris Evans is Professor of History at the University of South Wales. He is interested in industrialization as a global process and slavery/emanci-pation in the nineteenth century. With Göran Rydén he is currently lead-ing the project 'Places for making, places for taking: metals in the global world, 1630–1820'. His publications include *Slave Wales: The Welsh and Atlantic Slavery 1660–1850* (2010) and with Göran Rydén, *Baltic Iron in the Atlantic World in the Eighteenth Century* (2007).

Notes

1. The Swedish word *bruk* historically denotes industrial development in the countryside. It implies a combination of landed property, supplying raw materials such as charcoal, and an industrial community where manufacturing took place.
2. Dag-bok öfver En Resa till Roslags Bergslagen hållen år 1753 af Christer Berch. Handskriftsavdelningen M 172, Kungliga Biliioteket, Stockholm. (Quoted as Berch 1753.)
3. See foremost M. Isacson. 1987. *Verkstadsarbete under 1900-talet: Hedemora verkstäder före 1950*, Lund: Arkiv Förlag; A. Johansson. 1988. *Arbetets delning: Stocka sågverk under omvandling 1856–1900*, Lund: Arkiv Förlag.
4. The best general treatment of Swedish economic development in the eighteenth century is still E.F. Heckscher. 1949. *Sveriges ekonomiska historia från Gustav Vasa. Andra delen: Det moderna Sveriges grundläggning*, Stockholm: Albert Bonniers Förlag. For a more modern discussion see L. Magnusson. 1996. *Sveriges ekonomiska historia*, Stockholm: Tiden Athena.
5. For a good introduction to the field see M. Peltonen. 2000. 'Ledtrådar, marginaler och monader: Förhållandet mellan mikro- och makronivå i historieforskningen', *Historisk Tidskrift för Finland* 85(3), 251–64; and G. Levi. 2012. 'Microhistory and the Recovery of Complexity', in S. Fellman and M. Rahikainen (eds), *Historical Knowledge: In Quest of Theory, Method and Evidence*, Newcastle upon Tyne: Cambridge Scholars Publishing, 121–32.
6. G. Levi. 1991. 'On Microhistory', in P. Burke (ed.), *New Perspectives on Historical Writing*, Cambridge: Polity Press, 97–119.
7. L. Colley. 2007. *The Ordeal of Elizabeth March: A Woman in World History*, New York: Pantheon Books; M. Ogborn. 2008. *Global Lives: Britain and the World 1550–1800*, Cambridge: Cambridge University Press.
8. E. Rothschild. 2011. *The Inner Life of Empires: An Eighteenth-Century History*, Princeton: Princeton University Press, quotations from pp. 7 and 162.
9. One important exception to this pattern is P. Linebaugh and M. Rediker. 2000. *The Many-Headed Hydra: Sailors, Slaves, Commoners, and the Hidden History of the Revolutionary Atlantic*, Boston: Beacon Press.
10. A general treatment is found in K.-G. Hildebrand. 1992. *Swedish Iron in the Seventeenth and Eighteenth Centuries: Export Industry before the Industrialization*, Stockholm: Jernkontoret.
11. C. Evans and G. Rydén. 2007. *Baltic Iron and the Atlantic World in the Eighteenth Century*, Leiden: Brill.
12. At a bruk leaseholding peasants and crofters (in Swedish *torpare*) paid their rents in kind, usually charcoal, or by labour services, usually in haulage. For a discussion of the Swedish/ Finnish term *torpare/torppari* in relation to the late nineteenth century, see chapter 7.
13. En liten handbok angående Leufsta Bruk &c. Wälborne Herren Herr Carl de Geer, wid ankomsten i Orten af En Des Tienare, öfwerlemnat 1739, written by Eric Touscher (and quoted as Touscher 1739) Leufsta Arkivet, vol. 152, Riksarkivet, Stockholm.
14. G. Rydén. 2002. 'Vallonbruk, vallonsmeder och vallonsmide – en precisering av ett forskningsläge', in A. Florén and G. Ternhag (eds), *Valloner – järnets människor*, Hedemora: Gidlunds Förlag, 109.
15. R. Bredefeldt. 1994. *Tidigmoderna företagarstrategier: Järnbrukens ägar- och finansieringsförhållanden under 1600-talet*, Stockholm: Almqvist & Wiksell International; G. Haggrén. 2001. *Hammarsmeder, masugnsfolk och kolare: tidigindustriella yrkesarbetare vid provinsbruk i 1600-talets Sverige*, Stockholm: Jernkontoret. From a Scandinavian perspective one can also point towards the small iron industry in Norway, organized along the same lines – in bruk – as in Sweden.

16. Touscher 1739, Berch 1753 and the business accounts from Leufsta Bruk, Leufsta Bruksarkiv, Lövsta. Note that some of these commodities might have been delivered on other days as well.
17. Touscher 1739.
18. Berch 1753.
19. B. Douhan. 1985. *Arbete, kapital och migration: Valloninvandringen till Sverige under 1600-talet*, Uppsala: Acta Universitatis Upsaliensis.
20. Berch 1753.
21. Douhan, *Arbete, kapital och migration*.
22. Berch 1753, Touscher 1739, Förteckningar över arbetare 1749–1762, Leufsta Arkivet, vol. 152, Riksarkivet, Stockholm, and business accounts from Leufsta Bruk, Leufsta Bruksarkiv, Lövsta.
23. Berch 1753 and business accounts from Leufsta Bruk 1753, Leufsta Bruksarkiv, Lövsta.
24. von Stockenström, Salomon, Beskrivning öfwer wårt Swenska stångjernsmide innefattande så wäl den tyska smides processen som äfwen ställning och arbete uti Walon Hammaren Jemte Smält Ståls Beredningen författade efter en på Wällof: Jern Contoirets bekostnad gjord resa genom Riket af SalvStockenström, Öfwermasmästare. 1777, Jernkontoret arkiv, Fullmäktige, F IIa: Riksarkivet, vol. 24.
25. Evans and Rydén, *Baltic Iron*.
26. Business accounts from Leufsta Bruk, Leufsta Bruksarkiv, Lövsta.
27. S. Fritz. 2010. *Jennings & Finlay på marknaden för öregrundsjärn och besläktade studier i frihetstida storföretagande och storfinans*, Stockholm: Kungl. Vitterhets Historie och Antikvitets Akademien Handlingar.
28. Angerstein's extensive comments on the local non-ferrous sector are found in T. Berg and P. Berg (eds). 2001. *R. R. Angerstein's Illustrated Travel Diary, 1753–1755: Industry in England and Wales from a Swedish Perspective*, London: Science Museum, 258–67.
29. Berg and Berg, *R. R. Angerstein's*, 258–67.

References

Berg, T. and P. Berg (eds). 2001. *R. R. Angerstein's Illustrated Travel Diary, 1753–1755: Industry in England and Wales from a Swedish Perspective*, London: Science Museum.

Bredefeldt, R. 1994. *Tidigmoderna företagarstrategier: Järnbrukens ägar- och finansieringsförhållanden under 1600-talet*, Stockholm: Almqvist & Wiksell International.

Colley, L. 2007. *The Ordeal of Elizabeth March: A Woman in World History*, New York: Pantheon Books.

Douhan, B. 1985. *Arbete, kapital och migration: Valloninvandringen till Sverige under 1600-talet*, Uppsala: Acta Universitatis Upsaliensis.

Evans, C. and G. Rydén. 2007. *Baltic Iron and the Atlantic World in the Eighteenth Century*, Leiden: Brill.

Fritz, S. 2010. *Jennings & Finlay på marknaden för öregrundsjärn och besläktade studier i frihetstida storföretagande och storfinans*, Stockholm: Kungl. Vitterhets Historie och Antikvitets Akademien Handlingar.

Haggrén, G. 2001. *Hammarsmeder, masugnsfolk och kolare: tidigindustriella yrkesarbetare vid provinsbruk i 1600-talets Sverige*, Stockholm: Jernkontoret.

Heckscher, E.F. 1949. *Sveriges ekonomiska historia från Gustav Vasa. Andra delen: Det moderna Sveriges grundläggning*, Stockholm: Albert Bonniers Förlag.

Hildebrand, K.-G. 1992. *Swedish Iron in the Seventeenth and Eighteenth Centuries: Export Industry before the Industrialization*, Stockholm: Jernkontoret.

Isacson, M. 1987. *Verkstadsarbete under 1900-talet: Hedemora verkstäder före 1950*, Lund: Arkiv Förlag.

Johansson, A. 1988. *Arbetets delning: Stocka sågverk under omvandling 1856–1900*, Lund: Arkiv Förlag.

Levi, G. 'On Microhistory', in P. Burke (ed.), *New Perspectives on Historical Writing*, Cambridge: Polity Press, 1991, 97–119.

————. 'Microhistory and the Recovery of Complexity', in S. Fellman and M. Rahikainen (eds), *Historical Knowledge: In Quest of Theory, Method and Evidence*, Newcastle upon Tyne: Cambridge Scholars Publishing, 2012, 121–32.

Linebaugh, P. and M. Rediker. 2000. *The Many-Headed Hydra: Sailors, Slaves, Commoners, and the Hidden History of the Revolutionary Atlantic*, Boston: Beacon Press.

Magnusson, L. 1996. *Sveriges ekonomiska historia*, Stockholm: Tiden Athena.

Ogborn, M. 2008. *Global Lives: Britain and the World 1550–1800*, Cambridge: Cambridge University Press.

Peltonen, M. 2000. 'Ledtrådar, marginaler och monader: Förhållandet mellan mikro- och makronivå i historieforskningen', *Historisk Tidskrift för Finland* 85(3), 251–64.

Rothschild, E. 2011. *The Inner Life of Empires: An Eighteenth-Century History*, Princeton: Princeton University Press.

Rydén, G. 'Vallonbruk, vallonsmeder och vallonsmide – en precisering av ett forskningsläge', in A. Florén and G. Ternhag (eds), *Valloner – järnets människor*, Hedemora: Gidlunds Förlag, 2002, 107–35.

CHAPTER 2

'FOREST MEN'
How Scandinavian Loggers' Understandings of 'Real Men' and 'Real Work' are Rooted in Personal Narratives and Popular Culture about Forest Life

Ingar Kaldal

Life in the forest has long been the subject of some of the most resonant stories, from ancient folk tales about nymphs and trolls to popular reality television series about 'axe-men' and 'heli-loggers'. As a lifeworld, the forest has been extensively mythologized in narratives told in very different contexts. In everyday speech, *skogen*, the forest in the Scandinavian languages, provides metaphors for 'natural life', 'solid material', 'healthy products', and – most relevant for this contribution – 'real work' and 'real men'.

The aim of this contribution is to explore how men's forestry work has been constituted culturally during the twentieth century, and how themes from life and work in the forest have also been used by forest workers to portray themselves as 'forest men'. In various contexts, loggers and other men in woodland communities refer to themselves – and are referred to by others – using similar terms. In Norwegian, for example, *skogens mann* (man of the forest) denotes a man closely bound to the forest and to life in the forest, often as a *tømmerhogger* (logger), but also as a hunter or even as one who loves just being in the forest.[1]

These issues in Scandinavian loggers' lives have been thoroughly analysed in some major studies. The Swedish ethnologist Ella Johansson in her doctoral thesis, *Skogarnas fria söner* (Free Sons of the Forests) (1994), focused on masculinity and modernity in the logging culture of

Norrland in Sweden, while historian Paul Tage Halberg gave his 1993 monograph on the history of Norwegian forest workers and their union the title *Den stolte sliter* (The proud hard worker).[2] Freedom, pride and masculinity, as well as some particular kinds of modernity and tradition, were, according to these studies, the determining characteristics of forest men's lives. At the same time, these studies show how complex, ambiguous and multiple the meanings of 'free' and 'proud' could be in loggers' culture. My aim is to explore these complex meanings further.

The analysis will be based on oral personal history, popular culture and a wide range of scholarly literature written about forest work. I collected most of the oral material from the communities Trysil and Värmland in a forest-dominated region that straddles the national border between Norway and Sweden. During the late 1990s I interviewed about 100 people in this region, men and women, most of them old enough to remember changes since the 1930s, but some young enough to still be in the first part of their working life.

My findings suggest that examining narrative aspects of the data is useful when analysing the cultural meanings of work. When workers talk about their work, their stories give information on several levels, from singular facts to traces of what aspects of life have meant in the culture where those stories have been shaped and shared. The best evidence for understanding the cultural meanings of work may often be found in the most historically unreliable and mythologized parts of what people say about their lives.

First I will sketch out a few points about the importance of forestry and forest workers socially, politically and symbolically in Scandinavian societies, mainly in Norway.

Forest, Society and Labour Politics

Long before industrialization, forestry was one of the main export trades in Norway. Others were the fisheries, mining and shipping; the oil economy became important after 1970. Until mechanization changed logging in the 1960s (see below), thousands of men were employed in the forests. Although statistics combine forest workers with other occupations and do not take seasonal variation into account, available figures show that 150,000 to 200,000 Swedes may have been employed in forest work at the end of the 1930s.[3] In Norway about 36,000 men, at most, were employed in forestry around 1950; by 1970, their numbers had fallen to 9,000.[4]

Forest workers worked with hand tools and their horses' muscular energy. The tasks of cutting down trees, delimbing and debarking them and transporting the logs from the forest to the river were done with simple technology; mainly axes, handsaws and horse-drawn equipment. Forest work was seasonal work, with tree harvesting taking place in the winter and *fløtning* or log driving on the rivers down to sawmills or cellulose or paper mills taking place during the spring weeks when snow melting in the mountains made the rivers run in spate. During the rest of the year, the same men worked at other, diverse tasks in their rural communities, from farm work to the building of houses, roads and so on.[5] But many men saw the forest as the main source of their livelihoods as well as their self-identity. As ethnologist Ella Johansson has written, the typical Swedish worker of the late 1800s and early 1900s was not working in a factory and living in a city; he was a forest worker living in a rural community.[6]

Many aspects of life in Scandinavian woodland communities could easily be described as traditional. Until about fifty years ago many tasks were done in the same ways as they had been for generations. In logging, even though some important changes were introduced with the first motorized equipment in the 1950s, the basic characteristics of the work remained the same.[7] When chainsaws and tractors replaced handsaws and horses, the work was still carried out and organized in much the same way as before. And the work still consisted mainly of strenuous manual tasks. More fundamental changes came in the 1970s, when much larger machines replaced many manual tasks and almost entirely eliminated the need for the large workforce of earlier generations.

At the same time, many aspects of forest men's lives could be seen as modern a long time before technology changed these same lives forever. In the nineteenth century, loggers' culture was already characterized by mobility, flexibility, competition, market relations and money.[8] The individualized, flexible aspects of the work as well as the wage settings may have been some of the reasons why loggers were difficult to organize in unions. Loggers were used to thinking of their work as being determined by individual capacities and seasonal changes more than by collective action. Here, individuality was not only something modern, but also a part of tradition.

Other modern aspects of the loggers' ways of living were their patterns of consumption. When loggers were absent from home for weeks during the winter season, living in small cabins near their logging sites, they often brought with them food they had purchased, such as sugar, white bread and coffee. These commodities were not commonly found on everyday tables in rural working-class homes until later in the twentieth century. Thus, foodstuffs more generally used for feasts or in affluent homes were eaten by poor loggers during their working days.[9] And while farm labourers received some of their wages as food, loggers bought their food with their own cash, earned through work.[10]

Forest workers were also important for the labour movement, although for Norwegian forest workers the breakthrough of trade unionism did not come until the end of the 1920s, twenty-five years later than for most groups of factory workers. Strong, durable unions for loggers were established only after several years of very militant class conflicts between loggers' unions and forest owners. One reason these conflicts became so intense was that some forest workers supported right-wing organizations, such as *Arbeidets Frihet* (Freedom to work), and refused to join the trade union; and some forest workers willingly worked as strike-breakers. The most violent conflicts occurred between union members and strike-breakers, often guarded by the police. In spite of these conflicts – or because of them – forest workers' unions grew strong very quickly. Before 1940, *Norsk skog- og landarbeiderforbund* (the Norwegian union of forest and agricultural workers) – known in everyday speech as *Skog og land* (Forest and Land) – had recruited about 30,000 members. By this time, it had become one of the biggest unions within the national federation of unions in Norway. It continued to be a major force through the 1950s, the same decade as factory employment reached its peak. In 1960, 23,000 people belonged to *Skog og land*, but from then on their numbers decreased. By 1988 – the year the forest workers' union merged into a common trade union, Fellesforbundet, for multiple groups of workers – only 6,000 remained.[11]

During the 1930s, loggers were one of the main groups supporting the political rise of social democracy. In the mobilization of popular support for these new governments, the decentralized network of loggers' unions played an important role, recruiting thousands of voters in rural parts of the country. Forest workers were one of the main groups who best illustrated the slogan of the new social democratic governments formed across the Nordic region during the 1930s, expressed in Norway as 'By og land – hand i hand' (City and countryside – hand in hand).

Several aspects of the loggers' working lives fit almost perfectly into the labour movement's conception of 'the real': manual, masculine work done under strenuous conditions for poor wages. Loggers worked for powerful, and in some regions very wealthy, employers, with whom they experienced more violent and long-lasting conflicts than any group of factory workers ever did. Perhaps, most importantly, the loggers' difficult working conditions made them not only politically self-confident, but also proud of being masters of such hard work. Even today, when few do the same forest work as was done in the past, every Labour politician who can relate some experience of logging is easily held up as an example of 'the real'. The best known example in Norway is the president of the Norwegian parliament from 2009 to 2013 Dag Terje Andersen, always speaking his rural dialect with his upper lip filled with snuff. His well-known background as a forest worker often seems to be the main character trait mentioned in the media.

Many aspects of loggers' lives were different from what is commonly known as working-class culture among industrial workers. Within loggers' culture, themes of individuality and collectivity exist together in stories and memories. These themes are threads of meaning that exist not as opposites, but as complements that show multiple and mutually constitutive ways of living and working. Although individual contracts along with a focus on individual work achievements may have delayed the formation of unions, such practices did not prevent forest workers from experiencing and expressing egalitarianism and solidarity.

While working, loggers competed with each other every day, and every hour of every day. The success of each man's work was measured by the number of cubic metres of wood cut, since, similar to piecework, this determined the wages earned. At the same time, loggers had multiple, sometimes contradictory relationships with their employers. Individuals with control over forest property were often very powerful, whether they represented a company, with all its might and influence, or whether they were private forest owners themselves. In small communities, these major forest owners were well-known public figures, with clear signs of affluence, power and position.[12] Thus, when conflict broke out, everyone knew who was on 'the other side'. These close, transparent social relations could both strengthen the collectivity and harden the conflict; they could also nurture a social hatred so strong that it could take generations to overcome.[13] Even many decades later, during my interviews with them in the 1990s, some old forest workers hesitated to talk about conflicts before 1940, since the transparency of their forest communities included knowledge of who had collaborated with the 'wrong' side.[14]

Nevertheless, loggers often thought of themselves as self-made men. Identifying themselves as free and proud were relevant ways of thinking not only about work and labour relations, but also about their own ability to live close to nature and to accomplish what nature claimed of their bodies – from managing deep snow in the forest, to sleeping in cold, wet cabins. In interviews with older loggers, one often hears almost never-ending accounts about the nature of the forest: how men coped with weather (snow) and landscape during specific logging seasons, remembered many years later to the nearest degree of frost or metre of snow depth.

These memories show the loggers to be not only workers and men, but 'forest men', men with a competence and feeling for the forest as landscape, nature and lifeworld. Their relation to nature – just as much as their relation to markets and employers – made loggers think about themselves as 'their own bosses'.[15]

Growing Up to be Forest Men

For Scandinavian loggers who retired during the last part of the twentieth century, a common way to begin their life stories was to go back to their first memory of joining their father in the forest, and most importantly of receiving their first, basic experience of the forest as workplace. This theme appeared in almost every interview I conducted with old men about their working lives. Some of them had grown up in the 1920s, but even those who had started their working lives in the 1950s would often tell of their first memories of work in the forest as boys, even as young as seven or eight years of age.[16] This was possible until certain technological changes occurred, for, as long as most of the timber work was done with hand tools, young boys could perform some tasks in the logging process such as debarking.[17] When there were log drives to float timber down rivers, loggers removed bark from the logs to prevent them from sinking. When trucks took over in the 1960s, logs were transported with the bark on. Debarking had been a task suitable for young boys because it was less dangerous than cutting down trees.

Boys and men alike used a special tool (Norwegian *barkespade*), a long stick with a sharp metal knife-like implement on the end, to remove the bark from the log. With this tool, they were more likely to avoid injuring their hands or legs than if they wielded an axe or a saw. Within this theme of beginning work in the forest as a boy, debarking is presented as the first phase in the process of turning boys into what they were determined to become: mature loggers who could work with and then succeed their fathers: 'I went with my father; he cut down the trees and I debarked. I could not use the axe the first time, and I was not allowed to fell trees; but later ... and after some time, I got my own tools. The first time, I used my father's tools'.[18]

Debarking was not a small task; some estimate that it claimed about half the amount of time required by the entire logging process.[19] Thus, debarking was not a task reserved for children, but a time-consuming job where young and old worked together. It was more the first step to becoming a mature forest man than it was a part of childhood. Debarking effectively initiated boys into the realm of men. Although it was less dangerous than felling trees, debarking was hard work. As one logger remembered:

> My dad taught me the debarking, ... and how to debark both sides of the log [with a spud]. ... it was crooked wood ... hard to get the bark off ... and it had to be done accurately at that time ... [there] had to be no bark left on the log ... and the bark could be frozen ... even that had to be handled. [20]

The harder the trials were, the more convincing they sounded with regards to what made men out of boys. This initiation and transformation is one of the themes that shows the teleological nature of the life stories of forest men: how older loggers saw what happened in their earlier lives as pre-phases for what would happen later and indeed as focal points for their entire life story. Thus, boys became sons not only of forest men but also of the forest.[21] In the stories of older loggers, boys and men become organic figures: boys grow up to be what they were meant to be from the very beginning.

Thus, even painful experiences could be remembered with honour. Memories of stifled tears shed in the cabin at night, aching muscles, clothes wet and frozen stiff and temperatures so low that hair stuck to the timber wall of the cabin during the night: all could, in later memories, fit the same free and proud discourse. These experiences were hard, but when managed well, they brought respect – and self-respect – to men who had been through it and had grown up to master it.[22]

Putting Down Roots in a Woodland Community

There were different kinds of loggers. Some were single and free to take jobs wherever they were offered, while others were married and had their own house or farm. Mobile loggers who moved long distances for work were more usually found in Sweden and Finland, where big companies employed more loggers (as in the United States and Canada).[23] Where logging sites were far away from the loggers' homes, young boys could not join their fathers in the forest so often. But as the Finnish ethnologist Hanna Snellman has written about timber floating in the Kemi river region in northern Finland, even there young boys could learn much about handling timber in the water when the logs passed through their home communities on the river. Balancing on a log in the water was part of what made young men growing up in those communities consider themselves to be superior to southern men.[24]

In Norway, loggers were more likely to combine forest work with maintaining a small farm with two or three cows. For these men, finding work close by was more important. Until car transportation made commuting easier, most loggers lived in cabins during the logging season, so absence from home and family was a common experience.

Some aspects of this logging life could be compared to other activities close to nature, such as hunting or fishing. But the loggers were far away, 'out there' in a literal sense, making a living for themselves and their families. Their motivation for succeeding in their work was orientated towards home and family, and to the place where they lived between logging seasons. Thus, the stories older loggers tell about the hardships of forest life, from hard work to simple cabin conditions to exile far from home, strengthened their ties not only to the forest where their fight for a living was carried out, but also to the local communities, where the results of their work took on material form.

Another aspect of forest life that strengthened loggers' ties to their woodland communities was that loggers had loggers as neighbours. What they had in common and were able to talk about after logging seasons ended and before new ones began were not only their jobs, which were often in different forests, but also their experience and qualifications that characterized them as forest men. They were connected, however, not to the specific local forests where they worked, but to the forest as a general idea, a cultural realm. Since this connection represented cultural capital that was highly valued in woodland communities, it must have strengthened the loggers' ties to those same communities.

Many stories also mythologize those ties. Although thousands of men left woodland communities for factory work in cities, and before 1920 for America, those who have remained told me about their choice as if it were their only alternative. A forest man was not made for industrial and urban life. On the contrary, he was destined to face problems in a factory, controlled by the clock, doing work dictated by machines, in rooms with no fresh air. In the memories of men who had grown old in a woodland community, anecdotes often mentioned their failed attempts at industrial life. Speaking of his younger days when he tried a factory job in a city, one man from Värmland told me: 'After only one week I quit and went home'. Another man from Trysil spoke of hearing about job openings in the forest after he had worked just a few weeks in a factory: 'Then I think I was the very first one to pack my rucksack and go back to the forest, and there I stayed, for all the years to come'.[25] By focusing on how short a time they lasted in the factory and how resolutely they decided to go back to the forest where they 'belonged', loggers mythologized their ties to the forest, the work in the forest and the forest community in their stories.

Another theme underpinning the image of loggers as rooted in forest life is that of loggers' knowledge and competence. In the stories, forest men were qualified to perform a wide range of tasks connected to the forest. Here the forest is a broad label, referring not only to the forest as nature or place, but also to tools and activities related to living as men in forest communities. In the stories, loggers' competence as forest men is practical, based on hands-on work and seeing how other work-ers were performing the tasks rather than on reading or other forms of book-based learning. The ethnologist Kjell Hansen writes that in a for-est region in Sweden the distance between forest and school was very far.[26] Knowledge based on reading books and men known for reading or writing books were spoken of with scepticism but also with some pity. [27] Some stories portray such men as helplessly unfit for the forest:

> There were some ... who came here, and did not know forest work ... and who did not fit in ... and maybe they became artists later, or writers ... They could sit down and write a poem, but got nothing done ... And they had to work in the forest ... but were unsuitable ... Not every man could be in the forest ... some made one cubic [metre], others made five ... You could see it when they worked ... the rhythm ...[28]

Stories of strangers who did not fit in were told not only with regards to the physical work, but also in regards to the culture of the logging camps. A logger from Värmland speaking about his first years in the for-est during the 1950s remembered that,

> There was a man from Stockholm who was in the forest and whom the log-gers regarded as peculiar, because this Stockholmer ... put on pyjamas when he went to bed, which none of us did. We slept in our underpants and when it was very cold, we slept with our trousers on.[29]

The more the stories describe forest men's cultural capital as difficult to exchange for a life in factories and cities or in school-based occupations, the more they strengthen the ties to the forest and the forest community. In this forest environment, forest men could be what they were predeter-mined to be, and the value of their culture was realizable. Thus, growing up to be forest men and growing roots in the forest community were two aspects of the same cultural process.

Loggers' memories and narratives not only present the men as forest men rooted in a forest society, but also show their forest man characteristics

Illustration 2.1 Working in the forest. Arbetarrörelsens arkiv och bibliotek, Sweden, Lantarbetaren. Unknown photographer.

as right and natural. Stories that focus on the many men who gave up their forest roots and succeeded in different work do exist, but confirm that the men had indeed given up their roots or that they were not real forest men after all. A school teacher from Värmland told me why he became a teacher: he had tried logging with his father for two weeks when he was young and realized that he cut in one day only half the amount of timber that his father did. Thus his choice of occupation seems to be explained not by what he wanted to be but by what he could not be.[30]

In this way, stories told by and about forest men naturalize the image of 'how they are', and make them seem not only rooted to the forest world, but also unchangeable. Major changes, though, were on the way; what happened then to forest men's culture?

A Culture Undermined and Rebuilt

Over the last fifty years, life in Scandinavian forest communities has changed radically. In regions with substantial spruce forests (in Norway the southern, eastern and middle regions; in Sweden from Norrland to Småland in the south), logging was the main source of wage income for the majority of men during the winter season. Even today logging is economically important in some of those communities, but few men are now employed in the industry. Moreover, these men work very differently from loggers in the past: they drive heavy machinery that accomplishes tasks that until the 1960s required the work of many men. Such motor-driven logging machinery came into Scandinavia much later than in North America, where steam engines known as donkeys, locomotives and other heavy machinery were already making logging more industrial in the late 1800s.[31]

During the last decades in Trysil, more people have been employed in tourism than in forestry: one of the largest alpine ski centres in Norway is located there. In other parts of the same woodland regions, such as northern Värmland, people have found it difficult to find any work for long periods of time. After 1970 many younger people moved away from these communities, and the region's percentage of elderly residents increased.

For many loggers, these changes brought not only the loss of income and livelihoods but also of honour and self-respect. Some changes undermined the men's cultural capital, masculinity and self-identity: men had problems finding a job, and they also had problems finding a spouse, since more women than men moved away. In interviews with women and men from Trysil and Värmland, comparable gender differences emerged. When speaking about what their children had done, mothers talked with optimism about children who completed their education and found positions, while fathers hinted, albeit sceptically, at their acceptance that such choices were necessary after all.[32]

Many reasons lie behind these gender differences. For young men, moving away may have been a greater, more alienating cultural break from a masculinity that was strong and dominant in their home milieu. Meanwhile, young women in forest communities had for generations been used to leaving home to take jobs as servants, possibly returning when they married. For young women, ties to their communities were thus about marriage and family, which they could establish anywhere. For men, local belonging was defined more by occupation and a masculinity that was specific to the forest community. For sons of loggers, educating themselves academically would be a major cultural break.

One alternative way to experience some of the cultural codes of the forest man was to hunt. During the weeks of the autumn elk hunt, the forest was a place where many men in the woodland communities continued to experience themselves as 'real' men.[33] Although few of them got their living from logging, they could acquire some self-respect through putting into practice their hunting competence and their knowledge of the culture connected to the forest. Going 'home' for a few days during the hunting season could thus after all be a chance for young men to see themselves in some way as forest men.[34]

Experiencing the cultural recognition of being forest men became more difficult from the1960s and 1970s. New machines such as mechanical harvesters, wood processors, feller bunchers and slashers could accomplish the entire logging process with little manual work and only a few operators. Harvesters, for example, operate on four huge wheels, and are equipped with a moveable arm with an element at the end that cuts and delimbs the tree, cuts the resulting log into suitable lengths, and stacks the wood into waiting trucks that haul it away. Every timber-harvesting machine eliminated the jobs of several men. And the work that was done with the harvesters was fundamentally different from logging in the past. Machine operators still thought of themselves as forest men, but what constituted this term of identity was changing. Not only did the operators of these new machines require formal education and certification, but this new forestry also gradually required new kinds of competencies. In a workplace where book knowledge had been shunned, workers now had to take courses. The new forest machines thus also made impossible and irrelevant the identity-building stories that told how forest men began their work as boys in the company of their fathers.

There were aspects of the new work, however, where the old cultural codes could be adapted and experienced. First, machine driving was still hard, dirty work. Although men sat in warm or air-conditioned cockpits as they worked, some manual tasks had to be undertaken outside the machine. Getting dirty and expending a lot of manual effort was still part of the normal working day. And although the new work was connected to heavy machinery and was thus in one way industrialized, it was far from being controlled as it was in factories. Drivers could still talk about themselves as being free men: they were not proletarians under control of the machinery but free men controlling powerful machines.

Second, the physical and biological landscape of the forest was much the same. The big machines cancelled out some of the challenges of weather conditions and they made logging a year-round activity, but loggers still had to 'read' the forest. In the newer as well as the older logging, failing to see what were the best ways of proceeding with the work in a given terrain could cause a lot of trouble and result in much wasted effort. For new machine drivers, understanding the landscape was different from what it had been for older loggers. Modern knowledge of ecology thus became part of the expected competence for forest workers, although even here, given the older loggers' stewardship of nature, there were aspects of continuity. Young trees had always represented a future resource.[35] One logger from Trysil remembered the time when clear cutting (cutting down all the trees in an area) was a normal practice: 'Cutting down young spruce trees was like killing small children'.[36] Another aspect of older loggers' ecological concern was their appreciation for the aesthetic qualities of the forest. When the first big machines arrived, the older loggers commented that the harvesters left behind very ugly scars in the landscape.[37]

A third aspect of continuity featured the economy. Some kinds of private entrepreneurship had always been part of logging.[38] Older loggers owned their own tools and equipment. And even after organizing themselves in unions, loggers had individual contracts drawn up between themselves and forest owners. The loggers' will to take economic risks had also long been present. New machine operators often owned their own machines, or they owned several machines, which were operated by paid drivers. This practice made some workers act as tradesmen or entrepreneurs with big investments. At the same time, they were hard-working loggers, often working longer days than their forefathers had been able to, because their new machines could operate after sunset with artificial light and because the machines had to be used for as many hours as possible to make enough money to pay the bank loans that funded their purchase.

Other changes, though, represented more fundamental breaks with the past. Men who were still working in the forests in the 1960s and

1970s were not living in cabins, unless they took jobs very far from home. They could easily drive home at night by car. Thus, an important social arena for building a collective culture disappeared. In addition, the log drives to float timber down rivers ended. Until truck transport took over, every spring many men had worked together to get logs to the mills. Even more than the felling of trees, the log drives were characterized by teamwork. Now, the logs were moved by trucks driven by men working alone from morning till night.

Insofar as the operators of the new forest machines could think of themselves as men inheriting some of the older characteristics of forest work, the stories about 'good workers' in the past, often with an heroic sheen, could shed light on the image of the men they still wanted to be: hard-working men, fighting the good fight not with a group of men but with their machines, interacting closely with the forest, nature and landscape to support themselves and their families. And insofar as their competence could be seen as forest-specific, their work could still nurture their roots in the forest community. For those men, their forest jobs could provide the life experiences necessary for them to speak of themselves, still, as forest men.

Conclusion

My picture of the Scandinavian logger corresponds with those presented by Ella Johansson and Paul Tage Halberg, on whose studies my analysis in this chapter depends. Further exploring the representation of the logger, my work details how important themes in the loggers' culture have been formed narratively and how these themes have been affected by the fundamental changes of the 1950s and beyond.

Even though most of the large numbers of loggers employed in Scandinavia until the 1960s engaged in multiple types of work throughout the year, they defined themselves as loggers. The forest was their main theme when they talked about what made men out of boys, what constituted their masculinity and what tied them to the communities where they belonged. Work in the forest filled only one part of their work year, but they used their stories about forest life, almost exclusively, to create and maintain their identities. To understand why the memories of these men could be so dominated by their forest experiences, one must focus on both narrative content, with its repetition of themes, and narrative function: why loggers told such stories, and how they used their stories to constitute their culture.

The two narrative themes discussed above – boys joining their fathers in the forest and forest life having formed them as forest men – are, themselves, material used by the men in the process of culture-building. By preserving past everyday experiences connected to a selected occupation in ways that made the work seem self-evident – the rightful path to choose, the 'real' work, and the way to teach boys to be 'real' men – Scandinavian loggers' stories naturalize loggers' culture. The logger-storytellers could have chosen to narrate events from any one of the many different jobs they had during the year, but they chose one part of their lives only, and for forest men that was the forest life and, most of all, their forest work.

When changes in technology and employment made it difficult for them to build their identities on the same old stories, they still had some aspects of their work that were similar, and these continuous cultural practices made it possible for loggers to present themselves as the inheritors of their fathers' culture. But, as with all changes in cultural heritage, some aspects of culture are given new meanings when transferred to new owners and used in new contexts.

Labour historians should take more seriously the culture-producing effects of the narratives told by and about workers in different contexts. Stories told in occupational cultures serve as resources and guidelines for living. They have given men the ability to ascertain right and wrong in their personal lives, and they have made forest men think and act in specific ways as men, workers, fathers, sons, husbands, breadwinners and members of society. Thus the tales labour historians collect from workers today will help us write a more robust, complex and inclusive history in the years ahead.

Ingar Kaldal is Professor of History at the Department for Historical Studies at the Norwegian University for Technology and Science (NTNU) in Trondheim. His main research interests are the history of work and everyday life, social and cultural history, historical theory and methodology. His doctoral thesis (1994) was about work and the social milieu in two pulp and paper mills in the period 1920–1970. A full list of publications is available at: http://www.kaldal.net/ingar/prod.htm.

Notes

I thank my colleague Dr Margaret R. Yocom, folklorist and Associate Professor Emerita of English at George Mason University, Fairfax, Virginia, United States, for serving as my editor. A specialist in the cultural history and traditions of forest life in New England, she not only corrected my English but also commented critically and constructively on the content of this chapter. Thanks to her my work is more interesting and readable.

1. Another term, *skogskar* ('forest chap' or 'forest guy' [*kar*=chap, guy, fellow]) has been applied more specifically to men who work in the forest. Other words may have been used for 'kar' in different local dialects.
2. E. Johansson. 1994. *Skogarnas fria söner: Maskulinitet och modernitet i norrländskt skogsarbete*, Stockholm: Nordiska museets Handlingar, 118; P.T. Halberg. 1993. *Den stolte sliter: Skog- og landarbeiderne 1900 til 1990 – en kamp for likeverd*, Oslo: Fellesforbundet seksjon Skog og Land.
3. Johansson, *Fria söner*, 9.
4. The number of men in Norway employed in forest work and paid by wages grew from about 16,000 in 1900 to 30,000 in 1930; their numbers peaked around 1950 with about 36,000. In 1960, there were 27,000 men; in 1970, only 9,000. See Halberg, *Stolte sliter*, 623. Around the mid 1900s, there were about 6.5 million inhabitants in Sweden and 3 million in Norway, but these figures indicate little about the importance of the forestry workers in forestry-dominated regions.
5. For a good illustration of how the working year consisted of many, varying tasks and jobs, see E. Svensson. 1998. *Människor i utmark*, Lund: Studies of Medieval Archaeology 21, 177.
6. Johansson, *Fria söner*, 9. Many results from the same project are presented in English in E. Johansson. 1990. 'Free Sons of the Forest: Storytelling and the Construction of Identity among Swedish Lumberjacks', in R. Samuel and P. Thompson (eds), *The Myths We Live By* London/New York: Routledge, 129–42.
7. Traditional aspects of logging are also discussed in A. Tomczik. 2008. '"He-men Could Talk to He-men in He-man Language": Lumberjack Work Culture in Maine and Minnesota, 1840–1940', *History* 70(4), 697–715.
8. Johansson, *Fria söner*, 26–28, 39–41.
9. Johansson, *Fria söner*, 83.
10. Johansson, *Fria söner*, 69–92.
11. Halberg, *Stolte sliter*, 614. Most of the members of *Skog og Land* were employed in forestry, while a small minority had jobs in farming and gardening.
12. P.T. Haberg. 2002. *I skogens favn. Gravbergskogen: Borregaard Skoger i 100 år. 1902 – 2002*, Elverum: Borregaard Skoger AS, 75–98.
13. Halberg, *Stolte Sliter*, 140–45.
14. This hesitation to speak of conflicts was very noticeable during many of my interviews with old men in Trysil and Värmland during the late 1990s.
15. Halberg, *Stolte sliter*, 26ff and Johansson, *Fria söner*, 56–57.
16. See also Halberg, *Stolte sliter*, 213.
17. Halberg, *Stolte sliter*, 421.
18. Translated from interview quoted in I. Kaldal. 2000. 'Skog, arbeid og dagligliv i kvinners og menns fortellinger fra Trysil og Nord-Värmland etter 1930', in I. Kaldal et al. (eds), *Skogsliv. Kulturella processer i nordiska skogsbygder*, Lund: Historiska Media, 85–118, quotation 92 in Swedish: *'Jag var med pappa, han fällde, och jag barkade ... yxa vet jag inte om jag fick använda den första tiden ... fälla fick jag inte i början, men sen ... och efter nogot hade jag väl eget verktyg ... första tiden brukade jag min fars verktyg'.*
19. A. Vevstad (ed.). 1991. *Trysil kommuneskoger 100* år, Trysil: Published by Trysil Kommune, 90; Johansson, *Fria söner*, 44; see also E. Johansson. 1989. 'Beautiful Men, Fine Women and Good Workpeople: Gender and Skill in Northern Sweden', *Gender and History* 1(2), 208.
20. Translated from interview quoted in Kaldal, 'Skog, arbeid og dagligliv', 93. A spud is a hand tool used to remove bark from logs. It has a wooden handle between 30cm and 1.2m long, with an attached curved metal blade. Quotation in Swedish: *'Det var farsan som lärde mig att barka åt båda sidorna ... at man kunde växla mellan varje ... det var*

knotig tall detta ... det var rent svårt at få av barken ... och det var noga med att barka på den tiden ... fick inte vara igjen någon bark kvar ... och så var barken frusen ... men det fick gå det också'.

21. The title of Ella Johansson's doctoral thesis, 'Free Sons of the Forests', underscores this point.

22. Kaldal, 'Skog, arbeid og dagligliv', 93; Johansson, 'Beautiful Men', 205; Johansson, *Fria söner*, 154–55.

23. Johansson, *Fria söner*, 117–20; H. Snellman. 2005. 'Reality and Romance as Historical Portrayals', in H. Snellman (ed.), *The Road Taken. Narratives from Lapland*, Inari: Kustannus-Puntsi, 27–39; see also H. Snellman. 2000. 'Flottningsepoken i Norra Finland', in I. Kaldal et al. (eds), *Skogsliv: Kulturella processer i nordiska skogsbygder*, Lund: Historiska Media, 63–84.

24. H. Snellman. 2005. 'The Challenge of Differences', in H. Snellman (ed.), *The Road Taken: Narratives from Lapland*, Inari: Kustannus-Puntsi, 70.

25. Translated from interviews quoted in Kaldal, 'Skog, arbeid og dagligliv', 100–1. Quotation in Norwegian: *'da trur jeg at jeg var den første til å pakke sekken og reiste til skogen ... og der har jeg fortsatt for ettertida'.*

26. K. Hansen. 1998. *Välfärdens motsträviga utkant: Lokal praktik och statlig styrning i efterkrigstidens nordsvenska inland*, Lund: Historiska Media; K. Hansen, 2000. 'Mellan inordning och motstånd. Om formering av lokala identiteter i nordsvenska skogsbygder', in I. Kaldal et al. (eds), *Skogsliv: Kulturella processer i nordiska skogsbygder*, Lund: Historiska Media, 118–45.

27. For example, see H. Børli. 1997. *Med øks og lyre: Blar av en tømmerhoggers dagbok*, Oslo: Aschehoug, 70–80.

28. Translated from interview quoted in Kaldal, 'Skog, arbeid og dagligliv', 99. Quotation in Swedish: *'Det fanns dom som kom hit och inte kunde skogsarbete ... och som inte hade något där att göra ... och kanske blev dom konstnärer i stället, eller författare ... dom satt och skrev dikter ... dom kom ingen väg ... och måste arbeta i skogen ... men dom var inte lämpliga där ... och inte alla kunde vara i skogen ... kanske högg dom bara en kubik mens en annan högg fem ... det kunde du se på arbetet ... på takten'.*

29. Translated from interview quoted in Kaldal, 'Skog, arbeid og dagligliv', 107. Quotation in Swedish: *'stockholmare som var i skogen, och dom tyckte det var så konstigt, för denna stockholmaren ... satte på sig pyjamas när han la seg ... det var det ingen andra som hadde, vi låg i kalsongerna ... och var det riktigt kallt, låg vi med byxorna på'.*

30. Kaldal, 'Skog, arbeid og dagligliv', 99.

31. For further reading see: K. Druschka. 1992. *Working in the Woods: A History of Logging on the West Coast*, Madeira Park: Harbour Publishing; T.J. Karamanski, 1989. *Deep Woods Frontier: A History of Logging in Northern Michigan*, Detroit: Wayne State University Press; D.C. Smith. 1972. *A History of Lumbering in Maine, 1861–1960*, Orono: University of Maine Press; Tomczik, 'He-men Could Talk to He-men'. For a study of how logging has been remembered and mythologized in personal and public memories in the north-west logging regions of the United States, see R.E. Walls. 1997. 'The Making of the American Logger: Traditional Culture and Public Imagery in the Realm of the Bunyanesque', Ph.D. dissertation, Indiana University. For more information about the history of American forestry, see The Forest History Society at http://www.foresthistory.org/

32. Kaldal, 'Skog, arbeid og dagligliv', 102–3.

33. L.M. Bye. 2009. '"How to be a Rural Man": Young Men's Performances and Negotiations of Rural Masculinities', *Journal of Rural Studies* 25(3), 278–88; L.M. Bye. 2010. 'Bygdas unge men: En studie av bygdemenns forhandlinger om og utforming av "rurale maskuliniteter", Ph.D. dissertation, Norwegian University of Science and Technology.

34. Bye, '"How to be a rural man"'; Bye, 'Bygdas unge menn'. This pattern is also confirmed in interviews conducted for the project that resulted in Kaldal, 'Skog, arbeid og dagligliv'.

35. T.E. Bruvoll. 1998. 'Skogbruk og skogsarbeid i Snåsa: Kulturelle og sosiale endringar i ei skogsbygd frå 1940- til 1970-åra', MA dissertation, Norwegian University of Science and Technology.
36. Translated from interview quoted in Kaldal, 'Skog, arbeid og dagligliv', 112. Quotation in Norwegian: *'å hogge smågran var som å drepe små barn'.*
37. Halberg, *Stolte sliter*, 360, 422.
38. Johansson, *Fria söner*, 54–56.

References

Bruvoll, T.E. 1998. 'Skogbruk og skogsarbeid i Snåsa: Kulturelle og sosiale endringar i ei skogsbygd frå 1940- til 1970-åra', MA dissertation, Norwegian University of Science and Technology.

Bye, L.M. 2009. '"How to be a Rural Man": Young Men's Performances and Negotiations of Rural Masculinities', *Journal of Rural Studies* 25(3), 278–88.

———. 2010. 'Bygdas unge men: En studie av bygdemenns forhandlinger om og utforming av 'rurale maskuliniteter', Ph.D. dissertation, Norwegian University of Science and Technology.

Børli, B. 1997. *Med øks og lyre: Blar av en tømmerhoggers dagbok*, Oslo: Aschehoug.

Druschka, K. 1992. *Working in the Woods: A History of Logging on the West Coast*, Madeira Park: Harbour Publishing.

Halberg, P.T. 1993. *Den stolte sliter: Skog- og landarbeiderne 1900 til 1990 – en kamp for likeverd*, Oslo: Fellesforbundet seksjon Skog og Land.

———. 2002. *I skogens favn. Gravbergskogen: Borregaard Skoger i 100 år. 1902 – 2002*, Elverum: Borregaard Skoger AS.

Hansen, K. 1998. *Välfärdens motsträviga utkant: Lokal praktik och statlig styrning i efterkrigstidens nordsvenska inland*, Lund: Historiska Media.

———. 'Mellan inordning och motstånd: Om formering av lokala identiteter i nordsvenska skogsbygder', in I. Kaldal et al. (eds), *Skogsliv: Kulturella processer i nordiska skogsbygder*, Lund: Historiska Media, 2000, 118–45.

Johansson, E. 1989. 'Beautiful Men, Fine Women and Good Workpeople: Gender and Skill in Northern Sweden', *Gender and History* 1(2), 200–12.

———. 'Free Sons of the Forest: Storytelling and the Construction of Identity among Swedish Lumberjacks', in R. Samuel and P. Thompson (eds), *The Myths We Live By*, London/New York: Routledge, 1990, 129–42.

———. 1994. *Skogarnas fria söner: Maskulinitet och modernitet i norrländskt skogsarbete*, Stockholm: Nordiska museets Handlingar 118.

Kaldal, I. 'Skog, arbeid og dagligliv i kvinners og menns fortellinger fra Trysil og Nord-Värmland etter 1930', in I. Kaldal et al. (eds), *Skogsliv. Kulturella processer i nordiska skogsbygder*, Lund: Historiska Media, 2000, 85–118.

Karamanski, T.J. 1989. *Deep Woods Frontier: A History of Logging in Northern Michigan*, Detroit: Wayne State University Press.

Smith, D.C. 1972. *A History of Lumbering in Maine, 1861–1960*, Orono: University of Maine Press.

Snellman, H. 'Flottningsepoken i Norra Finland', in I. Kaldal et al. (eds), *Skogsliv: Kulturella processer i nordiska skogsbygder*, Lund: Historiska Media, 2000, 63–84.

_____. 'Reality and Romance as Historical Portrayals', in H. Snellman (ed.), *The Road Taken. Narratives from Lapland*, Inari: Kustannus-Puntsi, 2005, 27–39.

_____. 'The Challenge of Differences', in H. Snellman (ed.), *The Road Taken: Narratives from Lapland*, Inari: Kustannus-Puntsi, 2005, 62–71.

Svensson, E. 1998. *Människor i utmark*, Lund: Studies of Medieval Archaeology 21.

Tomczik, A. 2008. '"He-men Could Talk to He-men in He-man Language": Lumberjack Work Culture in Maine and Minnesota, 1840–1940', *History* 70(4), 697–715.

Vevstad, A. (ed.). 1991. *Trysil kommuneskoger 100 år*, Trysil: Published by Trysil Kommune.

Walls, R.E. 1997. *The Making of the American Logger: Traditional Culture and Public Imagery in the Realm of the Bunyanesque*, Ph.D. dissertation, Indiana University.

CHAPTER 3

DIVERSE, RATHER THAN DESPERATE
Housewifization and Industrial Home Work in Sweden, 1906–1912

Malin Nilsson

This chapter explores the question of how normative perceptions of gender and work can affect the terms of women's labour force participation. Specifically, it examines a theoretical claim made by feminist theorist Maria Mies, that industrial homeworkers[1] have been more exploited than other workers because they have been ideologically constructed as being primarily housewives and not workers. I approach Mies' theoretical claim by exploring two questions derived from her housewifization theory. First, were the industrial homeworkers ideologically constructed as housewives? And second, was this an accurate picture – that is, were they secondary workers with supplementary incomes that were not important for the subsistence of the family? To answer these questions, I use the case of early twentieth-century Sweden and employ two different types of empirical materials: a qualitative material consisting of legal documents, newspaper articles and social pamphlets from 1906 to 1910, and a dataset based on interviews with women industrial homeworkers from 1912. The results showed that Swedish homeworkers were not described as housewives in the contemporary Swedish debate, nor could they be considered housewives based on the interview material. The qualitative material revealed an intense public debate on industrial homeworkers in early twentieth-century Sweden. However, instead of describing homeworkers as housewives, the sources largely described them in terms of being the 'poorest of poor' workers and exploited victims of the emerging garment industry. The interview material revealed a diverse labour force, of which the majority of the workers were unmarried and could not be considered housewives. Also among the married homeworkers, the incomes from industrial homework often formed a significant part of the household income.

During the last three or four decades of labour history, as in many other fields of social science, much research has focused on trying to understand social and economic change beyond large universal structures. During the 1960s and 1970s many studies on structure implied a tendency to regard workers, and especially poor workers, as an undifferentiated grey mass of victims, passively affected by large economic structures. From the late 1970s, however, the focus shifted towards a closer examination of historical actors as rational, strategic decision makers, without denying the limits set by the structures within which they make these decisions. Post-structuralist labour history has made space for gender in labour history, and has reintroduced the household and family as an important aspect for understanding labour.[2] This chapter follows in the path of this development by focusing on social and economic change reflected in the interrelations between gender, family and labour. The chapter provides new empirical data and discusses two aspects that still need further exploration, both in Nordic labour history and internationally: the home-based remunerated work of women and the work of married and older women in the labour market.

Industrial Homework and 'Housewifization'

Over more than a century, and across the globe, industrial homeworkers share some common features: their gender and their exposed, unregulated and informal status in the labour market. Mies suggests that 'housewifization' could explain their precarious situation. According to her definition, housewifization is 'a process by which women are socially defined as housewives, dependent for their sustenance on the income of a husband, irrespective of whether they are de facto housewives or not'.[3] In this process of housewifization, the work of women is increasingly described as an activity rather than an occupation and the income derived from it as supplemental rather than crucial to one's subsistence. As a consequence, women workers become separate from 'normal' workers and thus marginalized and unprotected in the labour market.[4] According to Mies the ideological construct of homeworkers as 'housewives' rather than 'workers' is what makes them different and disadvantaged. An entire chapter could be devoted to exploring the meaning of the term housewife in the Swedish setting, both in a literal and contextual sense. I have used an applied definition of 'housewife' in this chapter, fully based on Mies' definition. Mies defines a housewife according to two characteristics: a) being married; b) one's income is supplementary to that of a male breadwinner and not important for the subsistence of the family.[5]

Mies' theory of housewifization proposes a universal process where the interactions of gendered divisions of labour and industrial capitalism intersect and make industrial homeworkers an exceptionally vulnerable group. The theoretical concept of 'housewifization' was developed during Mies' work on industrial homeworkers at the time of expanding industrialization in India in the 1980s.[6] Mies' study is not entirely clear as to the origin of the 'propagandation of the housewife ideology'.[7] According to Mies, in Narsapur the ideology was introduced during colonial times via the Christian and Victorian values of the nineteenth century and later spread by exporters and traders, who wanted access to cheap and flexible labour.[8] The lived effects of the ideology are well documented in her study, but it is not always clear where and how these effects are evidenced or characterized. According to Mies, housewifization originated in industrializing Western Europe and is present in all industrializing countries.

To my knowledge there has been only one empirical study on housewifization and industrial homeworkers besides Mies' own study. Elisabeth Prügl has studied the housewifization of industrial homeworkers in Brazil, Pakistan, Turkey, Thailand and Britain after 1970.[9] She shows that housewifization – as in the construction of homeworkers as nonworking, dependent housewives – was present in all five countries, at least on the surface. She also found that they were defined as housewives although the homeworkers had regular incomes and paid for basic household items.[10] Both Mies' and Prügl's studies use contemporary cases but, as previously noted, Mies claims this process to be present in every country going through industrialization. This study will explore this claim further from a historical perspective.

Historical studies of gender and industrial homework have been in line with these studies, primarily focusing on industrial homework as work within a strong single breadwinner model where women were not seen as primary workers. Eileen Boris has studied industrial homeworkers in the industrializing United States, Britain, France and Germany, and claims that it is the gendered construction of women as being 'naturally' subordinate in the family and the labour market that enables industrial homework to exist.[11] Boris claims that, '[m]arried women with small children whose husbands failed to earn adequate incomes (through unemployment, disability, or low wages) composed the majority of

homeworkers in these countries'.[12] Cynthia Daniels in her study of New
York City immigrants in the early twentieth century claims that, '[m]
ost homeworkers were married women with children whose husbands
brought in inadequate wages and whose cultural traditions or family responsibilities kept them home'.[13] In a similar fashion, women's industrial
homework in Sweden has been almost exclusively dealt with as work
done as a consequence of a strong single breadwinner model. Previous
accounts of industrial homeworkers in Sweden portray industrial homeworkers as married women working in their homes for small sums of
money, complementing a male breadwinner.[14]

Methods and Materials Used in this Chapter

To explore the ideological constructions on housewifization I have used
official records, political pamphlets and newspaper articles from 1906 to
1910. In total thirty-three texts were analysed. These included two books:
Gerda Meyerson's *Svenska hemarbetsförhållanden* (The Conditions of
Swedish Industrial Home Work) from 1907 and *Anteckningar till frå-
gan om hemarbetets eller hemindustriens reglering genom lag* (Notes on
the Issue of Legislation on Home Work and Home Industries) written
by Moritz Marcus on behalf of the governmental Yrkesfarekommittén
(committee on occupational hazards) 1909. The study also included
two official records: the governmental bill for the regulation of labour
in industrial homework, dated 1909, and the arguments for the bill,
also dated 1909. The twenty-nine newspaper articles I study were all
published in Swedish newspapers around the time of the exhibition on
industrial homework in Stockholm in October 1907. They were collected by the Centralförbundet för Socialt Arbete (National Association
of Social Work, CSA), who organized the exhibition.[15]

There are two assumptions made in Mies' housewifization theory;
that industrial homeworkers are described as housewives (i.e., married
with supplementary incomes) and that they are in fact not housewives.
Three operational questions were used to see if these theoretical predic-
tions were true in the case of early twentieth century Sweden. Are the
homeworkers described as married women in the text? Are their incomes
homework described as secondary or complementary in the text? Are the
homeworkers described using the term 'worker' *(arbetare/arbeterska)*
throughout the text?

To investigate whether the industrial homeworkers at this time really were married women with supplementary incomes I have used the
original interviews conducted in connection to a survey on the social

and economic conditions of industrial homeworkers in Sweden 1912. The interviews hold detailed information on the individual homeworker regarding marital status and income, as well as the income of all other family members by year. In Sweden, the survey was carried out by Socialstyrelsen (National Board of Health and Welfare) in 1912. Sweden was not the only country that made surveys of industrial homeworkers at this time, but it seems to have been one of the few countries to complete a large nationally representative survey with a large number of interviews conducted with individual homeworkers.

As detailed individual-level data require considerable time to compile, the study has been limited to the urban Gothenburg area. In the 1910s Gothenburg was an industrial city with a large and diverse labour market and several garment and textile industries. A total of 366 interviews were conducted with industrial homeworkers in Gothenburg. Of these, 290 were found in the archive, 276 of which were with women workers. These make up the sample of interviews used in this study.

Ideological Constructions of Women Industrial Homeworkers in Sweden: Were They Described as Housewives?

The simple answer to the question of whether women industrial homeworkers in Sweden were described as housewives in public debate at this time in Sweden is that they were not. In fact, in none of the legal documents, books and newspaper articles on industrial homework from 1906 to 1920 were they described as married women or secondary earners. If anything, they were described as unprotected and exposed workers who fell victim to a harsh economic system. Descriptions of married industrial homeworkers as secondary earners were present a few times in the material; however in those cases this was mostly to emphasize that their income, even if complementary, was important to the family. The social activist Gerda Meyerson (1866–1929) wrote in her book on the working conditions of homeworkers in 1907:

> In several cases the work hours are so long, for the married women as well, that we must assume that their earnings must constitute a crucial income, for the earning of which the household work must be set aside.[16]

Rather than ideologically constructing homeworkers as housewives, many authors focused on other factors to explain their low pay and precarious situation. Lack of knowledge about the situation of homeworkers, both among the workers themselves and in society more generally, was the main target of several of the analysed texts. Most notably, the proposals for legislation focused on the registration of homeworkers with the explicit aim of giving homeworkers more information on the situations of other homeworkers. However, demands for the registration of homeworkers were also likely to be for tax reasons.

Another problem concerned the lack of information about how much money the 'middleman' took. In the legislative proposals as well as newspaper articles there was a concern that employers did not know how much money the homeworkers made after the 'middleman' had taken his share. The underlying assumption was that if only the employer knew how little the homeworkers actually earned, their wages would go up. In the 1909 proposal to revise the laws regarding women and children's work in industry, we can read that if the employers had to keep detailed registers of all homeworkers, the middleman and hence the 'sweating system' would disappear:

> In ensuring that these obligations are met, the employer would gain an understanding of the workers with whom he does not come into personal contact, which in itself could lead to an interest in these workers' wage conditions, and the employer may then consider avoiding the middleman and instead be in direct contact with the worker, as it is the employment of the middleman that is considered to be the main reason for the "sweating system" characteristic of industrial home work.[17]

Consumers formed another targeted group responsible for the harsh conditions of homeworkers. In particular, female consumers were accused of constantly demanding cheaper clothing and thereby causing the 'sweating' of homeworkers. In *Aftonbladet*, one of Sweden's biggest newspapers, a contributor called 'Sidsel' wrote after visiting an exhibition on the situation of industrial homeworkers in Stockholm in October 1907 that,

> The result is an ever lower income for those performing this work, a downward spiral that will not stop until the cause is removed; the public's petty, and in some people – especially women – almost manic desire for haggling. And besides this, their awkward idle lust for ready-made clothing of the poorest quality rather than making their own garments out of good fabric or at least buying clothes for their actual value and – as far as possible – in cash.[18]

There was a consensus in the public debate on industrial homeworkers. The homeworkers were depicted as victims or workers, but not as wives. Who might be expected to hold an opposite view, and why were they not represented in these sources? Following Mies' argument we should assume that employers had an interest in keeping down the wages of industrial homeworkers. They, more than anyone, would have something to gain from portraying industrial homeworkers as housewives and not workers. However no such characterizations are to be found in these sources. I found one letter from an employer in one of the boxes of assorted documentation in the archive of the national industrial homework survey. It is addressed to the industrial homework survey administration in 1912, and the content could be an indication that marital status really was used as a means to justify low wages:

> I have 160 seamstresses working in their homes ... I have paid them 18,678.02 krona during 1911. However these are all younger married women (wives of tram drivers) and they do not live exclusively on this income.[19]

However this quote is the only one that expresses this attitude. There were thirty-three texts of various lengths in my sample and in only one of them were the homeworkers described as being married women with children. No employers were present in the material except when the previously mentioned Gerda Meyerson was interviewed by one of the newspapers during the exhibition on industrial homework in Stockholm in October 1907. She then described how several employers attending the exhibition had said that it gave a false account of the homeworkers' situation. They claimed that industrial homeworkers earned good money in fact.

Were They Housewives?

The average industrial homeworker in Gothenburg was not married, nor did she have a male primary breadwinner in her household. Out of all the industrial homeworkers in the interview sample, about one in four had a husband with an income at home, while out of the married homeworkers, around two thirds had a husband with an income in their household. In several interviews there were comments made by the interviewer regarding the absence of a husband's income. For instance, in some cases they stated that the husband was ill or that he had abandoned his wife, emigrated to America or that he was a 'drunkard'. The women who did have a husband present were married to salesmen, seamen, carpenters, artisans and barbers, but most commonly to men engaged in some type of manual work. For the husbands that did have a reported income, the average annual earnings were SEK 950, which was slightly below the

average earnings of a male factory worker.[20] Of all the industrial homeworkers, about ten per cent lived alone. Amongst those who were unmarried, most lived together with an elderly parent and/or siblings or
other relatives. With a few exceptions, those who lived with an elderly
parent were the only breadwinner in the family. However, when they
lived with siblings there were also other incomes in the household. There
are several examples of sisters who formed small informal producer cooperatives and lived and worked together, often, but not always, for the
same employer.

The mean annual income for industrial homeworkers in the interviews
was SEK 1,120. However, as there were many homeworkers who earned
little but only a few who earned a high income, the average is not a very
good measure of the incomes of the homeworkers here. The median
income of SEK 500 gives us a somewhat better description, although
in general the incomes varied a lot and the standard deviation from the
mean and median is large. When the information on their incomes and
occupational structure is examined more closely, three main groups of
industrial homeworkers appear. These women had more than a similar
income structure; they also shared other features such as age, marital
status and the products made. Let us take a closer look at these women.

Women embroiderers made up the first group. In this group, incomes were low and working hours irregular. More often than others
these women stated that incomes and hours worked varied too much
for them to be able to state how much they earned or worked in a year.
Nevertheless many of them worked throughout the greater part of the
year and the ones who did state working hours in the interviews worked
on average between eight and nine hours a day. The women in this first
group were in general younger, unmarried women living at their parents'
house or older women who often but not always came from wealthier
households. A handful of them stated that they only did needlework to
have something to keep them busy. This is the group where we would
expect to find the real 'housewives' of this dataset. However, the few
women who were married in this group had husbands with working-class
occupations and low wages. Nevertheless, in this group, incomes were
rarely sufficient to make a living and their incomes were complementary;
if not to a husband's income, then to poor relief, pensions, saved capital,
to income from other relatives or to other income from their own work.

One example from this group was a 54-year-old single woman living
with her younger sister. This woman had been making various kinds
of embroidered goods for different employers for about thirty years,
and she had never held another occupation. She worked irregularly the
whole year and most often around six hours a day. Her yearly wage was

around SEK 400. She worked in her bedroom, which was brightly lit by two big windows and a kerosene light. In the winter she had a tile stove to warm her and the rent for the whole apartment was SEK 500 per year. The sisters lived in a fairly large two-room apartment in a better area of Gothenburg and shared the tasks of cooking and cleaning between them. The woman's sister lived off a small amount of capital and they both sometimes received help from a brother. Their father had owned a factory in another part of Sweden and they seem to have managed financially. However, the interviewer emphasized that both sisters seemed to be very nervous and of poor health.

The second group consists of women who made undergarments. On average, the women in this group worked between eight and nine hours a day. They made similar products but the piece rate varied according to type and quality, and possibly also as a result of having negotiated different rates. This was the biggest group, but it could also be divided internally into married and unmarried women. The married women in this group often had small children and their husbands had more or less regular incomes. These married women could be found on the lower side of the income spectrum.

A typical example of a married woman in this group would be informant no. 213, who was thirty-six years old and made undergarments. She lived with her husband and their four small children in their one-room and kitchen apartment, for which they paid SEK 198 per year. Their six square metre kitchen was the room where two of her children slept, but it was also the place where she worked all year round. She had been working as a homeworker for six years and did not state any previous occupation. In summer and autumn, she worked around eight hours a day, but during winter and spring her working hours increased to between ten and twelve hours a day. She had bought her sewing machine for SEK 85 and hoped to be able to use it for at least ten years. She paid for needles and thread at a cost of about SEK 0.5 per dozen garments. It took her about two days to make a dozen camisoles *(daglinnen)* and every week she went by tram to drop them off at her employers and receive SEK 2.40 per dozen. In total she earned around SEK 200 a year, while her husband worked at a local brewery and made SEK 1,100 a year. The homeworker was stated as being of good health, but her oldest child, a daughter of twelve, had a lung disease – most likely tuberculosis.

Unmarried women and married women whose husbands had left them had the highest wages in this group, but they still worked long hours for low pay. However, even though these women were not married they seldom lived alone, but most often with other relatives such as siblings or elderly parents. A typical example of this category is informant no. 226. She was a forty-year-old woman who made finer undergarments. She and her sister, who was also a seamstress, lived in a one-room and kitchen apartment for which they paid SEK 216 a year. They both worked in their rather large kitchen, which was lit by one big window

Illustration 3.1 Seamstress. Drawing by Carl Larsson, published in *Casper*, 17 March 1877. Arbetarrörelsens arkiv och bibliotek, Sweden.

and in the evenings by a kerosene light. This woman worked ten hours a day all year round except during July, August and September when she worked nine hours a day. Both she and her sister had an annual income of around SEK 600. The woman had been working as a homeworker for ten years, but before that she had worked as a seamstress in a shop. She also had vocational training in a sewing atelier. The sisters worked for different employers and received about SEK 8.4 per dozen garments, before deducting the SEK 0.80 they spent on needles and thread. Her sister was described as healthy but the homeworker as 'weak'.

The third and last group of workers consists of the women who made coats. These women were in general unmarried; they were themselves employers of other women and they had occupational training. On average they were also slightly younger than the other women. They all lived geographically close to one another. Several rented a small shop or an extra room nearby or attached to the home where they worked. Almost all worked for the same company, Wettergrens, which was located close to where they lived and worked. Many of them had worked in the company's factory before and/or had received professional training there. These women worked on average eleven hours a day all year. A few worked parts of the year in the factory. One example from this group is no. 84, a 29-year-old unmarried woman making coats. She lived with her elderly mother close to the small shop where she worked. The shop had two windows; it was lit by gas and heated by a tiled stove. In the shop she had sewing machines owned by Wettergrens, but she had to pay for gas, rent, needles and silk thread herself. She also employed four other women between the ages of fifteen and twenty-five. One coat brought in between SEK 4 and SEK 6. It is not really clear how much of that money went to her employees. They, as well as she, worked ten hours a day all year around. She herself made about SEK 1,400 a year and she was also a member of a *sjukkassa*, or health insurance society.

These coat makers illustrate well the complexity of determining who was really a homeworker. They were employees, but also employers. In addition they did not always work out of their own home. Nevertheless, in the survey it was their relationship to the employer that defined them as homeworkers. It was not really significant whether they worked in the rooms that they lived in, or whether work took place in a small shop nearby. It was the position of being subcontracted that made them homeworkers. There was one thing, however, that really differentiated these women from the other homeworkers: their income. Some of these women earned substantially more than the average homeworker. Belonging to the group who made coats and employed other women was highly correlated with earning higher wages. Women could make some money by making simpler garments and coats by themselves at home, but to make much more money they needed to make coats and have a shop and employees.

Housewifization and the Case of Sweden

None of the texts analysed described the homeworkers as primarily being married women with secondary incomes, nor were the majority of the homeworkers in this sample married women with secondary incomes. In about two-thirds of the texts the homeworkers were explicitly described as workers. Most importantly they were described in the official records as workers and covered by protection for all women workers.

Nevertheless, even if they were not described as housewives, this does not exclude the possibility that the process of housewifization affected industrial homeworkers in a more indirect way. Sweden in this period was a society moving towards a single male breadwinner model. Several studies have shown how the single breadwinner norm set up gender bars for women in the Swedish labour market. However, the results in this chapter suggests that in the case of Sweden before the First World War, 'housewifization' is not a sufficient explanation for the precarious situation of the industrial homeworkers.

Another conclusion of this chapter is that industrial homeworkers did not form a uniform group; not in their own time, not over time nor during different phases of industrialization. This case reveals a diverse labour force, which does not fit easily into the previous descriptions of homeworkers. They were not exclusively exploited nor housewives; rather they were a heterogeneous group that represented many different characteristics and, just as other groups in the labour market, they differed in age, skills and socio-economic status. However, one thing binds the homeworkers together with all the other studies of homeworkers over time and space. This is the interconnections between their gender, their place of work and their unprotected and unregulated situation in the labour market. In the early twentieth century, as well as today, we know that one's home can be an important place for economic activity. In order to understand this type of work it is important to recognize the multitude of activities that take place there as well as the diversity of the workers that perform them.

Malin Nilsson works at the Unit for Economic History, Department of Economy and Society at Gothenburg University. She defended her doctoral thesis, entitled *'Taking Work Home: Labour Dynamics of*

Women Industrial Homeworkers in Sweden during the Second Industrial Revolution' in March 2015. Her main areas of interest are the history of women's work, time allocation and labour supply, and the economics of gender.

Notes

1. While there are different types of homework, the focus in this study is on industrial homework – referring to industrial production executed in the home (or at another place chosen by the worker) for money and for an employer.
2. L. Tilly and J. Wallach Scott. 1987. *Women, Work, and Family*, New York: Methuen; T.K. Haraven. 1990. 'A Complex Relationship: Family Strategies and the Processes of Economic and Social Change', in A.F. Robertson and R.O. Friedland (eds), *Beyond the Marketplace: Rethinking Economy and Society*, New York: Aldine de Gruyter, 215–44; C. Goldin. 1979. 'Household and Market Production of Families in a Late Nineteenth Century American City', *Explorations in Economic History* 16(2), 111–31; N. Folbre. 1987. 'Family Strategy, Feminist Strategy', *Historical Methods: A Journal of Quantitative and Interdisciplinary History* 20(3), 115–18.
3. M. Mies. 2012. *The Lace Makers of Narsapur*, Spinifex Press, 200.
4. M. Mies. 1998. *Patriarchy and Accumulation on a World Scale: Women in the International Division of Labour*, London: Zed, 118.
5. Mies, *The Lace Makers of Narsapur*, 124.
6. Mies, *The Lace Makers of Narsapur*, Preface to the 2012 edition.
7. M. Mies. 1982. *The Lace Makers of Narsapur: Indian Housewives Produce for the World Market*, London: Zed, 119.
8. Mies, *The Lace Makers of Narsapur*, 38.
9. E. Prügl. 1996. 'Home-Based Workers: A Comparative Exploration of Mies's Theory of Housewifization', *Frontiers: A Journal of Women Studies* 17(1), 114–35.
10. Prügl, 'Home-Based Workers', 129.
11. E. Boris. 1994. *Home to Work: Motherhood and the Politics of Industrial Homework in the United States*, Cambridge: Cambridge University Press, 2.
12. E. Boris and E. Prügl. 1996. *Homeworkers in Global Perspective: Invisible No More*, New York: Routledge, 20.
13. E. Boris and C.R. Daniels. 1989. *Homework: Historical and Contemporary Perspectives on Paid Labor at Home*, Urbana: University of Illinois Press, 3.
14. C. Carlsson Wetterberg. 1986. *Kvinnosyn och kvinnopolitik: En studie av svensk Socialdemokrati 1880–1910*, Lund: Arkiv, 44; R. Frangeur. 1998. *Yrkeskvinna eller makens tjänarinna?: Striden om yrkesrätten för gifta kvinnor i mellankrigstidens Sverige*, Lund: Arkiv, 49; S. Hedenborg and U. Wikander. 2003. *Makt och Försörjning*, Lund: Studentlitteratur, 98; L. Karlsson. 1995. 'Mothers as Breadwinners: Myth or Reality in Early Swedish Industry?', *Uppsala Papers in Economic History* 39, 27; K. Åmark. 2005. *Hundra år av välfärdspolitik: Välfärdsstatens framväxt i Norge och Sverige*, Umeå: Boréa, 73–74.
15. The articles were found in the CSA archive in the National Archive in Stockholm and were labelled 'newspaper clippings on the industrial homework exhibition'. It is important to note that I was not personally involved in the selection of these articles. However, the organizers of the exhibition appear to have scanned all major Swedish newspapers for entries relating to industrial homework or to the exhibition itself, without apparent selection biases (positive as well as negative views are represented).

16. '... *I flera fall är äfven för de gifta kvinnorna arbetstiden så lång, att förtjänsten torde utgöra en synnerligen nödvändig inkomst, för hvars ernående det husmoderliga arbetet måste åsidosättas.'* in G. Meyerson. 1907. *Svenska Hemarbetsförhållanden: En undersökning utförd som grund för centralförbundets för socialt arbete hemarbetsutställning i Stockholm, oktober 1907*, Stockholm: n.p., 47.

17 '*Genom en dylik vidsträckt registreringsskyldighet skulle nämligen arbetsgifvaren beredas kännedom äfven om sådana arbetare, med hvilka han ej kommer I någon personlig beröring, hvilket möjligen hos arbetsgifvaren kunde väcka intresse för dessa arbetares lönevillkor och tanke på att med mellanmannens förbigående träda I direkt förbindelse med arbetarne. Då anlitandet af mellanman väl just är att anse som en hufvudsklig anledning till det för hemindustrien vanligen utmärkande "svettningssystemet"',* in M. Marcus. 1909. *Bihang till Betänkande afgifvet den 9 december 1909 af den af Kungl: Maj:t den 20 januari 1905 tillsatta Kommittén för revision af lagarna angående skydd mot yrkesfara och angående minderårigas och kvinnors användande till arbete i industriellt yrke m. m.*, Stockholm: n.p., 171.

18. '*Och* så blir följden än ytterligare afknappad dagspenning åt dem som utföra tillverkningen – en fortgårende rörelse nedåt, hvilken ej kan upphöra förrän orsaken uteblir: detta allmänhetens lumpna prutbegär, hos somliga – synnerligen bland kvinnorna – nästan mani. Och jämsides härmed deras opraktiska lättjefulla lust att köpa fördiggjorda kläder af de tarfligaste kvalitet hellre än att själfva förfärdiga dem af fullgodt stoff eller betala sådana till fullt värde samt – så vidt möjligt – betala kontant', in Sidsel, 'En Lärorik Hemarbetsutställning', *Aftonbladet*, 9 October 1907.

19. '*jag har 160 hemsömmerskor och betalt till dessa under 1911 18.678:02 kr. Dock är dessa yngre gifta kvinnor (spårvagnsfruar) som ej uteslutande lefva av denna förtjänst'.* He also adds that he did not employ any middlemen: '*några mellanhänder betjäna jag mig ej av!'* Letter from Yngve Östberg, June 10 1912. In archive: Socialstyrelsen 4:e byrån, byrån för pris- och socialvårdsstatistik 1913–1961; H2BD Svensk hemindustri; Ref. code: SE/RA/420267/420267.05/H 2.

20. The average annual earnings for a male factory worker in 1911 were SEK 1,246. The average annual earnings of a female textile factory worker in Sweden was around SEK 600. E. Lundberg, I. Svennilson, and G. Bagge. 1933. *Wages, Cost of Living and National Income in Sweden 1860–1930. Vol. 2, Wages in Sweden 1860–1930*, Stockholm Economic Studies 3a, London: P.S. King, 48.

References

Åmark, K. 2005. *Hundra år av välfärdspolitik: välfärdsstatens framväxt i Norge och Sverige*, Umeå: Boréa.

Boris, E. 1994. *Home to Work: Motherhood and the Politics of Industrial Homework in the United States*, Cambridge: Cambridge University Press.

Boris, E. and C.R Daniels. 1989. *Homework: Historical and Contemporary Perspectives on Paid Labor at Home*, Urbana: University of Illinois Press.

Boris, E. and E. Prügl. 1996. *Homeworkers in Global Perspective: Invisible No More*, Routledge.

Carlsson Wetterberg, C. 1986. *Kvinnosyn och kvinnopolitik: En studie av svensk socialdemokrati 1880–1910*, Lund: Arkiv.

Folbre, N. 1987. 'Family Strategy, Feminist Strategy', *Historical Methods: A Journal of Quantitative and Interdisciplinary History* 20(3), 115–18.

Frangeur, R. 1998. *Yrkeskvinna eller makens tjänarinna? Striden om yrkesrätten för gifta kvinnor i mellankrigstidens Sverige*, Lund: Arkiv.

Goldin, C. 1979. 'Household and Market Production of Families in a Late Nineteenth Century American City', *Explorations in Economic History* 16(2), 111–31.

Haraven, T.K. 'A Complex Relationship: Family Strategies and the Processes of Economic and Social Change', in A.F. Robertson and R.O. Friedland (eds), *Beyond the Marketplace: Rethinking Economy and Society*, New York: Aldine de Gruyter, 1990, 215–44.

Hedenborg, S. and U. Wikander. 2003. *Makt och försörjning*, Lund: Studentlitteratur.

Karlsson, L. 1995. 'Mothers as Breadwinners: Myth or Reality in Early Swedish Industry?', *Uppsala Papers in Economic History* 39.

Lundberg, E., I. Svennilson and G. Bagge. 1933. *Wages, Cost of Living and National Income in Sweden 1860–1930. Vol. 2, Wages in Sweden 1860–1930*, Stockholm Economic Studies 3a, London: P.S. King.

Marcus, M. 1909. *Bihang till Betänkande afgifvet den 9 december 1909 af den af Kungl: Maj:t den 20 januari 1905 tillsatta Kommittén för revision af lagarna angående skydd mot yrkesfara och angående minderårigas och kvinnors användande till arbete i industriellt yrke m. m*, Stockholm: n.p.

Meyerson, G. 1907. *Svenska Hemarbetsförhållanden: en undersökning utförd som grund för centralförbundets för socialt arbete hemarbetsutställning i Stockholm, oktober 1907*, Stockholm: n.p.

Mies, M. 1982. *The Lace Makers of Narsapur: Indian Housewives Produce for the World Market*, London: Zed Press.

———. 1998. *Patriarchy and Accumulation on a World Scale: Women in the International Division of Labour*, London: Zed.

———. 2012. *The Lace Makers of Narsapur*, Spinifex Press.

Prügl, E. 1996. 'Home-Based Workers: A Comparative Exploration of Mies's Theory of Housewifization', *Frontiers: A Journal of Women Studies* 17(1), 114–35.

Sidsel. 'En Lärorik Hemarbetsutställning', *Aftonbladet*, 9 October 1907.

Tilly, L.A. and J. Wallach Scott. 1987. *Women, Work, and Family*, New York: Methuen.

Archives

National Archives (Riksarkivet), Stockholm: Socialstyrelsen 4:e byrån, byrån för pris- och socialvårdsstatistik 1913–1961; H2BD Svensk hemindustri; volym 7–39; Ref. code: SE/RA/420267/420267.05/H 2

Centralförbundet för Socialt Arbete; Klipp rörande sociala ämnen; volym 5. Bunt 5. Hemarbetsutställningen 1907. Ref. code: SA/RA/73026/L III a.

CHAPTER 4

HOUSEMAIDS OF THE PAST AND AU PAIRS OF TODAY IN DENMARK
Do They Have Anything in Common?

Helle Stenum

The au pair system in Denmark is based on the Council of Europe's 1969 Agreement on Au Pairs.[1] The system was previously restricted to young Western women, often from the middle classes, who would live for a year with foreign families before starting their higher education or entering marriage. Until the end of the 1990s, the system languished, but around that time there occurred a major increase in the number of migrants utilizing the au pair arrangement. This time, however, the au pairs were largely Filipino women.[2] Since the end of the 1990s, the number of non-EU citizens who have received residence permits as au pairs in Danish private homes has increased substantially: from 316 au pair residence permits issued in 1996 to close to 3,000 in 2008. The vast majority of these migrants are women from the Philippines, but countries such as the Ukraine, Russia and Nepal are also represented in the statistics (Table 4.1).

Thus, the past ten years of au pair migration to Denmark concerns, in most cases, women from the Global South who migrate to affluent countries in order to work and remit money to their families. The employers in Denmark are often families with small children where the parents practise a dual career lifestyle. Migration to Denmark now takes place in a transnational space, where national regulations about immigration and emigration, personal networks, new communication technologies and global and national inequalities all play a role, and

Table 4.1 Residence permits granted to au pairs 1996–2011

Year	1996	1999	2003	2004	2005	2006	2007	2008	2009	2010	2011
All au pairs	316	528	1233	1500	1471	1793	2207	2937	2773	2649	2409
Filipino au pairs		21	246	490	612	955	1510	2163	2165	2140	1950
% of au pairs = Filipino		4	20	33	42	53	68	73	78	81	81

Source: Danish Immigration Service

where the social organization of childcare, family relations and gendered work all have great importance. The discourse in the Philippines around motherhood, au pair migration and leaving one's own children to work abroad in order to support them is part of this social process, as is the Danish discourse of gender equality, career, motherhood and employing au pairs.

Although it is organized as a so-called cultural exchange, Denmark's au pair system functions in effect as a migrant worker programme.[3] There is one key struggle over definition in the legislative regulation of the au pair system and the political and media discourse about the presence of au pairs, both transnationally and nationally. This is the issue of whether the au pair is regarded as a housemaid or a person participating in a cultural exchange. The transnational struggle over definition resulted in the Philippines – between 1998 and 2012 – prohibiting its citizens from emigrating to Europe to work as au pairs because the government viewed their working conditions as unacceptable. The Philippine government wanted citizens working abroad as au pairs to be recognized as migrant domestic workers, but gave up the ban in 2012.

The national struggle over definitions plays itself out politically as an ambivalence between what is work and what is not work. The Danish authorities attempt to maintain the social and legislative construction that the au pair is not working but participating in a cultural exchange. The au pair's residence permit is contingent on her living with her host family as live-in help. Paid work and the labour market are not present in the formal legislative framework, where the au pair does not receive a Danish work permit, but only a residence permit valid for a maximum of twenty-four months. Moreover, the money for the work carried out by the au pair is not defined as a wage, but as so-called pocket money, which is not subject to collective agreements between employers and employee organizations, but was set at a minimum rate of DKK 3,200 per month (EUR 430) by the government on 1 January 2013. On the other hand, as the subsequent regulations indicate, the au pair work is in some respects administered as a labour market relationship. For example, the pocket money the au pair receives is subject to income tax and the host family must take out work-related accident insurance like other employers. Furthermore, the employment is covered by the Danish compulsory vacation law.

Domestic work in the private home is not subjected to any form of control or inspection, however, and it is uncertain how the working environment laws operate; for example, in cases of sexual harassment or smoking. The work of the au pair is considered 'household chores' with maximum hours of thirty hours per week or five hours work per day. Any work beyond the set working time and outside the host family is defined as illegal and can lead to the revocation of the residence permit and a fine.

Moreover, there are increasing signs that this construction cannot function uniformly in the social contexts where au pair employment actually occurs. For example, it has become increasingly common for Danish property advertisements to rename a basement guest room as the 'au pair room', while accounts of successful Danish businesswomen will mention that there is an au pair on the home front, and that she often rescues their career by taking on the household chores. Ambivalence in the perception of the role of an au pair as work or non-work is also found in the attitudes of au pair employers. In interviews with the Danish daily newspaper *Information*, in connection with the 2010 International Women's Day on 8 March, several Danish middle- and upper-class women expressed their enthusiasm for the au pair scheme:

> Danish women achieve a more unhindered and equal access to the labour market and career by hiring an au pair as household help … Our au pair is like a teenage daughter. There are also some duties which come with having a grown teenage daughter … I am rich, she is poor. That is the essential thing … She obtains a better [life] working for me than in her home country… It is about purchasing freedom on the home front.[4]

No men were interviewed in this series of articles. The women saw themselves as pioneers of their liberation as 'career women', but expressed discomfort at having to relate to the outside world's interpretation of the au pair relation in a mistress-servant perspective. 'I have become used to being criticized as the middle-class woman who exploits poor women', one of them said. To speak of a return to master-servant relations creates unease among middle-class Danes. In the typical historical narrative, this is something 'we' have left behind 'us' at an earlier stage of development, and 'this kind of thing' belongs to a period where women did not have rights and were not equal. Despite neo-liberal erosions in recent decades, equality is still an essential construction in the national political space.

As a migration researcher I have attempted to historicize the management of migration, including the management of au pair migration, in order to bring new insights to both contemporary and historical debates. It has been extremely interesting and valuable to conduct a study of au pair migration in Denmark and then to investigate the extent to which regulation and practices from the period between 1870 and 1920, characterized by the 'invention' of the international migrant and the high point and the beginning of the demise of paid live-in domestic work in Denmark, can be compared to today's salaried, gendered, live-in domestic worker arrangement known as 'the au pair system'.[5] This chapter asks whether it is useful to compare present-day legislation, discourse and experiences of paid, live-in domestic workers with the conditions of paid domestic servants a hundred years ago, and how potential historical presences of power and regulatory mechanisms, relations and social productions can illuminate present-day conditions.

Between 2007 and 2008, I carried out the first qualitative study of the Danish au pair system, interviewing in English a group of twenty-four mostly Filipino au pairs, six host families and eight key informants with knowledge of the au pairs' situation. About half of the au pairs interviewed were between twenty-one and twenty-four years of age and the other half in the range twenty-five to twenty-nine years. The twenty-one Philippine au pairs were from many different regions; some from rural areas, others from urban areas. Of all twenty-four au pairs interviewed, seventeen had partly or fully completed higher education. The qualifications covered a broad span, including university degrees. Five (all Filipinos) of the twenty-four au pairs interviewed had children between one and four years old.

Based on my empirical study of au pair migration, the first part of this chapter will deal with the experiences and conditions affecting au pair life in Denmark. In the second part I will compare these experiences and conditions with the social practice and legal frameworks affecting paid, live-in domestic workers in the period between 1870 and 1920. The sources here will include historical analyses, legal texts, narrative accounts, memoirs, etiquette books and newspaper articles.

The Home as Workplace

That the au pair's work takes place in the private home is not without importance for the present day struggle over definition. Also important is the fact that the au pair often comes from economically poorer parts of the world and belongs to a non-Western minority ethnic group. That the work that the au pair carries out is still gendered as women's work is also important.[6] In a detailed study of migrant domestic work in Europe, Helma Lutz warns against considering the housework and care work market as 'just another labour market'.[7] According to Lutz, the household and care work market is characterized by the intimate character of the social sphere in which the work is carried out and the social construction of housework and childcare as women's work. Furthermore the special emotional and personal relationship between employee and employer often creates a high degree of personal dependency.

The organization and practice around housework and childcare in the family can today be seen as an intersection of the welfare regime, labour market organization, the division of labour and the degree of equality between the sexes.[8] With the Danish au pair arrangement being organized as live-in work, two factors give this domestic work a special character. First, the au pair's workplace is in the home of the host family. Second, the au pair's workplace is also her home, which can mean that the separation between work and private life can be very difficult.

A home is often connected with private, not public, life and when the home also functions as workplace, this private life character will typically dominate. It is a closed space and thereby also a closed workplace. What takes place within the four walls of the home is normally of a private character. The public normally has no access to the home and is therefore unable to monitor how the home functions as workplace for those employed there. For domestic workers, private homes are often a one-person workplace, filled with emotions and special traditions.

The empirical study reveals that in the au pair contract, work in the home is called domestic chores and the wages termed pocket money.[9] The work tasks are specified as laundry, cooking, childcare, and cleaning, etc. Most of the families in my study used a schedule specifying tasks for each day. 'And they'll give me a schedule of what I should do in that day, for example Monday I'll clean the bathroom upstairs and vacuum downstairs and then I can do ironing at night' (Nelly).[10] One of the interviewed au pairs, Lynn, explained that her role was more like that of a housekeeper, as she was the one who was in control of what was to be done in the house. The only daily task was shopping and cooking in the evening, when she and the family ate together. Lynn emphasized that she thought it was a great advantage that she could control her work routine, and she was very happy with her family, which consisted of a single father and his son. She thought that the absence of a female employer in the house was what gave her a degree of self-determination and relative freedom.

In the vast majority of cases, however, the daily management of the au pair's work was carried out by the female employer, when there was one in the home. From the au pairs' accounts, it appeared that the management style was in many ways relatively detailed and controlling. The workload imposed upon the au pairs varied substantially, as the types of work tasks also differed. Nancy was happy with her family and stated that she did not work any more than the stipulated five hours per day, while other au pairs had a workload and a type of work that was significantly longer. Ellain cleaned, washed clothes, ironed, babysat on occasion, washed windows and generally worked much more than the five hours per day. She was also asked to do some gardening work.

There was a great difference in the amount of work assigned to the au pair employees, but also in the types of work tasks. According to Danish regulations, the au pair's working week should not exceed thirty hours over six days, with a maximum five hours work per day. Some of the interviewees worked off the books alongside their work for the family, and for one of them – Susan – it meant that her workday could reach twelve to fourteen hours. For Susan, the workload for the host family was large, and the demands on her increased considerably during the time she was with the family. She had a child to support in the Philippines and sent a large portion of her salary home to her mother, who cared for her daughter. The fact that she knew that she was violating the au pair regulations and that it could endanger her residence permit meant she did not question her situation with the host family. She was afraid that the host family would report her for illegal work; that she would be expelled and thereby lose the ability to support herself and her family back in the Philippines.

Another element of work and the organization of work for the au pair employee was that as long as the au pair resided in the home work and leisure time often blended into each other. For example, if the employer were to ask whether the au pair would help the family bake bread after dinner, was this considered work or leisure time? The work was often organized in skewed time periods with breaks of a few hours duration, but without the possibility to use this interval as genuine free time. Even during her free time, the au pair was often expected to remain in the home in order to help out if there was an unexpected need, such as a child becoming ill. The au pairs felt it was difficult to express opposition to the employer's organization of the work, especially in light of the fact that their residence in Denmark was tied to a specific family.

Workplace as Home

For the au pair it is not her choice to live at her workplace with the host family, but a condition for obtaining a Danish residence permit. The physical framework for the au pair employees' private residence varied greatly, but most of the informants interviewed had access to their own dwelling or own room. The quality of the au pair's dwelling ranged from a small room of ten square metres, the small room that adjoined an office area separated only by a glass pane and curtains, or a basement room placed between spiders and storage cupboards, to one's own apartment with bathroom, kitchen and private entrance. Many of the au pairs lived in basement rooms.

A home and the feeling of having a home have a lot to do with privacy and intimacy. This applies to one's private space and the possibility of deciding who to let in and who to keep out. It applies to the possibility of choosing the food one eats and having access to privacy in connection with personal hygiene. Further, it applies to the possibility of creating one's own social space with whomever one wants, receiving guests and having the chance to be left in peace at predictable, fixed times of the day or week.[11]

To many au pairs, creating this kind of separation between work and private life proved difficult. They found it difficult to obtain the feeling of being truly off-duty and free, even when they were in their rooms. This required the establishment of a set of clear boundaries, physical and psychological, between the au pairs' workplace and their home, between their work tasks and their free time. However, the nature of live-in domestic work made it highly difficult to establish a clear-cut boundary between activities that were work and activities that were voluntary. This is because certain features of au pair work are tied to emotional relations between the employer and employee and because the au pair was prevented from leaving the home to gain privacy, or because she found it difficult to gain privacy simply by retreating to her own dwelling area. The regulation of the au pair scheme meant that the au pair was tied by her residence permit, which required that she lived with her employer that is only the employer with whom she had a contract. The possibility of choosing an alternative living arrangement was non-existent, and the chances of switching to a different employer would depend on the au pair's ability to find a new one within a certain time limit, as well as the renewed approval of the Danish Immigration Service.

One au pair explained how it was difficult for her to set boundaries for taking time for herself. Instead of having Sundays as a fixed day off, they gave her time off from 6pm on Friday to 5pm on Saturday, which meant that she could see her friends only until Saturday afternoons. 'They are holding my time', she complained.

Another aspect connected with the workplace-home connection involves access to food and conditions for meals. Some of the au pair informants mentioned that food was a problem and that they went to bed hungry or woke up hungry at night. Filipino food traditions differ from those in Denmark, and the au pairs often found that it was difficult to obtain the food to which they were accustomed. One factor is the food that is served; another is the communication that takes place around the dinner table. In some homes, the dinner conversation took place in English while in others it was in Danish. Not surprisingly, the au pair employee would feel excluded if the conversation took place in Danish, given that even if she attended and paid for language classes she would normally obtain only very limited language skills.

Access to the bathroom is another area connected to private life and intimacy. In one instance, the au pair employee was denied access to the bathroom after 8pm, which she found frustrating because she preferred bathing in the evening, as she had done in the Philippines.

When the workplace is one's home, there often occurs a blending of rules for the au pair's behaviour in the workplace and in private life. This was expressed in rules regarding which parts of the house were off limits to the au pair employee, how the au pair could spend her free time, whether guests were permitted in the room, whether the host family should be informed if the au pair had a boyfriend or where she went at weekends. In one case, the female host employer was upset after discovering that the au pair she had hired had a Danish boyfriend.

Housemaids of the Past and Au Pairs Today

In my attempt to historicize the phenomenon of the new au pairs, I will primarily emphasize the experiences and accounts of the position of 'domestic servant' and the relationship between mistress and servant. Moreover, I will also briefly discuss the formal regulation of this relationship through legislation.

My historical perspective begins around the end of the nineteenth century and the early twentieth century, when domestic work constituted the main occupation for women in the labour market. It ends at the beginning of the 1950s, when privately paid and organized domestic work in private homes was more or less phased out, due to the growth of the modern welfare state and the increased entry of women into the labour market. Both in Europe and in Denmark, the period from the 1880s to the 1920s represents the high point for paid private domestic work and the onset of a significant decline in the number of women hired as domestic labour, especially by the urban middle and upper classes.[12]

The relationship between servants and housework in Denmark was formally regulated by the *Tyendeloven* (servant law) of 1854, which was replaced by the *Medhjælperloven* (assistance law) in 1921. The 1854 servant law can be seen as part of increasing state influence and control over domestic labour and an increasing liberation of the individual as legal subject.[13]

The *Skudsmålbogen* (judgement booklet) was a key regulatory mechanism in the control over labour mobility. The booklet was held by individual servants and was essentially the complete documentation of previous work experience. It had to be stamped by the police and fines were imposed on the servant if the booklet was lost. Until its elimination in 1921, 'the judgement booklet' was hated by the servants, and it came to regulate their mobility as a group in a manner that was stricter than the controls applied to the rest of the working class.

According to the 1854 servant law, the domestic worker was a juridical subject only to a limited degree, and was not a political subject as an individual. In 1915 she became a political subject following the introduction of universal suffrage. In 1921 the special mobility controls were removed for Danish servants with citizenship and the domestic worker thereby emerged from the confines of the household to become a political, juridical and 'governable' subject, rather than, as earlier, a subject subordinated to strong direct control and included in the household as a social unit.

Differences and Similarities

Even though there would seem to be great differences in the social context, material level and social norms, this journey back gave me new perspectives on both the housemaids in today's migrant domestic work and new perspectives on the migrant domestic servant of the past. The housemaid of the past became visible in the migrant domestic workers of today, the au pairs, and today's migrant domestic workers became visible in the housemaids of the past. It is especially the latter that surprised me when I studied accounts of young Danish women who had left home to work as household servants.

The narratives and descriptions of life as housemaids in the years around 1900 express a quite consistent pattern around a specific subjectification of the live-in domestic worker as primarily female and working-class. This is seen in the archives, in historical analyses and descriptions, in legal judgments, in fictional accounts and in personal memoirs.[14] Even though the physical framework and conditions both for practical life in general and domestic work in particular have changed considerably over the past century, there are striking parallels between the historical housemaids living and working in a gendered asymmetrical power relationship as live-in domestic workers and the accounts from today's Filipino au pairs.[15] This is true, for example, of the feelings of loneliness, foreignness, homesickness and longings for family and networks.[16] There are also parallels in the importance of and often disappointment about the condition and location of the room that the housemaid was given, which was often placed next to the kitchen and toilet, for example.[17] The women's lack of free time to themselves,[18] since they were often compelled to sleep together with the children at night, is also recognizable, as is the overwhelming burden of work. Themes of social control over the servant's food, hygiene, time spent outside the house and her possible boyfriends were likewise present and are comparable with the accounts of the au pairs.[19]

Københavns Tjenestepigeforening (Copenhagen servant girls' association) fought to acquire recognized and professionalized status.[20] The association's 1895 demands show that working hours, wages for overtime, suitable room and board, days off and free evenings were high on the agenda. The structuring of the housemaid's work into specific tasks conducted at certain specific times and in a specific fashion is recognized in Louise Nimb's edifying novel *Karen* from 1895, where the bourgeois Nimb advises how a housemaid should live and work. Nimb's description of the housemaid's work resembles a modern work schedule:

> I begin my weekly cleaning on Wednesday with the Captain's room ... the windows are opened, the plants carried down into the kitchen, along with the lamps, the coal box, the fender and all the other metal things that had to be shined. Naturally, the ashes were emptied from the oven and the ash box and the stove were brushed with a dry brush.[21]

Based on narrative accounts, literature, etiquette books, newspapers and magazines, Haastrup describes how housemaids experienced the internal division of labour within the individual household and the ambivalent emotional relations that existed between the housemaid and the mistress of the house.[22] Haastrup shows how different strategies developed based on their differing class-based and gendered roles, and there are parallels here with the life practice of today's Filipino au pairs. In 1893 the former housemaid Sophie Helsted published an instructional guide for aspiring housemaids, emphasizing the importance of always smiling and never contradicting or arguing with the master.[23] My au pair informants have also spoken of the smile that must always be present, and of their anxiety about disagreeing or expressing dissatisfaction. They often used a cultural explanation for their lack of assertion: 'you don't do that in the Philippines'. Nevertheless, the expectation of docility is clear on both sides of the power relation and forms a part of the common cultural construction of being Filipino. While this does not mean that Filipino women accept or subordinate themselves to the conditions, it is certainly an expression of a strategy based on the relatively weak position in which they find themselves as au pairs.

Even though the housemaids of a century ago managed to establish a trade union, it was difficult to assemble members and it was not possible for the association to offer concrete support to individual housemaids. Vammen notes that 'frequent shifts of workplace were the housemaids and home assistants' most important liberation attempts'. It was frequently the only realistic possibility when it concerned applying one's will when faced with strong control by the master and unsatisfactory conditions.[24] The au pairs of today have no formally recognized association and the strategy for them is completely parallel. If they are dissatisfied, the only realistic way for them to change their situation is to find a new host family. However, changing jobs is more complicated than it was for the Danish housemaid of the last century, due to the fact that control over paid domestic work now takes place primarily through migration regulations; in other words the Danish housemaid could not be expelled from the country if she did not have work.

Rosa Berg: Transnational Domestic Worker

Not only do experiences and relations as live-in domestic workers cut across different periods of time but so too do experiences and accounts of national and transnational mobility. Such mobility characterized the life of young Rosa Berg, for example. Rosa Berg's memoirs recount her early life as a housemaid.[25] At the age of fifteen in 1902 she became an internal migrant by travelling 80 km from the harbour town of Korsør, where she lived with her poor family, to Copenhagen. Over the years, she worked in different homes, after which she emigrated to Scotland, then to London and onwards to the United States to work as a domestic worker. After six years in the United States, she returned to Copenhagen.

Her memoirs focus on the work load, the management and social control by the female head of the household, the employers' occasional sexual harassment and humiliating treatment, the hypocrisy of the middle and upper classes about social norms of conduct and sexuality, and the significance of the room and the frequent uprooting as the only real possibility to alter her work and living situation. It is also striking that many of the migrant experiences and strategies that she describes resemble experiences and strategies used by today's Filipino au pairs. For several years, Rosa Berg sent money home to her mother in Korsør. She was part of a migrant network, both when she travelled to Copenhagen and when she maintained contact with other girls from Korsør, and in the expansion of the network in Copenhagen. When she emigrated to England and later to the United States her network expanded to become transnational. This network played a role both in giving mutual aid and support and in making contacts with other migrants and workplaces. In London, for example, Rosa found a job for a friend from Korsør at the hotel where she herself worked. Rosa travelled as a migrant domestic worker without making decisions about whether she should settle down or not, and she returned to Denmark in a way that today's 'circular' migrant returns to the home country.

Conclusion: The Housemaid of the Past and the Au Pair of Today

It has been very exciting and productive to rediscover elements of today's migrant domestic worker in the Danish servant girls of the past. It is also a matter of concern that this historical experience is largely ignored in the literature. Like so much else, it is an expression of our general methodological nationalism, where transnational processes have been interpreted as irrelevant and left out of the collective national memory.[26] Rosa Berg's memoirs are a vivid example of how the transnational migration practice is not a new phenomenon. Her memoirs show how the experiences of domestic work and the asymmetrical power relations connected to the live-in arrangement resembled each other across the national contexts in which she found herself.

The report of the Husassistentkommissionen (home assistant commission) from 1943 concluded that household work was necessary for the health and well-being of the population and for society.[27] Domestic labour was still uniformly gendered as female, but the class-based division of labour of earlier years, between middle-class or bourgeois women and the lowly housemaids, was breaking down. In 1949, the law on *husmoderafløser* (housewife substitute) was passed as a new standard for paid domestic labour in private homes, and in 1953 the women who continued to work in private homes were given a collective formal status (later on primarily as home carers) and were redefined as participants in the general labour market.

At the end of the 1990s, paid live-in domestic work reappeared in Demark in a new form: as au pair migration. The migration regime and the regulation of migration created frameworks for the reintroduction of paid live-in domestic workers into private homes in the twenty-first century. Paid domestic work in private homes has been reprivatized and re-individualized in the form of live-in au pair domestic work. The working conditions of the twenty-first century domestic worker have certainly changed but her position as paid live-in worker in a private home is in many ways comparable to that of the housemaid prior to 1921. The au pair of today – in terms of migration restrictions and her position as a migrant – is defined primarily by her subordinate position in a household. Without the household taking her in as au pair, her residence in Denmark would be illegal, and she has no right to work and live outside the household. She has limited social rights, such as the right to use the health system; she has no political rights and no chance to obtain these rights. Her rights as a worker are more or less suspended because her work is not defined as work. She is defined as a part of the family, her work consists of 'chores' and her wages are 'pocket money'. Her residence permit functions as a control over her mobility, resembling the old judgement booklet because it is decisive for her possibilities of work.

There are no doubt great differences in the life practice of today's Filipino au pair and the housemaid of the past. However, if one understands the au pair as labour, as a domestic worker in the national territory, then she can be seen as being subordinated to a governmental rationality that has more in common with a premodern or feudal context than a modern regulatory rationality based on the idea of individual freedom and individual rights.[28] The au pairs of today are subordinated to a comprehensive mobility and residential control regime by virtue of their position as temporary migrants. This contributes to positioning them as an underclass in Denmark. The migration regime is thus able to establish a parallel regulatory universe in the national space, which apparently functions more or less smoothly in relation to the dominant equality and rights-based discourse elsewhere in Danish society. Inequality thus becomes institutionalized, rationalized and grounded in the au pair's otherness rather than in differences of class, gender, skill or qualifications.

At the level of practice, it is thought-provoking that many of the experiences of live-in domestic workers are recognizable across different historical eras and geographic and national contexts. This underscores the strength and continuity of the social mechanisms operating to sustain this power relationship. These are constituted in the employment relation between the paid live-in domestic worker and the employing family. The rising middle-class rationalization of au pair employment as a so-called win-win situation, where Danish pocket money replaces Philippine subsistence wages 'for everyone's benefit', reinforces the subjectification of the au pair as transnationally accessible cheap household and care labour, anchored in a global social inequality that 'we' cannot change. A transnational and historicized approach can open up new memories of 'we' that also includes migrant domestic workers and a more power sensitive concept of 'we' that includes class, gender and migrant status.

Helle Stenum has a Ph.D. in migration studies and is external lecturer at Roskilde and Aarhus universities. She also works as an independent consultant and activist. Her research interests include the management of labour migration; marginalized migrants; technologies and production of difference; processes of inclusion/exclusion; the historicization of migration – racialization, whiteness and gender in memory; and silence about the Nordic colonial past. Recent publications include 'Bane and Boon; Gains and Pains; Dos and Don'ts ... Moral Economy and female bodies in Au Pair Migration' in R. Cox (ed.), *Sisters and Servants* (Palgrave, 2014) and (with A.O. Farah) 'Danish-Somalis in Copenhagen' (Open Society Foundation, October 2014).

Notes

An earlier Danish version of this chapter can be found in H. Stenum. 2010. 'Fortidens tjenestepiger og nutidens au pairs. Har de noget til fælles?', *Arbejderhistorie 2*, 66–83.

1. Council of Europe. 1969. 'European Agreement on Au Pair Placement', Strasbourg, 24 October.
2. For an excellent study and description of female Filipino immigration to Denmark see N.T. Andersen. 2013. *Profession: Filippiner – Kvinder på arbejde i Danmark gennem fire årtier*, København: Tiderne Skifter; N.T. Andersen. 2014. 'Filippinske hotelarbejdere i København fra 1960erne-1990erne', *Arbejderhistorie 1*, 7–29.
3. H. Stenum. 2011. 'Migration Management at the Margins. Transnationalized and Localized Government of Marginalized Migrants in Denmark: Au Pairs and Destitute EU Citizens', Ph.D. dissertation, Aalborg: Aalborg University.

4. M.L. Thorup. 2010. 'Vejen til et friere liv blev et nyt tabu', *Daily Information*, 8 March (in connection with International Women's Day).
5. See for example H. Stenum. 2011. 'Abused Domestic Workers in Europe: The Case of Au Pairs', research paper, Brussels: European Parliament's Committee on Civil Liberties, Justice and Home Affairs; Stenum, 'Migration Management at the Margins'; H. Stenum. 2010. 'Au Pair Migration: Transnational Production of Corruption and New Nordic Inequalities', in L.W. Isaksen (ed.), *Globalizing Welfare. Gender, Care and Migration in Nordic Societies*, Lund: Nordic Academic Press, 23–48.
6. See for example B. Ehrenreich and A. Hochschild (eds). 2002. *Global Woman: Nannies, Maids and Sex Workers in the New Economy*, New York: Metropolitan/Owl Books; B. Anderson. 2000. *Doing the Dirty Work*, London: Zed Books; B. Anderson. 2007. 'A Very Private Business. Exploring the Demand for Migrant Domestic Workers', *European Journal of Women's Studies* 14(3), 247–64; H. Lutz (ed.). 2008. *Migration and Domestic Work*, Aldershot: Ashgate; H. Stenum. 2008. *Au Pair in Denmark: Cheap Labour or Cultural Exchange*, København: Foa; Stenum, 'Au Pair Migration'; R. Lister and F. Williams (eds). 2007. *Gendering Citizenship in Western Europe*, Bristol: The Policy Press.
7. Lutz, *Migration and Domestic Work*.
8. See for example M. Daly and K. Rake. 2003. *Gender and the Welfare State*, Cambridge: Cambridge Polity; F. Williams and A. Gavanas. 2008. 'The Intersection of Childcare Regimes and Migration Regimes: A Three-Country Study', in H. Lutz (ed.), *Migration and Domestic Work*, Aldershot: Ashgate.
9. Udlændingeservice 2010: AU1, Del 2: Au pair kontrakt. Retrieved 23 April 2016 from www.nyidanmark.dk
10. All names of informants are pseudonyms.
11. N. Constable. 1997. *Maid to Order in Hong Kong: Stories of Migrant Workers*, Ithaca and London: Cornell University Press; J. Rollins. 1985. *Between Women: Domestics and Their Employers*, Philadelphia: Temple University Press; J. Ardano. 2003. 'Maternalism in Mistress-Maid Relations:_The Philippine Experience', *Journal of International Women's Studies* 3(4), 154–77.
12. R. Sarti. 2008. 'The Globalisation of Domestic Service – An Historical Perspective', in H. Lutz (ed.), *Migration and Domestic Work*, Aldershot: Ashgate, 77–98; T. Vammen. 1986. *Rent og Urent*, København: Gyldendal.
13. A.F. Jacobsen. 2008. *Husbondret: Rettighedskulturer i Danmark 1750–1920*, København: Museum Tusculanums Forlag.
14. Historical analyses, descriptions and legal judgements are found in B. Broch, D. Dahlerup, B.K. Hansen and T. Vammen (eds). 1982. *Kvinder i Opbrud: En kildesamling om land-og bykvinder i arbejde og forening omkring år 1900*, København: Gyldendal; K. Skovbjerg. 1983. *Da kvinden blev borger*, København: Dansklærerforeningen; Vammen, *Rent og Urent*; B. Possing. 1980. *Arbejderkvinder og kvindearbejde i København ca. 1870–1906*, Aalborg: Aalborg Universitetsforlag, Serie om kvindeforskning nr 2.; L. Haastrup. 1984. *Husarbejde – kvindearbejde: Tjenestepiger – husmødre. 1880–1925*, København: Institut for nordisk filologi; L.H. Jensen. 2001. *Kvindebevægelsen og de svenske tjenestepiger i Danmark*, Farum: Farum Arkiver og Museum; A.M. Knudsen. 2002. 'Det huslige arbejde – også et erhverv', *Statens Arkiver: Siden Saxo* 4(19), 40–46 ; N.G. Bardenfleth. 2004. *For lang og tro tjeneste: Det kvindelige velgørende selskab 1815–2004*, København: Nyt Nordisk Forlag; E. Blochs. 2000. 'Indvandringsboom, kontrol og diskrimination', in E. Blochs et al. (eds), *Over Øresund før broen – svenskere på Københavnsegnen i 300 år*, København: Lokalhistoriske Arkiver i Storkøbenhavn, 136–59. For fictional accounts and memories see: H. Strange. 1923–24. *Inger Prier*, København: Det Schønbergske Forlag; R. Berg. 1916. *En Tjenestepiges Erindringer*, København: Gyldendal; M. Christensen. 1983. En samtale mellem to husassistenter 1923', in K. Skovbjerg, *Da kvinden blev borger*, 64–65.

15. For example Vammen, *Rent og Urent*; Possing, *Arbejderkvinder og Kvindearbejde*; Haastrup, *Husarbejde – Kvindearbejde* and R. Berg, *En tjenestepiges erindringer.*
16. Vammen, *Rent og Urent*; Broch et al., *Kvinder i Opbrud.*
17. E. Damgaard and P.H. Moustgaard. 1970. *Et hjem – en familie: En etnologisk punktundersøgelse af et borgerligt københavnsk miljø o. 1980*, København: Nationalmuseet, Folklivstudier nr 3.
18. Vammen, *Rent og Urent*; Christensen, 'En samtale mellem to husassistenter'; Berg, *En tjenestepiges erindringer.*
19. Vammen, *Rent og Urent*; Possing, *Arbejderkvinder og Kvindearbejde*; Christensen, 'En samtale mellem to husassistenter'; Knudsen, 'Det huslige arbejde – også et erhverv'; Berg, *En tjenestepiges erindringer*; Haastrup, *Husarbejde – Kvindearbejde.*
20. Christensen, 'En samtale mellem to husassistenter'.
21. L. Nimb, *Karen* (1895) cited in Broch et al. (eds), *Kvinder i Opbrud*, 68–69.
22. Haastrup, *Husarbejde – Kvindearbejde.*
23. Broch et al. (eds), *Kvinder i Opbrud* .
24. Vammen, *Rent og Urent*, 75.
25. Berg, *En tjenestepiges erindringer.*
26. N. Glick Schiller and A. Wimmer. 2003. 'Methodological Nationalism, the Social Sciences, and the Study of Migration', *The International Migration Review* 3(37), 576–610.
27. Betænkning afgivet af den af Arbejds- og Socialministeriet nedsatte Husassistentkommission (1943).
28. For an extended discussion on the governmentality perspective see Stenum, *Migration Management at the Margins* or Stenum, *Fortidens tjenestepiger og nutidens au pairs.*

References

Andersen, N.T. 2013. *Profession: Filippiner – Kvinder på arbejde i Danmark gennem fire årtier*, København: Tiderne Skifter.

———. 2014. 'Filippinske hotelarbejdere i København fra 1960erne-1990erne', *Arbejderhistorie* 1, 7–29.

Anderson, B. 2000. *Doing the Dirty Work*, London: Zed Books.

———. 2007. 'A Very Private Business. Exploring the Demand for Migrant Domestic Workers', *European Journal of Women's Studies* 14(3), 247–64.

Ardano, J. 2003. 'Maternalism in Mistress-Maid Relations: The Philippine Experience',
Journal of International Women's Studies 3(4), 154–77.

Bardenfleth, N.G. 2004. *For lang og tro tjeneste: Det kvindelige velgørende selskab 1815-2004*, København: Nyt Nordisk Forlag.

Berg, R. 1916. *En Tjenestepiges Erindringer*, København: Gyldendal.

Betænkning afgivet af den af Arbejds- og Socialministeriet nedsatte Husassistentkommission. 1943.

Blochs, E. 'Indvandringsboom, kontrol og diskrimination', in E. Blochs et al. (eds), *Over Øresund før broen – svenskere på Københavnsegnen i 300 år*, København: Lokalhistoriske Arkiver i Storkøbenhavn, 2000, 136–59.

Broch, B., D. Dahlerup, B.K. Hansen and T. Vammen (eds). 1982. *Kvinder i Opbrud: En kildesamling om land-og bykvinder i arbejde og forening omkring år 1900*, København: Gyldendal.

Constable, N. 1997. *Maid to Order in Hong Kong: Stories of Migrant Workers*, Ithaca and London: Cornell University Press.

Council of Europe. 1969. 'European Agreement on Au Pair Placement', Strasbourg, 24 October.

Christensen, M. 'En samtale mellem to husassistenter 1923', in K. Skovbjerg (ed.), *Da kvinden blev borger*, København: Dansklærerforeningen, 1983, 64–65.

Daly, M. and K. Rake. 2003. *Gender and the Welfare State*, Cambridge: Polity Press.

Damgaard, E. and P.H. Moustgaard. 1970. *Et hjem – en familie: En etnologisk punktundersøgelse af et borgerligt københavnsk miljø o. 1980*, København: Nationalmuseet, Folklivstudier nr 3.

Ehrenreich, B. and A. Hochschild (eds). 2002. *Global Woman: Nannies, Maids and Sex Workers in the New Economy*, New York: Metropolitan/Owl Books.

Glick Schiller, N. and A. Wimmer. 2003. 'Methodological Nationalism, the Social Sciences, and the Study of Migration', *The International Migration Review* 3(37), 576–610.

Haastrup, L. 1984. *Husarbejde – kvindearbejde: Tjenestepiger – husmødre. 1880–1925*, København: Institut for nordisk filologi.

Isaksen, L.W. (ed.). 2010. *Globalizing Welfare: Gender, Care and Migration in Nordic Societies*, Lund: Nordic Academic Press.

Jacobsen, A.F. 2008. *Husbondret: Rettighedskulturer I Danmark 1750–1920*, København: Museum Tusculanums Forlag.

Jensen, L.H. 2001. *Kvindebevægelsen og de svenske tjenestepiger i Danmark*, Farum: Farum Arkiver og Museum.

Knudsen, A.M. 2002. 'Det huslige arbejde – også et erhverv', *Statens Arkiver: Siden Saxo* 4 (19), 40–46.

Lister, R. and F. Williams (eds). 2007. *Gendering Citizenship in Western Europe*, Bristol: The Policy Press.

Lutz, H. (ed.). 2008. *Migration and Domestic Work*, Aldershot: Ashgate.

Possing, B. 1980. *Arbejderkvinder og kvindearbejde i København ca. 1870–1906*, Serie om kvindeforskning nr 2, Aalborg: Aalborg Universitetsforlag.

Rollins, J. 1985. *Between Women: Domestics and Their Employers*, Philadelphia: Temple University Press.

Sarti, R. 'The Globalisation of Domestic Service – An Historical Perspective', in H. Lutz (ed.), *Migration and Domestic Work*, Hampshire/Burlington: Ashgate, 2008, 77–98.

Skovbjerg, K. 1983. *Da kvinden blev borger*, København: Dansklærerforeningen.

Stenum, H. 2008. *Au Pair in Denmark: Cheap Labour or Cultural Exchange*, København: Foa.

———. 'Au Pair Migration: Transnational Production of Corruption and New Nordic Inequalities', in L.W. Isaksen (ed.), *Globalizing Welfare: Gender, Care and Migration in Nordic Societies*, Lund: Nordic Academic Press, 2010, 23–48.

———. 2010. 'Fortidens tjenestepiger og nutidens au pairs: Har de noget til fælles?', *Arbejderhistorie: Tidsskriftet for Historie, Kultur og Politik* 2, 66–83.

———. 2011. 'Abused Domestic Workers in Europe: The Case of Au Pairs', research paper, Brussels: European Parliament's Committee on Civil Liberties, Justice and Home Affairs.

———. 2011. 'Migration Management at the Margins: Transnationalized and Localized Government of Marginalized Migrants in Denmark: Au Pairs and Destitute EU Citizens', Ph.D. dissertation, Aalborg: Aalborg University.

Strange, H. 1923–24. *Inger Prier*, København: Det Schønbergske Forlag.

Thorup, M.L. 2010. 'Vejen til et friere liv blev et nyt tabu', *Daily Information*, 8 March.

Udlændingeservice 2010: AU1, Del 2: Au pair kontrakt. Retrieved 23 April 2016 from www.nyidanmark.dk

Vammen, T. 1986. *Rent og Urent: Hovedstadens Piger og Fruer 1880–1920*, København: Gyldendal.

Williams, F. and A. Gavanas. 'The Intersection of Childcare Regimes and Migration Regimes: A Three-Country Study', in H. Lutz (ed.), *Migration and Domestic Work*, Aldershot: Ashgate, 2008, 13–28.

CHAPTER 5

TRADE UNIONISM IN DENMARK, 1870–1940 – FROM THE PERSPECTIVE OF WORK

Knud Knudsen

Labour historians have often contrasted the history of trade unionism 'from above' with the history 'from below' and it has been difficult to reconcile the two. 'History from above' is concerned with organizations and their conflicts with employers and the state, whereas 'history from below' focuses on the members of trade unions, the workplace, consent and conflicts at work. In this chapter, I argue that the gulf between history 'from above' and history 'from below' may be bridged, for instance, by studying the history of trade unions from the perspective of work and thus integrating the development of work and work experience into the history of the trade unions.

By applying a work perspective, I also seek to reconcile some of the basic ideas of social history with some of the insights of the new cultural history of the 1980s and 1990s. Insistence on the importance of social structures and collective agency was a basic idea of social history, in line with the constructivist notion of collective identities as a key idea in the new cultural history. Even though the new cultural history was to some extent articulated as a critique of the social history idiom, subsequent debates have shown that constructivist ideas and social history are not mutually exclusive.[1]

The work perspective includes both socio-economic and ideological issues. The socio-economic section of this chapter deals with the transformation of work during the second industrial revolution from the 1890s, and the argument is that across the different patterns of industrialization some general trends can be identified, which I see as the growth of modern, disciplined work. The two final sections of the chapter discuss the ideological dimensions of the concept of work as this was expressed in the agitation, the organizational structures and the politics of the trade unions. The argument is that trade unionism represented not merely the politics of skill but also a broader ideology of work, emphasizing the rights of labour in modern society.

Historiography

Until the 1970s, Danish labour history was dominated by the publications of the labour movement and the bulk of this was organizational history in the traditional sense of the term. In the 1970s, a new critical history of the labour movement emerged, still in the tradition of political history but now with a focus on the militant groups and the oppositional trends in the labour movement. Influenced by the English History Workshop movement and the ideas of 'history from below', research interest turned towards the social history of the working class, including the living and working conditions of urban and agricultural workers. The rediscovery of the collections of autobiographies of artisans and working people collected by the Danish National Museum in the 1950s also reinforced interest in the social and cultural history of workers.[2] The autobiographies have been a useful source in historical accounts of the trade unions, which include the perspective 'from below', including work experience.

Studies of work and trade unionism in Denmark are thus rooted in the tradition of social history. Nevertheless, the 'cultural turn' in the 1980s – presented in books by Gareth Stedman Jones, Patrick Joyce and Joan W. Scott among others[3] – also stimulated studies of work and these were further encouraged by feminist and gender history. The implications of the cultural turn were not only a critique of social history but also a constructivist approach to concepts such as class and gender, which proved particularly fruitful in studies of women's work. This can be seen for example in Marianne Rostgaard's analysis of the construction of new sexual divisions of labour in the textile and footwear industries.[4]

Paternalism was another issue in Danish studies in the 1990s, parallel to the international debate.[5] In his study of work and conflicts of work at the Burmeister & Wain (B&W) shipyard in Copenhagen in the period 1850–2000, Niels Jul Nielsen sketches 'the development from a paternalistic form of management to a formalized and institutionalized system of labour regulations'.[6] He argues that paternalism cannot be depicted as merely a reminiscence of the pre-industrial past but took new forms. The second issue of Nielsen's book was class. While the making of class had been a major theme in the social history of labour in the 1970s, diversity and heterogeneity were accentuated in the 1980s and 1990s. By the 1990s, the concept of class came under severe critique. In Denmark, some critics advocated the substitution of the concept of class altogether by the concept of 'life-mode'. Nielsen applied the theoretical ideas of the 'life-mode' approach to his study of B&W, arguing that internal differentiation – of wages, conditions, and orientations – characterized this stronghold of the Danish labour movement rather than the unity of class.[7]

Taken as a whole, the trends of labour history in Denmark – including the studies of work and trade unions – have followed the trends in international literature and research, though theoretical reflections have been rare in historical accounts of Danish trade unions.[8] While Danish labour historians were familiar with the classic books of the British Marxist historians and the German *Sozialgeschichte* in the 1960s, the so-called 'new' social history of the 1970s, represented for example by William Sewell and Christopher Johnson – who focused on proletarianization and radicalization of workers – had little impact on Danish labour history. By the late 1990s, political issues had regained momentum in Danish labour history, and this might be the reason why the international contributions to the study of class and labour did not receive the same attention in Denmark as elsewhere. The contributions by, for example, Sonya O. Rose and Kathleen Canning were discussed among feminist historians but had little impact on historical research at the turn of the century.

The concept of class has been a key issue in the international debate on labour history since the 1980s. Patrick Joyce definitely had a point arguing that the concept of class cannot be taken for granted, as it used to be in labour history. Yet the old dichotomies – heterogeneity or unity, sectionalism or class – have remained issues of debate. In the latest general account of the history of the Danish labour movement, published in 2007, class remains a key concept but the authors emphasize the variety of collective identities and the heterogeneity of class.[9] In an article contributing to the current debate about the concept of class in labour history, Lars K. Christensen argued that 'an understanding of modernity must include the realities of class'.[10] Class cannot explain everything, yet class cannot be ignored.

Comparative studies of international trade unionism are rare and even rarer if we look for trade union studies with a work perspective 'from below'.[11] The comparative project of a group of European scholars on the emergence of European trade unions before the First World War is therefore remarkable in a European context.[12] Yet in spite of their efforts to move beyond conclusions about the variety of organizational forms, the essays of this collection demonstrate the difficulties of comparisons.

In his 2005 book *A Crooked Line*, Geoff Eley noted that the move out of social history was 'both necessary and fruitful', but he also pointed to the costs.[13] In the heyday of social history in the 1970s, the concept of class provided an important common terrain in labour history. Today, such common terrain does not exist. Eley and Nield still insist, however, that both cultural and structural understandings need to be in play in social history.[14] Accepting the constructivist premises of the cultural turn does not inevitably imply a refusal of the impact of social structures. The work perspective draws attention to both social structures and ideology.

The Perspective of Work

It is crucial to note that work is not only a material category but also an ideology in modern society. Accordingly, the work perspective implies two levels of analysis: socio-economic and ideological. At the socio-economic level, the transformation of work during the second industrial revolution constituted the decisive socio-economic and structural preconditions of European trade unionism. The precise meaning of the concept of the 'second industrial revolution' can be, and has been, disputed. In the 1960s, it was a key concept in David S. Landes' writings about technological change and industrial development in western Europe. Landes pointed to late nineteenth century changes in the new chemical industries, the introduction of electric power, the combustion engines and motors as 'the cluster of innovations that is often designated as the second industrial revolution'.[15] The Danish economic historian Ole Hyldtoft has convincingly argued that it is meaningful to characterize the trends of Danish industrial development from the 1890s to the 1930s by the concept of 'the second industrial revolution'.[16] In the Danish context at least, the impact of the transformation of work and working conditions in the two decades before the First World War must form a constituent part of the explanations of the character, the organizational forms and the agenda of the unions.

At the ideological level, we have to consider the ways in which the trade unions transformed the individual experience of workers into collective identities, and how these collective identities were organized. The modern ideology of work was a bourgeois invention directed against the ideology of the inferiority of work. The distinction between the luxurious, idle and unproductive upper classes of society and the productive, working third estate was introduced into the political discourse of the Enlightenment. The citizen was the industrial citizen and good government was unthinkable without private property and the right of every citizen to enjoy the fruits of their own labour. The obligation to work was included in the revolutionary programme of the political revolutions of the late eighteenth century, and from the writings of the *philosophes*, the ideology of work and rights spread among the middle classes. The gospel of work became the ideology of the new industrial middle classes, and work was associated with a catalogue of social virtues and good habits – thrift, the spirit of self-help, etc.

From the industrial middle classes, the ideology of work passed into the theories and politics of the labour movement. If not before, then certainly at this point the concept of work became an issue of political contest. Work was, as phrased by the German socialist Lassalle, a human condition and workers knew no other principle than the principles of work and justice.[17] Trade unionists did not necessarily endorse the politics of social democracy, but they readily embraced the notion of 'Labour as the Source of Value'. Trade unions represented labour; they were the social movement of labour. The legitimacy of the union struggle was founded in the ideology of work. The argument in this chapter is that the basic ideology of Danish trade unions was an ideology of work, forged in socialist thinking and theory.

The Transformation of Work:
Uneven Development and Modernization

Looking at the history of European trade unionism before 1914, it seems obvious to relate the formation of trade unions to the development and spread of industry. The strongholds of the trade unions were in the industrialized societies in western Europe. No doubt, the progress of trade unionism was related to industrialization. Yet, the connections between industrialization and the trade unions cannot be seen as simple cause-and-effect connections. In the Danish context at least, the mutual influence of the transformation of work and trade union responses was a much more intertwined relationship.

Looking at industrialization from the perspective of work, we are confronted with a picture of diversity and divergent patterns of industrialization. 'Uneven development' was the concept that Raphael Samuel suggested in his brilliant article in the *History Workshop Journal* in 1977, and 'uneven development' and 'unevenness' are concepts that have been widely used since then. The conclusions of Samuel's article have also been widely accepted; for example, the claim that the industrial revolution cannot simply be identified with the destruction of the old crafts and the substitution of the skilled worker by the unskilled.[18] The obvious consequence of accepting the concept of unevenness was to emphasize the heterogeneous nature of the working class and of work experience. This was also the conclusion suggested by Patrick Joyce in *Visions of the People*, where he suggested that the 'revisionist notions of the development of industrial capitalism' placed the concept of class 'under heavy fire', as class was rooted in economic structures.[19] I would rather argue that the concept of 'unevenness' makes it imperative to rethink the relationship between industrialization and the formation of trade unions.

The recognition of the unevenness of industrialization does not automatically imply that all attempts at generalization must be abandoned. General trends can be observed, and if we were to make an attempt to conceptualize the transformation of work that took place during these years, modernization might be a useful concept. Modernization of work is a concept that refers to the new sense of time and work-discipline, to the specialization and the increased division of labour that was introduced in the workshops during these years. Across the various trades and occupations, working people shared a common experience: the emergence of modern, disciplined work as an integral part of a modernizing society.

The modernization of work occurred in Denmark as part of the transformation of work during the second industrial revolution. Technological innovations transformed work, often in ways that challenged existing crafts and skills. Minor trades such as turners and tanners, coach builders and wheelwrights disappeared more or less over a few decades. The work of the shoemaker was reduced to repairing factory-made boots and shoes produced by semi-skilled male and female operatives.[20] However, this was not the general pattern. In most major crafts and industries such as the building trades and the iron and metal industries skill survived as the basis of production, though in new and redefined ways. The work of the skilled plumber was transformed over a few decades, just as the production of tin goods was taken over by the factories employing semi-skilled women, and copper and tin roofs were substituted by tiled roofs; instead the plumber turned to water, heating and sanitation. In most cases, the redefinition of skills was less radical than the plumbers' experience. In the iron and metal industries, the traditional skills of the provincial blacksmiths – welding and hardening – were made obsolete by the introduction of machinery, and the number of blacksmiths declined in contrast to the growth of the skilled mechanics. In the graphic trades, the introduction of the typesetting machines did not dispense with the skilled worker, but work changed as 'ordinary work' increased at the expense of qualified work. The survival of skill in major crafts and industries was the basic precondition of the strength of craft-based unionism in Denmark.

The ideological impact of this is important. There is no evidence to suggest that workers considered industrialization to be a menacing evil. The unions did not lament 'the curse of the factory'. Industry was not the enemy; neither were the factories. Who and what was the enemy? Addressed to the unions, no doubt, the answer would be the 'market', 'competition' and 'capitalism', or compound variations of the three expressions: competitive capitalism, market economy and free competition. Competition was unfair, capitalism unjust and the market uncertain. Union leaders did not sympathize with any of these – the unfair, unjust and uncertain mechanisms of bourgeois society. However, there was nothing wrong with industry; industry was productive but capital was not. The ideology of work made union leaders accept industry, but not the market economy. Unionists entertained strong anti-capitalist sentiments and seemed to forget that industrialization was bound up with a market economy. In *Visions of the People*, Joyce coined the terms 'civilizing capital' and 'moralizing the market'.[21] The two terms fit the Danish context perfectly: the overall agenda of the trade unions was to remove the uncivilized and unfair implications of the capitalist market. Free competition and the capitalist market were the big evils.

In contrast to what might have been expected, the craft-character of Danish trade unionism was not weakened by the transformation of work from the 1890s. In Denmark, the trade unions had been in the making for more than two decades when industrialization accelerated in the second half of the 1890s. Because of their early formation, the unions were in place and prepared to engage in the conflicts that broke out as a consequence of the transformation of work. Therefore, we should perceive the development of industrial capitalism in the late nineteenth century not only as a socio-economic prerequisite for the development of the trade unions; at the same time, we should also see the transformation of work in the late 1890s as the first major challenge to the unions.

Rights of Labour: Agitating and Organizing

In a critique of the 'mechanical understanding of class formation' published in 1994, Sonya O. Rose quoted Geoff Eley, who argued that 'the "unity" of the working class, though postulated through the analysis of production and its social relations, remains a contingency of political agitation'.[22] A collective identity of class did not emerge automatically from the work experience of workers. I would assume that every experienced agitator around 1900 would subscribe to that. The agitators knew from experience that working people were not endowed with unlimited resources of solidarity as a birth-gift. It was the task of the agitator to rouse the spirit of solidarity; among the skilled workers, the task was to inculcate the collective identity of the trade among workers possessing the same skills.

We do not know whether the arguments of the agitators convinced anyone. The arguments of the agitator might not be identical with the motives of the people who joined the unions. However, the speeches of the agitators constitute a source of insight into the self-presentation of the unions. At this point, we may relate the Danish case to Antoine Prost and Manfred Bock's study of the different forms of self-representation in the British, French and German trade unions at the end of the nineteenth century. In France, as in Germany, the ethical dimension to labour discourse was important, and the Germans never ceased to pose 'the problem of equality of rights, both civil and trade union'. The British unions are characterized by the term 'economic trade unionism'.[23] In Denmark, we see both the economic pragmatism of the British and the German insistence on the rights of labour. The pragmatism was demonstrated in negotiations with the employers – the insistence on the rights of labour when addressing the members.

The papers of the unions in Denmark spoke the language of work. 'Capital would be nothing without labour; if labour withdrew from Capital, it would be dead, incapable of producing anything'. This was the message of an article in *Fagtidende for Smede og Maskinarbejdere i Danmark* (Journal of Blacksmiths and Metalworkers in Denmark) in September 1884. According to the article, the power of capital over labour in existing society was a product of 'the artificial and unnatural' arrangements of society.[24] Self-esteem and a strong sense of injustice were the motives of the agitating unionist, and work played a prominent role in the agitation and self-identification of the early trade unions.

Articles presenting arguments for union membership abounded in Danish trade union journals before 1914. Various arguments were advanced. First, the economic argument that membership would pay off; second, the moral argument that it was the duty of every respectable worker to be a member of the union; and third, the democratic argument that only the union could secure working people their influence upon their own conditions of work. The basic argument was, however, that workers had the right to advance demands for better working and living conditions. The language of rights slipped into the agitation of the trade unions: people who work have rights.

The arguments were more or less identical to this in speeches and pamphlets in the 1890s and in the 1920s. The critique of the system of free competition was omnipresent, and so was the message that only by means of the union could the workers obtain what were their proper rights. A pamphlet that Dansk Textilarbejderforbund (Federation of Danish Textile Workers) distributed to the workers in the mid Jutland region in the early 1920s – 'Why Everyone Should be a Member of the Union' (1924) – repeated the arguments of the 1890s. Workers should take part in decisions about their own conditions of work: 'Remember that no other values exist but those created by labour ... No capital is created without labour'. It was the duty of every worker to be organized in order to counterbalance the desire for exploitation of capital. Conditions of work and payment were best in trades with strong unions.[25]

The unions were organizations that cultivated a craft identity as well as the esteem of the trade. All along, the unions of unskilled workers developed a vocabulary that was more or less identical with that of the skilled unions. They also insisted upon the value of their work performance and on the value of their own skills, obviously forgetting that they were being identified by everyone else as workers who possessed no skills. However, an aspect would be missing if we see only craft identity and sectionalism. Both skilled and unskilled unions operated within the framework of an ideology of work and they therefore ended up representing the general interests of underprivileged people in their struggle to defend the rights of workers as a collective, irrespective of trade.

The content of the trade union journals leaves no doubt as to the weight of 'the work argument' in the agitation. Work was a key idea in the self-presentation and self-identification of the trade unions. The agitators and the unions translated the work experience of workers into a programme of the rights of labour. I see the ideology of work as the common ideological terrain of the trade unions, which served as the ideological framing of collective identities and of trade union politics.

The Dominance of Skill: The Structure and Agenda of Danish Trade Unions

The craft principle was dominant in the Danish trade unions from the outset and it survived until the 1960s. In consequence, the trade union movement was characterized by a large number of small local unions and small national federations.[26] Apparently, however small it might be, each trade had to have its own organization. Another characteristic aspect of the Danish trade union movement was the powerful federation of the unskilled workers. Dansk Arbejdsmandsforbund (federation of general workers in all industries) was established in 1897 and since then has been the big federation of the Danish movement. In the twentieth century the federation of the unskilled female workers, Kvindeligt Arbejderforbund (federation of general women workers in all industries) became another powerful organization. The co-existence of a few big federations at the top and a large number of medium-sized and very small organizations of craftworkers below characterized the trade union movement in Denmark before the Second World War. The American sociologist Walter Galenson noticed the 'relatively skewed' distribution of membership among the Danish trade unions, being characterized by a single large organization and a large number of very small unions.[27] Accordingly, a substantial number of the national federations were so small and so weak that their capacity to strike or resist a lockout was almost insignificant. They needed the support of the other federations.

A simple explanation of the dominance of the craft principle might be that the craft principle was introduced into the unions in the 1870s and 1880s when crafts played a pivotal role in the economy and in the labour market and once established, path dependency proved strong. The survival of the craft principle was supported by an organizational structure that proved successful. By the late 1890s, the centralized federations had become the powerful link in the organizational chain. Only the national federations had the authority to accept and to sign the collective agreements; only the national federations had the authority to make decisions about conflicts. A national central committee was established in 1898 with the foundation of De samvirkende Fagforbund i Danmark (central confederation of trade unions in Denmark). In comparison to the central organizations in other European countries, De samvirkende Fagforbund was a powerful construct. One of its primary tasks was to coordinate and to regulate strikes, and the authority of the national central was secured by the introduction of the principle of compulsory strike benefits according to fixed rules, which was unique in a European context. The Danish trade union movement thus succeeded in creating an organizational structure perfectly suited to a movement with many small and only a few big and powerful federations.

Higher wages and collective agreements were the first items on the agendas of the trade unions; in consequence, strikes – and the regulation of strikes – also became an issue. By the 1890s, shorter working hours (the eight hour day) became a third item. There were other issues that emanated directly from the conditions of work: for example the struggle against homework and the claims of the skilled unions for regulations of the conditions of apprenticeship. By the time of the second industrial revolution, however, the agenda of the trade unions had been set by the transformation of work. The recurrent controversies between the skilled and the unskilled organizations were a by-product of these changes. Attempts to solve these conflicts were made in 1899 in a series of talks between Dansk Smede og Maskinarbejder Forbund (federation of blacksmiths and mechanics), Dansk Arbejdsmandsforbund and Dansk Arbejdsgiverforening (Danish employers' association). The parties sought to agree upon definitions of skilled and unskilled work. However, the conclusions of these talks, settled in the March Agreement of 1900, appeared to be of no practical importance.[28] Besides such internal divisions and conflicts, the second industrial revolution posed a double challenge to the trade unions; first, the necessity of protecting the interests of the existing trades; and second, exploiting the new opportunities arising from the transformation of work. The skilled unions protected the work of the skilled workers against the intrusions of unskilled workers; they defended the dominance of skills and the traditional hierarchies of work – skilled in relation to unskilled, male in relation to female. The unions of unskilled workers sought to take advantage of the new opportunities offered by the second industrial revolution.

On the whole, the unions did not protest against the modernization of work. The trade unions did not complain about the disappearance of the primitive workshops of the old masters. In most cases, industry offered better conditions of work and higher wages. In 1905 the chairman of Dansk Skrædderforbund (Danish federation of tailors) advocated more discipline at work. In articles in the trade union journal on 'Our Rights and Duties' he declared that the 'good old days' were gone and that was good. He did not accept the idea that arriving late at work and leaving as he pleased should be regarded as an accepted privilege of the tailor. According to him, discipline at work was the precondition of the trade unions' claims for higher wages and stable conditions of work.[29]

The recognition of the unions – the employers' acceptance of the workers' right to organize – was the result of the general lockout in 1899. In return, the unions had to recognize 'the employers' right to manage work and to employ the number of workers they deem necessary'.[30] Since then, collective bargaining has become the general way of negotiating and regulating the conditions of work in the labour market. The collective agreements resulting from the bargaining reduced the insecurity caused by the market economy and it was a basic idea among unionists that the collective agreement should reflect the value of work performance. As the value of work increased, the workers were entitled to claim higher wages. The unions accepted wage differentials among workers. In their opinion, it was unacceptable if skills, diligence and abilities were not rewarded. Work performance was not the sole determinant factor. In mixed trades, the idea of the male breadwinner was another factor to be considered.

Concluding Remarks

In the historical literature about trade unions, the recurring negotiations between trade unions and employers and the political issues in relation to the state often dominate, leaving the impression that the agenda of trade unionism is to a large extent set within the triangular framework of the trade unions, the employers and the state. The dominant shadow of the centralized actors on the national scene might, therefore, obscure the impact of a fourth actor, the membership of the unions and the extent to which the agenda of unionism was set by conditions and conflicts of work.

The political agenda of the international trade union movement after the First World War – socialization – was framed within the ideology of work. In Denmark the programme of socialization was advanced as demands for workers' councils in industry, public control of commercial profits and public control of the business sector. The political idea of socialization was that the unions should have insight into the economy of the factories and the employers. No doubt socialization was an idea that was rooted in socialist theory. However, it was also founded in the ideology of work and derived from an idea of the rights of labour to a fair share of the produce. In 1933 Jakob Kr. Lindberg, who was the chief architect of the socialization programme in Denmark, published the book *Magt: En Bog om Arbejdets Ordning* (Power: A Book About the Organization of Work), in which he expounded the ideas of socialization as a practical step towards socialism.[31] The idea of socialization was born and reared in the ideological discourse of work.

Finally, it might be added that apparently ideas of respect and recognition of working people in society, vague as they might be, were an underlying motive of moderate trade union leaders. The ideal of the pragmatic union leader 'of the old school' in Denmark was not the radical or militant socialist but the well-respected citizen. The union leader would be proud when it was no longer possible to distinguish the worker from the master when taking a Sunday afternoon stroll. Good manners and disciplined conduct – at public meetings or in strained situations – were properties that the union leader appreciated, as well as not forgetting to vote for the Social Democratic candidate at elections. The unions regarded Socialdemokratiet (the Social Democratic Party) as their voice in Parliament and in municipal assemblies, as the party regarded the unions as a reservoir of supporters and an active resource of the party. As the mass organizations of the labour movement, the unions constituted the broad social basis of social democracy between the First and Second World Wars.

The aim of this chapter has been to bridge some inappropriate dichotomies of labour history – for example between 'history from above' or 'history from below' – between structural or cultural approaches, or between distinctions between trade unions as either organizations of narrow sectionalism or class struggle. In this chapter, I have focused on the decades of the second industrial revolution – which witnessed radical changes of work – in order to demonstrate how the conflicts of work set the agenda of the trade unions and established the basis for both narrow politics of craft and the general language of the rights of labour in modern society. Both were framed in the vocabulary of an ideology of work that emphasized the rights of labour. Ideology mattered. The ideology of work served as the framework of interpretation of work experience and provided the basis of trade union politics.

Knud Knudsen is Associate Professor at Aalborg University. He has published books and articles on labour history, historiography and the history of jazz. He is the author of 'Arbejdskonflikternes historie i Danmark: Arbejdskampe og arbejderbevægelse 1870–1940' (1999) and *Dansk fagbevægelses historie frem til 1950 – fra arbejdets perspektiv* (2011).

Notes

1. Cf. G. Eley and K. Nield. 2007. *The Future of Class in History*, Ann Arbor: University of Michigan Press; R. Spaulding and C. Parker. 2007. *Historiography: An Introduction*, Manchester: Manchester University Press, 32–37; D.M. MacRaild and A. Taylor. 2004. *Social Theory and Social History*, Houndsmill: Palgrave Macmillan, 118–46.
2. C.E. Andresen, J. Burchardt and F. Mikkelsen. 1979. *Arbejdererindringer*, Århus: Erhvervsarkivet.
3. For example G. Stedman Jones. 1983. *Languages of Class: Studies in English Working-Class History, 1832–1982*, Cambridge: Cambridge University Press; P. Joyce. 1980. *Work, Society and Politics: The Culture of the Factory in Later Victorian England*, Cambridge: Cambridge University Press; P. Joyce (ed.). 1987. *The Historical Meanings of Work*, Cambridge: Cambridge University Press; J.W. Scott. 1988. *Gender and the Politics of History*, New York: Columbia University Press.
4. M. Rostgaard. 1990. 'Hvordan kvindearbejde blev til kvindearbejde', in F. Mikkelsen (ed.), *Produktion & arbejdskraft i Danmark gennem 200 år*, København: Nyt fra samfundsvidenskaberne, 177–205.

5. M. Rostgaard. 2003. 'Industriel patriarkalisme som moderniseringsstrategi', *Den jyske Historiker* 102, 126–53.

6. N.J. Nielsen. 2002. *Virksomhed og arbejderliv – bånd, brudflader og bevidsthed på B&W 1850–1920*, København: Museum Tusculanum; and N.J. Nielsen. 2004. *Mellem storpolitik og værkstedsguld: Den danske arbejder – før, under og efter Den kolde Krig*, København: Museum Tusculanum.

7. Nielsen, *Virksomhed og arbejderliv*, 470.

8. Lars K. Christensen's two studies of trade unions in the metal and engineering industries in Copenhagen before 1914 and in the textile industry 1895–1940 were remarkable exceptions. Theories of modernization constituted the theoretical framework of his studies, and in both, autobiographies were used to characterize an emerging 'respectable' culture of work, in contrast to the undisciplined culture of the pre-industrial past. The textile workers' union is depicted as 'a truly modern institution'. See L.K. Christensen. 1998. 'Det moderne arbejde: Kulturelle og institutionelle forandringer af arbejdet i den danske tekstilindustri 1895–1940', Ph.D. thesis, Københavns Universitet, 333. Cf. L.K. Christensen. 1995. *Smedesvend og friherre: Maskinarbejde og arbejderkultur i København 1891–1914*, København: Selskabet til forskning i arbejderbevægelsens historie.

9. L.K. Christensen, S. Kolstrup and A.E. Hansen. 2007. *Arbejdernes historie i Danmark 1800–2000*, København: Selskabet til forskning i arbejderbevægelsens historie, 100.

10. L.K. Christensen. 2009–10. 'Den moderne arbejderklasse: Bidrag til en skabelsesberetning', *Arbejderhistorie* 3–1, 74.

11. In two comparative projects Gerd Callesen was the author of the contributions on Denmark: G. Callesen. 1990. 'Denmark', in M. van der Linden and J. Rohahn (eds), *The Formation of Labour Movements 1870–1914: An International Perspective*, vol. 1, Leiden: E. J. Brill, 131–60; G. Callesen. 1988. 'Die Gewerkschaftsbewegung in Dänemark. Traditionen der dänischen Gewerkschaftsbewegung', in W. Abelshauser, *Konflikt und Kooperation: Strategien europäischer Gewerkschaften im 20. Jahrhundert*, Essen: Klartext, 159–69.

12. J.L. Robert, A. Prost and C. Wrigley (eds). 2004. *The Emergence of European Trade Unionism*, Aldershot: Ashgate.

13. G. Eley. 2005. *A Crooked Line*, Ann Arbor: University of Michigan Press, 196. This move from social history to new cultural history was discussed further in *The Future of Class in History*, which surveyed the arguments for the moves and turns in the historiography of social history since the 1960s: see Eley and Nield, *The Future of Class*, 180–81, 195.

14. Eley and Nield, *The Future of Class*, 180–81, 195.

15. D.S. Landes. 1969. *The Unbound Prometheus*, Cambridge: Cambridge University Press, 4, 196, 235.

16. O. Hyldtoft. 2003. 'Den anden industrielle revolution', *Den jyske Historiker* 102–3, 42.

17. W. Conze. 1979. 'Arbeiter', in O. Brüner, W. Conze and R. Koselleck (eds), *Geschichtliche Grundbegriffe*, vol. 1, Stuttgart: Ernst Klett, 232.

18. R. Samuel. 1977. 'The Workshop of the World: Steam Power and Hand Technology in mid-Victorian Britain', *History Workshop Journal* 3, 8, 59.

19. P. Joyce. 1991. *Visions of the People*, Cambridge: Cambridge University Press, 4–6.

20. On the decline and growth of crafts 1897–1914, see *Danmarks Haandværk og Industri 1914. Statistisk Tabelværk* 5a(12), 34–41.

21. Joyce, *Visions of the People*, 87–113.

22. See S.O. Rose. 1994. *Limited Livelihoods: Gender and Class in Nineteenth-Century England*, Berkeley: University of California Press, 19.

23. A. Prost and M. Bock. 2004. 'Workers, Others and the State: A Comparison of the Discourse of the French, German and British Labour Movements at the End of the Nineteenth Century', in J-L. Robert, A. Prost and C. Wrigley (eds), *The Emergence of European Trade Unionism*, Aldershot: Ashgate, 183.

24. 'Teori og Praksis', *Fagtidende for Smede og Maskinarbejdere i Danmark*, No. 18 (September 1884).
25. *'Hvorfor bør man være Medlem af sin Fagforening?'*. 1924. Dansk Textilarbejderforbunds Arkiv. Agitationen, kasse 368.
26. J. Jensen and C.M. Olsen. 1901. *Oversigt over Fagforeningsbevægelsen i Danmark i Tiden fra 1871 til 1900*, København: F. E. Bording, 176.
27. W. Galenson. 1969. *The Danish System of Labour Relations*, New York: Russell & Russell, 31.
28. On the March Agreement see J.A. Hansen. 1913. *Festskrift i anledning af Dansk Smede- og Maskinarbejder Forbunds 25 Aars Jubilæum*, København: Danske Smede og Maskinarbejder Forbund, 75–91.
29. V. Arup, *Dansk Skrædderforbunds Medlemsblad*, no. 9, 'Vor Ret og vor Pligt'; no. 10, 'Hvad er Grunden'; and No. 11, 'Vor Ret og Pligt'.
30. Jensen and Olsen, *Oversigt over Fagforeningsbevægelsen i Danmark*, 140–44.
31. J.Kr. Lindberg. 1933. *Magt: En Bog om Arbejdets Ordning*, København: Martins Forlag.

References

Andresen, C.E., J. Burchardt and F. Mikkelsen. 1979. *Arbejdererindringer*, Århus: Erhvervsarkivet.

Callesen, G. 'Die Gewerkschaftsbewegung in Dänemark: Traditionen der dänischen Gewerkschaftsbewegung', in W. Abelshauser, *Konflikt und Kooperation: Strategien europäischer Gewerkschaften im 20. Jahrhundert*, Essen: Klartext, 1988, 159–69.

———. 'Denmark', in M. van der Linden and J. Rohahn (eds), *The Formation of Labour Movements 1870–1914: An International Perspective*, Leiden: E. J. Brill, 1990, 131–60.

Christensen, L.K. 1995. *Smedesvend og friherre: Maskinarbejde og arbejderkultur i København 1891–1914*, København: Selskabet til forskning i arbejderbevægelsens historie.

———. 1998. 'Det moderne arbejde: Kulturelle og institutionelle forandringer af arbejdet i den danske tekstilindustri 1895–1940', Ph.D. thesis, Københavns universitet.

———. 2009–10. 'Den moderne arbejderklasse: Bidrag til en skabelsesberetning', *Arbejderhistorie* 3–1, 55–74.

Christensen, L.K., S. Kolstrup and A.E. Hansen. 2007. *Arbejdernes historie i Danmark 1800–2000*, København: Selskabet til forskning i arbejderbevægelsens historie.

Conze, W. 'Arbeiter', in O. Brüner, W. Conze and R. Koselleck (eds), *Geschichtliche Grundbegriffe*, Stuttgart: Ernst Klett, 1979, 216–42.

Eley, G. 2005. *A Crooked Line*, Ann Arbor: University of Michigan Press.

Eley, G. and K. Nield. 2007. *The Future of Class in History*, Ann Arbor: University of Michigan Press.

Galenson, W. 1969. *The Danish System of Labour Relations*, New York: Russell & Russell.

Hansen, J.A. 1913. *Festskrift i anledning af Dansk Smede- og Maskinarbejder Forbunds 25 Aars Jubilæum*, København: Danske Smede og Maskinarbejder Forbund.

Hyldtoft, O. 2003. 'Den anden industrielle revolution', *Den jyske Historiker* 102–3, 18–46.

Jensen, J. and C.M. Olsen. 1901. *Oversigt over Fagforeningsbevægelsen i Danmark i Tiden fra 1871 til 1900*, København: F.E. Bording.

Joyce, P. 1980. *Work, Society and Politics: The Culture of the Factory in Later Victorian England*, Cambridge: Cambridge University Press.

———. 1991. *Visions of the People*, Cambridge: Cambridge University Press.

Joyce, P. (ed.). 1987. *The Historical Meanings of Work*, Cambridge: Cambridge University Press.

Landes, D.S. 1969. *The Unbound Prometheus*, Cambridge: Cambridge University Press.

Lindberg, J.Kr. 1933. *Magt: En Bog om Arbejdets Ordning*, København: Martins Forlag.

MacRaild, D.M. and A. Taylor. 2004. *Social Theory and Social History*, Houndsmill: Palgrave Macmillan.

Nielsen, N.J. 2002. *Virksomhed og arbejderliv – bånd, brudflader og bevidsthed på B&W 1850–1920*, København: Museum Tusculanum.

———. 2004. *Mellem storpolitik og værkstedsguld: Den danske arbejder – før, under og efter Den kolde Krig*, København: Museum Tusculanum.

Prost, A. and M. Bock. 'Workers, Others and the State: A Comparison of the Discourse of the French, German and British Labour Movements at the End of the Nineteenth Century', in J.L. Robert, A. Prost and C. Wrigley (eds), *The Emergence of European Trade Unionism*, Aldershot: Ashgate, 2004, 166–83.

Robert, J.L., A. Prost and C. Wrigley (eds). 2004. *The Emergence of European Trade Unionism*, Aldershot: Ashgate.

Rose, S.O. 1994. *Limited Livelihoods: Gender and Class in Nineteenth-Century England*, Berkeley: University of California Press.

Rostgaard, M. 'Hvordan kvindearbejde blev til kvindearbejde', in F. Mikkelsen (ed.), *Produktion & arbejdskraft i Danmark gennem 200 år*, København: Nyt fra samfundsvidenskaberne, 1990, 177–205.

———. 2003. 'Industriel patriarkalisme som moderniseringsstrategi', *Den jyske Historiker* 102, 126–53.

Samuel, R. 1977. 'The Workshop of the World: Steam Power and Hand Technology in mid-Victorian Britain', *History Workshop Journal* 3, 6–72.

Scott, J.W. 1988. *Gender and the Politics of History*, New York: Columbia University Press.

Spalding, R. and C. Parker. 2007. *Historiography: An Introduction*, Manchester: Manchester University Press.

Stedman Jones, G. 1983. *Languages of Class: Studies in English Working-Class History, 1832–1982*, Cambridge: Cambridge University Press.

CHAPTER 6

LABOUR MIGRATION AND INDUSTRIAL RELATIONS
Recruitment of Foreign-Born Workers to the Swedish Engineering Industry after the Second World War

Johan Svanberg

The recruitment of workers from abroad to Sweden after the Second World War was initiated by Swedish employers, in cooperation with the social democratic government and the national labour market authority. Thereafter, the trade unions concerned had to consider all the anticipated consequences of subsequent migrations. Theoretically, labour immigration may endanger trade unions' bargaining positions vis-à-vis employers, because it alters the relation between the supply of and demand for workers in the labour market. An influx of foreign-born workers may therefore thwart trade unions' endeavours to influence shop-floor issues; for example, the pace of work or piece wages. Immigration may be perceived by trade unionists as a threat to their overall agenda to restrict employers' exploitation of the workers.[1]

This chapter highlights labour migration from an industrial relations perspective. The overall aim is to analyse the relationship between Verkstadsföreningen (engineering employers' association) and Metallindustriarbetareförbundet (metalworkers' union, Metall), with the national Swedish labour market authority (Statens arbetsmarknadskommission, SAK; from 1948, Arbetsmarknadsstyrelsen, AMS) as a key state actor and important intermediary as regards labour recruitment from abroad to the Swedish engineering industry after the Second World War.

Empirically, the chapter draws upon internal source material from the organizations and authorities concerned; in particular, minutes, reports and correspondence. The enquiry aims chiefly to discern the main arguments of the employers' association and the trade union respectively for and against labour immigration to Sweden and to analyse how the labour market situation was perceived by the different actors during the early phase of the post-war boom.

An industrial relations perspective on labour migration, as suggested in this chapter, has not imbued the state of the art in Sweden or internationally. Previous research in Sweden has usually focused either on the trade union movement,[2] or on the employers (albeit to a much lesser degree)[3] or on state actors.[4] The perspective of this chapter may therefore also shed light on the development and consolidation of the corporatist Swedish labour market model.[5] One important argument in this chapter is that labour immigration was one of the first concrete issues after 1945 that the representatives of capital, labour and the state in Sweden could actually agree on. Because of the coincidence of their interests they could reach acceptable compromises, with substantial results as regards labour immigration.[6]

Verkstadsföreningen was the largest and the most important employers' association after the Second World War within the cross-industry and nationwide Svenska Arbetsgivareföreningen (Swedish employers' association, SAF). Among the main members of Verkstadsföreningen were several major export-oriented companies employing thousands of workers, such as Volvo, ASEA, SKF, Electrolux, LM Ericsson, as well as the large shipyards in Malmö and Gothenburg. The number of foreign-born individuals in Sweden increased from 100,000 – mainly war refugees – in 1945 to 200,000 in 1950 and 300,000 in 1960, largely due to the recruitment of these industrial companies.[7] The trade union counterpart of this employers' association, Metall, was hence deeply concerned by the process of labour migration to Sweden.

To begin with, this chapter discusses how industrial relations in the Swedish engineering industry were altered due to the great demand for workers after 1945. Thereafter the analysis is narrowed down to a focus on the recruitment of foreign-born workers, with special attention paid to the actual allocation of Italians and Sudeten Germans among different Swedish employers. How did Metall react to the employers' initiative to recruit foreigners? How did the trade union justify its reactions? Finally, this chapter highlights the process of labour immigration as a part of overall labour market policy in Sweden.

The Great Demand for Workers

Refugees arriving during the later part of the war were allocated carefully selected tasks in the Swedish labour market by the labour market authorities at national and regional level, in collaboration with interested employers. The refugees were primarily assigned to sectors with significant structural labour shortages: forestry, agriculture and the homes of well-to-do families. When the demand for workers continued to increase after the war, the strenuous work of the refugees had shown authorities and industrialists how the perceived shortage could be resolved by recruiting foreigners.[8] The reception of refugees during the war and the active recruitment of workers from abroad after the war should therefore be considered as two overlapping processes.[9]

Swedish industry experienced an increased demand for its products almost immediately after the war, both nationally and internationally. It was saved from the devastation of warfare, and ready to produce and export when a war-wrecked Europe was about to be rebuilt. During this boom, the (male) Swedish workforce proved insufficient to meet the increased demand for workers. At the beginning of 1946, a SAF publication calculated the shortage at 100,000 workers,[10] although this calculation was debated even when it was first published.

The shortage of workers was put on the agenda of Verkstadsföreningen in the early autumn of 1945. Indeed, the members of the board had great difficulties evaluating the future labour market situation, and could not agree on the prospects. While one of the directors, obviously with the post-First World War period in mind, anticipated an upcoming recession and therefore an increased supply of workers, another expected that the shortage would remain for quite some time. However, and more importantly, the powerful managing director of ASEA, Oscar Hellman, pointed out that employers 'should not talk so much about the shortage of workers'. Such declarations would only induce 'the workers to campaign for higher wages'.[11] Hellman thus put his finger on the changing nature of industrial relations: power was shifting to the advantage of the workers and the trade unions.

Transformed attitudes towards some kinds of work assignments seemed especially worrisome for the employers. One director noticed 'a serious shift away from heavy and hot tasks to easier engineering work'. Another employer reported to Verkstadsföreningen that it was difficult 'to maintain the workforce for heavy and dirty work' and a third one pointed out that it was almost 'impossible to get work done' late at night. On top of this it was stressed, certainly indignantly, that a 'disciplinary relaxation could be discerned', which meant that 'one had to deal with the personnel more gently than before'.[12]

In recurrent cases workers threatened their employers that they would collectively vote with their feet and resign if their wages were not increased or if working conditions were not improved.[13] Power relations in the labour market were thus shifting rather rapidly. Considering that the workers concerned had lost the great metal workers' strike, which had stirred up the Swedish labour market during the spring and early summer of 1945, such favourable negotiating conditions were a new experience for them. The great and unfulfilled demand for workers now opened up possibilities for many workers to refuse the most degrading tasks in favour of more enjoyable or perhaps better-paid work assignments. Workers all over the country comprehended and acted in accordance with their newly strengthened labour market position. This, in turn, created empty spots in the lowest ranks of the labour market hierarchy, which had to be filled in some way if production were to continue at the pace desired by the employers.

Altered Industrial Relations

A labour market characterized by a perceived shortage of workers and an increased rate of labour turnover certainly put the mutual loyalties of employers to a serious test. A vital task for Verkstadsföreningen during the post-war years, therefore, was to constrain the mutual competition among the employers for available (male) workers. The association opposed all employers who tried to attract workers from other fellow employers, with every means possible. A prohibition against advertising vacancies in newspapers was revived. Holiday bonuses, special vacation homes for workers, extra leisure time during the summer months and free buses to the workplaces were likewise strictly forbidden for anticompetitive reasons.[14] Companies that broke the employer code of loyalty and enticed workers with preferential treatment were threatened with fines and expulsion from Verkstadsföreningen.[15]

Another great problem for Verkstadsföreningen was that about 1,000 employers in the sector were not affiliated with the association. These companies were mostly smaller workshops that subverted the anticompetitive ambitions of the association by 'overpaying' the workers, at least according to other, angry employers.[16] The board of Verkstadsföreningen therefore urged its members to boycott all unaffiliated companies; the affiliates should neither collaborate with suppliers who were engaged in 'unfair competition', nor sell necessary tools or machinery to them.[17]

The otherwise cherished national aims of productivity and growth were accordingly put in the shadow of the employers' mutual interest of loyalty and anticompetitiveness. To break the loyalty between the employers would entail substantial financial costs.

In contrast to employers' understanding that a real shortage of workers existed, trade unionists in Metall considered the shortage as something more relative. According to these men – they were all men – it was mainly companies with poor working conditions, deficient wages and/or inadequate housing facilities that had problems recruiting as many workers as they required. The trade unionists stressed emphatically that if these shortcomings were rectified the unfulfilled demand for workers would disappear.[18]

Nonetheless, the altered labour market context strengthened the bargaining power of Metall. During the first post-war years, both the national trade union and the local branches around the country learned how to use the great demand for workers as a negotiation tool. With the perceived shortage of workers in mind, they could put the interests of the rank and file on the agenda. In contrast to the argument of his counterpart, the union's chairman Oscar Westerlund pointed out in the autumn of 1947 that the current labour market situation was better than ever and that besides the national agreement several and better wage agreements had recently been achieved at local level. 'The employers have been forced to pay higher wages to get any workers at all', Westerlund concluded.[19]

Besides threats to quit, the strategies used by workers to get their wage demands or work environment complaints met could include a temporary and collective decreased pace of work, or more or less spontaneous 'wildcat strikes' for a couple of hours.[20] Such actions were not a new phenomenon in the post-war era, but had been common since the early days of industrial capitalism. However, the great demand for workers after the Second World War created an important power resource for the workers and their trade unions. Industrial managers were forced to listen to the complaints and wishes of their employees much more seriously than ever before. Nevertheless, employers could counter the development in the labour market by increasing the total size of the labour force in Sweden. This could be done through recruitment of workers in other countries.

Employer Initiatives and Trade Union Opposition

The prospects of obtaining foreign-born workers were discussed within Verkstadsföreningen for the first time in April 1946.[21] During the following summer and autumn this was a recurrent theme on the agenda.

To begin with, the board members were rather doubtful. It was a common and explicit understanding among the employers that workers would generally oppose active labour recruitment abroad and that the trade unions had great influence with the social democratic government. Managing director of Verkstadsföreningen Georg Styrman pointed out, quite insightfully, that the workers would reject the idea, 'because they consider it to have an inhibitory effect on the wage trend'.[22]

In previous research there are different opinions as to whether the Swedish trade union movement actually opposed the initiatives of the employers to recruit foreign-born workers after the war.[23] Regarding Metall, however, there is no doubt that the national trade union rejected the first proposals from the employers. The issue was debated for the first time within this trade union in September 1946 – that is, about five months after the issue was raised within Verkstadsföreningen. The trade union explicitly opposed labour immigration for three reasons. Firstly, the decision was motivated by undefined problems, which apparently existed because of foreigners already employed in Sweden. Secondly, the trade union emphasized the general shortage of housing in many industrial communities and mill towns, and thirdly it stressed the costs associated with labour recruitment abroad. Instead of recruiting foreigners, the union chairman suggested an investigation of available but unused 'labour reserves' in Sweden.[24]

Hence, the preferred approach to the perceived shortage of workers initially differed between the employers' association and the representatives of the workers concerned. While Verkstadsföreningen did not consider any so-called domestic reserves seriously at this point in time, Metall emphasized – at least rhetorically – the labour market integration of married women, the elderly and those with minor disabilities.

In reality, however, the differences were not as profound as the rhetoric suggested. Those domestic reserves that Westerlund and other trade unionists pointed out were not realistic alternatives for Metall either. There is much research on this matter. In her pioneering study of female industrial workers in Sweden, historian Gunhild Kyle stresses that the trade unions' insistence that married women and other 'reserves' should have priority for vacancies during the 1940s was only empty words. Not until the 1960s was this rhetoric followed by any substantial policy. Employers' calls for easily mobile migrant workers, instead of married women, who were perceived as difficult to move and demanding extended childcare facilities for their labour market integration, were thus accepted in practice by the Swedish trade union movement.[25] Accordingly, perceptions of primary and secondary categories of workers influenced the trade unionists as well. The real industrial worker – the primary category – was a young or middle-aged man, born and raised in Sweden. Male and female migrants, married Swedish women, the elderly and those with minor disabilities were all considered to belong to the secondary labour reserves, which should only be drawn on when men from the primary category could not meet the existing demand. The trade unions generally appear to have been rather indifferent to how the employers actually chose between these reserves, and on top of the priority list of Verkstadsföreningen were male migrants.

Allocation of Italian Workers

In spite of the initial opposition from Metall, at the end of September 1946 Oscar Westerlund informed his fellow trade unionists that foreign-born workers would be recruited to Sweden. The social democratic government had appointed a special working group dealing with the issue (Beredningen för utländsk arbetskraft). By appointing representatives from the labour market authorities, the employers' associations and the trade unions to this group, the government attempted to create good conditions for developing consensus. According to the government's guidelines, all workers recruited to Sweden by the working group should be unionized and paid contractual wages in order to meet both parties' interests. But even so, when Westerlund presented the working group to his fellow trade unionists, he emphasized that the purpose was only to 'momentarily borrow some skilled workers from northern Italy'.[26] He obviously assumed a guest-worker programme. Bilateral agreements were then signed during 1947, not only with Italy, but also with Hungary and the occupation powers in Austria regarding Sudeten Germans. A few thousand workers were recruited to Sweden in line with these agreements.[27] Metall, as well as other national trade unions, thus had to react to the migrations that followed.

For a start, the social democratic government approved the recruitment of 500 Italian workers. SAK was commissioned to manage the drafts and allocate the workers, because the demand was certainly greater than 500 individuals.[28] In May 1947, SAK summoned a meeting with the national trade unions concerned. Here Metall could stress its opinion regarding those mills and industries that requested foreign-born workers:

> As regards the railway works in Falun we declared that we would not approve allocation to this company under any circumstances, because the company by itself is the reason for the prevailing difficulties. The company pursues a wage policy which must naturally lead to workers quitting to this great extent.[29]

Metall rejected the allocation of workers to two other companies as well, because of prevailing wage levels. ASEA, a fourth company, belonged to those employers that Metall approved of, but only under certain conditions: to receive any Italians the company had to take 'certain measures to make the situation tolerable for those workers who are already employed'.[30]

The strategy of attaching conditions to allocations can also be illustrated by a discussion between representatives of Metall and the company Storfors rörverk. After a preliminary allocation of fifty Italian workers, Edvard Vilhelmsson from the trade union visited the company for an inspection, together with C.W. Curtman from SAK. This resulted in criticism of the available accommodation as well as of the company's inadequate food-serving facilities. The temporary huts where the migrant workers were supposed to live consisted of ten rooms each, with an area of just seven square metres. They were unpainted on the inside and very simply furnished. The workers were supposed to share rooms with a partner, but according to Metall the accommodation 'must be considered particularly unsuitable for housing human beings'.[31]

Even though this attention to migrants' work and living conditions was genuine, the trade union had found a way to improve the situation for Swedish trade union members in general by putting these issues on the agenda. By highlighting the overall housing situation in connection with labour migration, the perceived shortage of workers could be used as a bargaining tool. To put it simply the message was: if you want more workers, give us better housing!

However, the issue of housing was perhaps also a viable trade union argument for rejecting allocation as a whole, and in the longer run for restricting overall immigration to Sweden. Even if Metall was not powerful enough to stop labour immigration, it was certainly able to influence the allocation of the recruited workers among interested Swedish employers. Another important aspect of the union's powerful position was the inclusion of an organization clause in the bilateral agreements of 1947. This meant that all workers recruited through these agreements were forced to join the appropriate trade union in Sweden.[32]

Allocation of Sudeten German Workers

In the autumn of 1947, Metall was informed that the government had approved the recruitment of 5,000 Sudeten Germans, of whom the lion's share would be metalworkers. The union, nevertheless, maintained that both SAK and the government 'should exercise the greatest caution

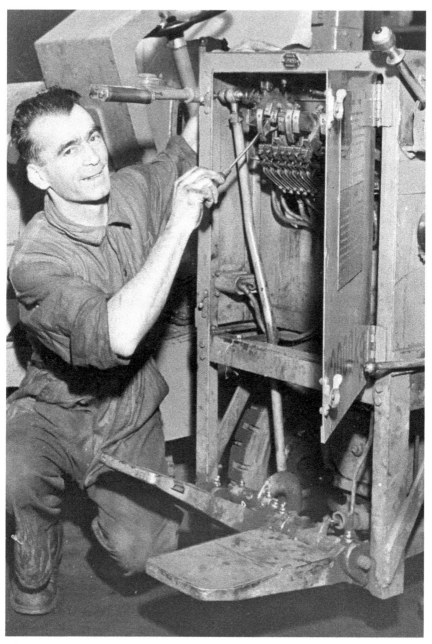

Illustration 6.1 Giuseppe Capello, migrant worker at ASEA in Västerås.
Arbetarrörelsens arkiv och bibliotek, VF Foto. Unknown photographer.

regarding the continued import of foreign-born workers'. The spokes-man Arne Geijer, later chairman of Metall, Landsorganisationen (Swedish trade union confederation, LO) and the International Confederation of Free Trade Unions, stressed that this caution was necessary because 'this import is not regarded as temporary'. He pointed out that 'the Sudeten German workers, who in practice do not have a home country, will settle permanently in Sweden', in some cases with their families. He also em-phasized that in the event of a recession, Swedish workers should have 'priority in all vacancies'.[33] This was stressed even though the migrants, unlike the Italians, were not perceived as guest workers and were obliged to pay the union dues.

However, the recruitments abroad continued despite the cautious op-position from Metall. The trade union was not, as stressed above, power-ful enough to successfully stop labour migration to Sweden completely, but the recruitment of Sudeten Germans was nevertheless restricted. Only about 1,800 migrants were transferred to Sweden, not 5,000, which was the initial goal.[34] At the same time, the trade union was given the op-portunity to influence the mobility of the Sudeten Germans in Sweden. Just as in the Italian case, Metall opposed allocation to certain employers:

> At these work places foreign-born workers are already allocated to such an extent, that significant irritation has occurred among the Swedish workers. To place more foreigners in these communities would only obstruct work and create such an atmosphere among the Swedish workers that we would be forced to intervene.[35]

Explicitly, only the number of foreigners already employed is mentioned as an argument against the allocation of Sudeten Germans. However, cer-tain social conflicts are implied. Much of this irritation among Swedish-born workers related to accusations of violations of different aspects of industrial working-class culture.

Union Affiliation, Working Pace and Affirmative Action

When Metall first opposed the idea of recruiting workers from abroad, Oscar Westerlund pointed out certain, but undefined, problems. He probably had non-unionized foreigners uppermost in his mind, among them, those who had come to Sweden as refugees at the end of the Second World War. Perhaps he was also referring to foreigners who violated other accepted standards in industrial working-class culture; for instance as regards the pace of work. Several local branches around the country complained about such issues. One example is branch no. 31, which reported to the trade union leadership in Stockholm that one company within its area of competence had employed many foreigners, mostly Estonians and Latvians, and that it had great difficulties unionizing them. Furthermore, the local branch maintained that the foreigners did not hesitate to 'tear down what the organization had built up, ruin the piecework wages and so on'.[36]

To clarify the situation, the national board of Metall initiated a nationwide inquiry among the local branches. This showed that about 60 per cent of all foreign-born workers, out of a total of about 5,500 at the workplaces concerned, were unionized, which should be compared with about 95 per cent among the Swedish-born. Arne Geijer, who analysed the enquiries, emphasized however that other complaints had been exaggerated and that the serious problems occurred only in a small number of communities.[37]

In addition to the issues of union membership and the pace of work, preferential treatment of the migrants by some employers was also a concern for many trade unionists. That especially Italians were given favourable treatments was, for example, underlined by one man from Borlänge in a meeting with fellow trade unionists at the headquarters of Metall:

> I strongly want to emphasize that foreign-born workers should be treated neither better nor worse than Swedish workers. At Domnarvets järnverk we have examples of foreigners who in some cases have been given benefits regarding housing and food that Swedish workers have not been able to acquire.[38]

Historian Jesper Johansson asserts that the Swedish trade union movement's self-understanding rested upon a male and monocultural frame of reference. It was assumed that the class positions of workers' families and their experiences of wage work would merge almost automatically into common interests shared by all workers regardless of ethnicity, gender and age. The need to assimilate foreigners who stayed in Sweden was taken for granted. Johansson maintains that the trade union movement emphasized that foreigners should adapt to the cultural standards of the Swedish majority society. But at the same time, and unlike the guest-worker programmes in West Germany and Switzerland, foreigners were granted almost all the same formal rights and benefits in Sweden as Swedish citizens.[39] By extension, the union starting point that everyone should be treated equally meant that every form of preferential treatment of migrants was opposed. However, the goal of equality was usually only highlighted when Swedish-born workers risked being treated worse than foreigners. The situation of foreigners at work and on the housing market was used as a tool by the trade unionists to put these issues on the agenda.

Recruitment, Economic Growth and the Welfare State

Recruitment of workers to Sweden according to the bilateral agreements of 1947 decreased during 1948. The demand for workers was, nevertheless, still unfulfilled. Labour migrations continued, chiefly from the other Nordic countries but also from countries outside the region.

In accordance with the bilateral agreements of 1947, recruitments had primarily been focused on skilled or semi-skilled workers. Meanwhile Verkstadsföreningen had concluded that the great demand for workers had resulted in a flight from heavy and dirty work, whenever Swedish-born workers could find more appealing tasks. Furthermore, the employers noticed a worrisome opposition among the workers to working late hours. Managing director Hans von Kantzow from Hallstahammar stressed, in line with this perception, that the employers should aim at a substantial 'import of foreign-born workers', but 'not skilled workers, since skilled work should be reserved for Swedish workers'.[40] At another meeting he pointed out, seemingly somewhat contradictorily, that Swedish industry was about to supply 'its need for skilled workers by foreigners, while Swedes had to take the bad jobs'. It was better, he stressed, to recruit foreigners and teach them to do unskilled or semi-skilled work.[41] It would thereby be possible to counter the flight from the lowest strata in the job hierarchy, and at the same time it would be possible to rationalize work processes with less resistance from native-born workers. Even if this individual actor belonged to the extremes within Verkstadsföreningen, the employers were thus influential when the ethnic divide of work became more rigid in Sweden after the Second World War.

Metall's opposition to labour immigration, which was obvious before the bilateral agreements were signed in 1947, was downplayed considerably by 1950. In November 1950, Arne Geijer informed the trade union board that it was still

> rather restrictive, but there has not been any possibility to completely reject the import of foreign-born workers. However, we have attempted to arrange it so that certain industries, which are important from an export point of view, have been allocated skilled people.[42]

After a few years of labour immigration the recruitments had, accordingly, become a part of an active labour market policy. The social democratic government and the trade union movement agreed that migrants should primarily be employed in export industries. Within Metall the connection between export revenues, national economic growth and welfare reforms for the benefit of its rank and file became more and more explicit:

> We must in this connection reckon with the fact that [the relative number of people of] working ages will decrease in our country ... and because we have to ensure the well-being of old people ... there must be investments in industry for production to adapt to present needs. With that follows, of course, an increased number of workers. When we cannot recruit Swedish-born workers to the industries, it follows that we must to some extent accept an influx of foreign-born workers to Sweden.[43]

To safeguard and expand the welfare system, young workers from abroad were apparently considered essential. This line of argument challenged the more restrictive attitudes within the trade union, and around 1950 it became stronger and more and more common.

By 1952, however, the post-war boom seemed to have come to an abrupt end. Around the country recruitments generally ceased, while cutbacks in production and in some cases even layoffs followed. In connection with this altered labour market, Metall also reformulated its immigration policy once again. The trade union now required the cancellation of all recruitment from abroad. It also asked AMS about its opinion on the 'foreign-born workers, who presently are employed in Sweden, when there will be a question of layoffs'.[44]

This open question can be interpreted in two different ways, depending on whether Metall had included the migrant workers as full members, or if they were still treated as a special and subordinate category although they paid their union dues. Accordingly, one possible interpretation is that the question was raised because of genuine concern about the migrants during this temporary economic slump. However, the analysis above points in another direction. Especially considering the Italians, a more appropriate interpretation would be that the economic problems highlighted the trade union's perception of the migrants as guest workers, and of a Swedish labour market that in the first place should be reserved for Swedes.

The answer from AMS to the trade union was, nevertheless, rather clear:

> Foreigners who already have been granted entry and work permits will have the right to stay in the country, if they prefer to do so, and this workforce ought to be treated in the same way as the Swedish workforce at layoffs.[45]

The post-war migrants were in Sweden to stay. But as to whether all workers really were equal and had the same rights, even AMS apparently hesitated a little with an 'ought to be' in the answer (instead of a 'will'). Ethnic equality was not self-evident in the early post-war era in Sweden.

Concluding Discussion

The great demand for workers altered industrial power relations in Sweden after the Second World War, in favour of the trade unions. Recruitment of workers in other countries was stressed by Verkstadsföreningen as the fastest and preferred method to increase the total size of the workforce in Sweden. Thereby the employers' association could supposedly relax the mutual competition for workers among its affiliates and counter the upward push on the wages as well as the Swedish-born workers' endeavours to gain power on the shop floors. The issue of labour migration was thus closely intertwined with labour market policy; labour migration was an issue that deeply affected industrial relations in Sweden overall.

The trade unionists within Metall managed to use the great demand for workers to their own advantage. In polemical exchanges with the employers they stressed that there was not a general shortage of workers in Sweden. The trade unionists pointed out that it was only some employers, mostly those who offered unsatisfactory working conditions, low wages and/or inadequate housing facilities, who had difficulties recruiting the required number of workers. In that way the trade unionists could use the unfulfilled demand for workers as a means to put other union issues on the agenda in their interactions with the employers.

Metall's initial opposition to labour recruitment from abroad was downplayed over time to become a more accepting line of argument. The trade unionists related immigration to increased industrial productivity and economic growth, which in the longer run and with fellow social democrats in the government would lay the foundation for anticipated welfare reforms. The trade unionists rallied behind the employers' argument that foreign-born men were preferable to other so-called native labour reserves. The gendered division of work – breadwinner/ homemaker – in practice excluded married women as an alternative, while the elevated pace of work eliminated the elderly and even slightly disabled workers as a realistic choice, at the same time as rationalizations and technical improvements took too much time to implement.

Yet, Metall's attitudes regarding labour immigration were ambivalent and full of contradictions. Mostly the migrations were accepted as necessary under prevailing labour market conditions, but occasionally the trade union tried to end the recruitments when the demand for workers seemed to decrease. Through this relatively restrictive attitude, the trade union tried to defend the newly won and much appreciated situation of full employment. The periods of widespread unemployment during the interwar years were close at hand and a part of every trade unionist's historical memory.

In any case, there was an obvious coincidence of interests between labour, capital and the state, as regards labour migration to Sweden. The trade unionists strove for improved working and living conditions for their rank and file; the employers required more workers for production to increase without a devastating wage drift; the social democratic government needed tax revenues for its planned welfare reforms. Because of the political power relations in Sweden at this point in time, the participation of all these three parties was necessary for reaching a mutually acceptable solution on the question of how the perceived shortage of workers should be resolved. The recurrent three-party discussions on these issues – between labour, capital and the state – therefore also contributed to the formation and consolidation of the Swedish labour market model in its corporatist form. Labour immigration was one of the first concrete issues where a sort of consensus could be reached between the parties in the Swedish labour market, and real results could be achieved.

Nevertheless, although a sort of consensus was reached about the necessity of labour immigration in general, divergent ideas about the scope and the conditions of the migrations continued to divide the parties. The representatives of Metall and Verkstadsföreningen put forward different opinions regarding the skills of the migrant workers. While some employers wanted to increase the recruitment abroad of so-called unskilled workers, Metall insisted that only skilled workers should be drafted in other countries during the early post-war years. In that way the trade union tried to counter the expected outcomes of the employers' interests – that is, a deepened ethnic divide of work in Sweden and perhaps also an even more divided working class along ethnic boundaries.

Johan Svanberg is a researcher at the Department of History, Stockholm University, specializing in migration history and labour history. His doctoral dissertation (2010) focused on Estonian Second World War refugees in the Swedish car industry, and his latest book (2016) deals with German migrants in the Swedish garment industry during the 1950s.

Notes

1. C. Guerin-Gonzales and C. Strikwerda (eds). 1998. *The Politics of Immigrant Workers*, New York/London: Holmes & Meier, chapter 1; R. Penninx and J. Roosblad (eds). 2000. *Trade Unions, Immigration, and Immigrants in Europe, 1960–1993*, New York: Berghahn Books, 4–13.
2. For example, J. Johansson. 2008. *"Så gör vi inte här i Sverige: Vi brukar göra så här"*, Växjö: Växjö University Press; Z. Yalcin. 2010. *Facklig gränspolitik*, Örebro: Örebro Studies in History.
3. See primarily J. Waara. 2012. *Svenska Arbetsgivareföreningen och arbetskraftsinvandringen 1945–1972*, Göteborg: Gothenburg Studies in Economic History.
4. For example, D. Frank. 2005. *Staten, företagen och arbetskraftsinvandringen*, Växjö: Växjö University Press; M. Byström. 2012. *Utmaningen. Den svenska välfärdsstatens möte med flyktingar i andra världskrigets tid*, Stockholm: Nordic Academic Press.
5. On the 'Swedish model', see, for example, P. Thullberg and K. Östberg (eds). 1994. *Den svenska modellen*, Lund: Studentlitteratur; P.A. Swenson. 2002. *Capitalists against Markets*, Oxford: Oxford University Press.
6. See also, L. Ekdahl. 2008. 'För medlemmarnas fackliga, ekonomiska och sociala intressen', in K. Bosdotter, R. Jansson and K. Misgeld (eds), *Det lyser en framtid*, Stockholm: IF Metall, 764–65.
7. L. Olsson. 2003. 'Hundra år av arbetskraftsinvandringen', in J. Ekberg (ed.), *Invandring till Sverige – orsaker och effekter*, Växjö: Växjö University Press, 9.
8. L. Olsson. 1997. *On the Threshold of the People's Home of Sweden*, New York: CMS; for example, 151–53.
9. Cf. K. Salomon. 1991. *Refugees in the Cold War*, Lund: Lund University Press, 197–206; D. Kay and R. Miles. 1992. *Refugees or Migrant Workers?*, London/New York: Routledge, 2, 9–10; M. Wyman. 1998. *DPs*, Ithaca: Cornell University Press, 188–91.
10. G. Ahlberg and I. Svennilson. 1946. *Sveriges arbetskraft och den industriella utvecklingen*, Stockholm: Industriens utredningsinstitut, 41.
11. VF:s överstyrelse, 27 September 1945, § 4. VF:s arkiv (Centrum för Näringslivshistoria), vol. AI:24. (All translations of quotations from Swedish in this chapter are the author's.)
12. VF till SAF, 17 October 1947; see also VF:s överstyrelse, 25 August 1950, § 4; 17 March 1950, § 13; 25 May 1950, § 6. VF:s arkiv, 'VF:s särskilda utredningar 1947' (sign. saknas) and vol. AI:29. Cf. T. Lundqvist. 2000. *Arbetsgivarpolitik under full sysselsättning*, Uppsala: Forskningsprogrammet Svensk modell i förändring, 36–37.
13. VF:s överstyrelse, 9 April 1946, § 5; see also 31 October 1945, § 8; 15 September 1949, § 4; 25 August 1950, § 4. VF:s arkiv, vol. AI:24–25, 28–29.
14. VF:s överstyrelse, 12 March 1946, § 19; 9 April 1946, § 5; 4 June 1946, § 10; 20 March 1947, § 14; 26 September 1947, § 9; 22 November 1950, § 18; VF:s cirkulär nr. 14/1946. VF:s arkiv, vol. AI:25–26, 29. See also C. Lundh. 2002. *Spelets regler*, Stockholm: SNS, 195; Lundqvist, *Arbetsgivarpolitik under full sysselsättning*, 32–3, 50–2; J. Svanberg. 2010. 'Då lördagar var lönsamma', in L. Berggren et al (eds), *Samhällshistoria i fokus*, Malmö: Big Bad Books, 32–49.
15. VF:s överstyrelse, 15 September 1949, § 6; 23 Maj 1951, § 8; 18 October 1951, § 4; 14 November 1951, § 5. VF:s arkiv, vol. AI:28, 30.
16. VF:s allmänna möte, 4 June 1946, § 11; VF:s överstyrelse, 22 October 1948, § 19. VF:s arkiv, vol. AI:25, 27.
17. VF:s allmänna möte, 4 June 1946, § 11. See also VF:s överstyrelse, 9 April 1946, § 5; 29 August 1946, § 3; 18 March 1952, § 8. VF:s arkiv, vol. AI:25, 28.
18. 'Rapport. Ang. arbetskraftsbristen vid järnbruken', 31 October 1946; see also 'Rapport. Ang. sammanträde med statsrådet Sträng', 22 July 1947; 'Rapport. Ang. sammanträde

inför statsrådet Möller', 26 February 1948. Sv. Metallindustriarbetareförbundets arkiv (Arbetarrörelsens arkiv och bibliotek, ARAB), vol. AIII: 92, 94, 96.

19. Metalls överstyrelse, 6 November 1947, § 8. Sv. Metallindustriarbetareförbundets arkiv, vol. AII:9.
20. For example, VF:s överstyrelse, 22 October 1948, § 6; 23 March 1949, § 11; 10 January 1950, § 10; 25 August 1950, § 8. VF:s arkiv, vol. AI:27–29; 'Rapport. Ang. Volvo, Pentaverken i Skövde', 5 July 1952. Sv. Metallindustriarbetareförbundets arkiv, vol. AIII:109.
21. VF:s överstyrelse, 9 April 1946, § 5. VF:s arkiv, vol. AI:25.
22. VF:s extra möte med södra kretsen, 3 September 1946, § 5. VF:s arkiv, vol. AIIb:5.
23. J. Nelhans (1973) stresses that the national trade unions opposed labour immigration (*Utlänningen på arbetsmarknaden*, Lund: Studentlitteratur, 29–30), while R. Tempsch and Johansson point out that a consensus developed between the parties in the Swedish labour market regarding a limited labour recruitment. See R. Tempsch. 1997. *Från Centraleuropa till folkhemmet*, Göteborg: Meddelanden från ekonomisk-historiska institutionen vid Göteborgs Universitet, 155–59; Johansson, *"Så gör vi inte här i Sverige"*, 123.
24. Metalls förbundsstyrelse, 5 September 1946, § 8. Sv. Metallindustriarbetareförbundets arkiv, vol. AIII:92. Also cited by Nelhans, *Utlänningen på arbetsmarknaden*, 139–40; Tempsch, *Från Centraleuropa till folkhemmet*, 156.
25. G. Kyle. 1979. *Gästarbeterska i manssamhället*, Stockholm: Liber, chapter 5; see also Y. Hirdman. 1998. *Med kluven tunga*, Stockholm: Atlas, 85, 186–95; Y. Waldemarson. 1998. *Mjukt till formen – hårt till innehållet*, Stockholm: Atlas, 125, 236–37.
26. Metalls förbundsstyrelse, 26 September 1946, § 7. Sv. Metallindustriarbetareförbundets arkiv, vol. AIII:92.
27. See A. Järtelius. 1987. *Drömmen om Sverige*, Västerås: Västerås kultutnämnd; Tempsch, *Från Centraleuropa till folkhemmet*; A. Lajos. 2008. *På rätt sida om järnridån?*, Växjö: Växjö University Press.
28. 'Sammanställning av hos arbetsmarknadskommissionen gjorda framställningar om italiensk arbetskraft', (odaterad). Sv. Metallindustriarbetareförbundets arkiv, vol. EI:55.
29. 'Rapport. Ang. överläggningar med statens arbetsmarknadskommission', 9 May 1947. Sv. Metallindustriarbetareförbundets arkiv, vol. EI:54.
30. 'Rapport. Ang. överläggningar med statens arbetsmarknadskommission'.
31. 'V.P.M. Angående eventuell placering av italiensk arbetskraft vid Storfors rörverk', 21 May 1947; 'Rapport. Ang. Storfors rörverk, Storfors', 31 October 1946, (quotation). Sv. Metallindustriarbetareförbundets arkiv, vol. EI:52.
32. W. Knocke. 2000. 'Sweden: Insiders Outside the Trade Union Mainstream', in R. Penninx and J. Roosblad (eds), *Trade Unions, Immigration, and Immigrants in Europe, 1960–1993*, 159.
33. 'Rapport. Ang. planerad import av sudettyska arbetare', 16 October 1947; see also 'Rapport. Ang. sammanträde å Arbetsmarknadskommissionen rörande import av sudettyska arbetare', 18 October 1947. Sv. Metallindustriarbetareförbundets arkiv, vol. AIII:95.
34. 'PM ang överföring av utländsk arbetskraft till Sverige 1946–1956', 21 December 1956. AMS:s arkiv, arbetsförmedlingsbyrån utlänningssektionen, vol. EVIIba:5.
35. Metall till AMS, 14 April 1948. *Metallindustriarbetareförbundets arkiv*, vol. EI:55.
36. Metalls förbundsstyrelse, 6 September 1945, § 9. Sv. Metallindustriarbetareförbundets arkiv, vol. AIII:89.
37. 'Rapport ang. utländsk arbetskraft inom metallindustrin', 13 November 1946. Sv. Metallindustriarbetareförbundets arkiv, vol. AIII:92.
38. Metalls överstyrelse, 5–6 May 1947, § 6; see also 31 May–1 June 1951, § 6. Sv. Metallindustriarbetareförbundets arkiv, vol. AII:9, 11.
39. Johansson, *"Så gör vi inte här i Sverige: Vi brukar göra så här"*, 136–37, 171, 368.

40. VF:s överstyrelse, 27 August 1948, § 4. VF:s arkiv, vol. AI:27.
41. VF:s överstyrelse, 25 August 1950, § 4. VF:s arkiv, vol. AI:29.
42. Metalls överstyrelse, 2 November 1950, § 5; see also 26 November 1948, § 7. Sv. Metallindustriarbetareförbundets arkiv, vol. AII:10.
43. Metalls överstyrelse, 2 November 1950, § 5. Sv. Metallindustriarbetareförbundets arkiv, vol. AII:10.
44. 'Rapport Ang. överläggningar rörande utländsk arbetskraft', 12 November 1952. Sv. Metallindustriarbetareförbundets arkiv, vol. AIII:110.
45. 'Rapport Ang. överläggningar rörande utländsk arbetskraft'.

References

Ahlberg, G. and I. Svennilson. 1946. *Sveriges arbetskraft och den industriella utvecklingen*, Stockholm: Industriens utredningsinstitut.

Byström, M. 2012. *Utmaningen*, Lund: Nordic Academic Press.

Ekdahl, L. 'För medlemmarnas fackliga, ekonomiska och sociala intressen', in K. Bosdotter, R. Jansson and K. Misgeld (eds), *Det lyser en framtid*, Stockholm: IF Metall, 2008, 764–65.

Frank, D. 2005. *Staten, företagen och arbetskraftsinvandringen*, Växjö: Växjö University Press.

Guerin-Gonzales, C. and C. Strikwerda (eds). 1998. *The Politics of Immigrant Workers*, New York/London: Holmes & Meier.

Hirdman, Y. 1998. *Med kluven tunga*, Stockholm: Atlas.

Johansson, J. 2008. *"Så gör vi inte här i Sverige: Vi brukar göra så här"*, Växjö: Växjö University Press.

Järtelius, A. 1987. *Drömmen om Sverige*, Västerås: Västerås kulturnämnd.

Kay, D. and R. Miles. 1992. *Refugees or Migrant Workers?*, London/New York: Routledge.

Knocke, W. 'Sweden: Insiders Outside the Trade Union Mainstream', in R. Penninx and J. Roosblad (eds), *Trade Unions, Immigration, and Immigrants in Europe, 1960–1993*, New York: Berghahn Books, 2000, 157–82.

Kyle, G. 1979. *Gästarbeterska i manssamhället*, Stockholm: Liber.

Lajos, A. 2008. *På rätt sida om järnridån?*, Växjö: Växjö University Press.

Lundh, C. 2002. *Spelets regler*, Stockholm: SNS.

Lundqvist, T. 2000. *Arbetsgivarpolitik under full sysselsättning*, Uppsala: Forskningsprogrammet Svensk modell i förändring.

Nelhans, J. 1973. *Utlänningen på arbetsmarknaden*, Lund: Studentlitteratur.

Olsson, L. 1997. *On the Threshold of the People's Home of Sweden*, New York: CMS.

———. 'Hundra år av arbetskraftsinvandringen', in J. Ekberg (ed.), *Invandring till Sverige – orsaker och effekter*, Växjö: Växjö University Press, 2003, 7–24.

Penninx, R. and J. Roosblad. (eds). 2000. *Trade Unions, Immigration, and Immigrants in Europe, 1960–1993*, New York: Berghahn Books.

Salomon, K. 1991. *Refugees in the Cold War*, Lund: Lund University Press.

Svanberg, J. 'Då lördagar var lönsamma', in L. Berggren et al (eds), *Samhällshistoria i fokus*, Malmö: Big Bad Books, 2010, 32–49.

Swenson, P.A. 2002. *Capitalists against Markets*, Oxford: Oxford University Press.

Tempsch, R. 1997. *Från Centraleuropa till folkhemmet*, Göteborg: Meddelanden från ekonomisk-historiska institutionen vid Göteborgs Universitet.

Thullberg, P. and K. Östberg (eds). 1994. *Den svenska modellen*, Lund: Studentlitteratur.

Waara, J. 2012. *Svenska Arbetsgivareföreningen och arbetskraftsinvandringen 1945–1972*, Göteborg: Gothenburg Studies in Economic History.

Waldemarson, Y. 1998. *Mjukt till formen – hårt till innehållet*, Stockholm: Atlas.

Wyman, M. 1998. *DPs*, Ithaca: Cornell University Press.

Yalcin, Z. 2010. *Facklig gränspolitik*, Örebro: Örebro Studies in History.

Archival Sources

AMS:s arkiv (Söderhamn): Arbetsförmedlingsbyrån utlänningssektionen: PM, 1956. vol. EVIIba:5

Arbetarrörelsens arkiv och bibliotek, ARAB (Flemingsberg): Svenska Metallindustriarbetareförbundets arkiv: Överstyrelsens protokoll, 1947, 1950–1951. vol. AII:9–11; Förbundsstyrelsens protokoll, inklusive bilagor, 1946–1948, 1952. vol. AIII:89, 92, 95–96, 109–110; Korrespondens, 1946–1948. vol. EI:52, 54–55.

Centrum för näringslivshistoria (Bromma): Sveriges Verkstadsförenings arkiv (VF): Protokoll och korrespondens, 1945–1951. vol. AI:24–25, 27–30; Protokoll södra kretsen, 1946. vol. AIIb:5; Utredningar, 1947. signum saknas.

Chapter 7

Land Agitation and the Rise of Agrarian Socialism in South-Western Finland, 1899–1907

Sami Suodenjoki

In the summer of 1904, the Finnish socialist leader Yrjö Mäkelin travelled from cottage to cottage in the province of Häme, south-western Finland, to canvass support for the socialist movement among the rural poor. When starting conversations with rural workers, he found it useful to bring up the recent assassination of Nikolay Bobrikov, who had served as the Governor General of Finland from 1898 until his death on 17 June 1904. Mäkelin, a devoted Finnish nationalist, considered Bobrikov the mastermind of the oppressive policies adopted in the Grand Duchy of Finland by the Russian government. While talking with the rural labourers of Häme, however, Mäkelin was astounded that many of them deeply mourned Bobrikov's demise:

> They still believe that if Bobrikov had remained alive and continued his work, he would have executed a redistribution of land and belongings, in other words, he would have taken from the rich and given to the poor. Such madness did not appear elsewhere than in such places where they read nothing, but there are, God help us, still extremely many such places.[1]

The quote from Mäkelin's travelogue shows his anxiety over landless people's apparent lack of national consciousness. Like many other socialist activists, he believed that the rise of socialism in the Finnish countryside was impeded by the rural inhabitants' ignorance and loyalty to the imperial regime. Yet while commenting on landless people's attitudes towards Bobrikov, Mäkelin touched on another major issue that socialists needed to tackle in order to gain the mass support of the rural proletariat. This issue was land ownership, the importance of which was reflected by the persistent circulation of land redistribution rumours in the countryside.

At the time of Mäkelin's tour in Häme, the socialist labour movement played only a minor role in the political life of Finland. Socialist ideas were gradually taking root, however, not only in the industrial centres but also in many rural areas. What was noteworthy in the rise of socialism in Finland was its concurrence with the collision between Finnish nationalists and the Russian government over the administrative autonomy of the Grand Duchy. The impact of this collision on the Finnish labour movement has been an important topic for Finnish historiography. Research has addressed the relationship of Suomen Sosialidemokraattinen Puolue (the Finnish Social Democratic Party, SDP) to the Russian government, and the particular way in which Finnish socialists combined class struggle with the defence of national autonomy.[2] Scholars have indicated that on the one hand, the socialist movement and the nationalist movement were closely integrated in Finland, but on the other hand, the labour movement benefited from the power struggle between the imperial authorities and the Finnish nationalist elite.[3]

While previous research on the relationship between the labour movement and imperial rule has focused on the views of socialist leaders and activists, some attention has also been paid to ordinary workers' conceptions of the political situation.[4] Some studies have even noted the appearance of pro-tsarist attitudes among agricultural workers and tenant farmers – that is, the rural people who were later the most responsive to socialism. These attitudes were expressed, for example, by the imperviousness of landless people to Finnish nationalists' agitation against imperial policies prior to 1905.[5]

Building on these previous findings, this chapter examines how the political clash between the Russian regime and Finnish nationalists fuelled landless labourers' protests and class consciousness at grass-roots level at the turn of the twentieth century. I argue that the rapid breakthrough of the socialist movement in Finland around 1905 would not have been possible without the preceding period of Russification, which gave the rural population new means and opportunities to engage in political action. By using sources such as rural people's letters to newspapers and their correspondence with the imperial authorities, I address the foundation of rural socialism in Finland. Although it has been recognized that the Finnish socialist movement was exceptionally agrarian in nature, these questions still require further elaboration.[6]

Map 7.1 South-western Häme

This analysis is confined to south-western Häme, officially the juris-
dictional district of Tammela, with eleven parishes and 58,000 inhabitants in the year 1900.[7] South-western Häme belonged to the core region
of Finland where urbanization and industrialization had been most rapid
in the late nineteenth century. Nonetheless, two thirds of the region's
inhabitants were still engaged in agriculture at the turn of the twentieth
century. Of the agricultural households, 13 per cent owned their own
land, whereas 26 per cent were tenant farmers *(maanvuokraaja)*.[8] The
remaining three-fifths of the households comprised cottagers *(mäkitupalainen)* and other agricultural labourers with their families. Not all
agricultural labourers are included in this figure, however, because many
farm servants and itinerant workers without their own dwelling do not
appear in the statistics.[9]

South-western Häme represented the part of Finland where the question of landownership was most acute at this time. It was a region where
a significant part of the land was owned by large manorial estates with
numerous tenant farmers and workers. In this respect, south-western
Häme resembled Skåne or the Mälaren valley in Sweden. Yet the region
was also inhabited by hundreds of independent peasant farmers whose
political position had been improved by the reforms of the national and
local governments in the 1860s. Moreover, the landowners had benefited economically from the penetration of the capitalist market system
into agriculture and forestry in the late nineteenth century. At the same
time, the landless population expanded rapidly and access to land became more difficult. These changes widened the gap between the various groups of the agrarian population, and increased tensions between
landowners and their tenants and agricultural labourers.[10]

This chapter examines how the evolving class conflict manifested itself
in the countryside and intertwined with the Finno-Russian conflict and
the rise of socialism during the years 1899–1907. The first two sections
of the chapter focus on how the political crisis created by Russification
presented landless labourers with a favourable opportunity to press the
domestic upper class into carrying out social reforms. As the landless
lacked formal representation in local and national politics, they turned
to traditional instruments of peasant protest, such as spreading rumours
and petitioning the imperial authorities.

In the third section of the chapter, I cover the concurrent penetration of the socialist labour movement in the countryside. Socialist agitators, aware of landless people's political significance, strove to address
the landownership question and unite the fragmented rural proletariat.
These efforts bore modest fruit, however, until the general strike of 1905
forced the Tsar to concede democratic reforms in Finland. The impact

of the strike is discussed in the fourth section, which describes the surge of organization among landless labourers and their alignment with the SDP in the parliamentary election of 1907. On the whole, the chapter elucidates how favourable twists in high politics turned landless people's informal protests into a strong backing for the socialists in a remarkably short period of time.

Finno-Russian Conflict-Boosting Rumours

The Grand Duchy of Finland had been part of the Russian Empire since 1809, but it enjoyed more administrative autonomy than any other region of the Empire. In February 1899, however, Tsar Nicholas II declared the so-called February Manifesto, which limited the Finnish Diet's influence in the implementation of imperial legislation in Finland. The manifesto was orchestrated by the recently appointed Governor General Bobrikov, who mainly needed it to introduce a conscription law that enabled the incorporation of the Finnish armed forces into the Russian army. Finnish nationalists considered the manifesto a flagrant violation of the autonomy granted to Finland by the Tsar. To reverse the manifesto and prevent further integration measures, they organized peaceful mass opposition. In only two weeks, a petition known as the Great Address *(suuri adressi)* gathered over half a million signatures. As the petitioners comprised a quarter of the Finnish adult population, the petition was cherished as an indication of Finnish unanimity against the imperial policies.[11]

Not all Finns, however, mobilized against the manifesto or signed the Great Address. The signatures of tenant farmers, in particular, were under-represented in the petition. In southern Häme, tenants comprised only 7 per cent of the petitioners; the most passive areas being the manorial parishes of Jokioinen and Ypäjä where less than 2 per cent of the tenants signed the petition. The low proportions imply that some tenant farmers deliberately shunned the petition to avoid taking sides in the infighting between the imperial government and the Finnish upper classes.[12] This view is echoed by the author Väinö Linna in his famous novel *Täällä Pohjantähden alla*, which has substantially influenced the popular image of early twentieth-century Finnish history. Linna, who sought inspiration for the novel from his birthplace in south-western Häme, represents some tenant farmers and cottagers as indifferent or hostile to the members of the upper class who collected signatures for the petition.[13] Linna's fictitious narrative bears a surprising similarity to some accounts written by rural workers soon after 1899. According to these accounts, many tenants and landless workers scorned the petition as an upper-class plot that deserved no support so long as the dominant groups overlooked their views on all other political issues.[14] Based on these accounts, the shunning of the Great Address seems more a protest against the local dominant groups than a statement of support for the imperial policies.

The view that the petition stirred underprivileged people to demonstrate against the domestic upper class is further supported by the simultaneous spread of rumours in the countryside. During the weeks following the introduction of the February Manifesto, rumours about a common redistribution of land swept through Finland. The rumours claimed that the Tsar would soon implement a nationwide land redistribution that would provide the landless with a plot of arable land either free of change or for an affordable price. These rumblings not surprisingly struck a chord with tenants and day labourers, who eagerly linked the manifesto with a long-awaited land reform.[15]

Examining rumours provides useful perspectives on the peasants' political behaviour. Rumours tend to run loose, particularly in an atmosphere of fear and political upheaval; in such circumstances they often overpower official information channels.[16] Rumours can be defined as improvised news that hypothesizes about unverified realities and fuses material from many sources: official and unofficial, literary and oral. As such, they represent a tactic for ordinary people to negotiate their way in society, or even an outright weapon of popular protest.[17]

The rumours that circulated in Finland 1899 can be traced, for example, by using rural letters to newspapers and citizens' complaints to officialdom. Both of these source types contain ample comments on the spread of unofficial news by local word-of-mouth networks. Although the authors of these texts sometimes treated rumours with disapproval or sarcasm, their texts give valuable insight into the content of the rumours and rural people's motives for their circulation.

Contemporaries who commented on the rumours in 1899 were well aware of the long tradition of whispers about land distribution in Russia. Particularly after the abolition of serfdom in the 1870s, rumours of a universal repartition of land had run loose around the Empire. In the Finnish provinces, similar rumours of land reform had circulated throughout the nineteenth century, often enhanced by crises in Finno-Russian relations. Nevertheless, previous rumours had always remained localized and scattered in Finland. It was only in the spring of 1899 that land redistribution rumours became widespread throughout the Grand Duchy, and south-western Häme was no exception. Although an official investigation found that the rumours did not gain as firm a foothold in

Häme as in some other parts of Finland, the rural police chiefs reported that the rumours were running wild in Urjala and Jokioinen for example.[18] In Urjala it was claimed that the forthcoming imperial law would grant every cottager the ownership of the land surrounding the cottage. According to some rumours, the landless did not even need to wait for the law to be implemented; they could immediately claim landownership by contacting certain agents in a nearby city.[19]

The rumours in Urjala and in many other regions associated the forthcoming land redistribution with the implementation of a 'Russian law' in Finland. This idea of the Russian law was based on rural inhabitants' vague conception of the collective land tenure system of Russian peasants known as *'mir'*.[20] In the electrified atmosphere following the February Manifesto in 1899, many rural inhabitants tended to interpret this old repartitional tenure as a general Russian landowning system that would come into effect in Finland and liberate the landless from their subordination. Spreading rumours was not, however, necessarily dependent on whether the rural inhabitants actually believed in the forthcoming land redistribution. Rather, the rumours should be understood as the landless people's attempt to use the discernible rupture in national power relations for their own purposes. Rumours offered them a means to put pressure on local landowners and to urge the state authorities to address the problems of landownership.

A Window of Opportunity for Petitioners and Denouncers

Upper-class Finnish nationalists considered the rumours about land redistribution a menace to their attempts to unify the people against the Russification policies. The nationalists therefore strove to suppress the wave of rumours by sending speakers to the countryside and publishing innumerable pamphlets and articles about the harmfulness of spreading rumours. To downplay the rumours, they also associated rumour-mongering with Russian pedlars who travelled around Finland. In doing so, however, the nationalists failed to take seriously the growing social tension related to the land question implied by the rumours. Thus, even though the countermeasures helped to attenuate the rumours by the summer of 1899, they did not eliminate the ultimate source of restlessness in the countryside.[21] This soon became evident when landless people's discontent found new expressions, some of which were much more explicit than vague rumours.

In south-western Häme, the discontent of landless people was manifested, for example, in 'counter-petitions' collected by the Kalvola

tenant farmer Adolf Nieminen in 1900. Nieminen's two petitions were
signed by sixty-seven landless labourers and tenant farmers from the sur-
rounding countryside. The petitioners praised the Tsar for the February
Manifesto, condemned the Great Address and appealed for an improve-
ment in landless people's conditions.[22] Both petitions were delivered to
Governor General Bobrikov personally by a former parish clerk, August
Erlund, who probably also aided Nieminen in formulating the petitions.
Erlund was locally well known as an advocate of the tenants' interests.
He had recently been sacked from his post as the parish clerk of Kalvola
and consequently employed himself as a 'land agitator'.[23]

Erlund and Nieminen's activities soon set them on a collision course
with the nationalists, who tended to stigmatize any Finns who collaborated with the oppressive Governor General as unpatriotic and corrupted. As a result, the pair was subjected to a fierce attack by the nationalist
newspapers.[24] The public gaze directed at Erlund and Nieminen also inspired a students' association from Helsinki to send agitators to Kalvola
in December 1900. The agitators, who went to acquaint themselves with
the local conditions and educate the landless population, gave the following report on their observations in Kalvola:

> What is most woeful is that besides moderate tenant farmers, there are many
> of those in the parish who live in hope of that golden land distribution.
> ... These people are led by the sacked parish clerk Erlund and the tenant
> Nieminen. These two gentlemen exercise downright provocation. ... Money
> is submitted to them regularly from Helsinki, which, by the way, they of-
> ten visit personally. It should also be mentioned that last summer they had
> brought along gendarmes to some religious gatherings. Furthermore, it
> seems that Nieminen has been given the task of nurturing itinerant pedlars.
> They [tenant farmers] said that there had once been 18 of them [pedlars] at
> his place at the same time.[25]

As the quotation indicates, the student agitators accused Erlund and
Nieminen of being funded by Bobrikov and of cooperating with the
hated Russian gendarmes *(santarmit)* and pedlars. By representing the
pair as unpatriotic exploiters of the rural poor, the agitators essentially
downplayed the existing tenancy conflict between the manor owners and
their tenants in Kalvola. This was symptomatic for the nationalist in-
telligentsia in general. The intellectuals' tendency to blame corrupted
individuals or foreign vagrants for provoking landless people implies a
failure to acknowledge the evolution of a clear-cut class conflict in the
countryside.[26]

By 1901, August Erlund and Adolf Nieminen had gained nationwide
publicity as collaborators of the imperial regime. Due to the bad press,

Nieminen was eventually evicted from his farm by an annoyed landlord and Erlund fell into outcast status in his community. These setbacks did not stop the pair from operating, however. Both men continued to communicate with the imperial government during the following years, requesting aid for themselves and for the rural poor of the region.[27] Erlund even engaged in composing land redistribution petitions to the Governor General on behalf of some illiterate tenants.[28] This brought him into still more disrepute as the newspapers proclaimed him to be a swindler who ripped off paupers with groundless promises.[29] Rather than being swindlers, however, Erlund and Nieminen probably truly aimed at improving the conditions of landless people, even if they were also motivated by the pursuance of personal prestige and financial support from the administration.

Erlund and Nieminen were not the only rural inhabitants of south-western Häme who engaged in political action by appealing to the imperial authorities. In 1902–1904, several lower-class people approached the Governor General's Chancery with denunciations accusing local upper-class individuals of conspiring against the imperial government.[30] Such letters became common at the same time as the implementation of the new conscription law in Finland, and they were mainly directed against the nationalist activists, known as Constitutionalists *(perustuslailliset)*, who had orchestrated boycotts against conscription in Häme.[31] These denunciations demonstrate that the Constitutionalist resistance to the government policies was far from unanimously supported by the rural population.

Letters of denunciation give valuable insight into internal tensions in local communities, for despite focusing on the conscription boycott, the letters usually carried other grievances as well. The denouncers included tenant farmers, agricultural workers and craftsmen who had personal disputes with landowners, bailiffs, priests or civil servants over issues such as evictions or debts.[32] For these lowly individuals, denunciations provided a means to argue for an administrative resolution in their favour or simply to cause harm to the individuals they were in dispute with.

An example of such a denunciation is provided by Vihtori Lindholm (1868–1918), a cobbler from Urjala, who wrote four letters to Bobrikov in the spring of 1903. In these letters Lindholm named several local landowners, a sawmill manager and a local priest as anti-government agitators who incited the local proletariat to boycott conscription. Moreover, Lindholm accused some local upper-class people of defaming the Tsar and the Governor General.[33] Lindholm justified these denunciations as loyalty to the imperial regime, but supporting evidence from his life story, such as trial documents and reminiscences, suggests alternative motives for the revelations. Lindholm's letter-writing seems to have been fuelled particularly by certain lawsuits that had led to him being jailed two years earlier. Apparently, the cobbler used denunciations to retaliate against the landowners and other upper-class people who had given negative testimonies against him in court or had otherwise contributed to his sentences.[34]

Amid the Finno-Russian conflict, mere rumours of denunciations were enough to generate political tensions and paranoia in local communities. Later on, during the general strike of 1905, several denouncers from south-western Häme were exposed when a crowd raided the gendarme station of Tampere and rummaged through its secret documents. In the patriotic atmosphere of the strike, nationalist newspapers published the names of the denouncers and stigmatized them as the henchmen of the oppressive regime.[35] As a result, these individuals became ostracized in their communities. Cobbler Lindholm, for example, was driven away from a popular meeting after being proclaimed as a traitor by the attendant crowd of local farmers and workers. He was also forced to repent publicly in the workers' association his intrigue with the imperial administration, in order to retain his membership of the association. Some years later, Lindholm therefore recalled the general strike as a personal tragedy rather than a celebration of democratic reforms.[36] He and others who had collaborated with the Russian regime became the losers of the strike, whereas for the Constitutionalists – and the socialist labour movement – the strike marked a triumph over tyranny.

The Socialist Movement Channelling the Protest

At the same time as the wave of land distribution rumours, petitions and denunciations, the socialist movement penetrated the countryside of Häme. Socialist ideas were promulgated by the itinerant agitators of Suomen Työväenpuolue (the Finnish Labour Party, from 1903 SDP) and by labour newspapers, whose circulation gradually increased from the 1890s. The labour newspapers gained a readership in the countryside, first and foremost by publishing rural letters that focused on the plight of the rural poor and the wrongdoings of the local elite. These letters were written mostly by local labour activists who themselves represented the rural proletariat, a group whose voice had been largely absent from the press before the end of the nineteenth century. Thus, the expanding labour press opened up a new public arena where working-class people who lacked full political rights were able to air their grievances and create class consciousness.[37]

The formation of working-class consciousness in south-western Häme was obviously linked with the escalating conflict between landowners and the landless. The status of tenant farmers became more insecure at the beginning of the twentieth century when landowners tightened rental terms or evicted their tenants in the fear that the forthcoming tenancy legislation would make leasing unprofitable. As shown above, tenants reacted to the insecurity by turning to rumour-mongering, petitions and denunciations. Tensions also emerged over the tenants' and agrarian workers' customary use of woodland, which caused an increasing number of litigations in the region.[38] All these developments benefited labour activists when canvassing for support among the landless for the socialist agrarian programme. The activists realized that in order to gain mass support, the SDP needed to respond to the rural proletariat's hunger for land. Hence, they tactically strove to adapt Marxist ideas of agriculture to suit the local circumstances. In this, the Finnish socialists followed the same path as their Scandinavian and German counterparts in seeking to win over the rural population by adopting a favourable stance towards small-scale farming.[39]

The rise of class politics in the countryside entailed a new form of collective protest, namely the strike. In the summer of 1903, several strikes of tenants and day labourers broke out in Finland. In June 1903, one of the biggest conflicts occurred in south-western Häme, where the day labourers of Jokioinen manor went on strike to shorten their working hours. The strike ended after two weeks when the manor's bailiff – fearing that the strike would extend to the manor's other estates – partly conceded to workers' demands. Later on in July 1905, the tenants of Kartanonkylä manor in Ypäjä also went on strike for better conditions and forced the manor owner to compromise. Conflicts such as these had a wide-ranging impact; they frightened numerous other landowners into cutting their labourers' working hours even before it was demanded.[40]

The agricultural workers and tenant farmers who engaged in collective action in 1903–5 were mostly unorganized. Nonetheless, their demands were sometimes backed by visiting socialist agitators or local workers' associations, as in the case of Jokioinen. In general, the SDP warned the agricultural labourers not to launch thoughtless strikes because they lacked the necessary muscle to push through their demands. Instead of striking, the party organs advised the rural proletariat to organize and promote their cause through negotiation.[41]

Despite the socialists' vigorous agitation, the organization of rural workers proved sluggish in south-western Häme. In total, six new workers' associations with a socialist programme were established between

1900 and 1904, but the membership of most of them remained low. Agricultural workers and tenants were reluctant to join the associations, as they justly feared discrimination by landowners and other dominant groups. Moreover, the organization was hampered by rural workers' religiosity even though socialist activists roundly reassured them that socialist ideology was in tune with Christianity.[42]

In particular, the socialists agonized over the mobilization of tenant farmers. Even if the tenants had been actively voicing their grievances via rumours and petitions, they lacked the kind of collective identity vis-à-vis landowners that would have been the prerequisite for concerted political action through workers' associations. Instead of organization, tenants tended to lean on the state, wanting the government, with its laws and statutes, to intervene in their personal relationships with landowners.[43] This faith in state intervention was a crucial factor behind the popularity of rumours about the Russian law in 1899 and the subsequent petitions to the Governor General. Labour party organs strongly deprecated the rural proletariat's resort to rumour-spreading and petitioning. From their viewpoint, involvement in such activities blatantly contradicted the aims of the socialist movement. For example, in an editorial of *Kansan Lehti* ('People's Journal'), Yrjö Mäkelin refuted the claims of some bourgeois nationalists that 'the labour movement was the instigator and spreader of land redistribution rumours'. He argued that instead of fostering rumours, the labour movement had effectively suppressed them through education.[44] Moreover, *Kansan Lehti* reprimanded landless people for pleading with the Governor General for land reform. According to the paper, the government would disregard such pleas and therefore the petitioners would receive nothing but the pity and contempt of their fellow citizens. Instead of vainly expecting help from officialdom, the labour organ argued, landless people could improve their lot only by organizing and furthering reforms patiently through legislation.[45]

A Surge of Organization after the General Strike of 1905

The SDP essentially argued that the problems of land ownership and tenancy could only be solved by a parliament elected under universal and equal suffrage. Hence, up until 1905, socialist agitators focused on mobilizing the rural poor in support of demands for rapid suffrage reform. This strategy was problematic, however, because as long as universal suffrage remained a distant dream, the socialist alternative did not appear very attractive to most tenant farmers and agricultural workers.

Things were to change, however, when the revolutionary situation in Russia spread to Finland with the general strike of November 1905. The strike forced the Tsar to suspend Russification measures and to concede universal and equal suffrage for both men and women in parliamentary elections.[46] As a result, the political horizon was suddenly filled with expectations of radical social reforms.

Although the general strike was largely a non-violent process, it produced considerable restlessness in south-western Häme. As communications were halted during the strike days, rural inhabitants suffered a news blackout and were thus left with only a vague understanding of the strike aims. This created favourable circumstances for rumours to resurface.[47] The press reported on tenants who grumbled 'that in Russia the land has been taken away from the rich and divided equally among the poor, and the same will happen here as well'.[48] Newspapers also noted that agitators were on the move in Häme again, luring landless people with promises of land redistribution.[49] Such reports indicate that the strike with its prospects of democracy and societal change inspired the rural

Illustration 7.2 Members of Honkola workers' association standing around their workers' hall in 1908. The Honkola workers' association (established in 1906) was one of the largest workers' associations in south-western Häme. Most of its members were tenant farmers and agricultural workers of the manor of Honkola. This particular manor and the workers' association inspired Väinö Linna in his novel *Under the North Star*. Linna was born in Honkola region. Courtesy of Alpo Hietanen.

poor to highlight the importance of landownership reforms and to apply pressure on the authorities once more through rumour-spreading.

During the following months, however, the rumours of the landless people gave way to a different kind of mobilization. In south-western Häme, like elsewhere in Finland, the membership of local socialist associations multiplied: by the end of 1906, as many as thirty-four workers' associations with 3,800 members existed in the region. This meant that more than one in ten adults had joined the SDP. Women, who had previously been all but missing from rural workers' associations, also now enrolled.[50] The enthusiasm for organization was due primarily to the suffrage reform. This reform would apparently bring within reach all of the social reforms yearned for by the landless once the unicameral Parliament started its work. In this atmosphere, the Social Democrats seemed to the landless to be the political group most able to realize the dreamed-of reforms in Parliament.

In the first parliamentary election with universal and equal suffrage in 1907, the SDP gained 37 per cent of the ballot in Finland. South-western Häme was the strongest area of support for socialism, with the Social Democrats winning 64 per cent of the regional vote. In the parish of Humppila, no less than 84 per cent of voters backed the socialists, and in the former strike areas of Jokioinen and Ypäjä, the socialists verged on 80 per cent of the vote.[51] These huge percentages imply that not only agricultural workers but also most tenant farmers aligned themselves with the SDP. Despite considerable differences in social position, both these rural groups were essentially connected by political subjugation and hunger for land, which made them responsive to the socialists' promise of radical reform. Yet the appeal of socialism in the Finnish countryside also owed much to the inefficiency of the other parties in addressing the land question. In this respect, the situation differed from Sweden, Norway and Denmark, where the liberals competed successfully for the support of the rural proletariat.[52]

Conclusion

Imperial integration policies turned south-western Häme into a battlefield of various agitators at the turn of the twentieth century. First, Finnish nationalist activists descended upon the countryside, striving to awaken national consciousness and quell pernicious rumours among the rural population. Second, a number of diverse advocates of landless people emerged to write up petitions and denunciations to the imperial government, thus representing a counterforce to nationalist agitation.

These land agitators blatantly capitalized on the conflict between the Russian regime and the Finnish nationalists while presenting themselves as landless people's spokespersons vis-à-vis the local dominant groups.

Finally, the rural population also encountered socialist agitators, who represented the SDP and its local branches. Many of the socialist activists sympathized with Constitutional nationalism and, at least officially, disdained the land redistribution rumours cherished by the agrarian lower class. Nonetheless, they appealed successfully to the very people who seemed the most resilient to the nationalist agenda and the most inclined to tsarism. Amid the political turmoil, socialists managed to convince the landless that it was not the imperial government that would help them; instead, agricultural workers and tenants could improve their conditions only by organizing and voting for the Social Democrats.

As this chapter has shown, several indications of landless people's discontent preceded the rise of the socialist labour movement in Häme. The discontent presented itself, for example, in the persistent rumours about the forthcoming Russian law and in the letters sent to Bobrikov's government. These expressions of discontent remained, however, too disconnected and fickle to imply the formation of a homogenous 'social movement' among the unlanded. It was only with the support of socialist labour organizations that landless people's campaigning became consistent, organized and programmatic, thus adopting the distinctive features of a social movement in the sense defined by Charles Tilly.[53]

Despite this organization, one can question altogether the meaningfulness of squeezing the rural protests of the turn of the twentieth century into the mould of a distinct movement. As Katrina Navickas argues, the new histories of collective action avoid reducing the complexities of collective actions to class-based 'riots' or 'movements'. Rather, these histories elucidate the geographically specific patterns of social conflict by stressing the constant negotiations, tensions and ambiguities involved in protest events.[54] As this chapter has illustrated, landless people's protests intertwined with imperial integration policies, nationalism and socialism in complex ways that cannot be grasped by confining oneself to the views of state officials and party elites. Instead, one needs to focus on local events and individual actors, who, despite belonging to the same 'class' or participating in the same collective actions, may have situated themselves in a very unorthodox way in relation to the political currents. Although the voices of the rank-and-file participants in protest events are often hard to recover, hints of their ideas can be found; for example, by tracing the rumours that spread in their local communities.

The specificity of the political struggle discussed in this chapter can be highlighted, for example, by contrasting it with the attempts of the

Swedish Social Democrats to unionize agricultural workers in Skåne at the beginning of the twentieth century. There, the Social Democrats resorted to a radical nationalist agenda to fight against the import of cheap labour from the Austrian province of Galicia.[55] In those circumstances the socialists apparently considered patriotic discourse essential in appealing to the rural working class. In south-western Häme, however, the reverse was true; the socialists confronted a rural proletariat who regarded Finnish nationalism with suspicion and looked to the Tsar for land reform. Nonetheless, the Social Democrats' ability to address the land question plausibly became their vehicle for introducing a socialist and nationalist discourse to the rural labouring classes of Häme.

The success of the Finnish socialists among the rural population had huge consequences; it helped the SDP gain a solid foothold in the Finnish political system from 1905. In fact, partly owing to the subsequent inability of Parliament to solve the land question, the Social Democrats were able to strengthen their agrarian support up until the revolutions of 1917–18. Not even the Civil War of 1918 – in which casualties were particularly high among the rural workers of south-western Häme – significantly dented the appeal of the socialist movement in the countryside. Thus, agrarian socialism proved to be a strikingly persistent phenomenon that characterized the political culture of Finland to an exceptional degree even by Nordic standards.

Sami Suodenjoki is a historian and postdoctoral researcher at the University of Helsinki. He currently works in the project *Fragmented Visions: Performance, Authority and Interaction in Early-Twentieth-Century Finnish Oral-Literary Traditions*, funded by the Academy of Finland (2014–17). Suodenjoki is also a member of the Finnish Centre of Excellence in Historical Research at the University of Tampere. His research interests include agrarian protests, popular organization and the interplay between citizens and the state in late nineteenth and early twentieth century Finland.

Notes

1. *'He nimittäin yhä vieläkin uskovat, että jos Bobrikoff olisi saanut elää ja jatkaa toimintaansa, olisi hän pannut toimeen maitten ja tavarain tasauksen, s.o.: olisi ottanut rikkailta ja antanut köyhille. Tällaista mielettömyyttä ei kyllä ilmennyt muualla kuin niissä paikoissa, joissa ei lueta mitään, mutta sellaisia paikkoja, Jumala paratkoon, on olemassa vielä tavattoman paljon'.* Y. Mäkelin. 1904. 'Kertomus matkasta Ruoveden ja Virtain pitäjissä kesä- ja heinäkuun ajalla v. 1904', Arvid Neovius' archive, folder 24. National Archives of Finland (NA).

2. J. Heikkilä. 1993. *Kansallista luokkapolitiikkaa: Sosiaalidemokraatit ja Suomen autonomian puolustus 1905–1917*, Helsinki: SHS; A. Kujala. 1989. *Vallankumous ja kansallinen itsemääräämisoikeus: Venäjän sosialistiset puolueet ja suomalainen radikalismi vuosisadan alussa*, Helsinki: SHS; A. Kujala. 1995. *Venäjän hallitus ja Suomen työväenliike 1899–1905*, Helsinki: SHS.

3. R. Alapuro. 1998. *State and Revolution in Finland*, Berkeley: University of California Press, 110–14; T. Polvinen. 1995. *Imperial Borderland: Bobrikov and the Attempted Russification of Finland, 1898–1904*, London: Hurst, 232–34; H. Soikkanen. 1961. *Sosialismin tulo Suomeen*, Porvoo: WSOY, 131–37.

4. For example, R. Alapuro. 1994. *Suomen synty paikallisena ilmiönä 1890–1933*, Helsinki: Hanki ja jää.

5. E. Jutikkala. 1977. 'Laittomat asevelvollisuuskysymys ja torpparikysymys', in T. Rantanen (ed.), *Historiantutkijan sana: Maisterista akateemikoksi*, Helsinki: SHS, 183–93; C.L. Lundin. 1981. 'Finland', in E.C. Thaden (ed.), *Russification in the Baltic Provinces and Finland, 1855–1914*, Princeton: Princeton University Press, 430–31.

6. Alapuro, *State and Revolution*, 117; D. Kirby. 1989. 'The Labour Movement', in M. Engman and D. Kirby (eds), *Finland: People, Nation, State*, London: Hurst, 196. So far, the most extensive accounts on the rise of agrarian socialism in Finland are included in V. Rasila. 1961. *Suomen torpparikysymys vuoteen 1909*, Helsinki: SHS, 1961; Soikkanen, *Sosialismin tulo Suomeen*.

7. The district includes the parishes of Akaa, Humppila, Jokioinen, Kalvola, Kylmäkoski, Somerniemi, Somero, Sääksmäki, Tammela, Urjala and Ypäjä.

8. The term 'tenant farmer' refers to a person who leased a plot of land from a landlord for a fixed period and paid an annual rent for it by labour or in cash. The tenant farmers encompass both leaseholders of a minor part of a farm *(torppari)* and a smaller number of tenants who held a whole farm *(lampuoti)*. In the English-language literature on Finnish history, *torppari* (cf. Swedish *torpare*) is usually translated as 'crofter', a term with a Scottish origin. However, this translation gives a misleading impression of the position of Finnish tenant farmers, who typically had more productive land than Scottish crofters. In fact, with regards to subsistence, the Scottish crofter was often closer to a Finnish 'cottager' *(mäkitupalainen)*, who occupied a cottage under tenure in return for labour but usually did not have enough arable land for subsistence farming.

9. H. Gebhard. 1913. *Maanviljelysväestö, sen suhde muihin elinkeinoryhmiin ja sen yhteiskunnallinen kokoonpano Suomen maalaiskunnissa v. 1901. Tilattoman väestön alakomitea. I*, Helsinki; Keisarillinen senaatti, table 2; Alapuro, *State and Revolution*, 43–47, 70–74. See also S. Heikkinen. 1997. *Labour and the Market: Workers, Wages and Living Standards in Finland, 1850–1913*, Helsinki: The Finnish Society of Sciences and Letters, 45–49.

10. Gebhard, *Maanviljelysväestö*, table 2; E. Jutikkala. 1969. 'Väestö teollistumisen alkuvaiheessa', in E. Jutikkala et al. (eds), *Hämeen historia* IV:1, Hämeenlinna: Hämeen Heimoliitto, 8–74: 58, 67; Alapuro, *State and Revolution*, 43–47, 70–74; M. Morell. 2011. 'Agriculture in Industrial Society, 1870–1945', in J. Myrdal and M. Morell (eds), *The Agrarian History of Sweden*, Lund: Nordic Academic Press, 169–78.

11. S.D. Huxley. 1990. *Constitutionalist Insurgency in Finland*, Helsinki: SHS, 145–47; Polvinen, *Imperial Borderland*, 82–84; A. Kujala. 2005. 'Finland in 1905', in J.D. Smele and A. Heywood (eds), *The Russian Revolution of 1905*, London: Routledge, 82–83; P. Tommila. 1999. *Suuri adressi*, Porvoo: WSOY, 153–56, 292.

12. M. Peltonen. 1992. *Talolliset ja torpparit*, Helsinki: SHS, 258–59; Tommila, *Suuri adressi*, 154–55, 159; S. Halkosaari. 1972. 'Etelä-Häme ja allekirjoitetut vastalauseadressit vuosina 1899–1901', MA dissertation, University of Tampere, 24–25.

13. V. Linna. 1959. *Täällä Pohjantähden alla* I, Porvoo: WSOY, 171–83.

14. M. Grönqvist, 'Viime vuoden tapahtumia', 1900, manuscript, 2:1–3, 3:1. Matilda Grönqvist's archive. Finnish Literature Society – Literary Archives; V. Lindholm, 'Elämän

raunioilla', 1909, letter. Archive of Urjala Workers' Association. Finnish Labour Archives (FLA).

15. K.J. Ståhlberg. 1899. *Berättelse om verkstäld undersökning angående utspridande af falska rykten i landet*, Helsingfors: Kejserliga Senaten, 3–6; S. Suodenjoki. 2010. *Kuriton suutari ja kiistämisen rajat: Työväenliikkeen läpimurto hämäläisessä maalaisyhteisössä 1899–1909*, Helsinki: SKS, 96–97.

16. A.A. Yang. 1987. 'A Conversation of Rumors: The Language of Popular Mentalités in Late Nineteenth-Century Colonial India', *Journal of Social History* 20(3), 485.

17. T. Johnston. 2011. *Being Soviet: Identity, Rumour, and Everyday Life under Stalin 1939–1953*, Oxford: Oxford University Press, xxxii–xxxiv; L. Viola. 1996. *Peasant Rebels under Stalin*, New York: Oxford University Press, 45–46; E.A. Aytekin. 2012. 'Peasant Protest in the Late Ottoman Empire: Moral Economy, Revolt, and the Tanzimat Reforms', *International Review of Social History* 57(2), 223–27.

18. Rasila, *Suomen torpparikysymys*, 139–43; Ståhlberg, *Berättelse om verkstäld undersökning*, 5. On land redistribution rumours in Russia see, for example, D. Field. 1976. *Rebels in the Name of the Tsar*, Boston: Houghton Mifflin, 24, 122–27.

19. 'Tietoja maanjakohuhuista', *Päivälehti*, 16 May 1899, 2.

20. H. Immonen. 1992. '"Kun Venäjän laki tulee" – sivistyneistö, kansa ja helmikuun manifesti', *Historiallinen Aikakauskirja* 90(2), 120–25; Tommila, *Suuri adressi*, 247–48.

21. Peltonen, *Talolliset ja torpparit*, 262–63; Suodenjoki, *Kuriton suutari*, 98–99.

22. A. Nieminen to Bobrikov, January and March 1900. D: Toiminta-asiakirjat. Artur Kniper's archive. NA.

23. Suodenjoki, *Kuriton suutari*, 103.

24. Suodenjoki, *Kuriton suutari*, 105–6.

25. 'Surkeinta kuitenkin on, että paitsi näitä niin sanoakseni maltillisempia torppareita on pitäjässä suuri joukko sellaisia, jotka elävät tuon kultaisen maan jaon toiveissa ... Heidän johtajanaan on virasta erotettu lukkari Erlund sekä torppari Nieminen. Nämä molemmat herrat harjoittavat suoranaista kiihotusta ... Rahoja lähetetään heille säännöllisesti Helsingistä, jossa muuten itsekin käyvät usein vierailemassa. Mainittakoon heidän toiminnastaan vielä, että viime kesänä jo olivat tuoneet santarmeja mukanaan muutamaan raamatunselitykseen. Niemisen tehtäväksi näyttää sitäpaitsi kulkukauppiaitten vaaliminen annettaneen. Niinpä kertoivat, että siellä kerrankin oli ollut hänen luonaan heitä 18 yhdellä kertaa'*. E. Laine and V. Bonsdorff, 'Kertomus Hämäläis-osakunnan kansanvalistusvaliokunnan toimeenpanemista luentokursseista Kalvolan ja Sääksmäen pitäjissä joululomalla 1900', 1901. Hd1: Kansanvalistus. Archive of Hämäläis-Osakunta. National Library of Finland – Manuscript Collection.

26. Cf. Peltonen, *Talolliset ja torpparit*, 264–65.

27. A. Nieminen to Bobrikov, 18 November 1901. Archive of the Chancery of the Governor General (KKK) 1902, section I, delo 13. NA; 'Tuhottavia papereita', *Tampereen Sanomat*, 12 November 1905, 2–3.

28. For petitions transcribed by Erlund see, for example, H. Lindgrén to Bobrikov, 9 June 1904. KKK 1904, section V, delo 27:103. NA; J. Kuusniemi to Obolenski, 14 August 1904. KKK 1904, section V, delo 27:186. NA.

29. 'Urjala', *Tampereen Sanomat*, 29 December 1905, 2–3; 'Petkuttajako liikkeellä?', *Aamulehti*, 30 December 1905, 2.

30. For example, J. Lehtonen to Bobrikov, 16 August 1902. KKK 1902, section I, delo 56. NA; K.O. Jalonen and H. Lindgrén to Bobrikov, 8 May 1903. KKK 1903, section V, delo 61. NA.

31. I. Hakalehto. 1979. 'Valtiolliset vaalit ja poliittiset puolueet', in E. Jutikkala et al. (eds), *Hämeen historia* IV:3, Hämeenlinna: Hämeen Heimoliitto, 258–72; Kujala, 'Finland in 1905', 84.

32. For example, O. Mäkilä to Bobrikov, 9 February 1904. KKK 1904, section V, delo 27:I. NA; H. Lindgrén to Bobrikov, 9 June 1904. KKK 1904, section V, delo 27:103. NA. See also S. Suodenjoki. 2014. 'Whistleblowing from Below: Finnish Rural Inhabitants' Letters to the Imperial Power at the Turn of the Twentieth Century', in A.C. Edlund, L.E. Edlund and S. Haugen (eds), *Vernacular Literacies: Past, Present and Future*, Umeå: Umeå University Press, 284–89.

33. V. Lindholm to Bobrikov, 24 March 1903, 26 March 1903, 29 March 1903 and 30 March 1903. KKK 1903, section I, delo 78:7. NA.

34. Suodenjoki, *Kuriton suutari*, 200–1.

35. Suodenjoki, *Kuriton suutari*, 199–203; E.I. Parmanen. 1941. *Taistelujen kirja IV*, Porvoo: Werner Söderström, 405.

36. V. Lindholm, 'Elämän raunioilla', 1909, letter. Archive of Urjala Workers' Association. FLA.

37. S. Suodenjoki and J. Peltola. 2007. *Köyhä Suomen kansa katkoo kahleitansa*, Tampere: Tampere University Press, 71–72, 130–31; Suodenjoki, *Kuriton suutari*, 128–31.

38. For example, records of regular affairs in Urjala and Akaa court district, 23 March 1904, § 16. Archive of Tammela jurisdiction. Provincial Archive of Häme; Suodenjoki, *Kuriton suutari*, 140–44. For woodland infractions as an indication of peasant resistance see C. Frías Corredor. 2007. 'Disputes, Protest and Forms of Resistance in Rural Areas: Huesca, 1880–1914', in J.A. Piqueras and V. Sanz Rozalén (eds), *A Social History of Spanish Labour*, Oxford: Berghahn Books, 209, 217.

39. Soikkanen, *Sosialismin tulo Suomeen*, 124–30; G. Callesen. 1990. 'Denmark', in M. van der Linden and J. Rojahn (eds), *The Formation of Labour Movements 1870–1914*, I, Leiden: E.J. Brill, 147–48; A. Thörnquist. 1989. *Lönearbete eller egen jord? Den svenska lantarbetarrörelsen och jordfrågan 1908–1936*, Uppsala: Uppsala University, 59–60; F. Sejersted. 2011. *The Age of Social Democracy: Norway and Sweden in the Twentieth Century*, Princeton: Princeton University Press, 132–35. For the evolvement of the agrarian programme of the SDP see P. Jussila. 2014. *Tilastomies torpparien asialla*, Tampere: THPTS, 94–194.

40. Rasila, *Suomen torpparikysymys*, 258–63, 271–79.

41. 'Maalaistyöväestölle', *Kansan Lehti*, 14 July 1903, 1–2; Rasila, *Suomen torpparikysymys*, 268–79.

42. Statistics of the Labour Party/SDP (Puoluetilasto) 1900–1907. FLA; Soikkanen, *Sosialismin tulo Suomeen*, 196–98, 203–5; Suodenjoki, *Kuriton suutari*, 163, 171–83.

43. P. Kettunen. 1986. *Poliittinen liike ja sosiaalinen kollektiivisuus*, Helsinki: SHS, 60.

44. '… työväenliike on maanjakojuttujen aiheuttaja ja levittäjä'. 'Työväenliikettä häväisty', *Kansan Lehti*, 28 May 1904, 1–2.

45. 'Hyljättävä tapa', *Kansan Lehti*, 7 May 1904, 1.

46. See chapter 8.

47. S. Suodenjoki. 2008. 'Suurlakon riitaisa yksimielisyys', in P. Haapala et al. (eds), *Kansa kaikkivaltias. Suurlakko Suomessa 1905*, Helsinki: Teos, 111–14.

48. 'He kertovat, miten Venäjälläkin muka on rikkailta otettu maa pois ja jaettu tasan köyhille ja sama asia on tekeillä täälläkin'. 'Maanjakoasia kummittelee', *Aamulehti*, 30 November 1905, 3.

49. For example, 'Urjala', *Tampereen Sanomat*, 29 December 1905, 2–3.

50. Puoluetilasto 1904–1906. FLA; Halkosaari, 'Etelä-Häme', 135; Suodenjoki, *Kuriton suutari*, 220.

51. Suomen Virallinen Tilasto XXIX, Vaalitilasto 1 (1907), table II.

52. B. Simonson. 1990. 'Sweden', in M. van der Linden and J. Rojahn (eds), *The Formation of Labour Movements 1870–1914*, I, Leiden: E.J. Brill, 99–100; E.A. Terjesen. 1990. 'Norway', in M. van der Linden and J. Rojahn (eds), *The Formation of Labour Movements 1870–1914*, I, Leiden: E.J. Brill, 117–18; Callesen, 'Denmark', 144–52; Sejersted, *The Age of Social Democracy*, 103–5.

53. C. Tilly. 2004. *Social Movements, 1768–2004*, Boulder: Paradigm, 3–4, 7, 13.
54. K. Navickas. 2011. 'What Happened to Class? New Histories of Labour and Collective Action in Britain', *Social History* 36(2), 197.
55. L. Olsson. 2009. 'From Galicia to Sweden: Seasonal Labour Migration and the Ethnic Division of Labour at the IFÖ Kaolin-Works in the Early Twentieth Century', in A. Steidl et al. (eds), *European Mobility*, Göttingen: V&R unipress, 44–45.

References

Alapuro, R. 1994. *Suomen synty paikallisena ilmiönä 1890–1933*, Helsinki: Hanki ja jää.

———. 1998. *State and Revolution in Finland*, Berkeley: University of California Press.

Aytekin, E.A. 2012. 'Peasant Protest in the Late Ottoman Empire: Moral Economy, Revolt, and the Tanzimat Reforms', *International Review of Social History* 57(2), 191–27.

Callesen, G. 'Denmark', in M. van der Linden and J. Rojahn (eds), *The Formation of Labour Movements 1870–1914*, Leiden: E.J. Brill, 1990, 131–60.

Field, D. 1976. *Rebels in the Name of the Tsar*, Boston: Houghton Mifflin.

Frías Corredor, C. 'Disputes, Protest and Forms of Resistance in Rural Areas. Huesca, 1880–1914', in J.A. Piqueras and V. Sanz Rozalén (eds), *A Social History of Spanish Labour*, Oxford: Berghahn Books, 2007, 197–220.

Gebhard, H. 1913. *Maanviljelysväestö, sen suhde muihin elinkeinoryhmiin ja sen yhteiskunnallinen kokoonpano Suomen maalaiskunnissa v. 1901: Tilattoman väestön alakomitea*, Helsinki: Keisarillinen senaatti.

Hakalehto, I. 'Valtiolliset vaalit ja poliittiset puolueet', in E. Jutikkala et al. (eds), *Hämeen historia* IV:3, Hämeenlinna: Hämeen Heimoliitto, 1979, 169–417.

Halkosaari, S. 1972. 'Etelä-Häme ja allekirjoitetut vastalauseadressit vuosina 1899–1901', MA dissertation, Tampere: University of Tampere.

Heikkilä, J. 1993. *Kansallista luokkapolitiikkaa: Sosiaalidemokraatit ja Suomen autonomian puolustus 1905–1917*, Helsinki: SHS.

Heikkinen, S. 1997. *Labour and the Market: Workers, Wages and Living Standards in Finland, 1850–1913*, Helsinki: The Finnish Society of Sciences and Letters.

Huxley, S.D. 1990. *Constitutionalist Insurgency in Finland*, Helsinki: SHS.

Immonen, H. 1992. '"Kun Venäjän laki tulee" – sivistyneistö, kansa ja helmikuun manifesti', *Historiallinen Aikakauskirja* 90(2), 117–27.

Johnston, T. 2011. *Being Soviet: Identity, Rumour, and Everyday Life under Stalin 1939–1953*, Oxford: Oxford University Press.

Jussila, P. 2014. *Tilastomies torpparien asialla: Edvard Gyllingin maatalouspoliittinen ajattelu ja toiminta suurlakon ja sisällissodan välissä*, Tampere: THPTS.

Jutikkala, E. 'Väestö teollistumisen alkuvaiheessa', in E. Jutikkala et al. (eds), *Hämeen historia* IV:1, Hämeenlinna: Hämeen Heimoliitto, 1969, 8–74.

———. 'Laittomat asevelvollisuuskysymys ja torpparikysymys', in T. Rantanen (ed.), *Historiantutkijan sana: Maisterista akateemikoksi*, Helsinki: SHS, 1977, 183–93.

Kettunen, P. 1986. *Poliittinen liike ja sosiaalinen kollektiivisuus: Tutkimus sosialide-mokratiasta ja ammattiyhdistysliikkeestä Suomessa 1918–1930*, Helsinki: SHS.

Kirby, D. 'The Labour Movement', in M. Engman and D. Kirby (eds), *Finland: People, Nation, State*, London: Hurst, 1989, 193–211.

Kujala, A. 1989. *Vallankumous ja kansallinen itsemääräämisoikeus: Venäjän sosialistiset puolueet ja suomalainen radikalismi vuosisadan alussa*, Helsinki: SHS.

———. 1995. *Venäjän hallitus ja Suomen työväenliike 1899–1905*, Helsinki: SHS.

———. 'Finland in 1905', in J.D. Smele and A. Heywood (eds), *The Russian Revolution of 1905: Centenary Perspectives*, London: Routledge, 2005, 79–93.

Linna, V. 1959. *Täällä Pohjantähden alla*, Porvoo: WSOY.

Lundin, C.L. 1981. 'Finland', in E.C. Thaden (ed.), *Russification in the Baltic Provinces and Finland, 1855–1914*, Princeton: Princeton University Press, 355–457.

Morell, M. 'Agriculture in Industrial Society, 1870–1945', in J. Myrdal and M. Morell (eds), *The Agrarian History of Sweden*, Lund: Nordic Academic Press, 2011, 165–213.

Navickas, K. 2011. 'What Happened to Class? New Histories of Labour and Collective Action in Britain', *Social History* 36(2), 192–204.

Olsson, L. 'From Galicia to Sweden: Seasonal Labour Migration and the Ethnic Division of Labour at the IFÖ Kaolin-Works in the Early Twentieth Century', in A. Steidl et al. (eds), *European Mobility*, Göttingen: V&R unipress, 2009, 39–49.

Parmanen, E.I. 1941. *Taistelujen kirja* IV, Porvoo: Werner Söderström.

Peltonen, M. 1992. *Talolliset ja torpparit: Vuosisadan vaihteen maatalouskysymys Suomessa*, Helsinki: SHS.

Polvinen, T. 1995. *Imperial Borderland: Bobrikov and the Attempted Russification of Finland, 1898–1904*, London: Hurst.

Rasila, V. 1961. *Suomen torpparikysymys vuoteen 1909*, Helsinki: SHS.

Sejersted, F. 2011. *The Age of Social Democracy: Norway and Sweden in the Twentieth Century*, Princeton: Princeton University Press.

Simonson, B. 'Sweden', in M. van der Linden and J. Rojahn (eds), *The Formation of Labour Movements 1870–1914*, Leiden: E.J. Brill, 1990, 85–102.

Soikkanen, H. 1961. *Sosialismin tulo Suomeen*, Porvoo: WSOY.

Ståhlberg, K.J. 1899. *Berättelse om verkställd undersökning angående utspridande af falska rykten i landet*, Helsingfors: Kejserliga Senaten.

Suodenjoki, S. 'Suurlakon riitaisa yksimielisyys', in P. Haapala et al. (eds), *Kansa kaikkivaltias. Suurlakko Suomessa 1905*, Helsinki: Teos, 2008, 101–20.

———. 2010. *Kuriton suutari ja kiistämisen rajat: Työväenliikkeen läpimurto hämäläisessä maalaisyhteisössä 1899–1909*, Helsinki: SKS.

———. 'Whistleblowing from Below: Finnish Rural Inhabitants' Letters to the Imperial Power at the Turn of the Twentieth Century', in A.C. Edlund, L.E. Edlund and S. Haugen (eds), *Vernacular Literacies – Past, Present and Future*, Umeå: Umeå University Press, 2014, 279–93.

Suodenjoki, S. and J. Peltola. 2007. *Köyhä Suomen kansa katkoo kahleitansa: Luokka, liike ja yhteiskunta 1880–1918*, Tampere: Tampere University Press.

Suomen Virallinen Tilasto XXIX. Vaalitilasto 1, 1907.

Terjesen, E.A. 'Norway', in M. van der Linden and J. Rojahn (eds), *The Formation of Labour Movements 1870–1914*, Leiden: E.J. Brill, 1990, 103–30.
Thörnquist, A. 1989. *Lönearbete eller egen jord? Den svenska lantarbetarrörelsen och jordfrågan 1908–1936*, Uppsala: Uppsala University.
Tilly, C. 2004. *Social Movements, 1768–2004*, Boulder: Paradigm.
Tommila, P. 1999. *Suuri adressi*, Porvoo: WSOY.
Viola, L. 1996. *Peasant Rebels under Stalin*, New York: Oxford University Press.
Yang, A.A. 1987. 'A Conversation of Rumors: The Language of Popular Mentalités in Late Nineteenth-Century Colonial India', *Journal of Social History* 20(3), 485–505.

Newspapers

Aamulehti
Kansan Lehti
Päivälehti
Tampereen Sanomat

Archival Sources

Finnish Labour Archives (FLA)
    Archive of Urjala Workers' Association
    Statistics of the Labour Party/SDP (Puoluetilasto) 1900–1907
Finnish Literature Society – Literary Archives
    Matilda Grönqvist's archive
National Archives of Finland (NA)
    Artur Kniper's archive, D: Toiminta-asiakirjat Arvid Neovius' archive, Folder 24
Archive of the Chancery of the Governor-General (KKK)
National Library of Finland – Manuscript Collection
    Archive of Hämäläis-Osakunta, Hd1: Kansanvalistus
Provincial Archive of Häme
    Archive of Tammela jurisdiction, Records of regular affairs 1904

CHAPTER 8

STRIKE IN FINLAND, REVOLUTION IN RUSSIA

The Role of Workers in the 1905 General Strike in the Grand Duchy of Finland

Marko Tikka

In October and November 1905, a general strike halted all of the Russian Empire. Russia's rural civil servants, urban bourgeoisie and the organized working population went on strike with the aim of breaking the autocratic, corrupt and petrified regime of Tsar Nicholas II.[1] The strike movement spread to the Empire's non-Russian areas, including the Grand Duchy of Finland. In Finnish historiography the events related to the Russian revolution of 1905 are referred to as a general strike, not a revolution.[2]

In Finland, the central accomplishment of the general strike was the 1906 suffrage reform that gave suffrage to men and women. Finland was among the very first nations in the world to adopt universal suffrage. But this was not the key motive for Finnish participation in the strike, nor was it seen as the most important accomplishment, either in contemporary writing or the subsequent decades of historiography on the strike. Why was this the case? One answer to this question concerns the role of the Finnish labour movement in the events of the strike in the Grand Duchy.

This chapter describes the activities of Finnish organized labour and illustrates the psychological significance of those activities for the Finnish labour movement. The chapter is based on a broader study that employed as its key sources texts produced during the general strike: minutes of political groups, manifestoes, notes and diaries. Domestic policy was the central factor determining how the strike was interpreted and also accounts for why the role of the workers in the strike was neglected for such a long time.[3]

The post-strike suffrage reform of 1906 gave the right to vote, first and foremost, to rural and industrial workers: the biggest population group left out of the assembly of the representatives of the estates (hereafter assembly) in the Grand Duchy of Finland. This group was politically well organized to an exceptional degree by 1906, although most individuals belonging to it had no right to vote in municipal or state elections.[4] The strategies this group employed to advocate for its goals and the emergence of political power based on numbers played a decisive role in the formation of the labour movement's organizational culture in the Grand Duchy of Finland in the beginning of the twentieth century.

In contemporary interpretations of the great strike as well as in later historical interpretations, the role and objectives of the labour movement have long remained marginal. The key reason for this was the interpretation emphasizing the national importance of the strike. In the opinion of those who wrote the history of the strike, it was above all a struggle for national rights. For a long time the events of the 1905 general strike in the Grand Duchy were portrayed in the Finnish historical interpretation as a reaction to the strike in the motherland Russia, but also as an action with Finnish national objectives. In this interpretation, the central background for the objectives and demands of the strike was seen to be the period preceding the general strike: the so-called first period of oppression when the motherland Russia sought to create an integrated administration between Russia and the Grand Duchy of Finland.

In February 1899, the Russian Emperor Nicholas II had issued a manifesto to Finland, which, from the Finnish perspective, trod roughshod over the country's rights. When Russia took Finland from Sweden in 1809, it left the Swedish laws of the country intact. During the nineteenth century, the Grand Duchy of Finland developed as an autonomous unit within the Russian Empire. The integration policy of the Russian Empire that started in the 1890s and the manifesto delivered to Finland in February 1899 interrupted this development.[5] When the Russo-Japanese War of 1904–5 temporarily weakened the Russian Empire, the long-simmering opposition in Russia rose to demand civil rights and a democratic regime. The Grand Duchy of Finland also joined the strike and demanded the restoration of the 'lawful conditions' that had preceded the February Manifesto.[6]

In this respect 'the people' meant the groups represented in the assembly – the nobility, the clergy, the bourgeoisie and the landowning farmers – and the struggle for the rights of these people. At the time, the labour movement and its demands did not fit well into the interpretation of a joint effort for 'all of Finland' and 'all Finns'. Rather, the labour movement has been seen as a troublemaker: instead of joining the common cause, it endangered the success of the 1905 general strike by pressing its own demands. This interpretation has its purposes. In Finnish historiography, the motives of the general strike were long viewed through the interpretation of one contemporary group, the Constitutionalists. The intention was to sweep under the carpet the fact that from the Finns' point of view the strike also involved domestic policy: the power struggle between the political groups in the assembly and the labour movement. Since the 1960s, and especially in the 1980s, Finnish research has started to emphasize the role and importance of labour movement actions in regard to the suffrage issue. [7] At the same time, researchers have adopted a broader perspective in looking at Russia's administrative actions directed towards integration in the Grand Duchy. It has been observed that in terms of administration the Grand Duchy of Finland did not differ very much from other national territories in the Russian Empire,[8] but the country's labour movement, operating quite freely, was actually an exception in Russia. The Finnish labour movement had been constructed on the basis of civic education, and before the general strike it had tried to steer clear of the separatist movements opposing Russia's authority. In doing so it had gained more freedom to act in Finland than was the case in Russia's other autonomous territories or in Russia itself. [9] Simultaneously, on the very brink of the general strike, the labour movement had grown into an organization that encompassed all of the Grand Duchy. At the beginning of the twentieth century, the key objective of the labour movement, aside from improving working conditions, was to demand important political rights for the workers. At the turn of 1904–5 that goal had become almost an obsession for the labour movement.

The Working Population and the Right to Vote

The Tsar of Russia had given the Grand Duchy of Finland her own assembly of the representatives of the estates, which had convened regularly since the 1860s. The estates were quickly joined by political groups overlapping the borders between estates. Nevertheless, the estates chose their own representatives to the assembly. The population outside the estates increased rapidly in Finland, and by the 1880s pressures for suffrage reform started to grow. Suffrage reform had been on the agenda of the assembly since 1897, but for various reasons passage of the reform had been postponed from one assembly to another.[10]

Actually, all the political groups in the assembly – the Suometar party, the Swedish party, and the Young Finns – supported the extension of suffrage from their own respective points of view. The Suometar party wanted to weaken the link between suffrage and the ability to pay tax so that they could take over the bourgeois estate, at the time controlled by the Swedish party. The Swedish party needed to maintain some level of tax-paying ability as a factor restricting voting rights. The zeal of the Young Finns to extend suffrage to the lower classes diminished at the same pace as the labour movement strengthened as a political force.[11] The labour movement also began to reject the separatism promoted by the Young Finns and the Swedish party together as the so-called Constitutionalists. The labour movement considered universal suffrage to be the primary means of strengthening the position of the Finnish working class.

A proposal for suffrage reform was presented to the assembly in 1900, based on expanding the assembly voting rights. According to the proposal, all registered, municipal taxpaying males over twenty-five years of age should get suffrage in state elections. They would gain the right to elect their representatives only in the two lower estates – the burghers and the farmers.

The proposal was considered too narrow and a counterproposal was presented to the assembly: K.J. Ståhlberg and Antti Mikkola proposed the omission of restrictions based on property. At the same time, they proposed national suffrage for all independent men of sufficient age.[12] This proposal did not proceed in the assembly, either. The inflamed administrative situation in the Grand Duchy made things more difficult. A part of the Young Finns had begun to actively hinder the functioning of the assembly. In their minds, the most important issue was to get back the autonomous rights of the Grand Duchy that had been subverted ever since the manifesto of February 1899. In the spring of 1905 the assembly therefore had the alternatives of choosing between suffrage based on property or suffrage for all adult males, or postponing the issue for further consideration.

Demands for suffrage reform grew stronger and stronger within the labour movement, which adopted the name Sosialidemokraattinen Puolue (Social Democratic Party, SDP) at a meeting in Forssa in 1903. They considered the right to vote to be essential in terms of social reform.[13] They also started to promote lowering the voting age from twenty-five to twenty-one years of age, an important strategy since a significant portion of the population under twenty-five years of age belonged to the working class. About half of the working population was younger than twenty-five.[14] The assembly understood that lowering the suffrage age would turn the existing political system of a society based on estates into a political struggle between political parties and different estates.

During the spring of 1905 the workers' demonstrations for suffrage strengthened, and in mid April, while the estates were handling the suffrage issue, more than 15,000 demonstrators, agitated by the labour movement, demanded universal suffrage in front of the House of the Estates.[15] The proposed bill was not accepted, as the bourgeois estate postponed the issue to the next assembly. In the spring of 1905, the working population marched in support of suffrage reform in several inland towns. In North Oulu and in East Vyborg, the army intervened brutally.[16] No wonder the labour movement considered the Russian strike of October–November the 'final struggle', where this demand for suffrage and a new diet simply had to be made reality.

According to the interpretation of the political groups represented in the assembly, the most essential thing was to oppose the oppressive policy of Russia and its interventions in the position of autonomous Finland. Only after that would it become possible to change the political system. Even that had its different degrees: just before the general strike the Finnish government and Finnish opposition would struggle for power for the first time in Finland's history. The Finnish party sitting in government took a passive stance on resistance, while the Young Finns, who were in the opposition, demanded active resistance. On the suffrage issue there were also other factors not mentioned aloud: the political groups of the assembly considered the reform to have potentially unpredictable consequences. This was the domestic policy situation of the Grand Duchy of Finland at the outbreak of the general strike in the autumn of 1905.

The Strike Breaks Out

The railway network of the Grand Duchy of Finland started from the Finland station in St. Petersburg. Railways were the fastest way to transport people and ideas in the Finland of the first years of the twentieth century.[17] For the general strike the railway was important in many respects: the railway telegraph played a key role in spreading strike information, and the trains manned by strikers transported strike leaders swiftly from one locality to another when necessary, even though traffic was otherwise at a halt. The railways also played a key role in the success of the strike: when the trains did not move, the military could not quickly suppress unrest.[18]

When the strikes began in St. Petersburg, a delegation of Russian strikers came to the Finland railway station in St. Petersburg to demand that the Finnish railwaymen join the strike. Higher officials among the railway employees took a passive attitude, but railwaymen worked actively in support of the strike.[19] This division became apparent right from the start: the officials initially failed to respond but eventually agreed to support the strike, while the railway workers joined it immediately. The news about the strike was confirmed in Finland within days. On Saturday 28 October the railway engineering shopworkers of Vyborg, the Finnish town nearest to St. Petersburg, gathered at the workers' hall to join 'the great strike of Russian workers'.[20] This was a decisive step in the Grand Duchy's joining Russia's strike movement.

When the civil servants, transport workers and shopworkers went on strike, the strike committees that were formed by Finns immediately after they had heard about the action assumed key leadership positions. The strike committee in Helsinki, the capital of the Grand Duchy, had a special role. Unlike similar groups in many inland towns, the Helsinki workers' associations that took part in the strike did not cooperate with the strike committees formed by the groups of the assembly; instead, they pursued a totally separate policy from the beginning of the strike.[21]

The Helsinki strike committee was formed by the leaders of the city's workers' associations, the labour press and the associations of print workers and railway workers. [22] In practice, the Helsinki strike committee controlled the leadership of the organized labour movement and the Social Democratic Party. The strike committee had contacts with the network of workers' associations, the labour press, the trade union movement and activist workers. On the other hand, the members of the strike committee were quite unknown to the political groups of the assembly, the political elite of the Grand Duchy and the administration of the motherland Russia. Their names were known for their writings in the newspapers but they were not personally familiar. This was the strength and weakness of the central committee. It controlled a vast social movement but had no political know-how whatsoever.

To become part of the general staff of the workers' strike was a stunning experience for these men and women, twenty to thirty years of age, who had gained social experience mainly within the workers' associations. Messages and requests for instructions sent to the Helsinki strike committee from all around the country show that the general staff had to assume responsibility for the strike in the entire labour movement of the entire Grand Duchy. The strike committee adopted as its new name the central committee of the national strike.[23]

The minutes of the central committee meetings record the developing situation. The committee even prepared for revolution (its wildest hope), as a line crossed out from the minutes shows: '... it was decided that the former government be overthrown, a new temporary government elected, and to summon a constitutional national assembly on the basis of general franchise, and if things proceed, to remove the former government from power and to appoint a temporary government ...'.[24]

When the situation became clearer, the workers' strike committee sought to summon a national assembly to displace the assembly of the representatives of the estates and to select its members through universal suffrage. The labour leaders clearly understood the weakness of their position. Without a determined approach they would have no say in the negotiations between the parties of the assembly and the highest representative of Russian power, Finland's Governor General. Partly because of this political weakness, they adopted the strike tactics of the trade union movement. They forwarded hard demands in order to persuade the political groups of the assembly to meet them at least halfway.

The central committee of the national strike found out that they were also expected to maintain public order. When the urban police departments joined the strike, the strike committee set up its own peacekeeping police, the National Guard. In Helsinki, the National Guard boasted 6,450 men. Half of them formed patrols; the other half belonged to various police sub-districts and to the railway employees' own peacekeeping companies.[25] By the third day of the strike, all Helsinki police stations were manned by the National Guard.[26]

The strike committee had many motives for establishing the National Guard. Keeping the peace was the most important of them, but the strike committee also feared armed conflicts between the Finns and Russian militia during the strike. Such conflicts would look like a rebellion against the Russian regime, which would undoubtedly be brutally suppressed.[27] Because the National Guard was quite strongly controlled by labour organizations, it was also used as an instrument of pressure against other political groups as the strike progressed.

The Russian Military Presence in Finland

The Governor General acted as the Tsar's representative in Finland. He commanded the Russian military forces stationed in Finland and at the same time led the Grand Duchy's senate. Finland's own army, which had operated within the Russian army as an independent unit, had been suppressed in 1901. After that year, the military units stationed on Finnish territory consisted of Russian, non-Finnish soldiers. The troops in Finland formed the 22nd Army Corps, led by Lieutenant General Anton von Saltza, and included two sharpshooter brigades and dragoon regiments, a general staff, signals staff, service troops, a field gendarme squadron and a Cossack battalion. The troops were situated in southern Finland, mainly in the three important towns of Helsinki, Vyborg and Hämeenlinna, with only small detachments stationed elsewhere in the country. The Army Corps had its headquarters in Helsinki; in addition, part of the sharp-shooter brigade and nearly 400 cavalry were stationed there.[28]

As in Russia in general, the military units were too dispersed and too small to control the unrest at the beginning of the strike.[29] Furthermore, the troops stationed in Finland lacked the experience of their counter-parts stationed in Russia in dispersing crowds.[30] For this reason the troops observed the development of the strike remarkably peacefully, viewed from the Finnish point of view.[31] Only in Vyborg, the town closest to St. Petersburg, did the Russian soldiers intervene in the strike by disarming the Vyborg National Guard.[32] This action took place without bloodshed, and the troops only detained individuals belonging to the strike leader-ship for a short time. The Army Corps commander Saltza later observed that the regime of the motherland was in the hands of his armed troops for almost the whole duration of the strike.[33]

The slackness of administration during the strike week resulted more from the mutual discord among the Russians than from the Finnish strik-ers. The army commander Saltza considered Governor General Obolenski a weak and undependable civil servant, not a soldier. Saltza, as well as a significant part of the Governor General's office staff, had been loyal to the heavy-handed former Governor General N.I. Bobrikov, who had been murdered in June 1904.[34] Trying to avoid the fate of his prede-cessor, Obolenski behaved more diplomatically towards the Finnish civil servants, and Saltza and many others regarded his actions as too lenient.

It seems that at no point did the military leadership consider the work-ers a threat; rather, it viewed as dangerous the Swedish-speaking and con-stitutional elite and small separatist groups operating in Finland.[35] Saltza's interpretation of the situation obviously proved quite accurate.

The Governor General and the Manifesto

The Finnish senate, controlled by the Suometar party and supportive of Nicholas II, resigned after the general strike broke out in Finland. At the same time, the strike in the motherland had already succeeded. On 30 October Nicholas II issued a manifesto in Vyborg, granting the citizens of the motherland a Parliament and civil rights. The general strike in Finland was only just beginning.

Governor General Obolenski summoned the councillor of state J.R. Danielson, Chancellor of Helsinki University, along with one of the Suometar party leaders and Baron R.A. Wrede, the Constitutionalist rector of Helsinki University, to a meeting. Obolenski explained the political situation in Russia and Finland.[36] The Governor General gave a mandate to both the opposition party Constitutionalists and the leaders of the Suometar-controlled senate to start constructing a manifesto to make the situation in Finland easier. The manifesto would be given a few days later as an Imperial Manifesto. Obolenski calculated that, in order to control these groups, he would have to be able to negotiate first and foremost with the government and the opposition – that is, the Suometar Party and the Constitutional Party. Obolenski did not consider the other groups to have political objectives.

Why were representatives of organized labour absent from this company? The reason was that neither the Governor General nor the political parties of the assembly took the working population seriously as a political group. Both Russian administrators and Finnish bourgeois groups assumed that negotiations could be pursued only with 'real' political groups, in other words the political parties operating in the assembly. From the Governor General's point of view, in November 1905 the labour movement represented anarchy and no official loyal to his Tsar would negotiate with anarchists. Until the demonstrations and riots of the spring and summer of 1905, Obolenski considered the organizational activities of the Finnish working population as politically goalless and no more significant than the actions of rabble loyal to the Tsar.[37] In the end, however, Obolenski decided to deal with the workers in diplomatic ways to spare the Grand Duchy from bloody unrest.

The Workers' Meeting Takes a Step towards Revolution – The Red Manifesto

The week of strikes elevated the former opposition party, the Constitutionalists, to power in the assembly. The Constitutionalists wanted labour to support the Constitutionalists' demands, although they were not ready to agree to labour's own demands in return.

In the political negotiations during the strike week the differences between the labour movement and the Constitutionalists came to a crisis over the question of suffrage. The labour movement accepted only a unicameral diet whose members would be elected through equal and universal suffrage. The Constitutionalists wanted voting rights reform to take place through the decision of the assembly.[38] The labour movement demanded that a preparatory national assembly be chosen by a meeting held at a marketplace. The Constitutionalists thought such a move would look like revolution, not only to Tsar Nicholas II, but to the Finnish political elite as well.

The workers took the next step. At their strike meeting in Helsinki on 1 November 1905, they demanded full freedoms of speech, printing, gathering and organizing, as well as the immediate dismissal of the representatives of the old administration. The most important demand was 'to call together a mass meeting, chosen by Finland's people with equal and universal suffrage. The meeting is to give Finland's people a new constitution and a unicameral Diet whose members are elected in a way where every citizen older than 21 years votes with one vote and is at the same time eligible for the Diet'.[39]

Representatives of different parties were to be included in the temporary government and charged with the tasks of restoring the peace and organizing relations with Russia's future council assembly, the Duma. The workers' meeting simultaneously gave itself the power to choose the members of the temporary government. Finnish strikers were now clearly divided into two camps: the organized labour movement and the Constitutionalist-led parties of the assembly.

In the end, the Constitutionalists dictated the details of the Imperial Manifesto to be given to Finland. The social conditions preceding the February Manifesto of 1899 were to be restored to the Grand Duchy; restrictions on freedoms of speech, printing and assembly were to be removed and an assembly of the representatives of the estates was to convene to prepare a diet based on equal and universal suffrage. Information concerning the content of the draft manifesto to be delivered to the Tsar sparked an open row between the strike committee and the Constitutionalists. In the opinion of the workers' strike committee, the Finns should now make the same demands as the Russian people, convening a national assembly to crush the earlier system of government.[40]

On the same day the Constitutionalists handed the draft to Governor General Obolenski, a strike train arrived in Helsinki from Pori via Tampere, transporting representatives of the Pori strike committee led by Eetu Salin, and the Tampere committee led by Yrjö Mäkelin. The Tampere representatives brought along the Red Manifesto, accepted in Tampere a day before. The Red Manifesto also contained the demand for a national assembly to serve as a temporary government.

The Red Manifesto also included an open threat. It stated that:

as the privileged classes from various parts of the country seem to be working enthusiastically to convene the Diet, the proletariat proclaims it can in no
circumstances accept a Diet that is formed according to the current parliamentary order. If the assembly of the representatives of the estates is called
together in spite of this warning, the working class of the country reminds the
propertied classes in good time that the events of these days will be repeated
immediately after the issuing of the call to the assembly.[41]

The demands for civil rights echoed earlier declarations. The manifesto did not demand separation from Russia: '... we have no particular
desire to separate from the great Russia if we only get guarantees that
the best elements of the Russian people take the governing of Russia's
empire in their hands'. It has been noted that the Red Manifesto primarily concerned domestic policy and was at the same time revolutionary in
its aspirations towards democracy: it was directed against the assembly
of the representatives of the estates and dictatorship – that is, the Tsar's
rule.[42] The goal of the Red Manifesto – in spite of its revolutionary nature – was universal suffrage.

The common goals foundered because of power struggles and political uncertainty among labour leaders. The arrival of the Tampere and
Pori workers surprised the Helsinki labour leaders, who, with their central committee of the national strike, had believed they were the leaders
of the general strike in all of the Grand Duchy. Now, other delegations
approached the central committee with the belief that they too came
from the headquarters of the strike and – even worse – wanted to give
advice to the Helsinki leaders.

Opinions outnumbered members in the workers' strike committee,
open disputes became commonplace and the 'more radical elements' –
the Tampere workers – of the committee started assuming leadership. A
prominent labour leader, the journalist Matti Kurikka, resigned from the
committee when worker activist Aukusti Rissanen demanded a decision
about whether the committee would support the Parliament reform offered by Constitutionalists or stand behind its own demands. Kurikka
proposed joining with the Constitutionalists if they would provide guarantees concerning suffrage and a unicameral diet. When it appeared that
the Constitutionalists were no longer able to give such guarantees, the
strike committee decided to maintain its original demands.[43]

Finally, the workers formed a temporary government, elected
by a meeting held in Rautatientori (Järnvägstorget) in Helsinki on 4
November 1905. Twenty-four people were elected, half of them representing the Constitutionalist group, nine the labour movement and three
the Suometar group. That same evening, the leaders of the workers'

strike central committee and the National Guard with their interpreters got to present their temporary government to the Governor General. His only comment was that the reforms were finished for the time being. However, Obolenski comforted the representatives of the workers by saying that in the future the bourgeois parties could no longer neglect the demands of the working population.

The disappointment felt by the workers manifested itself in the activities of the National Guard, which now assumed the nature of a political

Illustration 8.1 Finland and the Russian eagle, from *Brand* 7 (1906). The Swedish text reads 'When the fetter is broken, freedom is mine'. Arbetarrörelsens arkiv och bibliotek.

weapon more strongly than ever before. The Guard leadership adopted a cold attitude towards the news office of the Constitutional Party. When leaflets were handed out on Saturday 4 November 1905 giving information about the forthcoming Imperial Manifesto, the National Guard confiscated them and tore them up. Angered, the Constitutionalists accused the National Guard leadership and the working-class guardsmen of censorship.[44]

The Guardsmen also forcefully abducted woman servants from their work, demanding that they stay on strike. Bourgeois students decided to resign from the National Guard; they convened at the student hall and chose a separate student guard from among their own ranks.[45] Tensions were escalated by news of bourgeois individuals acquiring weapons. According to the information gained by the headquarters of the National Guard, weapons had been sold from weapons shops and the central committee thus decided to order fifty guardsmen to watch every weapons shop.[46] On the final day of the strike, the workers' strike guard and the bourgeois student guard came to within a hair's breadth of combat at Senate Square in the middle of Helsinki. The withdrawal of the National Guard from the threatening situation at the last moment prevented bloodshed.

Early in the morning of Sunday 5 November 1905, the ship *Eläköön* brought to Helsinki news of the manifesto Nicholas II had given. According to the expectations of the Constitutionalists, the manifesto rescinded the dictatorship statute, the preliminary censorship of the press and a number of other statutes restricting the freedoms of assembly, organization, speech and printing. The manifesto also ordered the senate to create a new parliamentary order based on equal and universal suffrage.[47] Obolenski had made only a few changes to the Constitutionalists' proposal. Maintaining the status of the Russian language as one of the official languages of the administration office was a notable difference, as the Constitutionalists had tried to overrule this statute for five years.[48]

Brief Defeat, Long Victory?

For the groups in the assembly, to which Finland's general strike had meant a struggle for national autonomy, the manifesto following the strike ended a harsh period of oppression in the way the educated Finnish elite actually wanted this transition to happen. The November manifesto rescinded the February manifesto of 1899 and the restrictions on civil rights enforced during the office of the previous Governor General N.I. Bobrikov.

But the members of the organized labour movement felt they had been betrayed. For the working population, the general strike had primarily been a struggle for suffrage. The end of the strike meant a defeat for them, as universal suffrage was still left to the goodwill of the 'ruling classes' in the assembly. It was precisely the lack of such goodwill that had stalled suffrage reform for seven years.

However, the defeat of the workers turned into a victory only one year later with parliamentary reform, elections and the forming of a unicameral Parliament. These victories proved even more lasting than those of the defenders of Finnish autonomy, which only a little while later foundered both in the Grand Duchy of Finland and in Russia under the tightening grip of the administration. Although legislative work in the Grand Duchy's Parliament came to a dead end almost every year with the discontinuation of the Parliament and ceased entirely during the First World War, the birth of the unicameral Parliament proved a lasting and significant change for the whole of society.

To the Finnish labour movement, the struggle for suffrage also spelled rapid growth for the movement itself. Unlike in Sweden, where the suffrage strike of 1902 and general strike of 1909 resulted in the division of the labour movement, the Finnish labour movement became more united and strengthened by the victory over suffrage reform and the active role it had taken during the general strike. In Finland the anarchist and syndicalist strains remained marginal in comparison with those in Sweden, for example. Only the dramatic years 1917–18 put a halt to this development and led to the division of the labour movement into Social Democrat and Communist wings after the civil war of 1918.[49] The membership of the labour movement and its political activity increased strongly during the years following the general strike. The number of local workers' associations alone multiplied by nine during the years 1905–6 and the number of members increased fivefold. The membership of the Social Democratic Party tripled in 1905 alone.[50]

It is true that this development meant not only the strengthening of the parliamentary political powers within the movement. Revolutionary elements, support for violent unrest and the use of workers' militia formed during the general strike as a means of pressure all increased as well. The labour movement and Suomen Ammattijärjestö (Finnish Federation of Trade Unions, SAJ), established with the movement's strong support in 1907, were considered the saviours to all the nation's problems forthwith. When that did not happen, the strikes grew into struggles involving thousands of people that could also turn violent.[51] In only a few years the strengthening labour movement grew into a real political movement, forcing other political groups, local decision-makers and employers to pay attention to its views. This development was largely a result of the labour movement's active role in the general strike.

For the active members of the bourgeoisie this development meant instability and a threat. In spite of the democratizing impact of the parliamentary reform on the Grand Duchy of Finland, the reform was considered negative. One manifestation of this is the policy towards history pursued by the bourgeois groups immediately after the strike. They started to emphasize strongly the national nature of the strike, beyond the national protest of the Grand Duchy of Finland for her autonomous rights. Other demands – like labour's struggle for the suffrage – were bypassed and left unmentioned. At most it was noted that the working population was the enfant terrible that had almost broken national unity with its selfish demands.[52]

In the months following the strike, underground activities increased. In Russia various opposition groups escalated their work, acts of terrorism against the regime of Nicholas II reached new heights, and unrest spread among the army much more widely than before October 1905.[53] In Finland the separatist groups became more important. They now split politically into the Red Guards close to the working population and the bourgeois separatists.

However, it is clear that the general strike left a legacy of new concepts and social possibilities. This legacy took concrete shape in the form of the unicameral Parliament. As in the general strike, the working population – albeit through their representatives – took their place in the Parliament as an equal part of society freely acting and expressing their demands to which the rest of society had to listen. This show of strength of the Finnish labour movement happened for the first time in the general strike and its impact on the movement was staggering.

The Finnish strike of 1905 was puzzlingly non-violent; it could almost be called a revolution by committee. Ordinary Finnish men and women had learned organizational skills in various cultural and trade associations and needed to take only a short step to enter the arena of public political activity. In the nature of their experience lay both their strength and their weakness: when interests clashed and decisions had to be made in a swiftly changing situation, the strike leadership dispersed.

Risto Alapuro has noted that the events surrounding the general strike correspond to Charles Tilly's definition of a revolutionary situation. For a moment, the Grand Duchy of Finland had, instead of a legitimate government, two competing groups struggling for governing power.[54] Perhaps for the contemporaries such a situation never existed, at least not for longer than the twelve hours that it took from the moment the Suometar-controlled senate publicly announced its resignation to the moment the Constitutionalists decided to create a draft for an Imperial Manifesto. Of course, even those twelve hours were a long time.

For contemporaries, the more important aspect of the Finnish strike of 1905 was its conceptual ramifications. In the general strike, politics emerged directly from people's everyday lives, not from a separate arena. The period of slightly more than one year from the general strike to the first parliamentary election amounted to the greatest moment in the Finnish history of organization.[55] The political parties and groups that still make up the Finnish party system today began during the years 1905–1907.

To Finns living in 1905, the general strike meant not only political victories but also the opening of entirely new social concepts and possibilities. In a society based on the estates – divided into those with land and power on the one hand and those lacking both on the other – the working population had been only an object, a means to an end, not a subject with an independent impact on society. When the working population performed, acted and expressed its demands during the general strike, the understanding of social privilege based on the God-given division of estates broke forever. There was another way to govern society, and the general strike had given people a glimpse of it. This transition in the thinking of the contemporaries was the biggest revolution of the general strike in Finland.

Marko Tikka is a Lecturer in History at the University of Tampere. His research interests are in twentieth-century Finnish history, especially the history of the 1918 civil war. Publications include *Kun kansa leikki kuningasta. Suomen suuri lakko 1905* (SKS, 2010).

Notes

1. On the Russian Revolution in 1905 see A. Ascher. 1988. *The Revolution of 1905: Russia in Disarray*, Stanford: Stanford University Press; A. Ascher. 1992. *The Revolution of 1905: Authority Restored*, Stanford: Stanford University Press.
2. On the general strike in Finland, see, for example, S. Roos. 1907. *Suomen kansallislakko I*, Helsinki: Alex. F. Lindbergin kustannus; H. Soikkanen. 1960. 'Suurlakko', *Historiallinen Aitta* XIV, 171–90; O. Jussila. 1977. 'Vuoden 1905 suurlakko Suomessa, sen historialliset edellytykset ja seuraukset', *Historiallinen Arkisto* 72, 71–92; A. Kujala. 1996. *Venäjän hallitus ja Suomen työväenliike 1899–1905*, Helsinki: SHS; A. Kujala. 1989. *Vallankumous ja kansallinen itsemääräämisoikeus: Venäjän sosialistiset puolueet ja suomalainen radikalismi vuosisadan alussa*, Helsinki: SHS; P. Haapala, K. Melkas, O. Löytty and M. Tikka (eds). 2008. *Kansa kaikkivaltias: Suurlakko Suomessa 1905*, Jyväskylä: Teos.
3. M. Tikka. 2009. *Kun kansa leikki kuningasta: Suomen suuri lakko 1905*, Helsinki: SKS. Unlike elsewhere in Russia, Finland did not use the Julian calendar in 1905, so the dates

correspond to the Gregorian calendar. The Julian calendar lags thirteen days behind the Gregorian calendar.

4. At the beginning of the twentieth century municipal suffrage was based on the ability to pay tax in the Grand Duchy of Finland. In state elections the suffrage was the privilege of the four estates: nobility, clergy, burghers and farmers.

5. On this, see O. Jussila. 2004. *Suomen suuriruhtinaskunta 1809–1917*, Juva: WSOY, 467–529, 596–634.

6. On resistance and Russification in English, see S. Huxley. 1990. *Constitutionalist Insurgency in Finland*, Helsinki: SHS; L. Lundin. 1981. 'Finland', in E.C.Thaden (ed.), *Russification in the Baltic Provinces and Finland 1855–1914*, Princeton: Princeton University Press, 357–457. Both of these represent mainly the earlier interpretation of history where the viewpoint relies strongly on Finnish, mainly constitutional interpretations.

7. Hannu Soikkanen was the first historian who wrote from this point of view. See H. Soikkanen. 1960. *Sosialismin tulo Suomeen*, Helsinki: WSOY, 224–34; H. Soikkanen. 1975. *Kohti kansanvaltaa 1: 1899–1937. Suomen sosialidemokraattinen puolue 75 vuotta*, Vaasa: Sos.dem. puolue, 78–91. After Soikkanen see: Kujala, *Venäjän hallitus*; Kujala, *Vallankumous ja kansallinen itsemääräämisoikeus*.

8. On this, see Jussila, *Suomen suuriruhtinaskunta*.

9. Kujala, *Venäjän hallitus*, 418–19.

10. R. Alapuro and H. Stenius. 1989. 'Kansanliikkeet loivat kansakunnan', in R. Alapuro, I. Liikanen, K. Smeds and H. Stenius (eds), *Kansa liikkeessä*, Vaasa: Kirjayhtymä, 30–39; A. Rasilainen. 1995. *Suostumus ja legaliteetti: Oikeus ja politiikka porvarissäädyn vaalioikeuden sääntelyssä 1869–1905*, Turku: Turun yliopisto, 173–76; A. Rasilainen. 1996. 'Työväenliike ja porvarillinen reformialttius äänioikeuskysymyksessä ennen vuoden 1906 uudistusta', in P. Kettunen, R. Parikka and A. Suoranta (eds), *Äänekäs kansa*, Väki voimakas 8, Työväen historian ja perinteentutkimuksen seuran vuosikirja, Helsinki: THPTS, 33–41.

11. See Rasilainen, *Suostumus ja legaliteetti*, 137–38.

12. Y. Blomstedt. 1969. *K. J. Ståhlberg. Valtiomieselämäkerta*, Helsinki: Otava, 174–82.

13. J. Mylly. 2006. 'Edustuksellisen kansanvallan läpimurto', in J. Mylly, *Suomen eduskunta 100 vuotta I*, Helsinki: Edita, 77–79 and 88–89.

14. M. Harjula. 2006. 'Kelvoton valtiokansalaiseksi? Yleisen äänioikeuden rajoitukset ja äänioikeusanomukset Suomessa 1906–17', *Historiallinen Aikakauskirja* 4, 368–81.

15. Tikka, *Kun kansa leikki*, 66–72.

16. Kujala, *Venäjän hallitus*, 361–63.

17. On railways in Russia and the Grand Duchy of Finland see A. Juntunen. 1997. *Valta ja rautatiet: Luoteis-Venäjän rautateiden rakentamista keskeisesti ohjanneet tekijät 1890-luvulta 2. Maailmansotaan*, Helsinki: SHS.

18. Tikka, *Kun kansa leikki*, 180–81.

19. See O. Riihinen. 1975. 'Suomen rautatieläisten liiton perustamiseen johtanut kehitys', in O. Riihinen, K. Hentilä and J.-J. Roos, *Rautatieläisten liiton historia 1: Vaikeat vuosikymmenet. Kehitys vuoteen 1930*, Tapiola: Weilin & Göös, 37–48; N. Nissinen. 1973. *100 vuotta rautatievirkamiesten järjestötoimintaa 1873–1973*, Pieksämäki: Rautatievirkamiesliitto, 80–85.

20. The description is mostly based on NA, Väinö Voionmaa Archive, folder 1, 'Yleiskatsaus rautatieläisten lakkoon Viipurissa' and 'Kokous Viipurissa', *Helsingin Sanomat* 31 October 1905, 'Strejk å finska järnvägen', *Hufvudstadsbladet* 30 October 1905.

21. T. Tuomisto. 1984. *Tienraivaajan osa: Sata vuotta Helsingin Työväenyhdistyksen historiaa 1884–1984*, Helsinki: HTY, 173–80.

22. Tuomisto, *Tienraivaajan osa*, 178–79.

23. Tikka, *Kun kansa leikki*, 189–90.

24. FLA, 1905–1906 Archive, 2§ 30.10.1905. General strike committee minutes copies.

25. K. Latinki (Väinö Voionmaa). 1905. *Kansalliskaarti: Muistoja sen ensimmäiseltä sota-retkeltä*, Helsinki: Punaisen kaartin kustannuksella, 32. On the 1905 guards see M.-L. Salkola. 1985. *Työväenkaartien synty ja kehitys punakaartiksi I*, Helsinki: VPK, 45–47.

26. 'Vapaustaistelu', *Työmies* 9 November 1905.

27. Latinki, *Kansalliskaarti*, 22; NA, Väinö Voionmaa Archive, The General Strike Diaries ('Suurlakkopäiväkirja').

28. M. Närhi. 1984. 'Venäläiset joukot Suomessa autonomian aikana', in P. Kurkinen (ed.), *Venäläiset Suomessa 1809–1917*, Helsinki: SHS, 166.

29. J.W. Daly. 1998. *Autocracy under Siege: Security Police and Opposition in Russia 1866–1905*, Illinois: Illinois University Press, 164.

30. See, for example, J. Bushnell. 1985. *Mutiny and Repression: Russian Soldiers in the Revolution of 1905–1906*, Indiana: Indiana University Press, 52–53.

31. There were certain exceptions. In Hämeenlinna, National Guardsmen who had arrested gendarmes got into an armed conflict that nearly resulted in the mobilization of the army. The chief of the local National Guard, Bruno Jalander, managed to pacify the situation. See B. Jalander. 1932. *Kenraali Bruno Jalanderin muistelmia Kaukaasiasta ja Suomen murroskaudelta*, Helsinki: Otava, 85–88.

32. H. Soikkanen. 1970. *Luovutetun Karjalan työväenliikkeen historia*, Helsinki: Tammi, 124–26.

33. O. Jussila. 1979. *Nationalismi ja vallankumous venäläis-suomalaisissa suhteissa 1899–1914*, Helsinki: SHS, 72.

34. On terrorism in Finland see A. Geifman. 1995. *Thou Shalt Kill – Revolutionary Terrorism in Russia 1894–1917*, Princeton: Princeton University Press, 31–32. Classic descriptions of murder are E.I. Parmanen. 1941. *Taistelujen kirja: Kuvauksia itsenäisyystaistelumme vaiheista sortovuosina*. II Osa, Porvoo: WSOY, 740–82; S. Zettelberg. 1988. *Viisi laukausta senaatissa: Eugen Schaumanin elämä ja teko*, Helsinki: Otava.

35. Jussila, 'Vuoden 1905 suurlakko', 210–11.

36. 'Suomalainen puolue ja kenraalikuvernööri', *Uusi Suomi* 7 November 1905.

37. On this see Kujala, *Venäjän hallitus*.

38. 'Merkillinen viikko ...' *Helsingin Sanomien Lisälehti* 7 November 1905.

39. 'Sotaväki tulee', *Helsingin Sanomat* 7 November 1905.

40. On the manifesto see Mylly, 'Edustuksellisen kansanvallan', 100–1; U. Kanerva. 1986. *Tampereen työväenyhdistys 1886–1986*, Tampere: TTY, 177–87; Tikka, *Kun kansa leikki*, 111–13.

41. The information in this section comes from: 'Merkillinen viikko ...', *Helsingin Sanomien Lisälehti* 7 November 1905; 'Julistuskirja Suomen kansalle', *Helsingin Sanomat* 7 November 1905; 'En arbetarproklamation till Finlands folk', *Hufvudstadsbladet* 7 November 1905 and 'Vallankumousliikkeen alku Helsingissä', *Työmies* 8 November 1905.

42. Mylly, 'Edustuksellisen kansanvallan', 100.

43. 'Hiukan selitystä', *Työmies* 10 November 1905; E. Aspelin-Haapkylä. 1980. *Kirovuosien kronikka: Eliel Aspelin-Haapkylän päiväkirja 1905–1927*, Helsinki: SKS, 70–71; K. Kalemaa. 1978. *Matti Kurikka: Legenda jo eläessään*, Helsinki: WSOY, 195–97.

44. Tikka, *Kun kansa leikki*, 119–23.

45. 'Ylioppilaiden suojakaarti', *Uusi Suomi* 7 November 1905.

46. FLA, 1905–6 Archive, 36 § 4.11.1905 General strike committee minutes copies.

47. The Manifesto was published in, amongst other places, *Helsingin Sanomien Lisälehti* 7 November 1905; *Helsingin Sanomat* 7 November 1905; *Työmies* 7 November 1905; *Uusi Suomi* 7 November 1905; and *Hufvudstadsbladet* 7 November 1905.

48. N.E. Setälä. 1918. 'Muistelmia ensimmäiseltä sortokaudelta ja sen päättymisestä', in *Murrosajoilta: Muistoja ja kokemuksia*, Porvoo: WSOY, 422–25.

49. On Sweden's strike see B. Schiller. 1967. *Storstrejken*, Göteborg: Scandinavian University Books; J.O. Berg. 2011. *På spaning efter en svensk modell: Idéer och vägval i arbetsgivar-politiken 1897–1909*, Enebyberg: Berg Bild Rum och Färg Förlag.

50. On the growth of the labour movement, see among others Soikkanen, *Kohti kansan-valtaa*, 110–19; P. Ala-Kapee and M. Valkonen. 1982. *Yhdessä elämä turvallisemmaksi: Sak:laisen ammattiyhdistysliikkeen kehitys vuoteen 1930*, Helsinki: SAK, 157–64.

51. For examples see Ala-Kapee and Valkonen, *Yhdessä elämä turvalliseksi*, 163–64, 200–5.

52. This interpretation is represented, particularly as regards the general strike, by the works of S. Roos, published immediately after the strike: Roos, *Suomen kansallislakko I*; S. Roos. 1909. *Sortovuodet ja suurlakko Oulun kaupungissa ja läänissä*, Oulu: Oulun kirjapaino-kirjansitomo ja Kirjakauppa Osakeyhtiö; S. Roos. 1910. *Kansallislakko Suomessa, Kuopion kaupunki ja lääni*, Kuopio: Oy Kuopion uusi kirjapaino. The importance of Roos's in-terpretations was emphasized because his works were largely used as sources of historical research on the general strike.

53. On military unrest see Bushnell, *Mutiny and Repression*; on terrorism Geifman, *Thou Shalt Kill* and on the general political development Ascher, *The Revolution of 1905: Russia in Disarray*.

54. R. Alapuro. 1988. *State and Revolution in Finland*, Berkeley: California University Press, 115.

55. R. Alapuro. 1994. *Suomen synty paikallisena ilmiönä 1890–1933*, Porvoo: WSOY, 96–99.

References

Ala-Kapee, P. and M.Valkonen. 1982. *Yhdessä elämä turvallisemmaksi: Sak:laisen ammattiyhdistysliikkeen kehitys vuoteen 1930*, Helsinki: SAK.

Alapuro, R. 1994. *Suomen synty paikallisena ilmiönä 1890–1933*, Porvoo: WSOY.

———. 1988. *State and Revolution in Finland*, Berkeley: California University Press.

Alapuro, R. and H. Stenius. 1989. 'Kansanliikkeet loivat kansakunnan', in R. Alapuro, I. Liikanen, K. Smeds and H. Stenius (eds), *Kansa liikkeessä*, Vaasa: Kirjayhtymä, 30–39.

Ascher, A. 1988. *The Revolution of 1905: Russia in Disarray*, Stanford: Stanford University Press.

———. 1992. *The Revolution of 1905: Authority Restored*, Stanford: Stanford University Press.

Aspelin-Haapkylä, A. 1980. *Kirovuosien kronikka: Eliel Aspelin-Haapkylän päiväkir-ja 1905–1927*, Helsinki: SKS.

Berg, J.O. 2011. *På spaning efter en svensk modell: Idéer och vägval i arbetsgivarpoli-tiken 1897–1909*, Enebyberg: Berg Bild Rum och Färg Förlag.

Blomstedt, Y. 1969. *K. J. Ståhlberg: Valtiomieselämäkerta*, Helsinki: Otava.

Bushnell, J. 1985. *Mutiny and Repression: Russian Soldiers in the Revolution of 1905–1906*, Indiana: Indiana University Press.

Daly, J.W. 1998. *Autocracy under Siege: Security Police and Opposition in Russia 1866–1905*, Illinois: Illinois University Press.

Geifman, A. 1995. *Thou Shalt Kill: Revolutionary Terrorism in Russia 1894–1917*, Princeton: Princeton University Press.

Haapala, P., K. Melkas, O. Löytty and M. Tikka (eds). 2008. *Kansa kaikkivaltias: Suurlakko Suomessa 1905*, Jyväskylä: Teos.

Harjula, M. 2006. 'Kelvoton valtiokansalaiseksi? Yleisen äänioikeuden rajoitukset ja äänioikeusanomukset Suomessa 1906–17', *Historiallinen Aikakauskirja* 4, 368–81.

Huxley, S. 1990. *Constitutionalist Insurgency in Finland*, Helsinki: SHS.

Jalander, B. 1932. *Kenraali Bruno Jalanderin muistelmia Kaukaasiasta ja Suomen murroskaudelta*, Helsinki: Otava.

Juntunen, J. 1997. *Valta ja rautatiet: Luoteis-Venäjän rautateiden rakentamista keskeisesti ohjanneet tekijät 1890-luvulta 2. Maailmansotaan*, Helsinki: SHS.

Jussila, O. 1975. 'Vuoden 1905 suurlakko Suomessa venäläisten silmin', *Historiallinen arkisto* 70, 208–18.

Jussila, O. 1977. 'Vuoden 1905 suurlakko Suomessa, sen historialliset edellytykset ja seuraukset', *Historiallinen Arkisto* 72, 71– 92.

———. 1979. *Nationalismi ja vallankumous venäläis-suomalaisissa suhteissa 1899–1914*, Helsinki: SHS.

———. 2004. *Suomen suuriruhtinaskunta 1809–1917*, Juva: WSOY.

Kalemaa, K. 1978. *Matti Kurikka: Legenda jo eläessään*, Helsinki: WSOY.

Kanerva, U. 1986. *Tampereen työväenyhdistys 1886–1986*, Tampere: TTY.

Kujala, A. 1989. *Vallankumous ja kansallinen itsemääräämisoikeus: Venäjän sosialistiset puolueet ja suomalainen radikalismi vuosisadan alussa*, Helsinki: SHS.

———. 1996. *Venäjän hallitus ja Suomen työväenliike 1899–1905*, Helsinki: SHS.

Latinki, K. 1905. *Kansalliskaarti: Muistoja sen ensimmäiseltä sotaretkeltä*, Helsinki: Punaisen kaartin kustannuksella.

Lundin, L. 'Finland', in E.C. Thaden (ed.), *Russification in the Baltic Provinces and Finland 1855–1914*, Princeton: Princeton University Press, 1981, 357–457.

Mylly, J. 'Edustuksellisen kansanvallan läpimurto', *Suomen eduskunta 100 vuotta I*, Helsinki: Edita, 2006, 47–102.

Nissinen, N. 1973. *100 vuotta rautatievirkamiesten järjestötoimintaa 1873–1973*, Pieksämäki: Rautatievirkamiesliitto.

Närhi, M. 'Venäläiset joukot Suomessa autonomian aikana', in P. Kurkinen (ed.), *Venäläiset Suomessa 1809–1917*, Helsinki: SHS, 1984, 161–80.

Parmanen, E.I. 1941. *Taistelujen kirja: Kuvauksia itsenäisyystaistelumme vaiheista sortovuosina. II Osa*, Porvoo: WSOY.

Rasilainen, A. 1995. *Suostumus ja legaliteetti: Oikeus ja politiikka porvarissäädyn vaalioikeuden sääntelyssä 1869–1905*, Turku: Turun yliopisto.

———. 'Työväenliike ja porvarillinen reformialttius äänioikeuskysymyksessä ennen vuoden 1906 uudistusta', in P. Kettunen, R. Parikka and A. Suoranta (eds), *Äänekäs kansa*, Väki voimakas 8, Työväen historian ja perinteentutkimuksen seuran vuosikirja, Helsinki: THPTS, 1996, 33–41.

Riihinen, O. 'Suomen rautatieläisten liiton perustamiseen johtanut kehitys', in O. Riihinen, K. Hentilä and J.-J. Roos, *Rautatieläisten liiton historia 1: Vaikeat vuosikymmenet. Kehitys vuoteen 1930*, Tapiola: Weilin & Göös, 1975, 19–55.

Roos, S. 1907. *Suomen kansallislakko I*, Helsinki: Alex. F. Lindbergin kustannus.

———. 1909. *Sortovuodet ja suurlakko Oulun kaupungissa ja läänissä*, Oulu: Oulun kirjapaino-, kirjansitomo- ja kirjakauppa-osakeyhtiö.

———. 1910. *Kansallislakko Suomessa, Kuopion kaupunki ja lääni*, Kuopio: Oy Kuopion uusi kirjapaino.

Salkola, M.-L. 1985. *Työväenkaartien synty ja kehitys punakaartiksi I*, Helsinki: VPK, 45–47.

Schiller, B. 1967. *Storstrejken*, Göteborg: Scandinavian University Books.

Setälä, N.E. 'Muistelmia ensimmäiseltä sortokaudelta ja sen päättymisestä', in *Murrosajoilta. Muistoja ja kokemuksia*, Porvoo: WSOY, 1918, 422–25.

Soikkanen, H. 1960. 'Suurlakko', in *Historiallinen Aitta* XIV, 1960, 171–90.

———. 1960. *Sosialismin tulo Suomeen*, Helsinki: WSOY.

———. 1970. *Luovutetun Karjalan työväenliikkeen historia*, Helsinki: Tammi, 124–26.

———. 1975. *Kohti kansanvaltaa 1: 1899–1937. Suomen sosialidemokraattinen puolue 75 vuotta*, Vaasa: Sos.dem. puolue.

Tikka, M. 2009. *Kun kansa leikki kuningasta: Suomen suuri lakko 1905*, Helsinki: SKS.

Tuomisto, T. 1984. *Tienraivaajan osa: Sata vuotta Helsingin Työväenyhdistyksen historiaa 1884–1984*, Helsinki: HTY.

Zettelberg, S. 1988. *Viisi laukausta senaatissa: Eugen Schaumanin elämä ja teko*, Helsinki: Otava.

CHAPTER 9

RADICALISM OR INTEGRATION
Socialist and Liberal Parties in Norway, 1890–1914

Einar A. Terjesen

The main question to be discussed in this chapter is to what extent Det norske arbeiderparti (the Norwegian Labour Party, DNA)[1] was integrated into Norwegian politics and society in its formative period up to about 1914.[2] The starting point is the thesis of the Norwegian historian Francis Sejersted (1936–2015), who argues that the political situation in the 1890s caused DNA to be more radical and oppositional than its Danish and Swedish counterparts.[3] For Sejersted this is an important factor in explaining the famous Norwegian radicalism around 1920. I dispute his argument and claim that at least up to the beginning of First World War DNA was significantly less radical than he assumes. Furthermore, I argue that the apparently exceptional strength of the radicalism in the 1920s was not an effect of exceptional radicalism in itself, but a result of the decentralized structure of the party and the lack of a strong social democratic leader. The disagreement is fundamentally about the timing of the integration of labour into society and about the question of revolution or reformism in the ideology of the Scandinavian labour movements.

Continuity or Change?

In 1849 the teacher Marcus Thrane (1817–1890) initiated labour associations in towns and the countryside across the eastern and southern parts of Norway. He also edited a newspaper. The movement took off and up to 1852 it is estimated that more than 30,000 men joined the associations for a shorter or longer time. That was about 10 percent of the adult male population in Norway. The main achievement of the Thrane movement was a petition to the Swedish king asking for universal suffrage and social reforms, which got 13,000 signatures. Thrane was arrested in 1851 and later sentenced to four years in prison. The movement withered away. It is impossible to establish any link between the Thrane movement and the labour movements that emerged in the 1870s and 1880s.[4]

Although DNA was founded as early as 1887, it became a political force only after the union between Norway and Sweden was dissolved in 1905. During the 1890s the Liberal Party, Venstre, maintained significant support among the workers and local trade unions. Venstre had its origin in the peasants' and the periphery's opposition to the civil service elite in the capital Kristiania (from 1925 named Oslo) and in Sweden. The party represented conflicting rural and urban interests. Liberal economic principles were not an essential part of the ideology. The main objectives were political democratization, including universal male suffrage and dissolution of the union with Sweden. These were also the most pressing political issues for DNA. DNA saw itself as part of the international socialist movement and maintained good relations to other social democratic parties, not least its Danish and Swedish sister parties. The two most prominent individuals in the party, the printer Christian Holtermann Knudsen (1845–1929) and the Danish brush maker and later merchant and mayor of Kristiania Carl Jeppesen (1858–1930), were both outspoken socialists. However, they never had absolute power. The party and its leadership included people with deep liberal inclinations and at times they may even have been in the majority.

After the turn of the century a radical opposition emerged in the labour movement. It did not see parliamentarianism as the only sustainable socialist strategy as the old leaders like Jeppesen and Knudsen tended to. In 1918 the opposition took over the leadership of DNA and for a few years dominated the labour movement with its non-parliamentarian rhetoric. The undisputed leader of the opposition was the painter Martin Tranmæl (1879–1967). He never aspired to be party chairman, but nevertheless up till the late 1940s he was one of the most influential people in the labour movement, mainly as editor of the national newspaper *Social-Demokraten* (from 1923 called *Arbeiderbladet*, today *Dagsavisen*) and due to his legendary informal authority.

A consequence of the victory of the opposition was that DNA joined the Communist International from 1919 to 1923 and that a right wing minority left the party. This led to the thesis of an exceptional Norwegian radicalism.[5] DNA was the only majority labour party in Europe with a substantial membership that joined the Comintern. But almost every-where the war and the Russian revolution radicalized the labour move-ment and led to a split in the socialist parties. What was special about Norway was not the radicalization in itself, but that radical forces in Norway gained a majority in the Party's leadership. The thesis about a special Norwegian radicalism is based on this formal takeover, not on any social analysis. In Norway it was the right wing that found itself in a minority and subsequently founded Norges socialdemokratiske arbeider-parti (Norwegian Social Democratic Labour Party). In most other coun-tries it was the left wing that constituted the minority. However, looking at the movement as a whole, the special position of Norway is not as ob-vious. For example, the left wing won majorities in all the Scandinavian socialist youth organizations. Everywhere the labour movement was di-vided between a revolutionary and a reformist wing, to keep in line with the most used contemporary and later rhetoric. The 'right socialists' re-joined DNA already in 1927.

In the literature on the Norwegian labour movement it is common to speak of a fundamental political and ideological change in the early 1930s when DNA discarded its revolutionary rhetoric and turned from being oppositional to seeking integration into society as well as the nation.[6] If we look at the situation just before the outbreak of the Second World War, the similarities between the labour movements in Scandinavia were certainly remarkable. In a Europe marked by economic crisis, dictator-ships and danger of war, the national labour movements in Denmark, Norway and Sweden were unique. Through parliamentary alliances with farmers' parties (Denmark and Sweden in 1933 and Norway in 1935), all three parties now participated in stable governments with Social Democratic prime ministers. A high level of trade union organization and national agreements between the organizations in the labour market secured peace in labour relations and gave the governments opportunity to act more freely (the Kanslergade Agreement in Denmark in 1933, Norway's Main Agreement of 1935 and the Saltsjöbaden Agreement of 1938 in Sweden).[7] The labour movements in Scandinavia signalled a democratic path out of the crisis. What later came to be called the Nordic model was initiated in this period.

In the short run the labour movements in Denmark and Sweden ex-hibited a more continuous reformist development than their Norwegian counterpart. But while it is usual to claim that DNA fundamentally changed its ideology in the early 1930s, more rarely discussed is the question of whether the takeover in 1918 represented an equally fun-damental ideological change in the opposite direction. It is agreed that DNA in the 1930s sought integration and left behind its class rhetoric for the benefit of talking about the 'nation' and the 'people'.[8] On the other hand, it seems to be accepted that the victory of the radical opposition only represented a change in strategy and tactics, not in overall ideological goals such as questions about class politics and integration. It is traditionally assumed that the party programme from 1891 signified that DNA from then on was a Marxist socialist party. In my view this programme had more symbolic than strategic value.

In my opinion the traditional view exaggerates the notion that the 1930s represent something quite new in the Norwegian labour movement. On the contrary, I argue that the mode of thought in the 1930s represented a return to what was common before the First World War. The wordings and the practical strategy were of course different, but that was due above all to different opportunities, not to fundamentally different mindsets. In terms of integration, I have argued that DNA both before 1918 and after 1930 ultimately strived for respect, both for the individual worker and the movement as a whole, through integration and cooperation.[9] In any case, seen from a historical perspective, the differences between the Scandinavian parties in the 1920s must not be exaggerated.

The Radicalization Thesis

The alleged Norwegian exceptionalism was brought to academic attention as early as 1922 in a famous article by the Norwegian historian Edvard Bull (1881–1932).[10] Bull was part of the radical opposition and was deputy chairman of DNA from 1923 until his death. Bull claimed that the Norwegian radicalism in the last instance could be explained by the nation's fast and late industrialization. The thesis was tested empirically in the 1960s and 1970s, but not conclusively substantiated. Thereafter the international comparative aspect was lost and historians turned towards explaining why the radicalism seemingly thrived in some types of industries and not in others.[11] Other historians have questioned whether there existed any substantial and united radicalism at all.[12]

In his major historical work *The Age of Social Democracy* (2011), the renowned Norwegian historian Francis Sejersted accepts the traditional thesis about the exceptionalism of Norwegian radicalism, but offers a new explanation for the difference in radicalism between Norway and Sweden.[13] Sejersted was originally an economic historian, but later specialized primarily in political subjects associated with democracy and the rule of law. From 1991 to 1999 he was chairman of the Norwegian Nobel Committee, representing the Conservative Party. For him the crucial question was not about different paths of industrialization, but differences in democratic development.

It is not disputed that democratization in Norway came early, at a time when DNA was only a marginal political force. First and foremost the extension of the suffrage could be attributed to Venstre. Venstre had established itself as a strong parliamentary party and thus left the Social Democrats with little political influence. In Sweden democratization came later, with the Social Democrats as the protagonists in the campaign for democracy, meaning that here the Liberal Party played a minor role. Social Democrats in Denmark and Sweden played a greater part in the democratization process than DNA and they gained government power before their party colleagues in Norway.

What I dispute, however, is that the strong 'left-liberal state' in Norway also marginalized the social democrats and almost necessarily strengthened their radicalism. According to Sejersted, the question of universal suffrage in Sweden had an 'unifying effect on the relationship between the Liberals and the Social Democrats' and 'the Social Democratic Party stood for universal suffrage', while in Norway universal suffrage for men was the achievement of Venstre alone and 'precisely the strong democratic tradition in Norway was part of the reason why it took such a long time for the Socialists (Social Democrats) to accept liberal democracy'.[14] And vice versa: 'An important precondition for the strong Left-liberal state in Norway, and the absence of the same in Sweden, was that in Norway the Social Democrats did not allow themselves to become integrated into the system as they did in Sweden. Precisely during this period DNA presented itself as a revolutionary party outside established society'.[15] Sejersted thereby postulates a connection between the strength of liberalism and social democratic radicalism. A somewhat similar argument can be found in an article by the social scientist Jostein Ryssevik.[16]

Table 9.1 Key dates in democratic development in Scandinavia

	Norway	Denmark	Sweden
Male suffrage	1898	1849	1909
Female suffrage	1913	1915	1919*
Introduction of parliamentary system	1884	1901	1917
First Social Democrats in parliament	1903	1884	1886
First Social Democrats in government	1928	1916	1917

*The first election in which Swedish women voted was in 1921.
Source: Elvander, *Skandinavisk arbetarrörelse*, 33.

Sejersted seems to assume the continuity of radical ideology from the foundation of DNA up to the early 1930s when the party indisputably followed a parliamentary strategy. According to him the party did not accept liberal democracy and opposed integration. From this point of view, DNA first became social democratic in the 1930s. This chapter will question this division.

A terminological clarification may be useful. The period before the First World War was the golden era of classical social democracy in Europe, a period when the international social democratic community in some ways was at its strongest and socialist ideals had not yet been put to a serious test. During this period the term social democracy was mainly used by the socialists as an organizational description, not an ideological one. Socialism was the ideology and the political socialist organizations constituted social democracy. The reason why the party in Norway was named Det norske arbeiderparti was not that it saw itself as more radical than its Swedish sister party, but that at its foundation in 1887 it did not consider itself a socialist party. That happened first in 1891.

Similarities and Differences

The relatively low level of violence in class conflicts in Scandinavian societies in the 1890s is important when we try to explain why the labour movements in these countries developed into strong social democratic movements. Democratic rights such as freedom of assembly, freedom of association and freedom of the press were well established and accepted. Already before 1910 the employers were generally beginning to accept labour organizations as representatives of workers' interests. The conflicts that took place despite this in the labour market and workplaces mainly ended peacefully. There were exceptions – in northern Norway especially – in remote communities relying on a single industry. But even if the military was mobilized in some instances, there was never a systematic outspoken violent alliance between the state and the capitalists.

The Swedish employers were stronger than those in Denmark and in Norway and launched a devastating attack on the trade unions in 1909. But even this lockout and the generally high level of strikes and lockouts in Norway and Sweden before the war and in the 1920s can be understood largely as a consequence of bargaining between workers and employers. The system of national collective agreements allowed local conflicts to expand easily to a national level and to include different industries.

On the other hand, the traditional conservative alliances between the army, the aristocracy, high-level civil servants and the upper bourgeoisie were stronger in the old great powers Denmark and Sweden than in Norway. This contributed to slower democratization in those countries than in Norway.[17] Both Denmark and Sweden had a two-chamber Parliament designed to safeguard the interests of the upper class.

A well-known similarity was that the working class in Scandinavia was spared serious ethnic, linguistic and religious differences between the countries as well as internally.[18] By cooperation through conferences and strike support across borders, the labour movements in Denmark, Norway and Sweden showed that what was similar was more important than what was different. We can assume that this solidarity really helped to minimize the danger of war between Norway and Sweden in 1905, although the labour movement was never put to the same direct test of international solidarity as it was at the outbreak of First World War. Within each country there was considerable ethnic, national and religious homogeneity. In many other countries such opposites could have significant organizational consequences.

Illustration 9.1 The May Day demonstration in the small mining community of Løkken verk in 1911. Arbeiderbevegelsens arkiv og bibliotek, Norway. Unknown photographer.

In his well-known historical and political model of Norway, the Norwegian political scientist Stein Rokkan writes of strong countercultures in the geographical periphery. He mentions few cultural conflicts within the national working class, however, except perhaps on the alcohol question. On the contrary, as Rokkan himself pointed out, where the countercultures were strong, the labour movement was weak. This was among Venstre's core areas, especially in the southern and western parts of Norway.[19] The Norwegian regional cultural diversity was not reflected in destructive cultural differences within the working class, but in geographical differences in support for the labour movement.

Nevertheless, Rokkan claims that crucial divisions were territorial and cultural and to some extent this was also true for the labour movement. Geographical differences within the labour movement occurred in all countries, not least in Norway. There were typically differences between centre and periphery; between the national centre and outlying areas. These differences were not primarily those of local identities or cultures but reflected a general and profound dissatisfaction with being controlled from above. In addition, the organizations in the periphery often represented other professions and industries with different interests than the organizations in the capital. The labour movement in Norway developed in geographically separate communities that eventually competed for power in the movement. Overall, up to about 1905, the local movements were less radical than the party leaders in the centre, while afterwards the local opposition was perhaps more radical until it took over the leadership in 1918. In 1903 DNA's first parliamentary representatives were all from northern Norway and from environments where the party leadership in the capital had little or no influence. Martin Tranmæl had his base in Trøndelag in the middle of Norway. The opposition of the periphery to the centre was not a particularly Norwegian characteristic – it was common in most countries, including Sweden – but it was stronger in Norway. The central leadership of the labour movement and parliamentary group in Sweden succeeded in determining the movement's ideology and politics to a far greater extent than the leadership in Norway.[20] We may say that while in all countries there was a clash of interests between the periphery and centre, it was primarily in Norway that the periphery gained decisive political influence.

The Labour Party and the Liberal Party

From the outset DNA followed an unequivocal parliamentary strategy despite its socialist programme from 1891. In its endeavour to achieve

parliamentary representation, DNA did not differ significantly from the
social democrats in Denmark and Sweden. The crucial difference, however, was that in Norway in the 1890s there existed a relatively strong
liberal labour movement, consisting primarily of liberal trade unions
and the two nationwide workers' organizations De forenede norske
Arbeidersamfund (The United Norwegian Workers' Society, DfnA) and
Norsk Fagforbund (Association of Norwegian Trade Unions).[21] It seems
that the existence of the two strands in the labour movement did not
promote any radicalization of the social democrats, rather the opposite.
Taking 1890 as the starting point, it was not preordained that a decade
later the socialist labour movement would clearly be dominant. Even after the turn of the century the liberals held a significant position among
the workers in certain geographical areas.

A characteristic of the Norwegian labour movement was that the socialists tried to conquer liberal workers' societies from within, rather than
establishing competing organizations as they generally seem to have done
in Sweden. In this respect the labour movement in Sweden was more oppositional and eager for battle than the labour movement in Norway.
Workers' societies could be found in several Norwegian towns, with the
largest and most important in the capital (Kristiania Arbeidersamfund).
Many of them had been founded by conservatives as apolitical paternalistic societies, which were later conquered by liberals before they were
taken over by socialists in the 1890s.[22] The societies were important because they were established discussion forums, often owned their own
buildings, and held other financial and material resources.

Socialists participated actively in liberal workers' organizations, including the national so-called Norske arbeidermøder (Norwegian
Workers' Meetings) that in practice was the general assembly of DfnA.
In 1891 the socialists dominated the proceedings. Christian Holtermann
Knudsen held a lecture on the eight hour day; Oscar Nissen (1843–
1911), a doctor who was part of DNA leadership, spoke about the working conditions of domestic servants, and Carl Jeppesen lectured about
'the modern labour movement and socialism'.[23] This became too much
for the liberals. In the future the workers' meetings closed their doors to
members of DNA, but accepted membership in Venstre.

A consequence of the socialists' endeavour to conquer the liberal organizations from within was the development of what has been called a
national labour banner tradition in Norway.[24] The international socialist
iconography is not predominant on Norwegian labour banners. The socialists conquered the banners of the old liberal organizations and used
them as their own, and new banners were mostly produced in the same
iconographic tradition. In Denmark and Sweden socialist iconography

seems to be more widespread. For example, in Norway the banners could be all kinds of colours, but in the two other countries they were predominantly red. In Norway the red flag was, so to speak, not always red. Whether this difference was due to strength or weakness, I will not discuss here. In any case, the explanation for this is not that DNA was more radical than its sister parties, but rather the opposite. It is also plausible to assume that the Norwegian strategy to conquer the organizations from within did not promote formal partnership on the national level. Paradoxically the clearer demarcation between liberals and socialists in Denmark and Sweden may have contributed to the possibility of closer political cooperation.

Another arena for competition between DNA and Venstre was the May Day celebrations. In several places throughout the country the liberals tried to 'steal the day' by taking the initiative. The main demand, the eight hour day, had wide common support, but the liberals were strongly opposed to 1 May as a day off from work. For them the nearest Sunday was a more suitable day for demonstrations. In Norway's third largest city, Trondheim, liberal workers arranged the first May Day demonstration in 1891. It was held on Sunday 3 May and the liberals dominated the celebration and the labour movement in the town up to 1897. In the town of Drammen, Venstre took the initiative in organizing the first May Day demonstration as late as 1898, which that year fell on a Sunday. In the capital, however, DNA arranged the demonstrations on its own from the first celebration in 1890.[25]

The demand for universal suffrage was an area of potential cooperation that led to major strategic and tactical disputes between socialists and liberals and inside the two parties.[26] Universal suffrage for both men and women was a fundamental requirement for the socialists, while the priority of the liberals was male suffrage. For the liberals the suffrage was primarily a means to achieve a parliamentary majority for dissolution of the union with Sweden. For the socialists universal suffrage was a prerequisite for the implementation of fundamental political and social change.

The struggle for universal suffrage had both a parliamentary and a non-parliamentary dimension. Since 1886 the socialists in Kristiania had led demonstrations on the Norwegian national day, 17 May, for the right to vote. For a few years liberal trade unions also participated in the marches. From 1892 the liberals held their own demonstrations. Elsewhere in the country there were also workers' demonstrations on 17 May. After the Parliament introduced universal male suffrage in 1898, the 17 May demonstrations were carried out partly as all women's events, partly in cooperation with DNA, but not with Venstre.[27]

At all elections during the 1890s both the liberal and the socialist workers' organizations put pressure on Venstre to place universal suffrage at the top of the agenda and to allow workers to nominate their own candidates on the election lists. While Venstre always refused nationally binding cooperation, until 1906 DNA more or less wholeheartedly endorsed cooperation – at least locally. Mostly, however, it came to nothing. DNA was, so to speak, 'forced' to present their own electoral lists or to call for an election boycott. The results were generally poor and in some instances the party even got fewer votes than it had members.

The recurring debate on whether or not to support the liberals came up again in the party congress of 1903.[28] The question was not whether the party was for or against a parliamentary road to socialism, but whether it was for or against electoral support of the then governing liberals. Against the advice of the party leadership, the majority also this time supported electoral cooperation. The leadership resigned and new leaders were elected. To some extent this reflected a change in the party composition. The party had gained members in areas where the liberal labour movement had been strong and many of them had only recently given up supporting Venstre. Two years later at the party congress in 1906, influenced by a new electoral system that harmed DNA, the mood had turned and the old leadership regained their positions. Even if the congress for the first time unanimously rejected election cooperation with other parties and criticized those who had taken over the leadership in 1903, this cannot be interpreted as a general radicalization. A radical opposition was beginning to emerge, but it was not yet a factor to reckon with. It was rather a reaction to Venstre's negligible interest in any cooperation and its now unambiguous appearance as a governmental capitalist party with marginal concern for the workers' situation. All in all, the absence of any electoral cooperation between Venstre and the Social Democratic Party was down to the refusal of the liberals, not any radicalism of the Social Democrats.

Democracy and Integration

One way to look at the difference between the countries is to examine to what extent the labour movement was integrated in the political system and in society. According to Stein Rokkan, we can distinguish different degrees of integration. He operates with several levels for the establishment of political parties.[29] The first level is legitimation. At this level, civil rights are recognized – that is, the movement's right to protest and to form an opposition to the established power. At the second level, incorporation, the free and equal right to elect representatives in the decision-making bodies is recognized. At the third level, representation, the right of parties to represent themselves in decision-making bodies is recognized. At the fourth level, the right to hold executive government power based on a parliamentary majority is recognized. This formal definition, based on terms of rights rather than the power to implement them, was established earlier in Norway than in Denmark and Sweden. It is therefore fair to say that the labour movement in Norway was at least theoretically integrated no later than the movement in Denmark and Sweden.

The integration of the labour movement was not unintended, but was on the contrary a result of a conscious strategy by the socialists. In countries like Denmark, Sweden and Norway, the majority of the labour movement in the 1890s regarded the Parliament as the most important political arena. The socialists had faith in the possibility of conquering the state through Parliament in order to implement reforms and introduce socialism. For them, socialism could and should be introduced by parliamentary majority. Universal suffrage and parliamentary representation was a common strategic goal for socialists and liberals, even if the social democrats went further in their democratic demands than the liberals. While the liberals in practice sought equality before the law, the socialists called for political equality.[30] In a classic article, the Swedish social scientist Göran Therborn claimed that the labour movement was the driving force of democratization, a view that has been confirmed but also modified by others.[31] It was the rise of the working class and the labour movement that put the issue of universal suffrage on the agenda, but nowhere was the movement strong enough to introduce democracy alone. It needed support from liberal parties that were already located inside the political system. The degree of the will of liberal parties to introduce democracy, and the degree of pressure from the socialist parties and trade unions, varied from country to country. Overall, it seems that in countries where it seemed possible to achieve power through parliamentary means, the labour movement chose this peaceful alternative.[32] The radicalism and the economic upturn after First World War in Norway was for a short time an exception that only proves the point. DNA never totally gave up parliamentary representation, but for a short period the party thought it could achieve socialism through direct action. When the movement again lost power, after a few years DNA returned to a wholeheartedly parliamentary strategy without fundamental change in the leadership. Martin Tranmæl became an outspoken parliamentarian democrat. Another integrative factor was ideology. To what extent was the socialist labour movement influenced by liberal thinking? It is not always fruitful to operate with a sharp distinction between liberalism and socialism if we want to understand the labour movement's mode of thought. The social democrats mixed concepts and terms from different traditions to come up with an ideology that was useful and gave meaning to their struggle. It is not fruitful to look for ideological consistency. More substantial, in my view, is that the ultimate goal for the labour movement in Norway in this period was not socialism or material gains, but first of all to gain respect for the individual workers and the collective class movement. This was seen as a step towards integration. It is fair to say that before the First World War the vast majority of the labour movement in Norway wanted integration, in the sense that the workers wished to be respected and regarded as equal partners in society.[33] This of course did not mean that material gains were unimportant, far from it, but that the driving force behind the demands was the endeavour to seek respect and self-respect.

The labour movement considered itself a legitimate participant in society and claimed a right and equal part in the national traditions. The red flag and the Norwegian national flag were not seen as contradictory, but as symbols of different things and were often used side by side. In the movement's most heroic period at the beginning of the 1920s, national symbols were also used, even if the red flag had never had greater prominence before and has not since. For example, the socialist children's organizations in Kristiania performed on 1 May dressed in national costumes and at the same time carried small red flags. It is a myth that the Norwegian labour movement first began to use national symbols in its arrangements and rhetoric in the 1930s.[34] Generally, much of the labour movement's cultural and enlightenment endeavour can be seen as a wish and a strategy for integration, not demarcation.

To what extent was social integration synonymous with political integration? Most people outside the movement have seen the Labour government as the ultimate proof of both the political and social integration of the labour movement into bourgeois society. The movement itself did not see it like that. For them, political integration – for example, a prime minster and government representing the labour movement – implied the possibility to change society. They desired integration into a new society, a society they themselves would shape. We can say that the very fact that the labour movement could obtain government power involved a violation of the classical bourgeois society that previously excluded such opportunities. It may be true that both liberals and socialists were behind a modernization project that required the integration of all groups in the new nation and that democracy was a way to integrate the entire population.[35] However, the nation the socialists desired to integrate into was not the same as the liberals. The socialists wished for fundamental economic and social change. That capitalism actually continued to exist despite the labour movement's political takeover and that the socialist goal was pushed far into the future and later abandoned is a different story.

Conclusion

Prior to 1914 there were no fundamental political differences between the social democratic parties in Denmark, Norway and Sweden. However, a significant difference between Norway and the other two countries was the power structure of the parties. With DNA the members and the periphery dominated at the expense of the central leadership. The composition and participation rules of the national congresses favoured the members and the districts. Furthermore, the parliamentary group was weak compared to the party leadership and not least the congresses. The periphery and the members were thus more powerful in Norway than in Denmark and Sweden.[36]

The party's old top leadership came mainly from a relatively narrow environment in the capital, an environment that was far removed from many of the members who held considerable power, because of the party's decentralized structure. The party's strategy to conquer liberal societies from within had in turn contributed to a diffusion of liberal thinking into the party. This strengthened the divergence and made the party less united and unified. During the years before the First World War the local opposition changed from being more moderate than the old Social Democrats to becoming more radical. The moderates gained the leadership of the party in 1903 but lost it again in 1906, not to the radicals, but to the old elite. Thereafter the radicals gained strength and took over the leadership in 1918. This divergence in the party membership persisted into the 1920s, but this time the new radical leadership managed to centralize the power structure of the party, paradoxically perhaps more in line with the conditions in the Social Democratic parties in Denmark and Sweden.

A second, but not independent, cause of the peripheral power in DNA was the lack of a strong leader. It was perhaps the most striking difference between DNA and the Social Democratic parties in Denmark and Sweden.[37] Even before 1914, Thorvald Stauning (1873–1942) in Denmark and Hjalmar Branting (1860–1925) in Sweden were well established and undisputed social democratic leaders. They were both party chairmen and at the same time leaders of the parliamentary group.

Both became prime ministers. Both held their positions for many years and could unite the parties on a social democratic platform.

Before 1914, DNA had no obvious leader with the same undisputed authority as Branting or Stauning. The typographer Ole O. Lian (1868–1925) might have been such a leader after the turn of the century, but his priorities were with the trade unions, and he became chairman of the Norwegian Federation of Trade Unions in 1906. He played an important part in stopping the radical opposition from gaining the same majority in the central trade union organizations as they did in DNA. The outspoken social democrats Christian H. Knudsen and Carl Jeppesen were undoubtedly the two most widely known and respected top leaders in DNA, but neither of them was a typical leader. Knudsen was the party founder and organizer, but rarely wanted to control the party. Unlike Knudsen, Jeppesen was a brilliant speaker, but lacked organizational authority. No one else stood out. Collectively, the leadership had little authority. It consisted largely of individuals, many of them with a background in Venstre and with important disagreements between them. The leaders had a tendency to withdraw from their positions when they were outvoted, only to resume their duties at the next opportunity.

No one in the old leadership could match the charismatic Martin Tranmæl from the radical opposition as a leading figure when he emerged just before the First World War. Tranmæl was then thirty-nine years old, compared to Knudsen, who was seventy-three and Jeppesen, who was sixty. After 1918 Tranmæl was the real leader of DNA even if he never became chairman. In reality the chairman had to have Tranmæl's blessing to do his job. The first person really to become party chairman in his own right was Einar Gerhardsen (1897–1987), who became chairman and prime minister in 1945. But it is symptomatic that Tranmæl took a central part in helping him into these positions.

In this chapter I have tried to show that DNA up to 1914 was no more radical than its Danish and Swedish sister parties. I have also argued that the radical turn in the party in 1918 can be seen as a result of the decentralized structure of the party and the lack of a strong social democratic leader. In the late 1930s the three parties showed remarkable similarities in both ideology and politics. To get there, DNA had had to pass through two programmatic changes. For the Danish and Swedish parties the continuity was more predominant.

Francis Sejersted's argument about liberal and socialist parties in Norway and Sweden implies that strong liberal parties correlate with radical socialist parties, and conversely that countries with weak liberal parties have moderate labour parties. As an alternative to Sejersted's view, I have tried to substantiate that this does not apply to Norway in the 1890s. In Denmark and Sweden democratization was a result of an alliance between the socialists and the liberals. The initiative lay largely with the labour movement. In Norway, Venstre was the leading force in the democratization, and DNA played no significant independent part. This difference, however, was not related to any difference in radicalism between the social democratic parties.

This chapter has also tried to show that the terms reform and revolution are meaningless as opposites if we are trying to understand the meaning in the ideology of social democratic parties. DNA, and I would guess also the Danish and Swedish parties, thought of themselves as both revolutionary and reformist at the same time. All three parties wanted integration into a new society, created on social democratic principles.

Einar A. Terjesen is retired Senior Advisor at the Labour Movement Archives and Library in Oslo, Norway (Arbark), where he specialized in the history of the labour movement up to 1920 and cultural aspects of the movement. His publications include works about the May Day celebrations, the Municipal Workers' Union from 1945 to 1995 and articles in the yearbook of Arbark *Arbeiderhistorie.*

Notes

1. DNA was, and still is, the Social Democratic Party of Norway. In 2011 the Party shortened its Norwegian name to Arbeiderpartiet. In English it is still called The Norwegian Labour Party.
2. This article is a revised version of E.A. Terjesen. 2005. 'Demokrati og integrasjon', *Arbeiderhistorie*, 73–101.
3. F. Sejersted. 2005. *Socialdemokratiets tidsalder: Norge og Sverige i det 20.århundre*, Oslo: Pax. Revised English edition: F. Sejersted. 2011. *The Age of Social Democracy: Norway and Sweden in the Twentieth Century*, trans. R. Daly, edited M.B. Adams, Princeton: Princeton University Press.
4. For an introduction to Norwegian society and labour movement before 1914, see E.A. Terjesen. 1990. 'Norway', in M. Linden and J. Rojahn (eds), *The Formation of Labour Movements 1870–1914*, Leiden: Brill, 103–30. The most comprehensive introduction to the Norwegian labour movement for this period, which incorporates much of the research up to mid 1980s, is E. Bull. 1985. *Arbeiderklassen blir til (1850–1900)*, Oslo: Tiden; Ø. Bjørnson. 1990. *På klassekampens grunn (1900–1920)*, Oslo: Tiden; P. Maurseth. 1987. *Gjennom krise til makt (1920–1935)*, Oslo: Tiden. For Marcus Thrane see also M. Ringvej. 2014. *Marcus Thrane: forbrytelse og straff*, Oslo: Pax.
5. O.-B. Fure. 1976. 'Synspunkter og historieteoretiske tendenser i forskningen om den norske arbeiderklasse og bevegelse i den radikale fase 1918–1933', *Tidsskrift for arbeiderbevegelsens historie* 1, 29–62; Bjørnson, *På klassekampens grunn.*
6. See especially H.F. Dahl. 1969. *Fra klassekamp til nasjonal samling*, Oslo: Pax.
7. N. Elvander. 1980. *Skandinavisk arbetarrörelse*, Stockholm: Liber.
8. Dahl, *Fra klassekamp til nasjonal samling.*

9. E.A. Terjesen. 1984. 'Marxismen og det norske sosialdemokratiet 1884–1910', *Vardøger* 14, 119–59.

10. E. Bull. 1922. 'Die Entwicklung der Arbeiterbewegung in den drei skandinavischen Ländern', *Archiv für die Geschichte des Sozialismus und der Arbeiterbewegung* 10, 329–61; E. Bull. 1922. *Arbeiderbevægelsens stilling i de tre nordiske land 1914–1920*, Kristiania: DNAs forlag; reprinted in *Tidsskrift for arbeiderbevegelsens historie* 1, 3–28. Edvard Bull was the father of the Edvard Bull, whose work is cited in note 4.

11. For example Ø. Bjørnson. 1979. 'Pengene eller livet: fagforeningshistorie frå Trondheim typografar og malarar 1890–1918', Ph.D. dissertation. Bergen: University of Bergen.

12. F. Olstad. 1988. 'Radikalisme?', *Arbeiderhistorie*, 47–61.

13. Sejersted, *Sosialdemokratiets tidsalder.*

14. Sejersted, *The Age of Social Democracy*, 62.

15. Sejersted, *The Age of Social Democracy*, 72–73.

16. J. Ryssevik. 1991. 'Party vs. Parliament', in L. Karvonen and J. Sundberg (eds), *Social Democracy in Transition*, Aldershot: Dartmouth, 15–48.

17. Ryssevik, 'Party vs. Parliament', 19.

18. N.F. Christiansen. 1995. 'Arbejderklasserne i de nordiske lande før 1920', *Arbejderhistorie* 3, 14–21.

19. S. Rokkan. 1966. 'Norway: Numerical Democracy and Corporate Pluralism', in R.A. Dahl (ed.), *Political Oppositions in Western Democracies*, New Haven and London: Yale, 80.

20. K. Östberg. 1990. *Byråkrati och reformism*, Lund: Arkiv.

21. E.A. Terjesen. 1991. 'Arbeiderbevegelse og politikk i 1890årene', *Arbeiderhistorie*, 21–52.

22. In some cases the societies have stayed 'apolitical' until today.

23. *Forhandlinger ved Det femte norske arbeidermøde, afholdt i Drammen 11te – 15de juli 1891* (1892), 6–7.

24. L.-A. Jensen. 2002. 'Norske fagforeningafaner – en egen fanetradisjon?', in P. Kettunen (ed.), *Lokalt och internationellt: Dimensioner i den nordiska arbetarrörelsen och arbetarkulturen*, Tammerfors: Sällskapet för forskning i arbetarhistoria i Finland, 193–216.

25. E.A. Terjesen. 1990. *Maidagen*, Oslo: Tiden.

26. H. Lange. 1962. *Fra sekt til parti*, Oslo: Universitetsforlaget.

27. According to advertisements and reports in *Social-Demokraten.*

28. DNA, protokoll 17. landsmøte, 1903.

29. S.M. Lipset and S. Rokkan. 1967. 'Cleavage Structures, Party Systems, and Voter Alignments: An Introduction', in S.M. Lipset and S. Rokkan (eds), *Party Systems and Voter Alignments: Cross National Perspectives*, New York: Free Press, 27–29; P. Flora et al. 1983. *State, Economy, and Society in Western Europe 1815–1975*, vol. 1, Frankfurt: Campus, 22.

30. D. Langewiesche. 1993. 'Liberalism and the Middle Classes in Europe', in J. Kocka and A. Mitchell (eds), *Bourgeois Society in Nineteenth Century Europe*, Oxford: Berg, 49, 61.

31. G. Therborn. 1973. 'The Rule of Capital and the Rise of Democracy', *New Left Review* 103, 3–41; R. Collier. 1999. *Paths toward Democracy*, Cambridge: Cambridge University Press; D. Rueschemeyer, E.H. Stephens and J.D. Stephens. 1992. *Capitalist Development and Democracy*, Chicago: University of Chicago Press.

32. S.M. Lipset. 1983. 'Radicalism or Reformism', *American Political Science Review* 77, 1–18; Ruschmeier, *Capitalist Development and Democracy.*

33. Terjesen, *Marxismen og det norske sosialdemokratiet.*

34. Terjesen, *Maidagen.*

35. F. Sejersted. 2004. 'Sosialdemokratiets tidsalder', *Nytt Norsk Tidsskrift*, 256.

36. Elvander, *Skandinavisk arbetarrörelse*; Ryssevik, 'Party vs. Parliament'; W. Lafferty. 1970. 'Partiideologi og gruppestruktur', *Historisk tidsskrift* 49, 161–90.

37. This is also emphasized by Elvander, *Skandinavisk arbetarrörelse*, 44 and 80.

References

Bjørnson, Ø. 1979. 'Pengene eller livet: fagforeningshistorie frå Trondheim typografar og malarar 1890–1918', PhD dissertation, Bergen: University of Bergen.
———. 1990. *På klassekampens grunn (1900–1920)*, Oslo: Tiden.
Bull, E. 1922. 'Die Entwicklung der Arbeiterbewegung in den drei skandinavischen Ländern', *Archiv für die Geschichte des Sozialismus und der Arbeiterbewegung* 10, 329–61.
———. 1922. *Arbeiderbevægelsens stilling i de tre nordiske land 1914–1920*, Kristiania: DNAs forlag. Reprint *Tidsskrift for arbeiderbevegelsens historie* 1 (1976), 3–28.
———. 1985. *Arbeiderklassen blir til (1850–1900)*, Oslo: Tiden.
Christiansen, N.F. 1995. 'Arbejderklasserne i de nordiske lande før 1920', *Arbejderhistorie* 3, 14–21.
Collier, R. 1999. *Paths toward Democracy*, Cambridge: Cambridge University Press.
Dahl, H.F. 1969. *Fra klassekamp til nasjonal samling*, Oslo: Pax.
Elvander, N. 1980. *Skandinavisk arbetarrörelse*, Stockholm: Liber.
Flora, P. et al. 1983. *State, Economy, and Society in Western Europe 1815–1975*, Frankfurt: Campus.
Fure, O.-B. 1976. 'Synspunkter og historieteoretiske tendenser i forskningen om den norske arbeiderklasse og – bevegelse i den radikale fase 1918–1933', *Tidsskrift for arbeiderbevegelsens historie* 1, 29–62.
Jensen, L.-A. 'Norske fagforeningafaner – en egen fanetradisjon?', in P.Kettunen (ed.), *Lokalt och internationellt. Dimensioner i den nordiska arbetarrörelsen och arbetarkulturen*, Tammersfors: SFFA, 2002, 193–216.
Lafferty, W. 1970. 'Partiideologi og gruppestruktur', *Historisk tidsskrift* 49, 161–90.
Lange, H. 1962. *Fra sekt til parti*, Oslo: Universitetsforlaget.
Langewiesche, D. 'Liberalism and the Middle Classes in Europe', in J. Kocka and A. Mitchell (eds), *Bourgeois Society in Nineteenth Century Europe*, Oxford: Berg, 1993, 40–60.
Lipset, S.M. 1983. 'Radicalism or Reformism', *American Political Science Review* 77, 1–18.
Lipset, S.M and S. Rokkan. 'Cleavage Structures, Party Systems, and Voter Alignments: An Introduction', in S.M. Lipset and S. Rokkan (eds), *Party Systems and Voter Alignments, Cross National Perspectives*, New York: Free Press, 1967, 27–29.
Maurseth, P. 1987. *Gjennom krise til makt (1920–1935)*, Oslo: Tiden.
Olstad, F. 1988. 'Radikalisme?', *Arbeiderhistorie*, 47–61.
Östberg, K. 1990. *Byråkrati och reformism*, Lund: Arkiv.
Ringvej, M. 2014. *Marcus Thrane: forbrytelse og straff*, Oslo: Pax.
Rokkan, S. 'Norway: Numerical Democracy and Corporate Pluralism', in R.A. Dahl (ed.), *Political Oppositions in Western Democracies*, New Haven and London: Yale, 1966, 70–115.
Rueschemeyer, D., E.H. Stephens and J.D. Stephens. 1992. *Capitalist Development and Democracy*, Chicago: University of Chicago Press.
Ryssevik, J. 'Party vs. Parliament', in L. Karvonen and J. Sundberg (eds), *Social Democracy in Transition*, Aldershot: Dartmouth, 1991, 15–48.
Sejersted, F. 2004. 'Sosialdemokratiets tidsalder', *Nytt Norsk Tidsskrift*, 250–63.

_____. 2005. *Socialdemokratiets tidsalder: Norge og Sverige i det 20.århundre*, Oslo: Pax.

_____. 2011. *The Age of Social Democracy: Norway and Sweden in the Twentieth Century*, trans. R. Daly, edited M.B. Adams, Princeton: Princeton University Press.

_____. 'Norway', in M. Linden and J. Rojahn (eds), *The Formation of Labour Movements 1870–1914*, Leiden: Brill, 1990, 103–30.

_____. 1990. *Maidagen*, Oslo: Tiden.

_____. 1991. 'Arbeiderbevegelse og politikk i 1890årene', *Arbeiderhistorie*, 21–52.

_____. 2005. 'Demokrati og integrasjon', *Arbeiderhistorie*, 73–101.

Therborn, G. 1973. 'The Rule of Capital and the Rise of Democracy', *New Left Review* 103, 3–41.

CHAPTER 10

'NORDEN' AS A TRANSNATIONAL SPACE IN THE 1930S

Negotiated Consensus of 'Nordicness' in the Nordic Cooperation Committee of the Labour Movement

Mirja Österberg

This chapter examines how cooperation between the Nordic social democratic organizations gave rise to its own brand of Nordicness in the 1930s, when those involved were able to discuss national questions from a joint Nordic premise. I argue that representatives of Nordiska arbetarrörelsens samarbetskommitté (the Nordic cooperation committee of the labour movement, SAMAK) created an image of a united Nordic labour movement in order to achieve certain political goals nationally and internationally. This negotiated consensus on Nordicness was constructed in a specific situation in order to respond to and cope with a specific problem. SAMAK was the transnational agent in the construction of a Nordic region.

Established in 1932, SAMAK involved the social democratic parties and the central trade union organizations in Sweden, Denmark, Finland and Iceland. They were all members of the Labour and Socialist International (LSI) and the International Federation of Trade Unions (IFTU), dominated by social democrats. This was in contrast to Det Norske Arbeiderpartiet (the Norwegian Labour Party, DNA) and De Samvirkende Fagforbund (the Norwegian central organization for trade unions, AFL), which were not affiliated to either of these international bodies. As LSI and IFTU membership was a precondition of full access

to SAMAK, the Norwegian labour organizations were denied membership in the committee until the late 1930s. Between 1921 and 1923,
DNA had been a member of the Third International, or Comintern,
and in the years 1923–1938 it remained internationally independent. It
was only when AFL joined IFTU in 1936 and DNA joined LSI in 1938
that the Norwegian organizations became full members of SAMAK. In
fact, the establishment of SAMAK has been explained as a method by
which the Swedish and Danish labour organizations put pressure on the
Norwegian labour organizations to join these international bodies.[1]

This chapter is a contribution to literature discussing the Nordic aspects of social democracy. Previous research has focused on SAMAK
from the angle of foreign policy at a time of tense geopolitical relations
in Europe, when fascism and communism were seen as threatening to
the survival of the social democratic movement and parliamentary democracy.[2] This chapter will instead examine how the Nordic aspect of
the labour movement was built in order to be used both at home and
abroad. This Nordicness was constructed out of the similarities that
were found among conflicting and rivalling national interests. This perspective has been explored by Klaus Petersen, whose research has shown
the importance of Nordic cooperation in constructing the notion of a
specific Nordic model of welfare. Once they had been established, similarities were turned into something Nordic.[3]

What made the annual or biannual SAMAK meetings special was that
the individuals involved understood them as private informal gatherings.
Any opinions that they voiced would remain within the circle of members only.[4] This made it possible to express conflicting views that never
appeared in public, while the committee's official press releases could be
used in political struggles as a means to press for changes in attitudes.[5]
This created a tension between the private and unofficial SAMAK discussions on the one hand and SAMAK's public and 'official' press releases
on the other, but it also gave the participants the possibility to negotiate
and to create an image of a united Nordic labour movement.

I will first briefly discuss the topic of Norden as a resource and will
then move on to the empirical part of the chapter, which demonstrates
how the Nordicness of the social democratic labour organizations was
constructed through Nordic social democratic cooperation within
SAMAK. The main body of the source material comes from the minutes of SAMAK, published by Krister Wahlbäck and Kersti Blidberg.
However, SAMAK was not the only Nordic social democratic arena,
and in 1935 and in 1938 the Nordic social democratic parties organized public mass gatherings under the heading of 'Days of Nordic

democracy'. Given the limitations of space, these debates on Nordic democracy will be touched upon only briefly.[6]

Norden as a Resource

Norden or the Nordic region comprises Denmark, Finland, Iceland, Norway and Sweden. The geographical term Scandinavia refers to the three Nordic countries of Denmark, Norway and Sweden.[7] In this chapter, I will make a clear distinction between Scandinavian and Nordic. While Scandinavia/Scandinavian is largely used synonymously with Norden/Nordic in the English-speaking world and refers to all five Nordic countries,[8] this usage is less common in the Nordic countries themselves.[9] It has been argued that Scandinavia was replaced by Norden between the world wars as a means of bringing Finland into the Scandinavian sphere.[10] Another term that the Nordic countries have themselves promoted abroad is 'the Northern Countries'.[11] *Nordisch* was a term used by the pan-German movement in the nineteenth century to refer to the 'true' unspoiled Germanic peoples of Norden. The term later came to be mostly associated with Nazism.[12]

It has been commonly accepted, especially since the emergence of the Nordic welfare states after the Second World War, that Norden today is a concept with unequivocally positive associations for almost everyone in the Nordic region.[13] We should nevertheless note that Norden should be seen as a temporal concept.[14] From the 1930s onwards, says the Finnish historian Pauli Kettunen, the Nordic countries understood Norden as a future code, '"the horizon of expectations" associated with modernization'. While Denmark's progressive social legislation represented modernization in the 1920s, in the 1930s it was Sweden that was identified as the centre of modernization from a social political and social democratic perspective. The class compromises of the 1930s between workers and farmers through political coalitions between social democrats and agrarian parties, and the consolidation of the practice of collective negotiations and agreements in the industrial labour markets, supported the idea that social security, economic efficiency and economic growth reinforced each other. Most notably in Sweden, the earlier self-image of a poor and peripheral country became detached from the concept of Norden, which now represented modernity.[15]

However, Norden also meant different things in different Nordic countries. From the 1930s in Finland, Sweden represented the basis for the future Finnish society.[16] In Iceland, the Nordic aspect of Alþýðuflokkur (the social democratic party) was met with scepticism, as internationalism and foreign dominance were in general seen as a threat to Icelandic independence.[17] Nordic cooperation was also perceived differently during different historical periods. Finland had gained independence in 1917, but it took until the end of 1935 for the Finnish government officially to adopt a Scandinavian orientation in its foreign policy. Nordic cooperation was not on the political agenda in Norway either after the personal union of Sweden and Norway was dissolved in 1905. Matters were complicated by the unsuccessful political pan-Scandinavian movement between the 1840s and 1860s[18] and Nordic cooperation had also been long fraught with tensions in the field of security policy.[19] On the other hand, the rise of the social democratic majority or coalition governments in Scandinavia increased the willingness for economic – and especially social – political cooperation.[20]

Moreover, the use of Norden as an idea by historical agents should be seen not only as a reflection of what might have been conceived as 'reality', but rather as 'projections of the political controversy in those countries where Scandinavian/Nordic models are debated'.[21] Foreign examples have always been used rhetorically when political innovations have been dismissed as doubtful, or promoted as models in order to stimulate political innovations.[22] The use of international comparisons, ideas or practices in a new context 'often implies changes in the original practice that will adapt it to its new environment',[23] so much so, perhaps, that the foreign origins of transferred ideas or practices become invisible.[24] Political transfers are therefore always innovations, which include 'translations' and appropriations.[25] The motivations for transfers are stimulated and conditioned by perceptions of the needs and interests that arise in a particular context.[26]

The notion of the 'Nordic' that was created in SAMAK was effective in domestic debates in Sweden, Finland, Norway and Denmark, since it referred to something transnational while simultaneously leaving room for a national element. Jussi Kurunmäki argues that Swedish and Finnish social democrats could in 1935 enhance their alignment with the national political tradition by making an implicit equation between Nordic and Swedish/Finnish. By referring to Norden it was therefore possible to play the national card twice. Furthermore, in 1935 the Swedish social democrats managed to colonize the concept of 'Nordic democracy', distinguishing the Nordic countries from the autocratic or dictatorial Europe while they nationalized their view of democracy.[27] In similar terms, Øystein Sørensen and Bo Stråth hold that 'the Nordic element was never independent in relation to national identities but always remained a constitutive element of them'.[28]

Constructing a United Nordic Labour
Movement in SAMAK

SAMAK was first and foremost established to steer the Norwegian labour organizations into the international fold. Beyond this, the cooperation committee had a twofold goal. The aim was to create Nordic unity in order to strengthen the possibilities for the small Nordic countries to influence decision-making in larger international arenas,[29] including the LSI, the IFTU and the International Labour Organization (ILO).[30] As Norbert Götz and Heidi Haggrén have argued, Norden has been an invaluable resource internationally as a shared identity that 'has been created through encounters between Nordic actors, but also through their common workings with the outside world'.[31] The second goal was to generate Nordic unity, which could be used at home to consolidate social democratic ideology and domination in the Nordic countries against what were understood as threats – that is, communism and fascism.[32] The split in the international labour movement between social democrats and communists also affected the Nordic labour movements, and the battles between communists and social democrats were particularly harsh in Finland and Norway. Another crucial aspect was to coordinate measures to alleviate unemployment caused by the economic crises of the early 1930s.[33]

Such goals, combined with the concern about the Norwegian labour movement's international position, provided the framework when in 1934 the individuals involved in SAMAK discovered a Scandinavian crisis policy and constructed an image of a united Nordic labour movement. This happened regardless of the fact that there were palpable tensions between the Nordic similarities that were identified and hopes of what the reality should look like.

The agenda for SAMAK's meeting in 1934 focused on two issues: reports of the current situation of the Nordic labour organizations and whether or not DNA would join the Socialist International. It is worth noting that although they were not full members of SAMAK until 1936/1938, the representatives of the Norwegian labour movement were regularly present as observers in SAMAK's meetings as of 1934. The meeting duly addressed the state of the Nordic labour organizations before proceeding to discuss whether or not DNA would join the Socialist International.

It was in this discussion that the Scandinavian delegates noticed similarities in their organizations' practices and goals. Per Albin Hansson, leader of Sveriges Socialdemokratiska arbetareparti (the Swedish Social Democratic Party, SAP) and prime minister from 1932–1936 and

1936–46, began the presentations by stressing that cooperation between the SAP and Bondeförbundet (the Swedish Farmers' League) was a successful way to solve the problem of unemployment for wage workers and farmers caused by the Great Depression. Hansson was followed by the leader of Socialdemokratisk Forbund (the Danish Social Democratic Party, SDF) and long-term prime minister (1929–1942) Thorvald Stauning. He began by arguing that '[o]ur politics has the same goal as in Sweden, namely to help agriculture and the unemployed'.[34] In response to Hansson's and Stauning's statements, Oscar Torp, leader of DNA, argued that DNA and the Swedish and Danish social democrats shared the unemployment policy goal of collaboration between wage workers and farmers. Torp concluded: 'we realize that we [in Norway] stand on similar ground'.[35]

The background for both Hansson's and Stauning's statements was the Danish Kanslergadeforliget (Kanslergade Agreement) of January 1933 and the Swedish krisuppgörelse of May 1933. The Kanslergadeforliget was named after the home address of Prime Minister Thorvald Stauning in Kanslergade (literally Chancellors' street) in Copenhagen, where the negotiations were completed. The Swedish krisuppgörelse, which means crisis settlement, was also referred to disparagingly as *kohandeln*, which literarily translates as 'the cow trade' or perhaps more precisely 'horse-trading', in other words a political compromise.[36] Both agreements were established between the national social democratic parties and the political parties advocating farmers' interests. The agreements were compromises over the goals of the unemployment policies of these two groups. The social democratic parties gained support for public investment in public work schemes, but in return they gave up the principle of free trade by accepting protective tariffs for some domestic agricultural products in order to improve farmers' economic circumstances.[37]

In contrast, DNA found itself in opposition until March 1935. This did not prevent Torp from incorporating DNA into this vision of a shared unemployment policy, because the party had discarded its strategy of class struggle and adopted a broader 'people's party' approach in a party conference in 1933. DNA's goal was now to combat unemployment through government action. As Jorunn Bjørgum argues, this shift away from a revolutionary strategy to a revisionist approach was brought about by the fear that the economic crises of the 1930s would win support for fascist groups in Norwegian society. The emergence of the Finnish extremist right-wing Lapua movement was used as an example.[38]

Yet, it is worth noting that while Torp stressed similarities between the Swedish and the Danish unemployment goals, DNA was not prepared to cooperate with a bourgeois party, which was what the Danish and

Swedish social democratic parties had done. DNA aimed instead at a parliamentary majority, as Torp mentioned during the debate.[39] Another interesting aspect is that Stauning – not the Icelandic representative Oddur
Olafsson – also included the Icelandic labour movement in the vision of
policies shared by the Nordic labour organizations.[40] However, although
the first 'green-red' government with farmers and social democrats held
power in Iceland from 1934–1938, the Icelandic social democratic party
was in such a weak position that it did not have the power to determine
the government's policies. The Icelandic party's influence was therefore
not comparable to that in Sweden and Denmark.[41]

While the Swedish, Danish and Norwegian trade union representatives
reassured each other with claims of shared goals and practices on unemployment, the delegates of the Finnish labour movements did no such
thing. The party secretary for the Suomen Sosialidemokraattinen Puolue
(Finnish Social Democratic Party, SDP), Karl Harald Wiik, concluded
that SDP had failed to achieve cooperation with a bourgeois party such
as Maalaisliitto (agrarian league). The fact that the SDP had won more
MPs in spring 1933 had not changed the situation.[42] In a similar manner,
Karl-August Fagerholm, representative of Suomen Ammattiyhdistysten
Keskusliitto (the Confederation of Finnish Trade Unions, SAK), underlined the weakness of the Finnish trade union movement.[43]

The background was that the Finnish labour market relations differed
from those in the Scandinavian countries in the 1930s and 1940s. Suomen
Työnantajain Keskusliitto (the Finnish employers' confederation, STK)
did not accept the practice of collective bargaining until January 1940,
and collective agreements were introduced only after the Second World
War. In the Scandinavian countries, basic agreements concerning a national system of collective agreements between the labour market parties
were already commonplace: in Denmark since 1899, in Norway since
1935 and in Sweden since 1938. Likewise, the position of SDP differed
from its sister parties.[44] In Finland, the SDP stayed in opposition, partly as
a consequence of the Finnish civil war in 1918, with the exception of the
social democratic minority government in 1926–27. The Finnish bourgeois parties identified the SDP as a threat to the nation in the wake of the
civil war between the socialist 'reds' and the bourgeois 'whites', which the
reds had lost. It was not until the formation of the 'Red-Earth' coalition
government in March 1937 of liberals, agrarians and social democrats
that the divisions in Finnish society slowly began to heal.

However, there were some new tendencies in SDP's economic programme that recalled the Scandinavian sister parties' practices, which
none of the Finnish representatives mentioned. One of their inner circle,
the future chair of SAK Eero A. Wuori, had already explored the crisis

policies of both the Swedish and the Danish social democratic parties during a study trip in the summer of 1933.[45] Wuori's report was circulated among the SDP's parliamentary members and both Wiik and Fagerholm must have known its contents as elected members of the Finnish parliament.[46] Also, SDP's written account for the Nordic cooperation committee reported on new tendencies in the SDP programme, which had been adopted in May 1933, such as the idea that the purchasing power of the vast majority would benefit the whole national economy.[47] In addition, Fagerholm, Wiik, the Finnish social democrat Reinhold Sventorzetski and also to some extent SDP's unofficial leader Väinö Tanner had promoted cooperation between workers and farmers in summer/autumn 1933 by using Swedish and Danish examples.[48] On the other hand, and despite these similar tendencies, contrary to the Swedish and Danish social democratic parties the Finnish SDP remained faithful to the principle of free trade and rejected any protective tariffs on agricultural goods in its economic programme of 1933.[49]

Nevertheless, although the Finnish delegates did not seem to be able or willing to include themselves in the construction of a Nordic narrative of how to overcome the problems of the economic depression, the Finnish SAMAK delegates were just as concerned as the other Nordic representatives about the meeting not producing any concrete results that could be shown to the rest of the world. SAMAK members had

Illustration 10.1 SAMAK meeting in Helsinki in 1935. In the picture are Martin Tranmæl, Magnus Nielsen, Gustav Möller, Alsing Andersen, Th Stauning, Johan Nygaardsvold, Väinö Tanner, Per Bergman, K.A Fagerholm and J.O Johansson. Arbetarrörelsens arkiv och bibliotek, Reportagebild.

conflicting views on a number of issues, which had become amply clear during the discussions on DNA's potential membership in the Socialist International and when debating the question of shortening the working week from forty-eight to forty hours.[50] It was therefore increasingly important for SAMAK to create something Nordic that the world – or at least the general public in the Nordic countries – could see. This perspective was particularly important to the Norwegians. In the internal debates, the unofficial leader of DNA, Martin Tranmæl,[51] concluded that '[m]any eyes are directed towards this meeting and we must therefore recognize what we have achieved'. Another representative of DNA, Magnus Nilssen, suggested that the meeting 'could agree upon elements that we share'. The Finnish social democrat Wiik also added that SAMAK had come together not to identify the differences among the Nordic labour organizations but to emphasize 'what we have in common and to achieve results that further support our cooperation'.[52]

Per Albin Hansson and Gustav Möller, the secretary of SAP and Minister of Social Affairs, also agreed with the previous SAMAK delegates' statements. However, they both felt Nordic cooperation had relevance not only for the social democratic movement in Norden: for them, Norden was also an agent in the international social democratic movement. As Hansson argued, the official declaration by SAMAK should also favour the future inclusion of DNA in the LSI, which would strengthen the international organization. Möller wondered if SAMAK could establish a joint Nordic front for democracy. After all, there was already a common front in unemployment questions. Such a democratic front would strengthen the Socialist International, Möller said, and benefit the labour movement in 'all countries'.[53] Norden could stand as a model for the defence of democracy.

Since it was impossible to build something 'Nordic' around specific details, the committee emphasized shared tendencies in the policies and goals of the Scandinavian social democratic parties and central organizations of trade unions. According to SAMAK's official press release, the meeting had shown that

> on the key domestic political questions – unemployment, support measures to ease agricultural depression, efforts to secure the social conditions of the working masses and to improve their living standard – the Nordic labour movements and trade unions *act in unison* and the labour organizations' policies are *completely similar* in all the countries.[54]

The press release quoted above also emphasized the joint Nordic defence of democracy, which had been mentioned by Möller, Hansson, Stauning and Torp.[55] What the SAMAK delegates of 1934 agreed upon were not specific unemployment policy practices, but rather a joint Nordic discourse that foregrounded cooperation between the 'working masses' in society – blue-collar workers and agricultural labourers. This cooperation was identified as essential to decrease unemployment and defend democracy. The press release therefore embraced both the Nordic similarities that the meeting had recognized and the delegates' hopes for the future. Hansson concluded: 'What matters is the willingness to bring this declaration into life. ... It is my sincere hope that the work in Norway will bear fruit and I share the hope that the whole labour movement will soon be included in the International'.[56]

Convincing Finns to Follow Scandinavian Cross-Class Policies

If the goal of a united Nordic social democratic labour movement in 1934 was to steer the Norwegian Labour Party towards membership of the LSI on a more reformist path, the goal had been partly fulfilled by the time of SAMAK's next meeting, held in Finland from 7 December to 9 December 1935. That is, a social democratic government had been formed in Norway in March 1935 at the same time as DNA had entered into a kriseforliket (crisis agreement) with the agrarian party. This arrangement bore similarities to the Danish kanslergadeforliget and Swedish krisuppgörelse. Compared to the previous year, SAMAK's meeting now had a rather high profile, because of the presence of three prime ministers: Per Albin Hansson (SAP) from Sweden, Thorvald Stauning (SDF) from Denmark and the Norwegian social democrat Johan Nygaardsvold (DNA) were all there. Väinö Tanner, the unofficial leader of the Finnish SDP, was also present at SAMAK's meeting and took a leading role when the Nordic social democratic leaders gave public speeches to their supporters in Helsinki Workers' House.[57] Just a few days earlier the Finnish government had declared a new official foreign policy based on a 'Scandinavian orientation' and neutrality in the aftermath of the weakness of the League of Nations. Members of SDP hoped that the adoption of the new foreign policy would strengthen their domestic position.[58]

Although Tanner had not participated in SAMAK's meetings in 1932–1934, he was thereafter a regular member in the late 1930s and early 1940s.[59] This indicates that Nordic cooperation became important for Tanner after 1935.[60] The explanation for this might have been that since the beginning of 1935 Tanner had been involved in different efforts to strengthen Finland's ties to Norden. First, since November 1934 he had been a member of the Nordic delegation that promoted economic cooperation between the northern countries. This delegation arranged its first meeting in February 1935.[61] Second, Tanner became a loose member of the group in Finland that from 1934 launched the new official foreign policy of 'Scandinavian orientation'.[62]

Again, there was a variety of topics on the agenda of the Nordic cooperation committee in 1935, but unlike in 1934, 'workers' and farmers' cooperation' was now an official item. It was not discussed spontaneously, as the year before. Since DNA had already proven its willingness to embrace reformism, the debate no longer dwelled on the efforts to establish common Nordic elements that would facilitate the Norwegians' inclusion in the LSI. Instead, the discussion now focused on convincing the Finnish social democrats to follow the Scandinavian example and establish political cooperation with Maalaisliitto. In addition to the shared economic interests of farmers and workers, the Swedish labour leaders also argued that this was the best way of defending democracy.

According to Nygaardsvold, Hansson and Stauning, the Finns needed to 'educate' the Finnish farmers of the benefits of worker-farmer cooperation. Nygaardsvold began by arguing that, '[t]hese two classes, which live by their own work, have learned to understand each other'.[63] Hansson continued by arguing that 'both working elements of the people should make the foundation for the future democratic politics', whereas according to Stauning '[c]o-operation between workers and farmers is natural and right'.[64]

Meanwhile, the Finns Tanner, Wiik and J.W. Keto all defended their current stance as resulting from Maalaisliitto's powerful position in Finnish society. The SDP was in opposition and had not managed to secure cooperation with any other political party. Tanner was also reluctant to give up the principle of free trade, since he was concerned that the SDP's voters would not understand such a new position. This would lie in the future, however, if collaboration with Maalaisliitto became reality. The Finnish leader was still hoping that a social democratic victory in the Finnish general election in the summer of 1936 might soften Maalaisliitto.[65] The SDP also suggested another alternative in its report to SAMAK, proposing a collaboration with Svenska Folkpartiet (the Swedish People's Party, SFP) or Kansallinen edistyspuolue (the National Progressive Party, ED). According to the SDP, these two liberal bourgeois parties, just like the SDP, promoted the interests of consumers.[66]

Tanner's opinions about the conflicting economic interests of workers and farmers did not discourage Hansson, Möller or Edvard Johansson, the chair of Landsorganisationen i Sverige (Swedish Confederation of

Trade Unions, LO) from seeking to convince the Finns that the Finnish farmers should be educated to understand the benefits of worker-farmer cooperation.[67] According to Johansson, a worker-farmer cooperation was an effective 'broad front for democracy'.[68] Möller argued that farmers could not be turned into socialists, but could instead be liberated from their opposition against the labour movement.[69] Hansson concurred that unconquerable principled disagreements should not exist, although occasional questions might disrupt the cooperation.[70]

By way of concluding this debate, the meeting produced a press release promoting the benefits of established worker-farmer cooperation in some of the Nordic countries. This, it was argued, had favourable economic consequences and was the best possible way of defending democracy. Interestingly, this part of the press release was formulated by the Finnish social democrat Wiik.[71] The formulation could therefore be interpreted as a negotiated consensus of what SDP should strive for. The press release also included a wish for success for the social democratic parties' general election campaigns the following year in Finland, Sweden, Denmark and Norway.

Despite the efforts of the Scandinavian leaders to convince the Finns to follow their example of worker-farmer cooperation, the issue no longer seemed as relevant in SAMAK's next meeting in 1936. SDP had gained victory in the 1936 general election, but the Finnish president Pehr Evind Svinhufvud, who had been a central figure on the 'white' bourgeoisie side in the Finnish civil war, refused to appoint a government with social democratic members.[72] However, the topic was only briefly mentioned, for other subjects dominated the agenda, such as shortening the working week or Nordic economic cooperation. The narrative changed to some extent, shifting from political cooperation between two groups to the victory of social democracy in Scandinavia with the farmers' support. This was portrayed as the future prospect for the SDP. However, the minutes of the 1936 SAMAK meeting also show that Hansson did not view the Swedish and Danish class compromises as identical. After all, he said, the Swedish agrarian party was conservative, whereas the Danish agrarian party Venstre was radical. According to Hansson, Swedish cooperation could continue only if Bondeförbundet supported the Swedish social democratic election programme.[73] Further, in SAMAK's next meeting in August 1937, the issue seemed even less pressing. The problem had already been solved. After the formation of the 'Red-Earth' coalition government, Finland could be included in the victorious vision of Nordic social democracy. As Hansson briefly declared at the opening of the meeting, 'We can now come together in shared delight of our victories. The labour movement in Norden has been consolidated and has gained a completely new position'.[74] Other subjects such as the issue of a forty-hour working week dominated the meeting.[75] The need for a united Norden was nevertheless continuously present in the following meetings of SAMAK in several other perspectives.[76]

Conclusions

The meetings of SAMAK enabled representatives of the Nordic social democratic labour movements to discuss urgent questions from a joint Nordic perspective. This paved the way for an idea of a common Nordic labour movement based on Nordic similarities. The idea of a united Nordic labour movement was created in 1934 in order to facilitate DNA's future accession to the LSI, but in 1935 the Scandinavian representatives seemed focused on getting the Finnish SDP to follow their example of worker-farmer cooperation. The benefits were portrayed as solving the problems of the Great Depression, but the outcome was also understood as the bulwark of parliamentary democracy. In 1936 and 1937, the Nordic topic appears to have lost its importance, which could be interpreted as a consequence of the strengthened and stabilized positions of the social democratic parties in Sweden, Denmark and Norway. The explanation as to why references to a Nordic labour movement were so useful was that 'Nordic' referred simultaneously in the four Nordic countries – with the exception of Iceland – to something transnational and national. By referring to shared Nordic values one could use the national card twice. However, creating an image of a united Nordic social democratic labour movement went further than fortifying the position of social democracy in Norden. For example, in 1934 Möller recognized the Nordic countries' example in defending Nordic democracy as a model for other countries to follow, which would benefit the labour movement in all countries. In this sense, as Kettunen has argued, Möller understood Norden as a future code associated with modernization. It also seems that Hansson saw DNA's membership in the Socialist International as consolidating the whole international social democratic movement. Norden was thus seen as an agent in the world.

The role of Finnish delegates is also interesting. Although previous research has viewed Finland as a passive observer in Nordic cooperation,[77] the 1930s SAMAK debates on worker-farmer cooperation raise different interpretations. The Finnish representatives may have spoken less than their Scandinavian colleagues, but the meeting in 1934 shows that Wiik, for example, was actively involved in the process of creating something Nordic. Although clear differences of opinion surfaced in the private discussions at SAMAK, all the members agreed on the importance of putting up a united front. One could therefore argue that the image of a united Nordic social democratic labour movement was a negotiated construction. In addition, the alternative views of the SDP representatives in 1935 on collaboration with a liberal bourgeois party instead of Maalaisliitto also demonstrates that the Finnish delegates, such as Tanner, were not merely the passive recipients of advice from their Nordic colleagues. They had a certain degree of independence. We therefore need further research on the Finnish representatives' involvement in Nordic cooperation. It would be particularly interesting to examine how the arguments used in the Nordic arena differed from those wielded in Finnish domestic debates.

Mirja Österberg is a researcher at the Centre for Nordic Studies, University of Helsinki. She is currently finalizing her Ph.D. thesis on the history of the Finnish social democratic party's Nordic orientation. Her research interests include the history of the welfare state and social democracy, transnational studies and Nordic cooperation.

Notes

1. K. Blidberg. 1984. *Splittrad gemenskap: kontakter och samarbete inom nordisk socialdemokratisk arbetarrörelse 1931–1945*, Stockholm: Acta Universitatis Stockholmiensis, 42–43; D. Putensen. 2002. 'SAI och SAMAK – växlande storlekar i den internationella och den nordiska dimensionen (1914–1945)', in P. Kettunen (ed.), *Lokalt och internationellt: Dimensioner i den nordiska arbetarrörelsen och arbetarkulturen*, Tammerfors: Sällskapet för forskning i arbetarhistoria i Finland, 137. Both DNA and AFL were eager to cut their international segregation and rejoin the Nordic cooperation from which they had been excluded as a consequence of their radicalization, which had led to the abolishment of the previous joint committee for the Scandinavian labour movements in 1912–1920. See: M. Grass. 1974. 'Arbetarskandinavism 1912–1920. Kommittéen för skandinaviska arbetarrörelsens samarbete, några aspekter', *Årbog for arbejderbevaegelsens historie* 4, 55–86.
2. Blidberg, *Splittrad gemenskap*.
3. K. Petersen. 2006. 'Constructing Nordic Welfare? Nordic Social Political Co-operation 1919–1955', in N.F. Christiansen et al. (eds), *The Nordic Model of Welfare: A Historical Reappraisal*, Copenhagen: Museum Tusculanum Press, 67–98; K. Petersen. 2009. 'Transnationale perspektiver på den nordiske vælferdsmodels tilblivelsehistorie 1900–1950', in S. Bjerrum Fossa et al. (eds), *Transnationale historier*, Odense: Syddansk Universitetsforlag, 174.
4. K. Wahlbäck and K. Blidberg (eds). 1986. *Samråd i kristid: Protokoll från den nordiska arbetarrörelsens samarbetskommitté 1932–1946*, Stockholm: Kungl. Samfundet för utgivande av handskrifter rörande Skandinaviens historia, 87, 125–26, 189, 286, 322–24, 349 [Minutes of SAMAK's meeting in 1936, August 1937, August 1939, January 1945].
5. Blidberg, *Splittrad gemenskap*, 77.
6. For contributions on the rhetoric of Nordic democracy see J. Kurunmäki and J. Strang (eds). 2010. *Rhetorics of Nordic Democracy*, Helsinki: Finnish Literature Society.

7.   Strictly the term Scandinavia refers in geographical terms to the Scandinavian peninsula consisting of Sweden and Norway but for cultural reasons Denmark is often included when this term is used.

8.   M. Hilson. 2008. *The Nordic Model: Scandinavia since 1945*, London: Reaktion, 12.

9.   U. Østergård. 1997. 'The Geopolitics of Nordic Identity – From Composite States to Nation States', in Ø. Sørensen and B. Stråth (eds), *The Cultural Construction of Norden*, Oslo: Scandinavian University Press, 31.

10. See also J. Kurunmäki. 2010. '"Nordic Democracy" in 1935: On the Finnish and Swedish Rhetoric of Democracy', in Kurunmäki and Strang, *Rhetorics of Nordic Democracy*, 75; J. Kurunmäki and J. Strang. 2010. 'Introduction: "Nordic democracy" in a World of Tensions', in Kurunmäki and Strang, *Rhetorics of Nordic Democracy*, 24.

11. 'The Northern Countries in World Economy: Denmark, Finland, Iceland, Norway, Sweden', Helsinki: Delegations for the Promotion of Economic Co-operation between the Northern Countries, 1937; G.R. Nelson. 1953. *Freedom and Welfare: Social Patterns in the Northern Countries of Europe*, Copenhagen: The Ministries of Social Affairs of Denmark, Finland, Iceland, Norway, Sweden.

12. Østergård, 'The Geopolitics of Nordic Identity: From Composite States to Nation States', 32.

13. Østergård, 'The Geopolitics of Nordic Identity: From Composite States to Nation States', 29.

14. K. Palonen. 2005. 'Political Times and the Temporalisation of Concepts: A New Agenda for Conceptual History', in L-F. Landgrén and P. Hautamäki (eds), *People Citizen Nation*, Helsinki: Renvall Institute, 50–64.

15. P. Kettunen. 2008. *Globalisaatio ja kansallinen me: Kansallisen katseen historiallinen kritiikki*, Tampere: Vastapaino, 151–53; Kurunmäki and Strang, 'Introduction', 23; P. Kettunen. 2011. 'The Transnational Construction of National Challenges: The Ambiguous Nordic Model of Welfare and Competitiveness', in P. Kettunen and K. Petersen (eds), *Beyond Welfare State Models: Transnational Historical Perspectives on Social Policy*, Cheltenham: Edward Elgar, 30; P. Kettunen. 2002. 'Inledning', in P. Kettunen (ed.), *Lokalt och internationellt: Dimensioner i den nordiska arbetarrörelsen och arbetarkulturen*, Tammerfors: Sällskapet för forskning i arbetarhistoria i Finland, 9.

16. Kettunen, *Globalisaatio ja kansallinen me*, 151–53.

17. On the other hand the Icelandic Communist Party managed to present itself as a defender of Iceland's independence by developing its own version of Icelandic nationalism. See R. Kristjánsdóttir. 2012. 'For Equality or Against Foreign Oppression? The Politics of the Left in Iceland Leading up to the Cold War', *Social Movements in the Nordic Countries since 1900: Moving the Social. Journal of Social History and the History of Social Movements* 48, 11–28. See also chapter 11.

18. L. Karvonen. 2005. 'Finland och Norden: det ständiga återvändandet till rötterna', in L. Häggman (ed.), *Finland i Norden: Finland 50 år i Nordiska rådet*, Helsinki: Pohjola-Norden, 18–19; M. Majander. 2004. *Pohjoismaa vai kansandemokratia? Sosiaalidemokraatit, kommunistit ja Suomen kansainvälinen asema 1944–51*, Helsinki: Suomalaisen Kirjallisuuden Seura, 55–56; F. Sejersted. 2005. *Socialdemokratins tidsålder: Sverige och Norge under 1900-talet*, Nora: Nya Doxa, 7–8, 175–81; R. Hemstad. 'Scandinavianism, Nordic Co-operation, and "Nordic Democracy"', in Kurunmäki and Strang, *Rhetorics of Nordic Democracy*, 180–82, 184–85.

19. K. Wahlbäck. 2000. 'Försvarsbundsförhandlingar 1948–49. Misslyckandet och det informella efterspelet', in B. Sundelius and C. Wiklund (eds), *Norden i sicksack: Tre spårbyten inom nordiskt samarbete*, Stockholm: Santérus, 31–44; N. Andrén. 'Säkerhetspolitikens återkomst: Om säkerhetspolitikens plats i rådsdialogen', in Sundelius and Wiklund, *Norden i sicksack*, 275–301. For a change concerning Nordic cooperation within the field of security policy see J. Strang. 2012. *Nordiska gemenskaper: En vision för samarbetet*, København: Nordiska rådet, 25, 36–40.

20. Petersen, 'Constructing Nordic Welfare?', 75–77, 86–94.

21. Ø. Sørensen and B. Stråth. 1997. 'Introduction: The Cultural Construction of Norden', in Ø. Sørensen and B. Stråth (eds), *The Cultural Construction of Norden*, Oslo: Scandinavian University Press, 21.

22. H. te Velde. 2005. 'Political Transfer: An Introduction', *European Review of History – Revue Européenne Histoire* 12(2), 205–21.

23. te Velde, 'Political Transfer', 208.

24. S. Nygård. 2008. *Filosofins renässans eller modern mystic: Bergsondebatten i Finland*, Helsingfors: Universitetstryckeriet, 11–14.

25. P. Clavin. 2005. 'Defining Transnationalism', *Contemporary European History* 14(4), 423.

26. N. Edling. 2008. 'Regulating Unemployment the Continental Way: The Transfer of Municipal Labour Exchanges to Scandinavia 1890–1914', *European Review of History: Revue Europeenne d'Histoire* 15(1), 27; see also M. Werner and B. Zimmermann. 2006. 'Beyond Comparison: *Histoire Croisée* and and the Challenge of Reflexivity', *History and Theory* 45(1), 30–50.

27. Kurunmäki, '"Nordic Democracy"', 60, 74–75.

28. Sørensen and Stråth, 'Introduction', 22.

29. Blidberg, *Splittrad gemenskap*, 45; Putensen, 'SAI och SAMAK', 137.

30. Blidberg, *Splittrad gemenskap*, 10–11, 51, 75.

31. N. Götz and H. Haggrén. 2008. 'Introduction: Transnational Nordic Alignment in Stormy Waters', in N. Götz and H. Haggrén (eds), *Regional Cooperation and International Organizations: The Nordic Model in Transnational Alignment*, London: Routledge, 1–22.

32. See for example Thorvald Stauning's and Gustav Möller's statements in the planning meeting of SAMAK in 1931, in Wahlbäck and Blidberg, *Samråd i kristid*, 15.

33. Putensen, 'SAI och SAMAK ', 137.

34. Wahlbäck and Blidberg, *Samråd i kristid*, 31. All quotes have been translated by the author and language checked by Pirkko Hautamäki.

35. Minutes of SAMAK's meeting in 1934; published in Wahlbäck and Blidberg, *Samråd i kristid*, 32.

36. K. Petersen, N.F. Christiansen and J.H. Petersen. 2013. 'The Danish Social Reform of 1933: Social Rights as a New Paradigm by an Accidental Reform?', in H. Haggrén, J. Raunio-Niemi, J. Vauhkonen, *Multi-Layered Historicity of the Present: Approaches to Social Science History*, Helsinki: University of Helsinki, 105; N. Edling. 2013. 'The Primacy of Welfare Politics: Notes on the Language of the Swedish Social Democrats and Their Adversaries', in Haggrén, Raunio-Niemi and Vauhkonen, *Multi-Layered Historicity of the Present*, 126.

37. A. Isaksson. 1996. *Per Albin: Partiledaren*, Stockholm: Wahlström & Widstrand, 239–40, 253–60; Sejersted, *Socialdemokratins tidsålder*, 96; K. Åmark. 2005. *Hundra år av välfärdspolitik: Välfärdsstatens framväxt i Norge och Sverige*, Umeå: Boréa, 62–63; Petersen, Christiansen and Petersen, 'The Danish Social Reform of 1933', 105.

38. J. Bjørgum. 2000. 'Krisen, fascismen og det norske arbeiderparti på 1930-tallet', in P. Kettunen, A. Kultanen and T. Soikkanen (eds), *Jäljillä: Kirjoituksia historian ongelmista. Osa 2*, Turku: Kirja-Aurora, 221–44.

39. Minutes of SAMAK's meeting in 1934 published in Wahlbäck and Blidberg, *Samråd i kristid*, 32.

40. Minutes of SAMAK's meeting in 1934 published in Wahlbäck and Blidberg, *Samråd i kristid*, 32, 29.

41. G. Jonson. 2001. 'The Icelandic Welfare State in the Twentieth Century', *Scandinavian Journal of History* 26(3), 254–55; Kristjánsdóttir, 'For Equality or Against Foreign Oppression?', 11–28.

42. Minutes of SAMAK's meeting in 1934 published in Wahlbäck and Blidberg, *Samråd i kristid*, 33; J. Mylly. 1989. *Maalaisliitto-Keskustapuolueen historia: Maalaisliitto 1918–1939*, Helsinki: Kirjayhtymä, 308, 310; H. Soikkanen. 1975. *Kohti kansanvaltaa: Suomen*

Sosialidemokraattinen Puolue 75 vuotta. 1-3, 1899–1936, Helsinki: Suomen sosiaalidemokraattinen puolue, 545.

43. Minutes of SAMAK's meeting in 1934 published in Wahlbäck and Blidberg, *Samråd i kristid*, 34–35. Edvard Huttunen, the chair of SAK, was the third Finnish representative at SAMAK's meeting.

44. P. Kettunen. 2001. 'The Nordic Welfare State in Finland', *Scandinavian Journal of History* 26(3), 226–47; Sejersted, *Socialdemokratins tidsålder*, 149–51, 157–61; Hilson, *The Nordic Model*, 35–37.

45. Soikkanen, *Kohti kansanvaltaa*, 561.

46. E.A. Vuori, 'The Economic Policy in Sweden 15.8.1933' and E.A. Vuori, 'The Economic Policy in Denmark 15.8.1933', private collection of Eero A. Vuori, Labour archive, Helsinki (TA) and private collection of Väinö Tanner, Riksarkivet i Helsingfors (RA); Minutes of SDP's parliamentary group 12.9.1933, Private collection of SDP's parliamentary group, TA.

47. Soikkanen, *Kohti kansanvaltaa*, 538–40.

48. *Arbetarbladet* 2.6.1933; *Valtiopäivät (VP). Pöytäkirjat 1933* [Proceedings from the Finnish Parliament]. 1935. Helsinki: Valtioneuvoston kirjapaino, 78, 1093–95; Soikkanen, *Kohti kansanvaltaa*, 584; J. Paavolainen. 1984. *Väinö Tanner. 3. Sillanrakentaja. Elämäkerta vuosilta 1924–1936*, Helsinki: Tammi, 315.

49. Soikkanen, *Kohti kansanvaltaa*, 538–40.

50. Minutes of SAMAK's meeting in 1934 published in Wahlbäck and Blidberg, *Samråd i kristid*, 38–39.

51. Sejersted, *Socialdemokratins tidsålder*, 154, 166.

52. Minutes of SAMAK's meeting in 1934 published in Wahlbäck and Blidberg, *Samråd i kristid*, 40.

53. Minutes of SAMAK's meeting in 1934 published in Wahlbäck and Blidberg, *Samråd i kristid*, 38.

54. Minutes of SAMAK's meeting in 1934 published in Wahlbäck and Blidberg, *Samråd i kristid*, 42 (italics added).

55. Minutes of SAMAK's meeting in 1934 published in Wahlbäck and Blidberg, *Samråd i kristid*, 30–33.

56. Minutes of SAMAK's meeting in 1934 published in Wahlbäck and Blidberg, *Samråd i kristid*, 43.

57. *Arbetarbladet*, 9 December 1935, 11 December 1935.

58. T. Soikkanen. 1984. *Kansallinen eheytyminen – myytti vai todellisuus? Ulko- ja sisäpolitiikan linjat ja vuorovaikutus Suomessa vuosina 1933–1939*, Turku: Turun yliopisto, 79.

59. Tanner took part in SAMAK's meetings in December 1935, November 1936, August 1937, August 1939, March 1940 and January 1943. Minutes of SAMAK's meetings in 1935–1945 published in Wahlbäck and Blidberg, *Samråd i kristid*.

60. Tanner had, however, been actively involved in the international cooperative movement since 1910 and was president of the International Cooperative Alliance from 1927–1945. See J. Paavolainen. 1977. *Nuori Tanne: 1. Menstyvä sosialisti. Elämäkerta vuoteen 1911*, Helsinki: Tammi, 403–5; J. Paavolainen. 1979. *Väinö Tanner: 2. Senaattori ja rauhantekijä. Elämäkerta vuosilta 1912–1923*, Helsinki: Tammi, 52; Paavolainen, *Väinö Tanner: 3*, 50–56, 135–40, 232–35. In addition, Tanner had also previously taken advantage of his personal Nordic contacts in order to strengthen SDP's position in various political struggles: see Paavolainen, *Väinö Tanner. 2*, 218–32; Soikkanen, *Kohti kansanvaltaa*, 319.

61. Paavolainen, *Väinö Tanner. 3*, 336, 345.

62. This inner circle consisted of the Finnish Foreign Minister Antti Hackzell, Field Marshal Carl Gustaf Mannerheim, Prime Minister Toivo Kivimäki and Juho Paasikivi; see Soikkanen, *Kansallinen eheytyminen*, 37–38. Tanner's task was mainly to meet members of

the Swedish Social Democratic Party in order to discuss the need for a more intense Nordic cooperation, especially concerning military aid. Paavolainen, *Väinö Tanner. 3*, 341.

63. Minutes of SAMAK's meeting in 1935 published in Wahlbäck and Blidberg, *Samråd i kristid*, 60–61.
64. Minutes of SAMAK's meeting in 1935 published in Wahlbäck and Blidberg, *Samråd i kristid*, 61–62.
65. Minutes of SAMAK's meeting in 1935 published in Wahlbäck and Blidberg, *Samråd i kristid*, 62–63.
66. SDP's report for SAMAK 7.12.1935, published in Wahlbäck and Blidberg, *Samråd i kristid*, 75–79.
67. Minutes of SAMAK's meeting in 1935 published in Wahlbäck and Blidberg, *Samråd i kristid*, 63–64.
68. Minutes of SAMAK's meeting in 1935 published in Wahlbäck and Blidberg, *Samråd i kristid*, 63.
69. Minutes of SAMAK's meeting in 1935 published in Wahlbäck and Blidberg, *Samråd i kristid*, 63–64.
70. Minutes of SAMAK's meeting in 1935 published in Wahlbäck and Blidberg, *Samråd i kristid*, 63.
71. Minutes of SAMAK's meeting in 1935 published in Wahlbäck and Blidberg, *Samråd i kristid*, 66.
72. Soikkanen, *Kansallinen eheytyminen*, 100–3. See chapter 8 in this volume on the general strike in 1905, which constituted a background for the Finnish civil war in 1918 and chapter 7 concerning the foundation of rural socialism in 1899–1907.
73. Minutes of SAMAK's meeting in 1936 published in Wahlbäck and Blidberg, *Samråd i kristid*, 81.
74. Minutes of SAMAK's meeting in August 1937 published in Wahlbäck and Blidberg, *Samråd i kristid*, 110.
75. Minutes of SAMAK's meeting in August 1937 published in Wahlbäck and Blidberg, *Samråd i kristid*, 111–21, 123–24.
76. See minutes of SAMAK's meetings 1937–1946 published in Wahlbäck and Blidberg, *Samråd i kristid*.
77. Blidberg, *Splittrad gemenskap*, 78.

References

Åmark, K. 2005. *Hundra år av välfärdspolitik:* Välfärdsstatens framväxt i Norge och Sverige, Umeå: Boréa.
Andrén, N. 'Säkerhetspolitikens återkomst: Om säkerhetspolitikens plats i rådsdialogen', in B. Sundelius and C. Wiklund (eds), *Norden i sicksack: Tre spårbyten inom nordiskt samarbete*, Stockholm: Santérus, 2000, 275–303.
Bjørgum, J. 'Krisen, fascismen og det norske arbeiderparti på 1930-tallet', in P. Kettunen, A. Kultanen and T. Soikkanen (eds), *Jäljillä: Kirjoituksia historian ongelmista. Osa 2*, Turku: Kirja-Aurora, 2000, 221–47.
Blidberg, K. 1984. *Splittrad gemenskap: kontakter och samarbete inom nordisk socialdemokratisk arbetarrörelse 1931–1945*, Stockholm: Acta Universitatis Stockholmiensis.
Clavin, P. 2005. 'Defining Transnationalism', *Contemporary European History* 14(4), 421–39.

Edling, N. 'Regulating Unemployment the Continental Way: The Transfer of Municipal Labour Exchanges to Scandinavia 1890–1914', *European Review of History: Revue Europeenne d'Histoire* 15(1), 2008, 23–40.

———. 'The Primacy of Welfare Politics: Notes on the Language of the Swedish Social Democratcs and Their Adversaries', in H. Haggrén, J. Raunio-Niemi and J. Vauhkonen (eds), *Multi-Layered Historicity of the Present: Approaches to Social Science History*, Helsinki: University of Helsinki, 2013, 125–50.

Grass, M. 1974. 'Arbetarskandinavism 1912–1920. Komittéen för skandinaviska arbetarrörelsens samarbete, några aspekter', *Årbog for arbejderbevaegelsens historie* 4, 55–86.

Götz, N. and H. Haggrén. 'Introduction: Transnational Nordic Alignment in Stormy Waters', in N. Götz and H. Haggrén (eds), *Regional Cooperation and International Organizations: The Nordic Model in Transnational Alignment*, London: Routledge, 2008, 1–22.

Hemstad, R. 'Scandinavianism, Nordic Co-operation, and "Nordic Democracy"', in J. Kurunmäki and J. Strang (eds), *Rhetorics of Nordic Democracy*, Helsinki: Finnish Literature Society, 2010, 179–93.

Hilson, M. 2008. *The Nordic Model. Scandinavia since 1945*, London: Reaktion.

Isaksson, A. 1996. *Per Albin. Partiledaren*, Stockholm: Wahlström and Widstrand.

Jonsson, G. 2001. 'The Icelandic Welfare State in the Twentieth Century', *Scandinavian Journal of History* 26(3), 249–67.

Karvonen, L. 'Finland och Norden: det ständiga återvändandet till rötterna', in L. Häggman (ed.), *Finland i Norden: Finland 50 år i Nordiska rådet*, Helsinki: Pohjola-Norden, 2005, 17–23.

Kettunen, P. 2001. 'The Nordic Welfare State in Finland', *Scandinavian Journal of History* 26(3), 225–47.

———. 'Inledning', in P. Kettunen (ed.), *Lokalt och internationellt: Dimensioner i den nordiska arbetarrörelsen och arbetarkulturen*, Tammerfors: Sällskapet för forskning i arbetarhistoria i Finland, 2002, 7–10.

———. 2008. *Globalisaatio ja kansallinen me: Kansallisen katseen historiallinen kritiikki*, Tampere: Vastapaino.

———. 'The Transnational Construction of National Challenges: The Ambiguous Nordic Model of Welfare and Competitiveness', in P. Kettunen and K. Petersen (eds), *Beyond Welfare State Models: Transnational Historical Perspectives on Social Policy*, Cheltenham: Edward Elgar, 2011, 16–40.

Kristjánsdóttir, R. 2012. 'For Equality or Against Foreign Oppression? The Politics of the Left in Iceland Leading up to the Cold War', *Social Movements in the Nordic Countries since 1900: Moving the Social. Journal of Social History and the History of Social Movements* 48, 11–28.

Kurunmäki, J. '"Nordic Democracy" in 1935. On the Finnish and Swedish Rhetoric of Democracy', in J. Kurunmäki and J. Strang (eds), *Rhetorics of Nordic Democracy*, Helsinki: Finnish Literature Society, 2010, 37–82.

Kurunmäki, J. and J. Strang. 'Introduction: "Nordic Democracy" in a World of Tensions', in J. Kurunmäki and J. Strang (eds), *Rhetorics of Nordic Democracy*, Helsinki: Finnish Literature Society, 2010, 9–36.

Kurunmäki, J. and J. Strang (eds). 2010. *Rhetorics of Nordic Democracy*, Helsinki: Finnish Literature Society.

Majander, M. 2004. *Pohjoismaa vai kansandemokratia? Sosiaalidemokraatit, kommunistit ja Suomen kansainvälinen asema 1944–51*, Helsinki: Suomalaisen Kirjallisuuden Seura.

Mylly, J. 1989. *Maalaisliitto-Keskustapuolueen historia: Maalaisliitto 1918–1939*, Helsinki: Kirjayhtymä.

Nelson, G.R. 1953. *Freedom and Welfare: Social Patterns in the Northern Countries of Europe*, Copenhagen: The Ministries of Social Affairs of Denmark, Finland, Iceland, Norway, Sweden.

Nygård, S. 2008. *Filosofins renässans eller modern mystic: Bergsondebatten i Finland*, Helsingfors: Universitetstryckeriet.

Østergård, U. 'The Geopolitics of Nordic Identity: From Composite States to Nation States', in Ø. Sørensen and B. Stråth (eds), *The Cultural Construction of Norden*, Oslo: Scandinavian University Press, 1997, 25–71.

Paavolainen, J. 1977. *Nuori Tanner: 1. Menestyvä sosialisti. Elämäkerta vuoteen 1911*, Helsinki: Tammi.

––––––. 1979. *Väinö Tanner: 2. Senaattori ja rauhantekijä. Elämäkerta vuosilta 1912–1923*, Helsinki: Tammi.

––––––. 1984. *Väinö Tanner: 3. Sillanrakentaja. Elämäkerta vuosilta 1924–1936*, Helsinki: Tammi.

Palonen, K. 'Political Times and the Temporalisation of Concepts: A New Agenda for Conceptual History', in L.-F. Landgrén and P. Hautamäki (eds), *People Citizen Nation*, Helsinki: Renvall Institute, 2005, 50–66.

Petersen, K. 'Constructing Nordic Welfare? Nordic Social Political Cooperation 1919–1955', in N.F. Christiansen, N. Edling and P. Haave (eds), *The Nordic Model of Welfare: A Historical Reappraisal*, Copenhagen: Museum Tusculanum Press, 2006, 67–98.

––––––. 'Transnationale perspektiver på den nordiske velfærdsmodels tilblivelseshistorie 1900–1950', in S. Bjerrum Fossa et al. (eds), *Transnationale historier*, Odense: Syddansk Universitetsforlag, 2009, 163–79.

Petersen, K., N.F. Christiansen and J.H. Petersen. 'The Danish Social Reform of 1933: Social Rights as a New Paradigm by an Accidental Reform?', in H. Haggrén, J. Raunio-Niemi and J. Vauhkonen (eds), *Multi-Layered Historicity of the Present: Approaches to Social Science History*, Helsinki: University of Helsinki, 2013, 105–24.

Putensen, D. 'SAI och SAMAK – växlande storlekar I den internationella och den nordiska dimensionen (1914–1945)', in P. Kettunen (ed.), *Lokalt och internationellt: Dimensioner i den nordiska arbetarrörelsen och arbetarkulturen*, Tammerfors: Sällskapet för forskning i arbetarhistoria i Finland, 2002, 129–49.

Sejersted, F. 2005. *Socialdemokratins tidsålder: Sverige och Norge under 1900-talet*, Nora: Nya Doxa.

Soikkanen, H. 1975. *Kohti kansanvaltaa: Suomen Sosialidemokraattinen Puolue 75 vuotta. 1-3, 1899–1936*, Helsinki: Suomen sosiaalidemokraattinen puolue.

Soikkanen, T. 1984. *Kansallinen eheytyminen - myytti vai todellisuus? Ulko- ja sisäpolitiikan linjat ja vuorovaikutus Suomessa vuosina 1933–1939*, Turku: Turun yliopisto.

Sørensen, Ø. and B. Stråth. 'Introduction: The Cultural Construction of Norden', in Ø. Sørensen and B. Stråth (eds), *The Cultural Construction of Norden*, Oslo: Scandinavian University Press, 1997, 1–24.

Strang, J. 2012. *Nordiska gemenskaper. En vision för samarbetet*, København: Nordiska rådet.

te Velde, H. 2005. 'Political Transfer: An Introduction', *European Review of History – Revue Européenne Histoire* 12(2), 205–21.

'The Northern Countries in World Economy. Denmark, Finland, Iceland, Norway, Sweden'.1937. Helsinki: Delegations for the promotion of economic cooperation between the Northern countries.

Wahlbäck, K. 'Försvarsbundsförhandlingar 1948–49: Misslyckandet och det informella efterspelet', in B. Sundelius and C. Wiklund (eds), *Norden i sicksack: Tre spårbyten inom nordiskt samarbete*, Stockholm: Santérus, 2000, 31–45.

Wahlbäck, K. and K. Blidberg (eds). 1986. *Samråd i kristid: Protokoll från den nordiska arbetarrörelsens samarbetskommitté 1932–1946*, Stockholm: Kungl. Samfundet för utgivande av handskrifter rörande Skandinaviens historia.

Werner, M. and B. Zimmermann. 2006. 'Beyond Comparison: Histoire croisée and the Challenge of Reflexivity', *History and Theory* 45(1), 30–50.

Archives and other sources

Arbetarbladet
Labour movements' archive, Helsinki, Finland (TA)
Private collection of E.A. Vuori
Private collection of SDP's parliamentary group
Riksarkivet i Helsingfors (RA)
Private collection of Väinö Tanner
Valtiopäivät (VP). Pöytäkirjat 1933 [Proceedings from the Finnish Parliament], Helsinki: Valtioneuvoston kirjapaino, 1935.

CHAPTER 11

FACING THE NATION

Nordic Communists and their National Contexts,
from the 1920s and into the Cold War

Ragnheiður Kristjánsdóttir

In his book about the down and outs in interwar London and Paris, George Orwell describes the Frenchman Fureux, a stonemason from Limousin:

> The queer thing about Fureux was that, though he was a Communist when sober, he turned violently patriotic when drunk. He started the evening with good Communist principles, but after four or five litres he was a rampant Chauvinist, denouncing spies, challenging all foreigners to fight, and, if he was not prevented, throwing bottles.[1]

Orwell found Fureux peculiar for what appeared to be his paradoxical political views. On the surface, and when sober, he was a communist internationalist, but alcohol transformed him into some sort of a nationalist. Orwell's sketch is in accordance with the widespread view that nationalism and communism are incompatible, that communists cannot or should not be nationalists. In theory, that might be true, but the praxis was more complex, and by comparing the way in which nationalism affected the politics of communists in the five Nordic countries, this chapter offers a more nuanced and comprehensive picture of communist nationalism.

While nationalism is not an ideology in the same sense as communism,[2] it has been defined as an ideology that 'imagines the community' as national, and asserts 'the primacy of this collective identity over others'.[3]

Nationalism can, in other words, be defined as a political programme, which implies that the duty of the nation's members 'to the polity which encompasses and represents the … nation overrides all other public obligations'.[4] Communism, on the other hand, is based on the Marxist premise that the human race is divided into classes with incompatible interests. Marxist and communist theory, so the story goes, has opposed nationalism as a political force on the grounds that it constructs barriers that obstruct the development of a universal class consciousness and thus the proletarian revolution.[5]

To be sure, such a view on the relationship between communism and nationalism immediately generates a number of interesting questions on how communist identity coexisted, mixed or collided with national identities. Even so, the interplay between nationalism and communism should not be approached as a question of absolute opposites. Recent studies have aimed at letting go of such dualist ideas, arguing instead for a thorough reading of instructions on nationalism given by the Comintern and Soviet Union as well as careful considerations about the dynamics at work within the nation states of respective communist movements. Scholars have claimed for some time now that the idea that communism and nationalism are mutually exclusive is a myth. Furthermore, it has been argued that in order to fully understand the interplay between communism and nationalism it is important to overcome the fragmentation of the field. Most studies to date have been limited to certain periods and countries. And as Martin Mevius has shown, the result has been that 'the comprehensive nature of communist appeals to national legitimacy remains hidden' and communist appeals to nationalism have wrongly been seen as an exception or novelty.[6]

Despite the internationalist commitment of communists and their peripheral place within the polity of their nation states, most of their battles were fought on the home front. And despite the fact that their ideological stance meant that they were sceptical participants in the politics of their nation states, they were time and again faced with the task of tackling nationalism and nationalist identities. As political actors within their respective nation states, they could, as we shall see, play a part in 'composing' and 'recomposing' nationalism.[7] Their relationship with nationalism may have been fundamentally different from that of other political organizations, but it was surely more sophisticated than that of Orwell's stonemason from Limousin.

The aim of the following comparison between the national contexts and labour politics of the five Nordic countries, and the way in which nationalism affected the politics of communists in each country, is twofold. As already stated, the primary aim is to add to our understanding of communist nationalism. At the same time, the comparison should contribute towards a better understanding of the different ways in which labour politics played out in Scandinavia (i.e., Denmark, Norway and Sweden) on the one hand and Finland and Iceland on the other.[8]

The focus is on two questions. First: how did the international commitment of the five Nordic parties affect their approach towards nationalism? Second: how did the nationalism and national identities within their respective nation states affect the rhetoric and discourse of Nordic communists? The first question regards the ideological and political toolbox provided by the international communist movement and the problematic relationship with Moscow. The second question concerns the extent to which they merged their communist internationalism with the nationalist discourse of their home countries. Engaging with recent research on nationalist communism, I propose that while the Marxist-Leninist and later Soviet stance on nationalism certainly affected the relationship between Nordic communism and nationalism, it was the domestic political context and the nature and place of nationalism in each country that defined the way in which the parties tackled nationalism.[9]

Nation and Labour

Labour historians have for a long time seen nationalism as one of the components of the political practice and theory of European social democracy. Labour movements based their political identities on the idea of class but were at the same time shaped by the nationalistic ideals that permeated European politics in the late nineteenth and early twentieth century. There is perhaps not consensus on when this merger occurred, for it depends on the point of view taken, as well as the region under consideration. Some scholars point to 1914, when most social democratic parties decided to support the war effort of their respective nation states. Others focus on how the Second World War changed notions of citizenship and paved the way for national welfare states throughout Europe. But all seem to agree that social democrats forged a link between socialism, democracy and liberal nationalism (i.e., progressive patriotism as opposed to reactionary nationalism).[10] And the most successful cases, it seems, were the social democratic parties of Denmark, Norway and Sweden, which came to power in the 1930s and set out to turn their respective nation states into a 'people's home' *(folkhemmet)*. As Francis Sejersted writes in his comparative study of social democracy in Norway and Sweden, 'the working class was integrated into the nation with the labor parties of the two countries becoming the governing parties'.[11]

The story of communism and nationalism is different. The first and most obvious complications were produced by the communist commitment to Moscow. At the same time as the internationalism of social democracy was giving way to identification with the nation state and its democratic institutions, the emerging communist movement sought its legitimacy from the Comintern rather than the legacies and traditions of the labour movements at home, thus severing the link between socialism, the expansion of democracy, and international class solidarity. And while communist commitment to the international movement can certainly not be reduced to a blind loyalty towards Stalin's regime, the way that communists accepted and promoted the foreign policy of the Soviet Union repeatedly put them in difficult positions at home. The most notable example in this context is the dilemma within the Nordic communist movement during the Winter War between Finland and the USSR. In Finland itself a number of communists fought for their native country against the Soviet Union, thus placing their national loyalties above their international ones.[12] But the fact that communists in the other Nordic countries decided to justify Stalin's move made it all too easy to accuse them of placing the interests of 'Soviet-Russia' above all else that they claimed to stand for at home, whether that was the 'common people' and 'labouring masses' of their native country or the principle of national self-determination.[13]

A second complication was the somewhat complex and fluctuating instructions given by the Comintern. While the principle of national self-determination was one of the core elements of Lenin's theses on the national and colonial question, adopted at the second Comintern congress in 1920, the general point of departure was a Marxist opposition to nationalism as an ideology that created a false sense of equality and thus obstructed the development of a universal class consciousness. Communists were to inform the workers of this 'bourgeois deception' and to stress that imperialist competition ruled out the possibility of national freedom under capitalism. The Comintern encouraged communists, however, to make exceptions to this general rule of opposing nationalism, given the right conditions. In accordance with Lenin's notion of the importance of colonial struggles, communists were to support national liberation movements in so-called oppressed and dependent countries as well as in backward (i.e., 'feudal' or 'semi-feudal') countries or countries that had not completed their 'bourgeois revolution'.[14]

As we shall see, in the case of Iceland, it was not always clear where this exception was applicable. And to further complicate matters, the emphasis of international communism shifted – most often due to changes in international politics. During the Popular Front (1935–1939) communist parties were urged to strike a patriotic note in their rhetoric and propaganda,[15] an emphasis that became problematic during the first two years of the Second World War. After the German invasion of the Soviet Union in 1941, the tide changed again; European communists were urged to define the struggle against Germany as a war of national liberation.[16]

Scandinavian Identities

Principally, then, Nordic communists had three options when confronting nationalism. First, they could ignore it as a force or issue insignificant to their struggle. Second, as Marxist-Leninist internationalists they could actively oppose it on the grounds that it was the main obstacle in their struggle for socialism. The third option was to look for ways to embrace or harness nationalism and to engage in composing and recomposing the nationalist discourse.

Until the advent of the Popular Front in 1935, a combination of the first two stances was what characterized the way in which the Scandinavian parties tackled nationalism. During the 1920s all three parties had for the most part cut loose from their roots within the respective national labour movements. Their legitimacy and political identity was primarily based on the idea that the Soviet Union was the fatherland of all workers, and their vocabulary was permeated by words and phrases originating in Moscow. Nationalism was to the communists a non-issue, or a political stance, which communists openly rejected.

In Sweden during the First World War, left-wing socialists, which later formed Sveriges Kommunistiska Parti (the Swedish Communist Party, SKP), sought ways to undermine the nationalism, which, in their view, characterized the age of modern industrial capitalism.[17] Also in Denmark, nationalism was seen as a threatening force. From the early years of the movement, and well into the 1930s, Danish communists objected to any affiliation to nationalist or patriotic feelings. We are of the kind, claimed Danish party leader Aksel Larsen in 1933, which hates the sound of the word fatherland.[18]

This is not to say, however, that all Scandinavian communists refrained altogether from any references to national identity. Sometimes they even referred to the working class as the genuine representatives of the nation. Nationalism as a political force could be one thing, and class patriotism another. Thus Swedish radicals and communists in the 1920s could claim, like the socialist Axel Danielson had done in the 1890s, that they were patriots of the social democratic kind.[19] In Norway, too, there are a few examples of nationalistic references in the discourse of the communist movement during the 1920s. When the communist Lars Evensen gave a speech on May Day 1927 in Odda he thus compared Lenin and the Norwegian working class with the medieval king St. Olav, who had crushed the icons of the heathen gods and imposed Christianity.[20] And in 1925 the communist journalist Olav Scheflo published a book in which he emphasized the similarity between the heroic Viking kings of Norway and the present labour movement, stressing the importance of the party basing its political programme on national traditions and values.[21]

But such views did not gain momentum within the Norwegian party; Scheflo's book came under hard attack.[22] And on the whole it can be argued that the way in which the leaders of the Scandinavian movement rejected nationalism indicates that they were acting in accordance with the Comintern line. In none of these countries could nationalism have been seen as a 'progressive' force – that is, related to the fight for independence from a foreign 'imperialist' power. At the same time, their stance reflects the respective national contexts. Nationalism was not an issue of central political importance during the early years of communism in Scandinavia, and insofar as it was, it did not yet chime with the central concerns of the labour movement.[23] In Denmark, nationalist feeling had been related to the gradual loss of the kingdom's territorial possessions since the middle of the previous century and later what has been called a peasant-farmer national identity – that is, the Grundtvigian 'emphasis on the unity of land, country, God and people (folk)'.[24] Similarly in Sweden, nationalistic aspirations were still related to the politics of the traditionalists rather than the liberals and socialists. When the union crisis between the dual kingdoms of Sweden and Norway resulted in Norway's declaration of independence in 1905 it hurt the nationalist pride of the traditionalists. And in the years leading up to the First World War, when defence was the dominant political theme, nationalist and patriotic feeling was primarily expressed in the discourse of the pro-militarist traditionalists but not the anti-militarist and modernist liberals and socialists.[25] In Norway this was different, as there had been a strong link between democratic reform and national independence and thus between nationalism and social democracy during the nineteenth century. But with the secession from Sweden in 1905, this link was severed; nationalism became associated with right-wing aspirations for securing Norway's position on the international arena.[26]

People's Home and Popular Front

During the interwar years in Scandinavia, the gap between the groups represented by the Left on the one hand and the rest of the nation on the other was bridged through a nation-building process in which the basis of Danish, Swedish and Norwegian national identity was redefined. Armed with the concept of *folkhemmet* (the people's home) – developed primarily by the Swedish social democratic leader Per Albin Hansson – the core of the labour movement gradually identified with nationalism.[27]

As already stated, the antipathy of Scandinavian communists towards nationalism cannot only be seen as a rather clear-cut implementation of the Comintern line; it also reflects the respective national contexts. However, while the social democratic labour movement was creating its own version of the nationalist discourse, Scandinavian communists did not engage in debating to what extent the labour movement should embrace and use national symbols. This points towards yet another explanation. Communists in Scandinavia were marginal in every sense, working in the shadow of an ever-expanding social democratic party. While the social democratic politicians were active participants in governing the nation state, the communists were on the national level a miniscule sect and had little capacity to integrate their communist and national identities.[28]

This was further established during the Popular Front period. When the Comintern called for the increased use of nationalistic elements in communist rhetoric and propaganda at the seventh Comintern congress in 1935, it took some time for the Scandinavian communists to implement the new line. Not until after May Day 1937 did the papers of Norges Kommunistiske Parti (Norwegian Communist Party, NKP) discuss the use of the national flag in labour parades.[29] By 1938 the NKP's stance on national symbols was in tune with that of Det Norske Arbeiderpartiet (the Norwegian Labour Party, DNA),[30] and after the Munich agreement the uncertain fate of Europe's small nations was further stressed. In September 1938 and January 1939 the Comintern issued resolutions to the NKP calling for a unification of all democratic forces in defence of Norwegian independence,[31] and in May 1939 the NKP's use of national symbols reached its climax. The party's official token for May Day placed the national and the red flags side by side and in the parade in Bergen the communist youth organization carried a portrait of the national poet Bjørnstjerne Bjørnson, clad in national colours and surrounded by young communist girls in national costume.[32]

As elsewhere in Europe, the changed circumstances following the non-aggression pact of 1939 between Germany and the Soviet Union caused an abrupt break with the Popular Front tactics. The NKP abandoned its ideas of a national democratic front against fascism and gradually became isolated from the rest of Norwegian politics.[33] After the Soviet invasion of Finland, a convincing emphasis on national independence became all but impossible. But this was a detour, so to speak, as the use of national symbols was resumed after the German occupation of Norway in 1940. The active resistance of communists against the occupying forces and Norwegian nazism was presented as a national struggle. One example was the new title of the communist paper, which from 1944 onwards was called *Alt for Norge* (Everything for Norway).

In Denmark and Sweden, the communist approach during the Popular Front, the pact period and the years of cooperation between the Soviet Union and Allied nations followed a similar path as in Norway. In the first decade or so of Swedish communism, its politics had to a certain extent been based on the traditions of the Swedish labour movement. But following a split in 1929, the identity and legitimacy of the party became further removed from the rest of the labour movement and more definitely linked with international communism. This changed during the Popular Front and then again after 1941, when the party actively set out to break out of its isolation in Swedish politics. It adopted a political programme more in tune with the reformism of social democracy, cut out terms such as 'the dictatorship of the proletariat' and systematically linked up with the history of the Swedish labour movement. Claiming to be a Swedish rather than a Soviet or Russian party, it replaced symbols of international communism – for example the hammer and sickle on the front page of its main newspaper – with national symbols. Most notably it adopted the Swedish flag, which appeared, for example, on the podium of party congresses in the late 1940s.[34]

The Danish party, like the Norwegian one, had responded rather hesitantly to Comintern's call for a Popular Front. But by the middle of 1937 – having received direct instructions from the Executive Committee of the Comintern (ECCI) – the tactics of the communal effort 'against the fascist threat towards democracy' as well as the threat to 'national independence' had kicked in.[35] In the programmatic text from 1938, the discourse was very much laid in the stream of Danish political democracy. The party emphasized its commitment to the struggle against the enemies of 'democracy, the people and the country'.[36] This line was re-established after the occupation in 1940. The central programmatic text from this period *'Vi kæmper for et sandt Demokrati'* (We fight for a true democracy) also tried to express the communist message within the democratic and national discourse.[37] The resistance against the German occupation was presented as an effort to reinstate Danish democracy; a struggle for Danish independence. And afterwards the feelings connected to this 'heroic' period continued to affect the communist position towards the Danish nation. The sense was that the party had stood for the national interests in a more deep and meaningful manner than the traditional nationalism of the ruling class. Theirs was a nationalism aimed at representing the interests of the majority of the people – the working class – together with the other parts of the nation that were willing to unite with them in that cause.[38]

Finland and Iceland

Before the independence of Finland in 1917 there had been a strong link between nationalism, the development of democracy and the labour movement. Advocating Finnish autonomy or independence was part of labour's quest for and defence of civil rights, democratic institutions and thus labour's possibilities to fight for social and economic reforms. This link between independence and the political aims of the social democratic party was secured further after the 1916 elections when Sosialidemokraattinen puolue (the Social Democratic Party, SDP) received a majority of the parliamentary seats and a leading position in the government or senate.[39]

This connection between the workers and the nation was injured in the nation-building process that followed Finnish independence in 1917 and the subsequent civil war. In the interpretation of the right wing, the civil war was depicted in nationalist terms as a war against the Russians for the independence of Finland. The Reds were eyed suspiciously. The new leadership of the SDP – which had been restructured by those who had opposed the revolution – had a tendency to conform to this view. Anti-Russian, anti-Soviet and anti-communist views were thus a constituent part of the nationalist discourse of the winners of the civil war.[40] Up to the autumn of 1944, Finnish communists were in many respects outcasts,[41] and it was only in the 1960s that this interpretation began to give way to a view where members of the communist movement were regarded as fully fledged members of the nation.

So while nationalist arguments were important in Finland at this time, communists were on the defensive and this position was reflected in the discourse, rhetoric and political activities of Finnish communists. Occasionally they met this situation by denying that the Finnish bourgeoisie was responsible for the country's independence, claiming instead that thanks were due to the Finnish and/or the Russian working class. Furthermore, communists did, at times, adopt Marxist-Leninist arguments on nationalism and imperialism, in order to respond to accusations of having fought against the independence of Finland during the civil war. Thus at some points they declared that Finland was still not independent, but was on the contrary under the economic dominance of a foreign imperialist or capitalist power. In the 1920s, Britain was seen as posing the greatest threat to Finnish independence, while this role was appointed to Germany in the 1930s. Such accusations reflected the foreign policy of the Soviet Union.[42] To begin with, communists openly rejected the use of national symbols such as the Finnish flag. But this was a rejection of the nationalism of the right wing, and by 1928 communists had acknowledged the importance of Independence Day, 6 December, by organizing their own festivities in the labour halls. But it was not until 1946 that the communist movement accepted the use of the national flag in its political activities.[43]

Like in Finland, and to some extent in Norway, Icelandic politics were very much dominated by nationalist arguments, and while communists were all along accused of being anti-nationalist puppets of a hostile international movement, their position within Icelandic society was in no sense as complicated as the position of communists in Finland. The most prominent and influential members of the communist movement were young students, brought up in the nationalist spirit of the years leading up to Iceland's independence in 1918. And unlike some of the non-privileged members of Icelandic society – for example, workers and seamen – who may have had a sense of standing outside the Icelandic nation, these young communists do seem to have identified themselves with the young Icelandic nation state.[44]

Even so, their approach was set within the framework of the international communist movement. In the early years, Icelandic communists had placed themselves within the Marxist-Leninist tradition by declaring their opposition towards bourgeois nationalism.[45] And in the first political programme of Kommúnistaflokkur Íslands (the Icelandic Communist Party, KFÍ), published just after it was founded in 1930, the party promised to expose the 'nationalist clamour' of the bourgeoisie.[46] An example of this policy in practice was the communist opposition to the celebration of the thousand years' anniversary of the medieval assembly Althing. The communists opposed the celebrations and denounced the much-cherished medieval constitution as having constituted one of the 'most dangerous forms of aristocratic rule known in the history of mankind'.[47] Correspondence between KPÍ and Comintern shows that this act had been carefully planned,[48] and the special edition of the communist periodical *Réttur*, dedicated to the 'struggle of the oppressed people of Iceland from the settlement of the island to the present', published on this occasion, seems to have been in the pipeline for over four years.[49]

The communist response to Althing's millennial anniversary thus fits well into the framework set by international communism. At the same time, however, the effort that they put into their acts, and the way that they presented their opposition, is an indication that for them, Icelandic nationalism was an important force that they should not ignore. In this respect their response differs from that of communists in Scandinavia, who had more or less refrained from the whole issue of nationalism in the 1920s and early 1930s. Furthermore, their stance indicates that their sense of the possibilities for making claims to the national heritage was different to that of their comrades in Finland, where it was more difficult to challenge the prominence of right-wing nationalism.

Indeed, it appears that we can trace the development of an alternative nationalist discourse back to the early years of the Icelandic communist movement. Right from the beginning, there was a clearly identifiable effort to link communist and nationalist arguments. A general attempt of this sort was manifest in the style and language of the party literature; for example, in frequent references to the deeds of those Icelanders that through the ages had fought against foreign dominance and disturbance. In a pamphlet issued by a small provincial branch of the party in 1933 it was thus stated that communists were assured that the 'labouring masses' of this province were still as eager fighters for freedom as their peasant ancestors, who had successfully driven away 'usurious English merchants' some centuries ago.[50]

Another manifestation of this effort is to be found in how the Icelandic communists tried to interpret the Marxist-Leninist doctrine in a way that justified a link between communist and nationalist arguments. This was not a straightforward exercise, since Iceland was an independent country and, according to the party literature, at the highest stage of capitalist development. As stated in a draft report by the Comintern – apparently the secretariat was perplexed by the political programme of the Icelandic party – Iceland was not a Danish colony.[51] Despite that, Icelandic communists argued that the capitalist stage in Iceland was characterized by the preponderance of foreign finance capital, which in practice meant that the nation's status was in fact similar to that of any other colony or semi-colony.[52]

After the War

By the end of the Second World War the successor of the KFÍ, the more broadly based Socialist Party founded in 1938, found itself in a relatively secure position within the Icelandic nation state. By then the party had

Illustration 11.1 Cover of the socialist-communist newspaper *Þjóðviljinn*, 17 June 1944, the founding day of the Icelandic Republic. Artist: Atli Már Árnason (1918–2006). It is a visual representation of what can be called the foundational premise of the radical left in Iceland, which since the 1920s had sought ways to bring Icelandic working-class politics, the struggle for national independence and the international communist revolution under a single banner.

also equipped itself with a version of the nationalist discourse where the labouring masses, most often referred to as *alþýða* – the English equivalent would be 'the common people', the Scandinavian one *folk* – were put at the centre. The party was practically the only political force opposed to the American military presence and Iceland's membership in NATO. This allowed it to play a distinct nationalistic tune that no doubt helped it to maintain its strength in the anti-communist atmosphere of the Cold War. But most important, perhaps, was the fact that the communists had found a broader organizational context, namely the Socialist Party, for their political struggle.

The same was true about communists in Finland, who managed to hold the strong position of the immediate post-war years within a broadly based left-wing party. The 1930s had seen an attempted reformulation of the social democratic approach to Finnish nationalism. Emphasizing the Marxist view that contemporary working-class politics were a continuation of the progressive bourgeois politics of the nineteenth century, they introduced the working class as the carrier of the best traditions of the national culture. In practice, to take one example, this policy included attempts to reinterpret the Finnish national epos, the *Kalevala*, to challenge the militarist right-wing interpretations. These reformulations were included in the communist discourse after the war. Events during the war had also called for a communist redefinition of Finland. As already mentioned, many supporters of Finnish communism had fought against the Soviet Union in the Winter War of 1939–40, and some even in the Continuation War of 1941–1944, thus showing in action that they placed the interests of the nation above those of the international. Furthermore, while Finnish communists had not abandoned all loyalties towards the Soviet Union, the legalization of Finnish communism in 1944 added to the ability of communists to participate in and attach themselves to discussions on the Finnish people and nation.[53]

As regards the Scandinavian communist parties, it turned out to be difficult for them to hold onto the success they had achieved at the end of the war. Even though the national turn taken by the Swedish party during the war seems to have led to a short term increase in party support and membership, it did not transform its position in the long run. Reaching out towards voters of the Social Democratic Party and trying at the same time to represent themselves as a feasible alternative to this ever more powerful rival proved all but impossible.[54] Communists in Denmark certainly tried to harness the political capital they had accumulated during the occupation, but it became ever more problematic for the party to maintain the image of being truly Danish as well as loyal towards the Soviet Union. In accordance with instructions from Moscow, the party continued to present itself as the true defender of Danish national interests, now against the 'monopoly capitalism' and 'dollar imperialism' of the United States and Britain. But this proved to be unconvincing. At the same time, the party had distanced itself from other political forces and by the late 1940s it had returned to the margins of Danish politics.[55]

In Norway too, communists aimed at drawing on their wartime experiences in order to establish themselves as a national political force with deep roots in Norwegian soil. The many party members who had died during the struggle for the country's independence helped to accentuate this point. The NKP claimed to be a party for Norway and the Norwegian people, and supported full national freedom and independence. With the rising confrontations between the Western powers and the Soviet Union by the end of the 1940s, the national rhetoric of the NKP was connected to the party's struggle against aggressive American capitalism and imperialism. In the party programme of 1953, NKP underlined its role as the true bearer of national sovereignty. In contrast to the bourgeois DNA, the NKP claimed to have held the standard of national freedom high in the struggle against the former's alleged national treason.[56] But as in Denmark, the communists' firm support of Soviet foreign policy meant that this national rhetoric was not taken seriously outside party circles.

Conclusion

Nationalism touched the five Nordic parties in different ways. The development in each case was determined by a combination of international and domestic factors. In the first years of the communist movement, nationalism was an inherent factor in Iceland and Finland, whereas the question had lost significance for the progressive forces in Norway, as well as in the old colonial powers Sweden and Denmark. This is reflected in the fact that nationalism was from the outset an important issue for Finnish and Icelandic communists, while it had less impact on the rhetoric and discourse of the Scandinavian communist parties.

Danish, Norwegian and Swedish nationalism came to the foreground when the international political situation called for a re-evaluation of the parties' tactics. Despite the fact that during the 1930s Scandinavian social democracy was embracing the idea of the nation, the increased communist emphasis on the national political discourse and turn towards nationalistic arguments seem to have been triggered by international developments, not by the national political context. The national tactics that communists had somewhat mechanically adopted during the

Popular Front were changed with the German occupation of Norway and Denmark and given a renewed emphasis in Sweden, also following the changed international circumstances. Communists were now actually and actively defending the democracy and 'progressive' traditions of their nation states. The experience of the resistance may have permanently changed the way that Danish and Norwegian communists related to the nationalism of their native countries. But in the long run it did not change the fact that Scandinavian communists remained marginal in every sense, working in the shadow of ever-expanding social democratic parties. While the latter were active participants in governing the nation state, the communists had little capacity to engage in other political issues except the ones advocated by Moscow.

It would be oversimplifying things to explain the strength of Finnish communists by pointing to how nationalism surfaced in their politics. Such an argument is more relevant in the case of Iceland. Nevertheless, and setting aside the question of causation, it is noteworthy that in the post-war years both Finnish and Icelandic communists integrated more successfully into the politics of their nation states than did their comrades in Scandinavia.

Ragnheiður Kristjánsdóttir is Senior Lecturer in History at the University of Iceland. She has written on nationalism, democracy and the politics of the Left. Her published works include 'The Politics of the Left in Iceland Leading up to the Cold War', *Moving the Social* 48 (2012); three chapters in *Þingræði á Íslandi* (2011) [On Parliamentarism in Iceland]; *Nýtt fólk. Þjóðerni og íslensk vinstri stjórnmál 1901–1944* (2008) [Nationalism and Icelandic Labour Politics]; and 'Communists and the National Question in Scotland and Iceland, c. 1930–1940', *The Historical Journal* 45(3) (2002). She is currently working on *A Concise History of Iceland* as well as a book on women and gender in Iceland in the twentieth century.

Notes

An earlier version of this text was produced as a part of a NOS-H project on Nordic Communism and I am indebted to all participants in the project. Furthermore, parts of the text on Norway are based on texts originally written by Ole Martin Rønning, what is said about Finland is based on texts from Tauno Saarela, and some of what is written about Denmark is based on Morten Thing's texts and ideas.

1. G. Orwell. 1933. *Down and Out in Paris and London*, London: V. Gollancz, chapter 17.
2. See R. Szporluk. 1988. *Communism and Nationalism: Karl Marx versus Friedrich List*, New York and Oxford: Oxford University Press, 7ff.

3. P. Spencer and H. Wollman. 2002. *Nationalism: A Critical Introduction*, London: Sage, 2.
4. E.J. Hobsbawm. 1992. *Nations and Nationalism since 1780: Programme, Myth, Reality*, Cambridge: Cambridge University Press, 9.
5. For Marxist theories on nationalism see W. Connor. 1984. *The National Question in Marxist-Leninist Theory and Strategy*, Princeton: Princeton University Press; E. Nimni.1991. *Marxism and Nationalism: The Theoretical Origins of a Political Crisis*, London: Pluto Press; E. Benner. 1995. *Really Existing Nationalisms: A Post-Communist View from Marx and Engels*, Oxford: Oxford University Press.
6. M. Mevius. 2009. 'Reappraising Communism and Nationalism', *Nationalities Papers* 37(4), 377–81.
7. Here I am referring to Craig Calhoun's notion of the nation as a discursive formation that is constantly being composed and recomposed. See his: *Nationalism* (Minneapolis: University of Minnesota Press, 1997), and more recent: *Nations Matter: Culture, History, and the Cosmopolitican Dream* (London: Routledge, 2007).
8. While my decision to group together the three Scandinavian countries (Denmark, Norway and Sweden) may blur out the differences between these countries, it should be clear from the following discussion that I am well aware of the different national contexts as well as the different development of labour politics in each of the Scandinavian countries. However, when placed against the other two Nordic countries (Finland and Iceland), they do have much in common. Let it suffice here to mention the strength of social democracy and weakness of communism in all three countries. In the period under discussion the social democrats in Scandinavia received between 30 and 50 per cent of the votes cast in general elections, while the support of communists hardly surpassed 5 per cent, except during the post-resistance upswing at the end of the Second World War. In Iceland, during the same period, the support for the social democrats never surpassed 20 per cent, while the communists received over 8 per cent in the late 1930s. And after the war, the Socialist Party, the more broadly based successor of the Icelandic Communist Party, became slightly bigger (measured in electoral support) than the social democrats (each party receiving between 15–20 per cent). In interwar Finland, social democrats had been strong (receiving up to 40 per cent of the votes cast). At the same time, notwithstanding the ban of the Finnish Communist Party (founded in Moscow in 1918), left-wing socialism and communism was rather strong and after the war communists worked within a broadly based movement known as The Democratic League of the Finnish People, which became one of the strongest parties in the country, receiving over 20 per cent of the votes cast. At the same time, the votes cast for social democracy were reduced to about 25 per cent.
9. As can be seen from this paragraph, I am not only looking at nationalism as an ideology (see endnotes 3, 4 and 5) but also as discursive formation and generator of identities (see endnote 7).
10. See M. van der Linden. 1988. 'The National Integration of European Working Classes (1871–1914)', *International Review of Social History* 33(3), 285–311; S. Berger and A. Smith (eds). 1999. *Nationalism, Labour and Ethnicity 1870–1939*, Manchester: Manchester University Press; M. Forman. 1998. *Nationalism and the International Labour Movement: The Idea of the Nation in Socialist and Anarchist Theory*, University Park, PA: Pennsylvania State University Press, 19–113. For the 'success of social democracy' in twentieth-century Europe, see S. Berman. 2006. *The Primacy of Politics: Social Democracy and the Making of Europe's Twentieth Century*, Cambridge: Cambridge University Press.
11. F. Sejerstad. 2011. *The Age of Social Democracy: Norway and Sweden in the Twentieth Century*, Oxford and Princeton: Princeton University Press, 8. For the similar process in Denmark see N.F. Christiansen. 1992. 'Socialismen og fædrelandet: Arbejderbevægelsen mellem internationalisme og national stolthed 1871–1940', in O. Feldbæk (ed.), *Dansk identitetshistorie*, 4 vols., Copenhagen: C.A. Reitzel, vol. 3, 512–86.

12. K. Rentola. 1998. 'Finnish Communism, O.W. Kuusinen, and their Two Native Countries', in T. Saarela and K. Rentola (eds), *Communism: National and International*, Helsinki: Suomen Historiallinen Seura, 169.

13. For examples of such accusations in Iceland see R. Kristjánsdóttir. 2008. *Nýtt fólk: Þjóðerni og íslensk verkalýðsstjórnmál 1901–1944*, Reykjavík: Háskólaútgáfan, 284–87.

14. J. Degras. 1956–1965. *The Communist International, 1919–1943: Documents*, 3 vols., London: Oxford University Press, vol 1, 139–40.

15. G. Dimitrov. 1951. *Selected Speeches and Articles*, London: Lawrence and Wishart, 39–114.

16. Mevius, 'Reappraising Communism', 385.

17. J. Bolin. 2004. *Parti av en ny typ? Skapandet av ett svenskt kommunistiskt parti 1917–1933*, Stockholm: Almqvist & Wiksell International, 57–61 and 402.

18. J. Jørgensen. 2005. '"Vort parti er et dansk parti". DKP og det nationale 1936–1952', *Arbejderhistorie* 2–3, 53.

19. I would like to thank Håkan Blomqvist for reminding me of this point. For a reference to Axel Danielson see: H. Blomqvist. 2006. *Nation, ras och civilisation i svensk arbetarrörelse före nazismen*, Stockholm: Carlssons, 100.

20. E.A. Terjesen and L. Jensen. 1990. *Maidagen: 1. mai-feiringens historie i Norge*, Oslo: Tiden norsk forlag, 115–16.

21. O. Scheflo. 1925. *Den røde tråd i Norges historie*, Oslo: Ny tid.

22. E. Lorenz. 1983. *Det er ingen sak å få partiet lite*, Oslo: Pax, 56–57.

23. For a general discussion of nationalism in the Nordic countries see, for example, H. Gustavsson. 1997. *Nordens historia: En Europeisk region under 1200 år*, Lund: Studentlitteratur, 209–14.

24. U. Østergård. 2004. 'The Danish Path to Modernity', *Thesis Eleven* 77(1), 34 and 39.

25. See, for example, N. Kent. 2008. *A Concise History of Sweden*, Cambridge: Cambridge University Press, 177–78; Sejerstad, *The Age of Social Democracy*, 66.

26. See A. Kirkhusmo. 2005. 'Sosialister og nasjonalister? Det norske Arbeideiderparti i 1905', *Arbeiderhistorie*, 5–27.

27. For this process see, for example, Berman, *The Primacy*, 162–67; S.I. Angell. 1994. *Fra splid til nasjonal integrasjon: Norsk nasjonalisme i mellomkrigstida*, Olso: Norges forskningsråd; H.F. Dahl. 1969. *Fra klassekamp til nasjonal samling – Arbeiderpartiet og det nasjonale spørsmål i 30-årene*, Oslo: Pax; Christiansen, 'Socialismen og fædrelandet'; J. Bjørgum. 1985. 'Det nasjonale spørsmål i norsk arbeiderbevegelse', *Tidskrift for Arbeiderbevegelsens Historie* 1, 99–130.

28. See M. Thing. 1993. *Kommunismens kultur*, 2 vols., Copenhagen: Tiderne skifter, vol. 1, 83; J. Bolin. 2002. '"Vi måste ha a viss nationell känsla" Den kommunistiska försvernsknins dilemma – första maj i Karlskoga', in H. Blomqvist and L. Ekdahl (eds), *Kommunismens hot og löfte: Arbetarrörelsen I skuggan af Sovjetunionen 1917–1991*, Stockholm: Carlssons, 138–39.

29. *Arbeideren* 7 May 1937; *Klassekampen* 17 May 1937; *Ny Tid* 17 May 1937.

30. *Arbeideren* 26 April 1938; *Arbeidet* 3 May 1938; *Arbeideren* 6 May 1938; *Arbeideren* 12 May 1938.

31. EKKI resolution on the Norwegian question. 15 September 1938, Moscow, Rossijskij Tsentr Kharenija I Izutsjenija Dokumentov Novejshej Istorii (Russian Centre for the Preservation and Study of Records of Modern History), Comintern Archive (RGASPI), 495-20-440, 127; EKKI to the NKP. 25 January 1939, RGASPI, 495-20-440, 161.

32. *Arbeidet* 5 May 1939.

33. T. Halvorsen. 1996. *Mellom Moskva og Berlin: Norges kommunistiske parti under ikke-angrepspakten mellom Sovjet-Unionen og Tyskland*, Oslo: Falken, 16–22.

34. Bolin, 'Vi måste ha', 138–42.

35. J. Jørgensen, 'Vort parti', 54–55.

36. A. Larsen. 1953. *Taler og Artikler gennem 20 år*, Copenhagen: n.p., 154.
37. See, for example, *Vi kæmper for et sandt Demokrati: En kortfattet Redegørelse for Hvad Kommunisterne vil!* (Copenhagen: Danmarks Kommunistiske Parti, 1943).
38. For the political identity of DKP during the occupation see, for example, M. Thing. 'DKP', Retrieved 30 August 2012 from http://www.leksikon.org/art.php?n=600
39. R. Alapuro. 1988. *State and Revolution in Finland*, Berkeley: University of California Press, 123–27, 158–61; J. Heikkilä. 1993. *Kansallista luokkapolitiikkaa: Sosiaalidemokraatit ja Suomen autonomian puolustus 1905–1917*, Tampere: Historiallisia tutkimuksia.
40. Alapuro, *State and Revolution*, 197–208.
41. On communism in Finland see chapter 12.
42. T. Saarela. 2008. *Suomalainen kommunismi ja vallankumous 1923–1930*, Helsinki: Suomalaisen Kirjallisuuden Seura, 643–46.
43. Saarela, *Suomalainen kommunismi*, 664–75. On the use of the Finnish flag, see K. Rentola. 1986. '"Ehkä mekin olisimme erehtyneet siihen …"'. SKP ja kansainvälisen kommunistisen liikkeen virtaukset 1944–48', *Tiede&Edistys* 11(4), 273–74.
44. Kristjánsdóttir, *Nýtt fólk*, 61–63, 215–17.
45. *Rauði fáninn* 7 (1924).
46. See *Hvað vill Kommúnistaflokkur Íslands?* (Reykjavík: Kommúnistaflokkur Íslands, 1931, 50); The programme's clause on nationalism has all the main points of the above-mentioned theses on 'the national question' accepted at the second Comintern congress in 1920.
47. E. Olgeirsson. 1930. 'Hvers er að minnast?', *Réttur* 15(2), 125. See also Kristjánsdóttir, *Nýtt fólk*, 221–45.
48. Report from KPÍ to K.I. 2 April 1930. RGASPI: 495-177–18, 4–5.
49. J. Guðnason (ed.). 1990. *Jafnaðarmannafélagið á Akureyri: Fundargerðabók 1924–32*, Reykjavík: Sagnfræðistofnun, 28; Kristjánsdóttir, *Nýtt fólk*, 224–28.
50. *Kotungur*, 1 (1933).
51. For a detailed discussion on the correspondence between the C.I. and KPÍ on this issue see Kristjánsdóttir, *Nýtt fólk*, 205–17.
52. IKP, *Hvað vill*, 2–13. It is interesting to compare this dialogue between the Comintern and Icelandic communists with somewhat similar communist discussions in Portugal on whether or not their country was a semi-colony. For that, see J. Neves. 2009. 'The Role of Portugal on the Stage of Imperialism: Communism, Nationalism and Colonialism (1930–1960)', *Nationalities Papers* 37(4), 485–99.
53. See T. Saarela. 2008. 'Bolshevization and Stalinization', in N. Laporte, K. Morgan and M. Worley (eds), *Bolshevism, Stalinism and the Comintern: Perspectives on Staliniziation, 1917–53*, Basingstoke and New York: Palgrave Macmillan, 201; and Rentola, 'Finnish Communism', 169.
54. Bolin, 'Vi måste ha', 143–48, 165–66.
55. For the national emphasis of the DKP after the war, see Jørgensen, 'Vort parti', 58–62.
56. See, for example, *Norges vei til fred, demokrati, nasjonal selvstendighet – til sosialismen, partiprogram* (Oslo: Norges kommunistiske parti, 1953, 29–30).

References

Alapuro, R. 1988. *State and Revolution in Finland*, Berkeley: University of California Press.

Angell, S.I. 1994. *Fra splid til nasjonal integrasjon: Norsk nasjonalisme i mellomkrigstida*, Olso: Norges forskningsråd.

Benner, E. 1995. *Really Existing Nationalisms: A Post-Communist View from Marx and Engels*, Oxford: Oxford University Press.

Berger, S. and A. Smith (eds). 1999. *Nationalism, Labour and Ethnicity 1870–1939*, Manchester: Manchester University Press.

Berman, S. 2006. *The Primacy of Politics: Social Democracy and the Making of Europe's Twentieth Century*, Cambridge: Cambridge University Press.

Bjørgum, J. 1985. 'Det nasjonale spørsmål i norsk arbeiderbevegelse', *Tidskrift for Arbeiderbevegelsens Historie* 1, 99–130.

Blomqvist, H. 2006. *Nation, ras och civilisation i svensk arbetarrörelse före nazismen*, Stockholm: Carlssons.

Bolin, J. '"Vi måste ha en viss nationell känsla" Den kommunistiska försvernsknins dilemma – första maj i Karlskoga"', in H. Blomqvist and L. Ekdahl (eds), *Kommunismens hot og löfte: Arbetarrörelsen I skuggan af Sovjetunionen 1917–1991*, Stockholm: Carlssons, 2002, 138–70.

———. 2004. *Parti av en ny typ? Skapandet av ett svenskt kommunistiskt parti 1917–1933*, Stockholm: Almqvist & Wiksell International.

Calhoun, C. 1997. *Nationalism*, Minneapolis: University of Minnesota Press.

———. 2007. *Nations Matter: Culture, History, and the Cosmopolitan Dream*, London: Routledge.

Christiansen, N.F. 'Socialismen og fædrelandet: Arbejderbevægelsen mellem internationalisme og national stolthed 1871–1940,' in O. Feldbæk (ed.), *Dansk identitetshistorie*, Copenhagen: C.A. Reitzel, 1992, 512–86.

Connor, W. 1984. *The National Question in Marxist-Leninist Theory and Strategy*, Princeton: Princeton University Press.

Dahl, H.F. 1969. *Fra klassekamp til nasjonal samling – Arbeiderpartiet og det nasjonale spørsmål i 30-årene*, Oslo: Pax.

Degras, J. 1956–1965. *The Communist International, 1919–1943: Documents*, London: Oxford University Press.

Dimitrov, G. 1951. *Selected Speeches and Articles*, London: Lawrence and Wishart.

Forman, M. 1998. *Nationalism and the International Labour Movement: The Idea of the Nation in Socialist and Anarchist Theory*, University Park, PA: Pennsylvania State University Press.

Guðnason, J. (ed.). 1990. *Jafnaðarmannafélagið á Akureyri: Fundargerðabók 1924–32*, Reykjavík: Sagnfræðistofnun.

Gustafsson, H. 1997. *Nordens historia: En Europeisk region under 1200 år*, Lund: Studentlitteratur.

Halvorsen, T. 1996. *Mellom Moskva og Berlin: Norges kommunistiske parti under ikke-angrepspakten mellom Sovjet-Unionen og Tyskland*, Oslo: Falken.

Heikkilä, J. 1993. *Kansallista luokkapolitiikkaa: Sosiaalidemokraatit ja Suomen autonomian puolustus 1905–1917*, Tampere: Historiallisia tutkimuksia.

Hobsbawm, E.J. 1992. *Nations and Nationalism since 1780: Programme, Myth, Reality*, Cambridge: Cambridge University Press.

Hvað vill Kommúnistaflokkur Íslands?. 1931. Reykjavík: Kommúnistaflokkur Íslands.

Jørgensen, J. 2005. '"Vort parti er et dansk parti". DKP og det nationale 1936–1952', *Arbejderhistorie* 2–3, 49–66.

Kent, N. 2008. *A Concise History of Sweden*, Cambridge: Cambridge University Press.

Kirkhusmo, A. 2005. 'Sosialister og nasjonalister? Det norske Arbeideiderparti i 1905', *Arbeiderhistorie*, 5–27.

Kristjánsdóttir, R. 2008. *Nýtt fólk: Þjóðerni og íslensk verkalýðsstjórnmál 1901–1944.* Reykjavík: Háskólaútgáfan.

Larsen, A. 1953. *Taler og Artikler gennem 20 år*, Copenhagen: n.p.

Lorenz, E. 1983. *Det er ingen sak å få partiet lite*, Oslo: Pax.

Mevius, M. 2009. 'Reappraising Communism and Nationalism', *Nationalities Papers* 37(4), 377–400.

Neves, J. 2009. 'The Role of Portugal on the Stage of Imperialism: Communism, Nationalism and Colonialism (1930–1960)', *Nationalities Papers* 37(4), 485–99.

Nimni, E. 1991. *Marxism and Nationalism: The Theoretical Origins of a Political Crisis*, London: Pluto Press.

Norges vei til fred, demokrati, nasjonal selvstendighet – til sosialismen, partiprogram. 1953. Oslo: Norges kommunistiske parti.

Olgeirsson, E. 1930. 'Hvers er að minnast?', *Réttur* 15(2), 123–38.

Orwell, G. 1933. *Down and Out in Paris and London*, London: V. Gollancz.

Østergård, U. 2004. 'The Danish Path to Modernity', *Thesis Eleven* 77(1), 25–43.

Rentola, K. 1986. '"Ehkä mekin olisimme erehtyneet siihen …". SKP ja kansainvälisen kommunistisen liikkeen virtaukset 1944–48', *Tiede&Edistys* 11(4), 27291.

———. 'Finnish Communism, O.W. Kuusinen, and their Two Native Countries', in T. Saarela and K. Rentola (eds), *Communism. National and International*, Helsinki: Suomen Historiallinen Seura, 1998, 159–81.

Saarela, T. 'Bolshevization and Stalinization', in N. Laporte, K. Morgan and M. Worley (eds), *Bolshevism, Stalinism and the Comintern: Perspectives on Staliniziation, 1917–53*, Basingstoke and New York: Palgrave Macmillan, 2008, 188–205.

———. 2008. *Suomalainen kommunismi ja vallankumous 1923–1930*, Helsinki: Suomalaisen Kirjallisuuden Seura.

Scheflo, O. 1925. *Den røde tråd i Norges historie*, Oslo: Ny tid.

Sejerstad, F. 2011. *The Age of Social Democracy: Norway and Sweden in the Twentieth Century*, Oxford and Princeton: Princeton University Press.

Spencer, P. and H. Wollman. 2002. *Nationalism: A Critical Introduction*, London: Sage.

Szporluk, R. 1988. *Communism and Nationalism: Karl Marx versus Friedrich List*, New York and Oxford: Oxford University Press.

Terjesen, E.A. and L. Jensen. 1990. *Maidagen: 1. mai-feiringens historie i Norge*, Oslo: Tiden norsk forlag.

Thing, M. 1993. *Kommunismens kultur*, Copenhagen: Tiderne Skifter.

———. 'DKP'. Retrieved 30 August 2012 from http://www.leksikon.org/art.php?n=600

van der Linden, M. 1988. 'The National Integration of European Working Classes (1871–1914)', *International Review of Social History* 33(3), 285–311.

Vi kæmper for et sandt Demokrati: En kortfattet Redegørelse for Hvad Kommunisterne vil!. 1943. Copenhagen: Danmarks Kommunistiske Parti.

Archives

Moscow, Rossijskij Gosudarstvennij Arkhiv Sotsialnoj i Polititsjeskoj Istorii, RGASPI (Russian State Archive for Social and Political History), Comintern Archive.

CHAPTER 12

TALLINN – STOCKHOLM – HAMBURG – COPENHAGEN – OSLO
The Northern Dimension of the Comintern's Global Network and Underground Activities, 1920–1940

Holger Weiss

This chapter provides an outline of the global communication network of the Third (communist) International or the Comintern with a special focus on its organization and outreach in northern Europe during the interwar period.[1] My aim is to identify and discuss underground activities in the Comintern's key northern hubs – that is, Tallinn (Reval), Stockholm, Hamburg, Copenhagen and Oslo. At different times, all of these locations hosted units and actors that were crucial for the operative planning and both the strategic and tactical implementation of the Comintern's global campaigns and activities. In addition, the Comintern was running a number of illegal underground bureaus and units around the world, including in several locations in northern Europe. Several of these units were especially set up to operate the Comintern's clandestine communications network, while others had been established for extraordinarily sensitive operations. Consequently, there was a need to organize and run a functioning and reliable communications network, with a particular emphasis on connecting Moscow with the Comintern's second operative centre in Berlin. Thus, although the arena and actors are located in northern Europe, my intention is not to focus on the activities of particular Nordic communist parties. It is, rather, firstly to highlight Lars Borgersrud's perspective on the 'glocal' aspects of the

Comintern's subversive and underground activities,[2] and secondly to present a Nordic/Baltic case study on Niels Erik Rosenfeld's seminal work on the underground apparatus of both the Soviet Union and the Comintern during the 1920s and 1930s.[3]

This chapter consists of three parts, which roughly correspond to the three periods of the northern activities of the Comintern's communications network and underground activities. In the first part, activities in Tallinn and Stockholm will be discussed. These two locations were two of the Comintern's earliest northern European hubs and were of special importance during the early 1920s when there were few possibilities for legal communist activities in Berlin. In the second part, the focus will be on Hamburg as the global gateway to the Comintern's communications network, especially through the activities of the International of Seamen and Harbour Workers (ISH), inaugurated in 1930. The northern and Baltic sections of the ISH were to be of the utmost importance for the Comintern in 1933, when several central operative units were moved to Copenhagen, including the ISH's headquarters. In the third part, the clandestine operations of the Organization Bernhard – that is, the Wollweber League – will be in focus. This organization had its headquarters in Oslo and had been established on the remnants of the ISH.

The Comintern and the Need for Global Communications

Established in March 1919 as a platform from which both to orchestrate the proletarian revolution and to coordinate global subversive activities, the Comintern emerged as the central unit for national communist parties with its headquarters in Moscow.[4] Along with the communist parties, other radical workers' organizations, such as the Red International of Labour Unions (RILU),[5] followed the Comintern's hierarchical organizational structure and became part of its apparatus.[6] Alongside the official communist parties, underground bureaus and departments, the so-called 'illegal apparatus' were to be established. These ultra-secret units were to maintain the links between Moscow, the national parties and other illegal apparatus as well as implement general political directives decided by the Comintern and, in case of emergency, to prepare the legal parties for the transition to illegal status.[7]

While the Comintern's architects envisioned a complex hierarchical system where the centre would be capable of linking up with the various national organizations, the reality proved to be far more complicated. The two greatest challenges were geography and post-war global political conditions. Only in a few places were communist activities legal or even tolerated by the national authorities. All bourgeois governments – in particular the French, British, U.S. and Japanese – branded the Bolshevik regime a challenge to existing national and international political stability. In some European countries, such as Finland and Poland, and in most of the colonies, communist activities were illegal,[8] while in other countries legal communist activities were under the close surveillance of the authorities and home security organizations.[9] The question for Moscow was how to organize a functioning system of communication between Comintern headquarters and the various national units and cells.

In principle, the Comintern could have made use of the network of Soviet Russian embassies and commercial missions abroad. The Soviet trade missions were used by both the Soviet Secret Service and the Department for International Communications (Otdel mezhdunarodnoi svyazi, OMS). The OMS was the liaison organization of the Comintern and maintained illegal connections both with foreign communist parties and the 'illegal apparatus', with the help of a staff of couriers.[10] The two units operated closely together and with the 'Bolshevization' of the Comintern in the late 1920s, the OMS became more or less the Kremlin's extended arm.[11] However, any direct and open connection with the Comintern was neither advisable nor strategically viable from a Soviet Russian perspective, as the Soviet government was trying to gain international recognition during the 1920s and early 1930s. Officially, therefore, the Soviet government distanced itself from the Comintern by claiming that Soviet Russia had no intention of interfering in other countries' internal affairs. Therefore, from the Kremlin's perspective, the use of the diplomatic postal service and other diplomatic channels was also inadvisable, although at times also necessary. Nevertheless, the various trade missions in particular were used as cover agencies for both Soviet and Comintern clandestine activities such as the directing of both financial support and political instructions to strikers, subversive underground groups and communist parties.[12]

However, there were situations or conditions when the Soviet missions either could not be used or did not exist. Logically, the utilization of ordinary postal or telegram services was not possible, nor was communication by radio or telephone advisable, as both could easily be – and certainly were – monitored and checked by the authorities. Instead, the Comintern used couriers, who would carry messages, instructions and money to any destination outside Soviet Russia. The infrastructure of its clandestine activities also included secure flats and places where subversive material could be printed and passports forged. Sometimes this could be done in Moscow, but it was far more effective to use underground as well as 'semi-legal' units outside Soviet Russia. The most effective way to do this was to use the facilities and workshops of those communist parties that could operate on a legal basis. Therefore, a plan to establish so-called Foreign Bureaus of the Comintern in several western European countries in order to promote and coordinate the 'World Revolution' had already been presented in 1919. Initially, such bureaus were to be established in Stockholm, Berlin, Vienna, Sofia and Amsterdam, while others were later established in New York (the Pan-American Bureau) and Mexico City (the Latin American Bureau) in 1920.[13]

In the Far East, Vladivostok emerged along with Shanghai and San Francisco as the main hub of the Comintern's communications network in the Pacific Rim during the 1920s.[14] In the West, Weimar Germany was of central strategic importance for the Comintern's global communication network in Europe and the Atlantic world. The capital of Weimar Germany was not only the 'gate to the West' for all kinds of refugees from post-revolutionary Russia but also the main site of the Comintern's legal activities. Berlin was a relatively free space for international activities, and a substantial number of communist organizations had set up their headquarters or secretariats there during the 1920s and early 1930s. Among others these included the European Bureau of the RILU and the Western European Bureau (WEB), the latter having been established after the Sixth Comintern Congress in 1929 to serve as the watchdog of the Executive Committee of the Comintern (ECCI).[15] The crucial question was how to establish reliable links between Berlin and Moscow.

Early Northern Relay Stations: Tallinn and Stockholm

During the early chaotic years of Weimar Germany, especially the years 1919–1921, when all activities of the German Communist Party (Kommunistische Partei Deutschlands, KPD) were banned several times by the authorities, two northern European countries provided ideal conditions for the Comintern's international ambitions. One of the Comintern apparatus' first hubs outside Soviet Russia was Tallinn (Reval), the capital of Estonia. In the wake of the collapse of the Russian Empire in 1917, Estonia experienced a period of political turbulence. Independence was declared in February 1918 only to be followed by German occupation a few weeks later. After the German collapse in late 1918, the Bolsheviks tried to invade the country but the Red Army was repulsed in 1919 and the Tartu (Dorpat) Peace Treaty of 2 February 1920 stabilized the relationship between Soviet Russia and Estonia.

The Estonian Communist Party (Eestimaa Kommunistlik Partei, EKP) was established in November 1920 as an underground party; its activities were explicitly subversive and its leadership had close links to the Bolsheviks. Not surprisingly, the Estonian government regarded the EKP as Moscow's 'Fifth Column'. On the other hand, the Bolshevik government was able to establish both an embassy and a commercial mission in Tallinn.[16]

The Bolsheviks' hub in Tallinn was of high strategic value. Estonia and Soviet Russia had a common border and, in contrast to either Finland or Poland, where communist activity was totally illegal and the Bolshevik diplomatic representation closely watched, conditions in Tallinn were tolerable. According to a German memorandum written in August 1921, Tallinn had by that time become the Bolsheviks' central propaganda centre. Its leading figure was Maxim Litvinov, officially the Bolshevik government's representative and head of the Soviet Commercial Mission in Estonia. However, according to this memorandum, Litvinov's diplomatic position was a mere facade for his clandestine political activities – that is, the coordination of the Soviet and Comintern propaganda apparatus in western Europe. He was in charge of an illegal and undercover printing press and information bureau in Tallinn. Under Litvinov's command, cells were also operating in Riga, Kaunas, Stockholm, Copenhagen, Berlin, Prague, Vienna and London. Communication between Tallinn and the various cells was organized through a special courier system.[17]

The 1921 memorandum provides a good insight into the structures of the early communication networks of both the Bolsheviks and the Comintern. While all activities were planned and determined in Moscow, their implementation was coordinated from Tallinn. The central relay station in Central Europe was Berlin, where a shipping company had been established. This company operated the shipping services between Stettin, Berlin's harbour, and Tallinn. Connections between the Baltic countries and Central Europe were vital during this period, as thousands of German and Austrian-Hungarian soldiers and prisoners of war were being repatriated from Russia via Tallinn and the Estonian border town Narva. However, Narva was not only a 'humanitarian bridge' in post-war Europe. It was also rather easy to hide a courier and a trunk of subversive material amongst the repatriates, and the secret services of the western European countries had every reason to believe that the undercover transfer of gold and money to the various communist parties was also being channelled this way.[18]

The Comintern's second northern relay station was Stockholm. Sweden had been a neutral country during the war and the communists could operate in the country legally and relatively freely.[19] The

Swedish Communist Party had joined the Comintern already in 1919 and had been reorganized in 1921 after internal rifts.[20] A Soviet Russian embassy as well as a Soviet Commercial Mission existed in Stockholm and there was a direct steam ferry connection between St. Petersburg/ Petrograd and Stockholm. In April 1919, the ECCI established its own special section, the Scandinavian Commission (Bureau), in Stockholm.[21] This Bureau, like its corresponding units in Berlin and Amsterdam, was to be the Comintern's official representative in western Europe. The Comintern's relay station in Stockholm seems, initially at least, to have been rather successful. Any person with either a Swedish passport or a visa issued in Sweden could move relatively freely throughout Europe. It was also relatively easy to print agitation and propaganda material by communist-owned or controlled printers in Sweden and to ship it out from Sweden.[22] In 1921, the operations of the Bureau were reorganized by the ECCI. Renamed the Section for International Liaison in Stockholm, or the Stockholm Bureau, its tasks were twofold. On the one hand, it was to continue its earlier activities, namely the transfer of money from Moscow to the Scandinavian and West European communist parties. On the other hand, it was also now instructed to organize the illegal transport of couriers and agitation literature from Soviet Russia to Europe. However, the Bureau was not functioning as well at this point and was soon reorganized and relocated to Oslo in 1923.[23]

However, neither the Estonian nor the Scandinavian relay station proved to be effective in the long run. Operations in Tallinn had to be closed down during the aftermath of the failed communist uprising and the banning of the EKP in December 1924. In Sweden, on the other hand, the Communist Party was paralysed by internal fights amongst its leadership over the relationship between the party and the Comintern. Due to the party's weak position as well as its continuing internal fights, the Comintern decided to close its bureaus in Scandinavia and to coordinate its communication network from Hamburg.

The Gate to the World: Hamburg and the Global Networks of Inter-Clubs

While in theory Soviet ships could handle the traffic of subversive material and individuals between Germany and Soviet Russia, this link was insufficient for running a global communication network. Therefore, Moscow was in need of reliable and influential partners on board the merchant fleets and amongst the harbour workers. However, the situation in the West was problematic, as about one third of the world's merchant fleet was in British hands and one fifth in American hands. In both countries the communist parties and communist-controlled unions were either weak or had only a marginal influence in the harbours and amongst the seamen. Even worse, the International Federation of Transport Workers (ITF) was controlled by the social democrats and the communists failed miserably in their attempt to get a foothold inside this union.[24] There also existed three other large national merchant fleets – the German, Norwegian and the Japanese – but communist activities amongst Japanese sailors were more or less impossible due to the Japanese government's anti-communist position. This left the German and Norwegian merchant fleets, both of which operated out of Hamburg.

Hamburg was an ideal place for subversive activities and the communists had a substantial influence on the working class and unemployed workforce there. The harbour area, in particular, was controlled by the KPD and communist labour unions.[25] Here, the key person was Albert Walter, an ex-seaman, who was one of the leaders of the German Maritime Workers' Union, which had joined the RILU in 1922.[26] Walter was thereafter commissioned by the RILU's General Secretary Alexander Losovsky to develop the International Propaganda and Action Committee of Transport Workers into the RILU's global platform.[27] This was achieved through Walter's second unit, the so-called International Port Bureaus.

Officially, the activities of the Port Bureaus were camouflaged under the pretext of being a meeting place for harbour workers and visiting seamen: the inter-club. The first inter-club had been organized in Leningrad in 1922 and served as a model for the one set up by Walter in Hamburg. Each club was to contain a library as well as a restaurant or bar where cheap food was served. During the evening, the inter-club staged theatre or film shows or organized other cultural events. More important was its function as a rallying point for radical seamen and communist agitators. By 1932, there existed fourteen inter-clubs in Soviet port cities, nine in Scandinavia, five in Germany, four in the United States and one each in Danzig (Gdansk), Belgium, the Netherlands, France, the United Kingdom, China, Australia and Uruguay.[28]

Walter was successful in his establishment of a global communication network. His strategy had been to establish small cells on board ships. This was achieved by the so-called Hamburg method. The basic idea was to establish a personal contact between an agitator and a seaman when a new ship arrived in Hamburg. A small group of functionaries and harbour activists boarded a ship in order to distribute leaflets and pamphlets amongst the crew. After contacts had been established, a close interaction between the inter-club headquarters and the crew was then expected in order to win over at least some of the crew to the cause of radical agitation. Most importantly, a report was written after each visit, listing reliable contacts and identifying potential partners for future cooperation. The names of individuals, cells and ships were thereafter collected in a catalogue. This catalogue, which already by the late 1920s included hundreds of individuals and ships, formed the central database of Albert Walter's communication network. Consequently, the OMS as well as the WEB and the European Bureau of the RILU regarded these ship cells as an ideal courier system that could be used for underground communications.[29]

The International of Seamen and Harbour Workers and its Northern Activities

Work on the waterfront was reorganized by the RILU in 1930. A new organization, the International of Seamen and Harbour Workers (ISH), was established in early October 1930.[30] During the Cold War, it was generally claimed that the ISH was a subversive organization focusing on clandestine and preventive operations in order to hamper the war preparations against the Soviet Union as well as communications between the centres in Moscow and Berlin and the rest of the world.[31] However, such a perspective has either downplayed or has actively ignored the RILU's explicit intention to establish a revolutionary trade union platform and a global alternative to the ITF.[32]

The headquarters of the new organization were located in Hamburg. The leading unit was the Executive Committee, which constituted the leading functionaries and secretaries in Hamburg as well as the leaders of the various national ISH sections.[33] The centres of mass agitation were the International Seamen's clubs and their number was to be vastly expanded.[34] Basically, each club was to consist of several national sections, each of them targeting a particular group of foreign seamen. In practice, only a few of these inter-clubs ever listed multiple sections. The most thorough reorganization occurred in Hamburg where an Anglo-American, a Scandinavian, a Latin and a Colonial section were set up.[35] In addition, there was a Baltic section but it was not located in the ISH building initially.[36]

The secretariat at the headquarters in Hamburg was the ISH's core unit and initially consisted of three members. The chair, George Hardy, was in charge of the *ISH Information Bulletin* as well as contacts with the Anglophone countries, India and the Far East. The secretary, Albert Walter, was in charge of the technical apparatus as well as work in

Scandinavia, the Baltic Sea countries and the German-speaking countries. The third member, Auguste Dumay, was in charge of connections with France, Yugoslavia, Greece, the Latin countries (Italy, Spain, Portugal) as well as work in French colonies in Africa and mandated territories in the Near East and Latin America.[37]

A reorganization of work at the headquarters in Hamburg followed sometime during the first half of 1931. The result was the establishment of a parallel unit and the arrival of a new mastermind at the ISH secretariat: Comrade Adolf.[38] This person was Alfred Bem alias Adolf Shelley, Moscow's representative and ISH Instructor. He was in charge of the so-called Illegal Secretariat – that is, the monitoring unit of the ISH (Legal) Secretariat of Albert Walter, located in a secret office in another part of the town.[39]

The ISH sections comprised about thirty affiliated national organizations, although many of them were not actually sections at all but rather 'threads of communications'. Only a few of the national sections, including those in Germany, France and the Scandinavian countries were financially self-sufficient. Other sections – for example, the U.S. section – received ISH funds for special purposes and individual actions, while the British, Baltic, Chinese and other sections were completely dependent on ISH subsidies. The Scandinavian sections were amongst the most important ones, especially the Danish and Norwegian revolutionary opposition unions.[40]

In Norway, the ISH's leading members were Arthur Samsing, Martin Rasmussen Hjelmen and Arne Halvorsen as well as Leif Foss, who was in charge of the inter-club in Oslo. The Norwegian Sjøfolkens RFO – that is, the communist trade union opposition group within the Seafarers' Union – was operating ten inter-clubs by 1932, in Oslo, Bergen, Tromsø and Narvik among other places. The organization had about 1,000 registered members, of which 250 were members of the Norwegian Communist Party.[41] In Denmark, on the other hand, the Danish Stokers' Union under the leadership of Richard Jensen and Georg Hegner was a highly prized affiliated union. Jensen, sometimes acting as a courier between Moscow and Hamburg, belonged to the ISH's central leadership.[42] By 1932, the campaign to establish cells on both Danish and Norwegian ships had been fairly successful, the largest ones being set up on the Marie Mærsk (DK) and the Anna Knudsen (NO).[43] In Sweden too, a revolutionary trade union section, Sjötransportarbetarnas röda fackliga opposition (RFO), had been established within the Swedish Seafarers' Union and was an affiliated section of the ISH, and in 1933 it had about 1,200 members.[44] Larger inter-clubs existed in Gothenburg and Stockholm.

The situation elsewhere in the Baltic Sea region was far more complicated. Communist activities were banned completely in Finland, and the
Finnish Seafarers' Union was closely controlled by reformists and socialists and was a member of the ITF. Work amongst Finnish seamen was
concentrated in Kiel, as this port was the main liaison centre for traffic
with Finland. A small revolutionary trade union group existed amongst
the seamen, although it had little influence and the ISH secretariat had
few direct links to it, if any. Nevertheless, underground communism was
a known fact in Finland and at least a few of the seamen were believed
either to have sympathized or backed the ISH's calls to replace the union's leadership before 1934.[45] The situation was similar in Poland and
the Baltic countries, although the ISH tried to agitate among Polish sailors via the inter-club in Danzig (Gdansk),[46] and in 1933 the majority of
the members of the Polish Seamen's Union as well as its leadership was
affiliated to the ISH.[47] Specific attempts were made to gain a foothold in
both the Estonian and Latvian merchant fleets.[48] While the Estonian case
proved difficult, the ISH was successful in infiltrating Latvian ships. By
the end of 1932, sections for Latvian seamen existed at the inter-clubs
in Hamburg, Antwerp, Danzig and Rotterdam, whereas cells or at least
members existed on thirty-two Latvian ships.[49] One year later, the ISH

Illustration 12.1 Postcard showing inter-club in Gothenburg during the first half
of the 1930s. Photographer unknown. Riksarkivet Sweden, SÄPOs arkiv.

claimed to control the majority of members in the Latvian Seamen's Union. The central person in charge of the Baltic countries was Ernst Lambert alias Michael Avatin (or Avotin).[50]

The operations at ISH headquarters and at some of the national sections were financed through funds from Moscow. Money was never transferred directly to Hamburg. Instead, the RILU established a secure communication network operating via Max Ziese in Berlin. Ziese would direct monthly payments to Albert Walter for the operations of the ISH and the International Trade Union Committee of Negro Workers (ITUCNW). Walter, in turn, would send subsidies to the various ISH sections via his courier system.[51] Occasionally, Richard Jensen served as courier between Moscow, Berlin and Hamburg.[52]

In accordance with the hierarchical rules of the Comintern apparatus, the various national units and their activities were to be coordinated, monitored and controlled by the centre. This was to be achieved by sending written instructions by couriers, by receiving written monthly reports on activities, and by visits of national functionaries to ISH headquarters. 'Travelling instructors' were sent to the national sections when they were to be reorganized, or in order to coordinate actions during a national strike. For example, Comrade Henry (Luigi Polano) was sent on a mission to Norway and Sweden in May 1931 with a mandate to co-manage the strike of the dockworkers in Oslo,[53] while Richard Krebs operated as ISH Instructor in Scandinavia in early 1933.[54]

One of the ISH's main structural problems was its dual position as both an independent and a communist-controlled union. Its links to the party apparatus were generally weak; this was the case not only in Hamburg but also characterized the relationship between the party and the various national ISH sections throughout the world. While most if not all of the leading comrades were party members, the majority of the rank and file was syndicalist rather than communist. At times, the ISH was even at loggerheads with other communist organizations in Hamburg, such as the Red Marine or even the local branch of the KPD. On the other hand, the independent position of the organization was advantageous from a strategic and tactical perspective. The ISH was not controlled by the party apparatus in Hamburg, nor were its sections taking any directives from the national parties or red union leadership. Nevertheless, the weak relationship between the ISH, its sections and the party was time and again considered to be a handicap, especially when the ISH secretariat tried to direct affairs in the sections. If Hamburg failed to influence the affairs of one section, the only avenue left was to ask the RILU and Comintern apparatus to intervene and settle the case.

1933: Copenhagen as the Comintern's New Centre

The dominant position of both Berlin and Hamburg as the Comintern's second centre came to an abrupt end in 1933. On 23 February 1933, the police launched a combined raid against communist bureaus in Berlin, including those of the WEB. A few weeks later, on 5 March 1933, the SA stormed the ISH premises in Hamburg. Communists were purged by both the police and Nazi troops and thousands were arrested and sent to concentration camps. All communist activities in Germany were declared illegal, and hundreds emigrated and went into exile in neighbouring countries, with 800 emigrating to Denmark. The Comintern's global communication network was seriously damaged, as all operations via Germany ceased.[55]

However, emergency plans for the relocation of the WEB (including the OMS bureau in Berlin) and the ISH to Copenhagen in case of a Nazi takeover in Germany had already been prepared in 1932. At closed meetings during the ISH's World Conference in Altona in May 1932, the decision was made that both the ISH's archives and operations would be transferred from Hamburg to Copenhagen if the activities of the organization were thwarted in Germany. Similar plans were made for the transfer of the WEB in case of an emergency. The two key figures involved in drawing up the plan were Richard Jensen and Ernst Wollweber, the leader of the ISH's German section.[56] In December 1932, Wollweber visited Jensen in Copenhagen in order to discuss this emergency plan further.[57]

The Berlin and Hamburg units were successfully relocated to Copenhagen in March and April 1933, while other KPD and Comintern bureaus were moved to Saarbrücken, Amsterdam, Prague and Paris. Most of its inner circle, including Adolf Shelley, had been able to escape to Denmark.[58] Wollweber was appointed as ISH Secretary and arrived in Copenhagen in late August 1933. Wollweber also headed the exiled regional unit of the KPD, the KPD/Abschnitt Nord.[59] Although the ISH secretariat was planning to continue its global operations, it soon had to realize that major structural changes were necessary, as its economic resources were extremely low. Consequently, its technical instructors were abolished, while the subsidies to its national sections as well as its financial support to strikers and strike campaigns had to be cancelled.[60]

Copenhagen served as the hub of the Comintern's communication network and as the centre for the RILU's maritime sections for about a year.[61] During the early years of the communist exile after February 1933, the new central European Bureau of the RILU was also based in Copenhagen.[62] Communist journals and pamphlets were printed in the

Danish capital and smuggled into Germany, either on board Danish ships or via Antwerp and Saarbrücken.[63] The Danish authorities seemed initially not to bother too much about the activities of the exiled Germans and the activities of the Comintern in Copenhagen. However, Copenhagen was not an ideal location for the focal point of a worldwide communication network, as the Danish capital had rather poor global connections. The headquarters of the WEB were therefore transferred to Paris in 1934, while those of the KPD/Abschnitt Nord ended up more or less in disarray.

The ISH's inability to fully engage in and monitor national strikes became evident during the seamen's strikes in Sweden and Finland in 1933. In both cases, the ISH tactics failed miserably and neither the ISH nor the underground Finnish organizations or the Swedish RFO was in any position to challenge the position of the reformists within the unions.[64] Similarly pathetic was the ISH's role in the Danish seamen's strike in April 1934.[65]

Even more problematic than the ISH's dismal performance during the Nordic strikes was the fact that its global system was difficult to operate from Copenhagen. This led to those national sections that were still in operation and not dependent on ISH subsidies to begin severing their ties from the ISH centre – not least due to the fact that the comrades in Copenhagen had not sent any instructions for months.[66] In fact, even its connections to Moscow were not functioning well, and with the transfer of Wollweber to the Soviet Union in mid 1934, activities in Copenhagen came to a standstill. By the end of the year, if not earlier, the ISH secretariat had been relocated to Antwerp.[67]

A further blow to the ISH's operations came with the Comintern's adoption of its Popular Front policy in 1935, which resulted in the subsequent dissolution of both the RILU and its various subcommittees, including the ISH. The idea was to push for a merger of the communist and reformist/syndicalist unions – that is, an amalgamation of both the ISH and the ITF. However, the ISH's illegal structures were not to be affected by this merger.[68]

Discussions between the ISH and the ITF achieved nothing, as the ITF simply did not want to discuss the amalgamation of the ISH into the ITF. The ITF thought that the ISH had outplayed its role by 1935, if ever it had had one. Since 1933, the former global network was barely functioning. Most of the inter-clubs, apart from those in Marseilles, Rouen, Dunkirk, Rotterdam, New York, Copenhagen, Esbjerg and Stockholm, no longer existed due to the lack of financial support from the ISH secretariat.[69] The final dissolution of the ISH is not even documented. It seems that by mid 1936 the ISH secretariat had ceased operations.

Adolf Shelley, who had supported the 'Popular Front tactics', was called to Moscow where he was charged for being both a 'Trotskyist' and a Polish spy and was sentenced to death, a fate he shared with several hundred others in the purges of the Comintern apparatus during the Great Terror.[70] Thereafter, the ISH existed only on paper and its fate was decided by the Secretariat of the Executive Committee of the Comintern, resulting in the dissolution of the organization on 27 May 1937.[71]

Nordic Postscript: Oslo and the 'Organization Bernhard'

Although the ISH no longer existed in 1936, some of its ship cells were still functioning and were being used for the transfer of illegal literature, agents and funds. Moreover, by utilizing whatever was left of the ISH network, Ernst Wollweber was able to set up his sabotage organization in 1935, officially called 'the Organization against Fascism and in Support of the USSR' but usually referred to as either the Organization Bernhard or the Wollweber League/Wollweber Group.[72]

Ernst Wollweber, who had been in charge of the inter-club in Leningrad in 1934, was instructed by the NKVD (People's Commissariat for Internal Affairs) to organize an international network for acts of sabotage against German, Italian and Japanese ships.[73] In late 1935, he returned to Copenhagen where he cooperated with Richard Jensen. Although the organization had no fixed headquarters, by 1936 Oslo had become the main centre for his operations – in part due to the fact that his wife, Ragnhild Wijk, was a Norwegian communist, and her sister Aagot Wijk was married to the Norwegian ISH leader Arthur Samsing (who, together with his wife, lived in Soviet Russia from 1933 to 1936). The remnants of the ISH cells in Norway, under the leadership of Martin Rasmussen Hjelmen, were also of strategic importance and Hjelmen was ordered by Wollweber both to organize and to lead the groups in northern Norway (Narvik) and in Sweden (Kiruna and Luleå).[74] The Swedish cells played a crucial role in the organization; for example, the dynamite used by the group in its sabotage acts was stolen from the LKAB (Luossavaara-Kiirunavaara Aktiebolag) iron ore mines in Kiruna.[75] Several leading individuals in the Wollweber League were former ISH functionaries, such as Josef Rimbertus Schaap, who was in charge of operations in Belgium and the Netherlands, and Ernst Lambert, who was in charge of operations in the Baltic and who replaced Schaap in 1939 as leader of the activities in Antwerp and Rotterdam.[76] Other leading members of the League were German communists who were living in exile in the Nordic countries, such as Karl Bergstätter, who served as Wollweber's liaison officer between the cells in France, Belgium, the Netherlands, Denmark and Sweden.[77]

After its first act of sabotage in 1936, the group attracted the attention of the Gestapo. In 1937, the Gestapo even believed that Wollweber's group was part of the ISH.[78] In 1938, the organization managed to sink two ships belonging to the Spanish Francoist government in the Danish port of Frederikshavn; in the same year, it carried out an act of sabotage against the German ship *Norderney* in Tallinn. In addition, Schaap and his men were active in the Netherlands and in Belgium. All together, Wollweber and his groups conducted twenty-one acts of sabotage against ships of fascist nations. The Gestapo, therefore, cooperated with the Belgian, Danish and Dutch police in order to uncover the organization's activities, and by 1939 the Wollweber Group had ceased its operations in all countries except Norway and Sweden. Hjelmen was caught by the Swedish police in February 1940 and deported to the Gestapo, first in Norway and then to Germany where he suffered in various concentration camps and was finally decapitated in 1944.[79] Wollweber himself was arrested by the Swedish police in May 1940 and charged by the Swedish authorities with having carried out acts of sabotage and was sentenced to prison, but the German authorities were never able to get their hands on him, as he was instead handed over to the Soviet authorities in 1944.[80] Schaap, who had been living in Copenhagen since the autumn of 1939, was jailed by the Danish authorities in August 1940 and later delivered to the German authorities, who tried and decapitated him in 1943. While operations ceased in Sweden, they continued in Norway under the name of the Osvald group and under the leadership of Asbjørn Sunde until 1944 when the NKVD ordered them to cease activities.[81]

Conclusion

The Comintern's objective was to establish a 'solar system' consisting of communist parties and organizations orbiting around the centre in Moscow. Alongside these structures, a set of illegal or underground apparatus were established whose function was both to monitor the legal activities of a party or a communist organization and to undertake clandestine activities. The need for smooth communications between the centre, the sections and the illegal apparatus, as well as between the illegal apparatus and the (legal) sections, was therefore of the utmost importance for the Comintern. However, the political situation after the First World War gave little room for the establishment of smooth communications between Bolshevik Russia and the rest of the world.

Both the Bolsheviks as well as the Comintern were branded by (most) European governments as a threat to the political order and stability. Communist activities were outlawed in many European countries, while in others they were tolerated but monitored by the authorities. Equally complicated was the official relationship between the Soviet Union and the Comintern: when the Bolshevik government tried to get diplomatic recognition from European countries, its relationship with an organization promoting world revolution was officially downplayed.

Communications between Comintern headquarters in Moscow and its sections and illegal apparatus had to be secure and secret. Neutral countries, such as the Scandinavian ones, became important hubs at various points during the interwar period, and the northern route via Copenhagen and Stockholm was initially preferred by both communists and Comintern couriers who were travelling to and from Soviet Russia. Communist activities in the maritime sector, especially the establishment of ship cells, added a further dimension to this secret communications system. The aim of the Comintern's maritime sector, first and foremost the IPAC Transport (International Propaganda and Action Committee of Transport Workers) during the 1920s and its successor, the International of Seamen and Harbour Workers, was to provide both a watertight network for the safe passage of couriers and a safe cover for various types of clandestine transactions.

This chapter has highlighted various important aspects of the Nordic hubs within the Comintern's communications network. A rough sketch has been given, starting with Stockholm and Tallinn in the early 1920s, continuing with Copenhagen in the mid 1930s and ending with Oslo in the second half of the 1930s. Although an outline of this northern European network can be provided, not much is known about the extent of the network apart from the fact that its agents and routes changed. The transit route from Sweden to Soviet Russia, via either Haparanda or Åbo (Turku) and then by train towards Leningrad, has not been touched upon at all – its existence was known about and it seems to have been used by communists, who (usually) used forged passports and fake identities to travel along this route.

It is difficult to establish exactly when the Comintern's northern European communication network ended. A major blow was the Nazi takeover in Germany in 1933, although this did not in itself end the 'solar system'. Another setback was the Comintern's own new Popular Front policy and tactics after 1935. The organization was further paralysed in 1936 when it became the target of Stalin's purges. Not much of the older northern European courier system seems to have remained intact at this point. However, a new one, the Organization Bernhard, marked the start of a different organizational setup, namely one that combined both Soviet and Comintern secret apparatus. Although officially working for the Comintern, this organization was in fact directed by the NKVD and was no longer focusing on communications but rather on both overt and covert sabotage operations against both fascist and Nazi regimes.

Holger Weiss is Professor of General History at Åbo Akademi University. He has published widely on African, global and Atlantic history, including *Between Accommodation and Revivalism: Muslims, the State and Society in Ghana from the Precolonial to the Postcolonial Era* (Finnish Oriental Society, 2008) and *Framing a Radical African Atlantic. African American Agency, West African Intellectuals and the International Trade Union of Negro Workers* (Brill, 2014).

Notes

1. An earlier and shorter version was published in Swedish, see H. Weiss. 2009. 'Stockholm – Hamburg – Köpenhamn: Nordeuropeiska noder i Kominterns globala kommunikationsnätverk, 1920–1933', *Historisk Tidskrift för Finland* 2, 139–69.
2. L. Borgersrud. 1994. 'Wollweber-organisasjonen i Norge', Ph.D. disseration, Oslo: Universitetet i Oslo; L. Borgersrud. 2001. *Die Wollweber-Organisation und Norwegen*, Berlin: Dietz. On the Nordic communist parties, see further K. Rentola and T. Saarela (eds). 1998. *Communism: National and International*, Helsinki: Finnish Literature Society; and chapter 11 in this volume.
3. N.E. Rosenfeldt. 2009. *The 'Special' World: Stalin's Power Apparatus and the Soviet System's Secret Structures of Communication*, 2 vols., Copenhagen: Museum Tusculanum Press; N.E. Rosenfeldt. 2012. 'Komintern og det hemmelige apparat', in J. Jørgensen et al. (eds), *Komintern og de dansk-sovjetiske relationer*, København: Arbejdermuseet & Arbejderbevægelsens bibliotek og arkiv, 81–128.
4. See further B.H. Bayerlein. 2004. 'Das neue Babylon: Strukturen und Netzwerke der Kommunistischen Internationale und ihre Klassifizierung', *Jahrbuch für Historische Kommunismusforschung*, 181–270.
5. Another acronym of the RILU is Profintern, which is a contraction of the Russian term 'Professionalye Soyuz Internationalnye'. Both words were in use, although the English, German (RGI), Swedish (RFI), French or Spanish (ISR) terms were always used in offical documents.
6. K. McDermott and J. Agnew. 1996. *The Comintern: A History of International Communism from Lenin to Stalin*, Basingstoke: Macmillan; R. Tosstorff. 2004. *Profintern: Die Rote Gewerkschaftsinternationale 1920–1937*, Paderborn: Schoeningh.
7. Rosenfeldt, *The 'Special' World*, vol. 1, 173–74.
8. "Red" refugees established the Communist Party of Finland in Moscow in the aftermath of the civil war in 1918. The party was a section of the Comintern and was illegal in Finland until 1944. However, cover organizations were established in Finland that participated in parliamentary and local elections: the Socialist Workers' Party of Finland in 1920 (illegal in 1923) and its successor, the Socialist Electoral Organisation of Workers and Smallholders, in 1924. Due to political pressure by the radical nationalist

and anti-communist Lapuan liike (Lapua Movement), the Finnish government declared all far-left activities illegal in 1930. See further T. Saarela. 1996. *Suomalaisen kommunismin synty 1918–1923*, Helsinki: Kansan sivistystyön liitto; T. Saarela. 2008. *Suomalainen kommunismi ja vallankumous 1923–1930*, Helsinki: Suomalaisen kirjallisuuden seura; and T. Saarela. 2015. *Finnish Communism Visited*, Helsinki: The Finnish Society for Labour History.

9. For a general outline, see Z. Steiner. 2005. *The Lights that Failed: European International History 1919–1933*, Oxford: Oxford University Press, 533–58.

10. Rosenfeldt, *The 'Special' World*, vol. 2, 220–24.

11. P. Huber. 1996. 'The Cadre Department, the OMS and the "Dimitrov" and "Manuilsky" Secretariats during the Phase of the Terror', in M. Narinsky and J. Rojahn (eds), *Center and Periphery: The History of the Comintern in the Lights of New Documents*, Amsterdam: International Institute of Social History, 122–52.

12. Rosenfeldt, 'Komintern og det hemmelige apparat'.

13. A. Yamanouchi. 2010. 'The Early Comintern in Amsterdam, New York and Mexico City', *The Journal of History* 147, 101–2, 116. Most of the bureaus were dissolved during the early 1920s; the Berlin Bureau or West European secretariat as late as 1925.

14. See further J. Fowler. 2007. *Japanese and Chinese Immigrant Activists: Organizing in American and International Communist Movements, 1919–1933*, New Brunswick: Rutgers University Press.

15. K. Schlögel. 1998. *Berlin Ostbahnhof Europas: Russen und Deutsche in ihrem Jahrhundert*, Berlin: Siedler.

16. S.P. Forgus. 1992. 'Soviet Subversive Activities in Independent Estonia', *Journal of Baltic Studies* 23(1), 29–46.

17. (Memorandum) Bolschewistische Propaganda, 1.8.1921, Swedish National Archives (SNA), Archives of the Ministry of Foreign Affairs (UD:s arkiv) 1920 års dossiersystem HP 1458, Den bolsjevikiska rörelsen: Sverige och utlandet, 1921, augusti-september. This document seems to have been written by a local informant and was handed to the Swedish Mission in Tallinn.

18. (Copy) Movement of Individuals and Gold to and from Soviet Russia via Narva, dated Reval 14.7.1921, SNA UD:s arkiv 1920 års dossiersystem HP 1458, Den bolsjevikiska rörelsen: Sverige och utlandet, 1921, maj-juli. On the repatriation of prisoners of war, see M. Housden. 2007. 'When the Baltic Sea was a "Bridge" for Humanitarian Action: The League of Nations, the Red Cross and the Repatriation of Prisoners of War between Russia and Central Europe, 1920–22', *Journal of Baltic Studies* 38(1), 61–83.

19. A. Kan. 2005. *Hemmabolsjevikerna: Den svenska socialdemokratin, ryska bolsjeviker och mensjeviker under världskriget och revolutionsåren 1914–1920*, Stockholm: Carlssons förlag.

20. J. Bolin. 2004. *Parti av ny typ? Skapandet av ett svenskt kommunistiskt parti 1917–1933*, Stockholm: Almqvist & Wiksell.

21. Yamanouchi, 'The Early Comintern', 104.

22. See further Weiss, 'Stockholm – Hamburg – Köpenhamn', 153–56.

23. L. Björlin. 2005. 'Mellan bolsjevism och socialdemokrati: Den kommunistiska rörelsen i Sverige och Komintern', *CoWoPa – Comintern Working Paper* 2. Retrieved 4 March 2013 from http://www.abo.fi/institution/en/media/7957/cowopa2bjorlin.pdf. On the transfer of money from Moscow to the Nordic communist parties, see M. Thing. 1998. 'The Communists' Capital', *Communist History Network Newsletter*. Retrieved 3 November 2016 from http://www.whatnextjournal.org.uk/Pages/History/DKP.html.

24. On the ITF, see B. Reinalda (ed.). 1997. *The International Transport-Workers Federation 1914–1945. The Edo Fimmen Years*, Amsterdam: Stichting beheer IISG.

25. L. Eiber. 2000. *Arbeiter und Arbeiterbewegung in der Hansestadt Hamburg in den Jahren 1929 bis 1939. Werftarbeiter, Hafenarbeiter und Seeleute: Konformität, Opposition, Widerstand*, Frankfurt am Main: Peter Lang.

26. H. Weber and A. Herbst. 2008. 'Walter, Albert Paul', in H. Weber and A. Herbst, *Deutsche Kommunisten: Biographisches Handbuch 1918 bis 1945*, Berlin: Dietz, 988.

27. H. Knüfken. 2003. *Von Kiel bis Leningrad: Stationen eines deutschen revolutionären Matrosen 1917–1930*, Berlin: Basisdruck, 210–12.

28. H. Rübner. 2003. 'Interklub, Bordzelle, revolutionärer Seeleutestreik: Die "Revolutionäre Gewerkschaftsopposition" in der Seeschiffahrt während der Weltwirtschaftskrise', *Archiv für die Geschichte des Widerstandes und der Arbeit* 17, 111–12.

29. Rübner, 'Interklub, Bordzelle, revolutionärer Seeleutestreik', 112, 114.

30. The best overview of the ISH's activities is presented in Borgersrud, 'Wollweber-organisasjonen'.

31. G. Nollau. 1961. *International Communism and World Revolution: History and Methods*, New York: Praeger. See further Borgersrud, 'Wollweber-organisasjonen', 2–5, 15–6.

32. Tosstorff, *Die Profintern*, 374.

33. CIC FO 10501 Report R-G44-50, page 5.

34. Draft Decisions: Basic principles [for work of the ISH], RGASPI 534/5/219, 81–84.

35. Resolution über die Tätigkeit des Hamburger Internationalen Klubs, no date, filed 15.3.1931, RGASPI 534/5/220, 158–61.

36. CIC FO 10501 Report R-G44-50, pp. 6, 14. According to Krebs, there existed a Finnish section in the inter-club in Kiel but his information is vague – he himself seems to have had no first hand information about its existence and so far I have found no traces of its activities among the Comintern files.

37. Duties and Tasks of Secretariat Members, filed 17.3.1931, RGASPI 534/5/220, 128–29.

38. See further the correspondence between George Hardy and Comrade Adolf, RGASPI 534/5/221, 162–74.

39. CIC FO 10501 Report R-G44-50, p. 2; R. Jensen. 1957. *En omtumlet tilværelse*, København: Fremad, 103; E. Nørgaard. 1975. *Revolutionen der udeblev*, København: Fremad; E. Nørgaard. 1985. *Drømmen om verdensrevolutionen: Komintern og de revolutionære søfolk*, Lynge: Bogan.

40. Borgersrud, 'Wollweber-organisasjonen', 41–52.

41. Borgersrud, 'Wollweber-organisasjonen', 57–58, 65.

42. On the activities of the ISH's Danish section see further Nørgaard, *Drømmen om verdensrevolutionen*.

43. List of members of the Scandinavian Section of the inter-club in Batumi, 1932, Archives of the Communist International, Russian State Archives of Socio-Political History, Moscow (RGASPI) 534/5/233, fol. 20–21.

44. Material über die ISH und über Arbeit unter den Seeleuten und Hafenarbeiter, 20.1.1934, RGASPI 534/5/241, fol. 70–88.

45. T. Soukola. 2003. *Riistorauhaa rikkomassa: Suomen Merimies-Unionin ja sen edeltäjien vaiheita 1905–2000*, Helsinki: Weilin+Göös, 99, 110.

46. Plan of Immediate Tasks, no date (ca late autumn 1930), RGASPI 534/5/219, fol. 54–57.

47. Material über die ISH und über Arbeit unter den Seeleuten und Hafenarbeiter, 20.1.1934, RGASPI 534/5/241, fol. 70–88.

48. Arbeitsplan der Estnischen Sektion des Baltischen Komitees der ISH für das Halbjahr Juli – Dezember 1932; Arbeitsplan der Lettischen Sektion des Baltischen Komitees der ISH für das Halbjahr Juli – Dezember 1932, RGASPI 534/5/234, fol. 1–4, 7–11.

49. Stand der Mitgliedschaft der RGO-Wassertransport auf den lettischen Schiffen am 1.12.1932, RGASPI 534/5/234, fol. 53.

50. Avatin, Die Lage in Lettland, 12.4.1935, RGASPI 534/5/242, fol. 147–48.

51. A. Walter, 25.1.33/Cross-Reference, BNA KV 2/1799.
52. J. Valtin. 1941. *Out of the Night*, New York: Alliance Book Corporation, 367; Jensen, *En omtumlet tilværelse*, 164.
53. Arbeitsbericht des Sekretariats der I.S.H., Hamburg 16.6.1931, RGASPI 534/5/221, 186.
54. Borgersrud, 'Wollweber-organisasjonen'.
55. On the Nordic exile of Germans from 1933, see E. Lorenz et al. (eds). 1998. *Ein sehr trübes Kapitel? Hitlerflüchtlinge in Nordeuropäischen Exil 1933 bis 1950*, Hamburg: Ergebnisse Verlag.
56. On Wollweber, see Borgersrud, 'Wollweber-organisasjonen'.
57. Nørgaard, *Drømmen om verdensrevolutionen*, 95, 97, 109.
58. Report by Adolf on the ISH secretariat's work in Copenhagen, 10.5.1933, RGASPI 534/5/236, fol. 53–54.
59. Borgersrud, 'Wollweber-organisasjonen', 75–77.
60. Jensen and Adolf, Umstellung des ISH-Budgets, no date, (c:a August 1933), RGASPI 534/5/236, fol. 81–85.
61. See further Borgersrud, *Die Wollweber-Organisation*; and Rosenfeldt, 'Komintern og det hemmelige apparat'.
62. Report in German concerning the reorganization of the RILU apparatus in 1933, no date, no author, RGASPI 534/4/459, fol. 10–11.
63. Borgersrud, 'Wollweber-organisasjonen', 78.
64. See further B. Svensson and E. Svensson. 1972. 'Sjömansstrejken 1933: bakgrund, förlopp och konsekvenser', *Arkiv för studier i arbetarrörelsens historia* 2(2), 3–26; Soukola, *Riistorauhaa rikkomassa*, 99–110.
65. Borgersrud, 'Wollweber-organisasjonen', 79.
66. Letter from the MWIU to Richard Jensen, no date, filed 22.XI.1933, RGASPI 534/5/236, fol. 126.
67. Borgersrud, *Die Wollweber-Organisation*, 49–51.
68. Memorandum über die Arten der internationalen Arbeit unter den Wassertransportarbeitern, 1.9.1935, RGASPI 534/5/243, fol. 83–88.
69. Bericht über die Internationalen Seeleute-Klubs und einige Vorschläge zu ihrer weiteren Tätigkeit, 31.3.1936, RGASPI 534/5/245, fol. 107–17.
70. Nørgaard, *Drømmen om verdensrevolutionen*, 137.
71. Protokoll (A) Nr 155 zusammengestellt auf Grund fliegender Abstimmung unter Mitgliedern des Sekretariats des EKKI am 27.6.1937, RGASPI 495/18/1206.
72. R. Szubanski. 1960. 'Sabotage Operations of the Pre-War Anti-Fascist League'. Retrieved 1 February 2013 from http://www.dtic.mil/cgi-bin/GetTRDoc?AD=ADA335012; Borgersrud, *Die Wollweber-Organisation*.
73. See further H. Dankaart and R. van Doorslaar. 1979. 'De activiteiten van een communistische sabotagegroep in Antwerpen en Rotterdam: De organisatie Wollweber (1933–1939)', *VMT Cahier* 1, 129–60. Retrieved 1 February 2013 from http://www.marxists.org/nederlands/thema/wereldoorlog2/1979sabotage.htm; Borgersrud, *Die Wollweber-Organisation*.
74. Borgersrud, 'Wollweber-organisasjonen', 41, 67–68.
75. On the Swedish cells of the Wollweber League, see further L. Gyllenhaal and L. Westberg. 2004. *Svenskar i krig: 1914–1945*, Lund: Historiska Media.
76. R. van Doorslaar and E. Verhoyen. 1986. 'L'Allemangne Nazie, la Police Belge et L'Anticommunisme en Belgique (1936–1944) – Un Aspect des Relations Belgo-Allemandes', *BTGN-RBHC* XVII (1–2), 97.
77. E. Verhoyen. 2012. '"De zaak Block en Celis". De moeizame relatie van de Antwerpse gerechtelijke politie met de Gestapo (1938–1941) – Deel 1', *Cahiers Inlichtingenstudies/Cahiers d'Études du Renseignment* 2, 22.

78. R. van Doorslaar. 1984. 'Anti-Communist Activism in Belgium, 1930–1944', *Socialist Register* 21, 114.
79. See further Borgersrud, *Die Wollweber-Organisation*.
80. M.F. Scholz. 2012. 'Wollweberligan: Ernst Wollweber', in K. Bosdotter (ed.), *Faror för staten: Politiska fångar på Långholmen 1880–1950*, Stockholm: Stockholmia förlag, 240–53.
81. Borgersrud, *Die Wollweber-Organisation*. On Sunde see his autobiography: A. Sunde. 2002. *Menn i mørkret*, new edition with preface by Lars Borgersrud, Oslo: Spartacus forlag.

References

Bayerlein, B.H. 2004. 'Das neue Babylon: Strukturen und Netzwerke der Kommunistischen Internationale und ihre Klassifizierung', *Jahrbuch für Historische Kommunismusforschung*, 181–270.

Björlin, L. 2005. 'Mellan bolsjevism och socialdemokrati: Den kommunistiska rörelsen i Sverige och Komintern', *CoWoPa – Comintern Working Paper* 2. Retrieved 4 March 2013 from http://www.abo.fi/institution/en/media/7957/cowopa2bjorlin.pdf.

Bolin, J. 2004. *Parti av ny typ? Skapandet av ett svenskt kommunistiskt parti 1917–1933*, Stockholm: Almqvist & Wiksell.

Borgersrud, L. 1994. 'Wollweber-organisasjonen i Norge', Ph.D. dissertation, Oslo: Universitetet i Oslo.

———. 2001. *Die Wollweber-Organisation und Norwegen*, Berlin: Dietz.

Dankaart, H. and R. van Doorslaar. 1979. 'De activiteiten van een communistische sabotagegroep in Antwerpen en Rotterdam: De organisatie Wollweber (1933–1939)', *Opstellen over de belgische arbeidersbeweging* 1, 129–60.

Eiber, L. 2000. *Arbeiter und Arbeiterbewegung in der Hansestadt Hamburg in den Jahren 1929 bis 1939. Werftarbeiter, Hafenarbeiter und Seeleute: Konformität, Opposition, Widerstand*, Frankfurt am Main: Peter Lang.

Forgus, S.P. 1992. 'Soviet Subversive Activities in Independent Estonia', *Journal of Baltic Studies* 23(1), 29–46.

Fowler, J. 2007. *Japanese and Chinese Immigrant Activists: Organizing in American & International Communist Movements, 1919–1933*, New Brunswick: Rutgers University Press.

Gyllenhaal, L. and L. Westberg. 2004. *Svenskar i krig: 1914–1945*, Lund: Historiska Media.

Housden, M. 2007. 'When the Baltic Sea Was a "Bridge" for Humanitarian Action: The League of Nations, the Red Cross and the Repatriation of Prisoners of War between Russia and Central Europe, 1920– 22', *Journal of Baltic Studies* 38(1), 61–83.

Huber, P. 'The Cadre Department, the OMS and the "Dimitrov" and "Manuilsky" Secretariats during the Phase of the Terror', in M. Narinsky and J. Rojahn (eds), *Center and Periphery: The History of the Comintern in the Lights of New Documents*, Amsterdam: International Institute of Social History, 1996, 122–52.

Jensen, R. 1957. *En omtumlet tilværelse*, København: Fremad.

Kan, A. 2005. *Hemmabolsjevikerna: Den svenska socialdemokratin, ryska bolsjeviker och mensjeviker under världskriget och revolutionsåren 1914–1920*, Stockholm: Carlssons förlag.

Knüfken, H. 2003. *Von Kiel bis Leningrad: Stationen eines deutschen revolutionären Matrosen 1917–1930*, Berlin: Basisdruck.

Lorenz, E. et al. (eds). 1998. *Ein sehr trübes Kapitel? Hitlerflüchtlinge in Nordeuropäischen Exil 1933 bis 1950*, Hamburg: Ergebnisse Verlag.

McDermott, K. and J. Agnew. 1996. *The Comintern: A History of International Communism from Lenin to Stalin*, Basingstoke: MacMillan.

Nollau, G. 1961. *International Communism and World Revolution: History and Methods*, New York: Praeger.

Nørgaard, E. 1975. *Revolutionen der udeblev*, København: Fremad.

———. 1985. *Drømmen om verdensrevolutionen: Komintern og de revolutionære søfolk*, Lynge: Bogan.

Reinalda, B. (ed.). 1997. *The International Transport-Workers Federation 1914– 1945. The Edo Fimmen Years*, Amsterdam: Stichting beheer IISG.

Rentola, K. and T. Saarela (eds). 1998. *Communism: National and International*, Helsinki: Finnish Literature Society.

Rosenfeldt, N.E. 2009. *The 'Special' World: Stalin's Power Apparatus and the Soviet System's Secret Structures of Communication 1–2*, Copenhagen: Museum Tusculanum Press.

———. 'Komintern og det hemmelige apparat', in J. Jørgensen et al. (eds), *Komintern og de dansk-sovjetiske relationer*, København: Arbejdermuseet & Arbejderbevægelsens bibliotek og arkiv, 2012, 81–128.

Rübner, H. 2003. 'Interklub, Bordzelle, revolutionärer Seeleutestreik: Die "Revolutionäre Gewerkschaftsopposition" in der Seeschiffahrt während der Weltwirtschaftskrise', *Archiv für die Geschichte des Widerstandes und der Arbeit* 17, 101–30.

Saarela, T. 1996. *Suomalaisen kommunismin synty 1918–1923*, Helsinki: Kansan sivistystyön liitto.

———. 2008. *Suomalainen kommunismi ja vallankumous 1923–1930*, Helsinki: Suomalaisen kirjallisuuden seura.

———. 2015. *Finnish Communism Visited*, Helsinki: The Finnish Society for Labour History.

Schlögel, K. 1998. *Berlin Ostbahnhof Europas: Russen und Deutsche in ihrem Jahrhundert*, Berlin: Siedler.

Scholz, M.F. 'Wollweberligan: Ernst Wollweber', in K. Bosdotter (ed.), *Faror för staten: Politiska fångar på Långholmen 1880–1950*, Stockholm: Stockholmia förlag, 2012, 240–53.

Soukola, T. 2003. *Riistorauhaa rikkomassa: Suomen Merimies-Unionin ja sen edeltäjien vaiheita 1905–2000*, Helsinki: Weilin+Göös.

Steiner, Z. 2005. *The Lights that Failed: European International History 1919–1933*, Oxford: Oxford University Press.

Sunde, A. 2002. *Menn i mørket*, Oslo: Spartacus forlag.

Svensson, B. and E. Svensson. 1972. 'Sjömansstrejken 1933: bakgrund, förlopp och konsekvenser', *Arkiv för studier i arbetarrörelsens historia* 2(2), 3–26.

Szubanski, R. 1960. 'Sabotage Operations of the Prewar Anti-Fascist League'. Retrieved 1 February 2013 from http://www.dtic.mil/cgi-bin/ GetTRDoc?AD=ADA335012

Thing, M. 1998. 'The Communists' Capital'. *Communist History Network Newsletter*. Retrieved 3 November 2016 from http://www.whatnextjournal. org.uk/Pages/History/DKP.html.

Tosstorff, R. 2004. *Profintern: Die Rote Gewerkschaftsinternationale 1920–1937*, Paderborn: Schoeningh.

Valtin, J. 1941. *Out of the Night*, New York: Alliance Book Corporation.

van Doorslaar, R. 1984. 'Anti-Communist Activism in Belgium, 1930–1944', *Socialist Register* 21, 114–29.

van Doorslaar, R. and E. Verhoyen. 1986. 'L'Allemangne Nazie, la Police Belge et L'Anticommunisme en Belgique (1936–1944) – Un Aspect des Relations Belgo-Allemandes', *BTGN-RBHC* XVII (1–2), 61–126.

Verhoyen, E. 2012. '"De zaak Block en Celis": De moeizame relatie van de Antwerpse gerechtelijke politie met de Gestapo (1938–1941) – Deel 1', *Cahiers Inlichtingenstudies/Cahiers d'Études du Renseignment* 2, 15–72.

Weber, H. and A. Herbst. 'Walter, Albert Paul', in H. Weber and A. Herbst, *Deutsche Kommunisten: Biographisches Handbuch 1918 bis 1945*, Berlin: Dietz, 2008, 988–989.

Weiss, H. 2009. 'Stockholm – Hamburg – Köpenhamn: Nordeuropeiska noder i Kominterns globala kommunikationsnätverk, 1920–1933', *Historisk Tidskrift för Finland* 2, 139–69.

Yamanouchi, A. 2010. 'The Early Comintern in Amsterdam, New York and Mexico City', *The Journal of History* 147, 99–139.

CHAPTER 13

DANISH CADRES AT THE MOSCOW PARTY SCHOOL, 1958–1960

Chris Holmsted Larsen

Approaching communist studies through a biographical and transnational historical perspective, this chapter investigates the communist Jens Otto Kiærulff Sand's (1915–1984) reflections during his stay at the Moscow Party School (MPS) from 1958 to 1960.[1] The intention is to present a representative picture of the Danish student's everyday life in the Soviet Union and interaction with Soviet society. In fact, it could be argued that Sand's experiences were representative of other Scandinavian communists' encounters with Soviet society. Sand, who had joined the party in the Stalinist high era of the 1930s, was in many ways a representative of the core of Danmarks Kommunistiske Parti (Danish Communist Party, DKP). During the German occupation, he had joined the Danish communist resistance movement Kommunistiske/Borgerlige Partisaner (Communist Partisans, KOPA/BOPA) and after the liberation he remained a dedicated communist who belonged to the upper echelons of the party but never entered the absolute leading inner circles. He did not originate from the middle or upper class, as did party ideologist Ib Nørlund (1917–1989) for example, but he was working class. He had a strong network in the party and was very outspoken in his political critique. After Moscow, he entered the party apparatus as a functionary, but quit because of political differences. In the late 1960s, he rose to become leader of the radical wing of the Vietnam Movement, where he spearheaded a policy that ran counter to his party's more moderate policies. As a consequence he was expelled in 1968, but continued to play a significant political role until the mid 1970s.

Like other political tourists and travellers during the Cold War, Sand met a carefully staged reality – a Potemkin village, which is a spectacle specially prepared in advance or refers to unrepresentative and propagandistic cultural showcases.[2] Sociologist Paul Hollander has described these particular strategies as 'techniques of hospitality' that consisted of two basic ingredients: firstly the screening of reality and the attempt to control what the visitor can see and experience, and second the way the visitor was treated with material and non-material privileges catering to psychological comfort and ego gratification.[3] Cultural showcasing was also utilized elsewhere, but other states were dwarfed by the staged Soviet display of social, economic and cultural power in terms of both scale and sophistication.[4]

In sum, these techniques were a set of tools that the regime applied to ensure that foreigners would go home with a carefully edited version of Soviet reality.[5] Hollander views eastbound political travel as a substitute for religious pilgrimage, but his conclusions were focused on Western intellectuals and not 'ordinary' communists – in other words the working class, which is the focus of this chapter.[6]

As will be argued in this chapter, communist students had better opportunities to form more nuanced impressions of Soviet society than was the case for other visiting political delegations. This was partly due to the longer duration of their stay, which made it difficult to prevent encounters with real Soviet society. This loophole in the staged Potemkin village was furthermore a product of the acquisition of language proficiency. Since all classes were taught in Russian, the students were required to learn the Russian language quickly. Thus, the Danish students were able to communicate with the Soviet population outside the extensive and ideologically managed system of guides and interpreters. Finally, it was expected that foreign communists were able to suppress ideologically unwanted impressions or at least keep these on a confidential level.

Therefore, Scandinavian communists constituted a special category of political travellers. They differed from other delegations and visitors by their relatively uniform communist worldview and they were expected to support the host's projection of so-called 'real existing socialism'. Several cases of Danish political tourists' experiences and reflections are analysed in Iben Vyff's Ph.D. thesis, but this study did not include the special category of communist students, who often stayed in the Soviet Union for a period of one to two years.[7] Predating this study, historian Bent Jensen has argued much along the lines of Hollander – that is, with an outspoken interest in the most extreme cases of 'fellow travellers' lured by the communist utopia.[8] A more nuanced study can be found in Morten Thing's doctoral thesis on Danish communist culture, but again this study is primarily focused on communist intellectuals and not working-class communists.[9] A broader and transnational evaluation of the political and ideological impact of west European communists' political schooling in the Soviet Union, during the Cold War, is still missing.[10]

Background to the Political Schooling Programmes

In 1925, the chairman of the DKP Aksel Larsen (1897–1972) became the first Danish communist to be selected for prolonged schooling at the West University and the International Lenin School (ILS) in Moscow.[11] He was to be the first of hundreds of Danish communists who attended lengthy political schooling in the Soviet Union until the end of the Cold War. In 1961, the Danish Security and Intelligence Service (PET) estimated that around seventy-one Danish communists had been enrolled in special Soviet party schools since 1957.[12] The increased interest that the Danish secret services had in the eastbound travel activity was related to the decision that the Communist Party of the Soviet Union (CPSU) took in 1954 to expand its domestic party school with a special section for its foreign communist allies.[13] This was in effect a revival of the ILS, which, from its creation in 1926 until its closure in 1938, had educated more than 3,500 communist students from fifty-nine different countries.[14]

This revival made it possible for DKP to send selected cadres on longer schooling programmes. After graduation the students would re-enter their national party, where they were expected to strengthen the party apparatus. At the ideological level, the schooling was intended to create a more advanced understanding of the principles of Marxism-Leninism and to strengthen international solidarity. In reality, the end goal was to secure the student's loyalty vis-à-vis the Soviet brand of communism.[15] In 1954, DKP established a schooling committee, which was to strengthen the schooling programmes and ensure the selection of suitable students. Furthermore, it was the committee's responsibility that the cadres would be reinserted into an appropriate function in the party upon their return.

However, it was only after 1956 that it became possible to send cadres on longer courses abroad.[16] This could be seen as an apparent ideological revitalization of the traditions of the Comintern, which had been abolished by Stalin in 1943. This renewed effort in political schooling was closely coordinated between DKP and the CPSU. In recognition of its significance, DKP's international secretary Ib Nørlund was put in charge of the project. As the prime ideologist of the party and a powerful 'grey eminence', this was an obvious choice. Nørlund held a near monopoly on the ideological relations to the CPSU, who in turn regarded him as a never-wavering ally.[17] Party secretary Ingmar Wagner (1921–1997) was tasked with practical matters, which included correspondence with the Soviet embassy and practical arrangements. Ideally, prolonged political schooling should strengthen the organizational skills and ideological values of the party's elite cadres. This was to be achieved not only through indoctrination into the official Soviet version of Marxism-Leninism, but also through professional, social and cultural activities such as visits to model factories and institutions. An understanding of transnational purpose and solidarity would be achieved through fraternal interaction with individuals and groups of other nationalities who attended these special party schools.

It is a difficult task to assess which role these activities played afterwards, both in terms of internal political and organizational developments and regarding the external dynamics of the Cold War. In a Danish context, this has not been the subject of a separate study, but in a larger study of Denmark's position during the Cold War, the Danish Institute for International Studies (DIIS) provided the following overall assessment: 'The importance of the schooling for the communists' political fighting ability in Denmark was relatively great. Based solely on the relatively large number of Danish students who followed these courses, it can be concluded that schooling activities abroad constituted a substantial foundation for DKP'.[18]

In October 1958, Sand and his family arrived in Moscow as part of the second batch of Danish communists who had been given the opportunity to participate in a 12–15 month stay at the MPS.[19] They left Denmark in a special period when their party was struggling for its very survival. Nikita Khrushchev's (1894–1971) 'secret speech' in 1956 had triggered a fierce party struggle between reformists headed by Larsen, and dogmatic communists headed by Nørlund. Eventually, after a prolonged struggle that decimated the party ranks, the dogmatic faction won the upper hand with Soviet support and consolidated their supremacy at the party congress in October 1958. As a consequence, Larsen and the reformist faction were expelled from the party, which was announced in the party paper on 16 November 1958.[20] In February 1959, Larsen responded by founding a new socialist party Socialistisk Folkeparti (Socialist People's Party, SF). The DKP was left in a state of crisis and isolation for the next ten years. After this dramatic showdown, Nørlund needed to assure absolute loyalty from the Danish students in Moscow, who were desperately trying to keep track of the changes back at home.

The sources that have made it possible to recount these experiences are Sand's own letters.[21] These have been preserved by his family and can roughly be divided into three categories. The first category contains the letters sent to his own family, primarily to his daughter who had to return prematurely to Denmark. The second category is those sent to his friends and comrades back home and these are generally unsentimental in tone and marked by friendly familiarity. It is primarily in this category of letters that a critique can be found.[22] The last category of letters consists of reports to Danish party leadership. These letters were handled with secrecy to avoid them being intercepted by PET, and they were carried by personal courier to their destination. These reports are important, because they provide a problem-oriented picture of everyday life for the students. They paint a picture of the problems that Danes experienced in their abrupt encounter with Soviet society. The shortcomings of Soviet life were illuminated further by the fact that Danish communists arrived from a welfare state with a relatively high standard of living, even for the working classes. To complicate matters, the guests had been brought up with a keen eye for identifying political deceit and systemic weaknesses in their home countries.

Sand and his comrades arrived during a significant historical Soviet period. Khrushchev's 'secret speech' in 1956 paved the way for a domestic political thaw and a new generation of apparatchiks who desired to reform Soviet society within a communist framework. These 'children of the twentieth Party Congress' held a rejuvenated belief in a communist future and simultaneously the Soviet Union experienced significant economic growth, which boosted patriotism and gave the Soviet citizen access to more and better consumer goods.[23] The Danish students witnessed this special period from the front row and the optimistic faith in the future affected them. An example is Sand's reflections on the Soviet progress in space, symbolized by sputnik, which was highlighted as evidence of the growing Soviet superiority over the United States and capitalism.[24]

Organizing the Group

Shortly before arrival, Sand was elected spokesperson, meaning that together with two other group members he made up the group's leadership. Sand was a natural choice, since he was the oldest and most experienced. He was also responsible for corresponding with the DKP and acted as a liaison officer in relation to the local authorities.[25]

Ideally, schooling was intended to be a reward to the most promising and best-qualified party members, for example those who possessed good organizational skills and demonstrated leadership potential. But in reality matters were more complicated. In the first report back home, this became evident:

> It is my impression that we must be more careful in the selection of suitable comrades for the future schooling programmes – we should avoid turning this into a skip for flawed characters. I am very well aware of the difficulties in getting people over here … We have comrades here who are in no way capable of ignoring minor problems and who, through petty criticism, have stretched the patience of the entire group.[26]

In the same report, specific problems were described in detail: a comrade was denounced as being a 'drunkard' who was 'hopelessly opposed to collectivism'.[27] Subsequently, Sand recommended dismissal and repatriation, but the school was not thrilled with this solution and neither was the DKP in fact. The problem was that a forced expulsion could damage the overall effort to find sufficient students to fill the national quotas. So, poor communist or not, repatriation was not an option. Five months later, a similar report made its way to Nørlund's desk. Sand described similar problems, but also expressed a more diplomatic understanding of the sensitive issue.[28] Sufficient recruitment was hampered by the problem that very few of those who were of Sand's age and equipped with his experience wished to go abroad. Communists with a sufficient level of human and ideological skills were often working and also had families that they did not want to leave or uproot. Furthermore, they were aware that Soviet living standards could not match life in Denmark, even though being a foreign communist in Moscow was a very privileged existence. Therefore, although these courses were intended for the best, they were in reality less attractive and the quotas were often made up with less-qualified candidates.

Adapting to Soviet Everyday Life

The foreigners' settlement caused numerous problems of both a practical and cultural nature. Sand was no exception, and since he brought his family, Lis and Kira Sand, he was to experience additional problems. After only four months, his fifteen-year-old daughter Kira had to be sent back to her grandparents in Copenhagen. Prior to the Sands' arrival, the hosts had promised that she could attend an international school, but she was dumped in a standard Russian school even though she was unable to speak a single word of Russian. She was not equipped with a school uniform and was expected to attend school for between six and seven hours every day. After several complaints, she was eventually moved to a boarding school, where the only compensation for her linguistic problems was being placed with much younger classmates. She recounted this experience in a later interview: 'It was the most terrible thing that I have ever been exposed to in my entire life. It was terrible, terrible and terrible to a degree which could make you completely anticommunist'.[29]

Her father made a great effort to convince his daughter of the superiority of communism and sought to soothe her bad experiences with the Soviet reality. The failure of his daughter's integration was problematic for Sand, who afterwards had to explain why his family could not bear to live in 'the workers' homeland'.[30] Despite a diplomatic letter to the DKP, he had no illusions regarding the real cause of the problems and in a subsequent letter to a personal friend the tone was different in its straightforwardness:

> Each day, she sits 6 hours in a class together with 38 Russian children and does not understand anything of what is happening. The absolute majority of teachers are rigid and schematic and do not help her settle in at all, which is obviously difficult with 38 other children in the class ... I really don't want her to hate everything Soviet. They had promised to take care of her spare time too (comrades, you know), but this has not happened yet (after 4 months!!).[31]

Again, this indicates that the Danish students were not completely ignorant of the flaws of Soviet society. They were aware, however, that if this criticism was voiced in public, it would immediately be turned against them. Criticism was therefore mostly reserved for correspondence between trusted friends, family and comrades. These problems were not the last, for five months after their arrival Lis Sand was hospitalized because of goitre.[32] Because of this and her daughter's problems, she could no longer follow the lessons at the party school. She was offered an extra holiday or a stay at a sanatorium, but rejected this. Only then was it agreed that she could be prematurely released from the contract.[33] As a consequence of these problems, Sand decided to step down as leader of the group.[34]

Language, Lectures and Teaching

The first obstacle was the Russian language, since mastering this was a precondition for attending the other classes. In his first letter to Nørlund, Sand remarked that there had been some general adjustment difficulties. But although these had been overcome, the language still caused major problems. The opening of the school was set for 10 February 1958 and the first three months were devoted to an intensive language course involving five hours of study per day. Originally, it had been planned that the group would make a longer visit to Leningrad, but this was cut short due to the linguistic problems. Thereafter, the students were divided into four classes of approximately five students each. The intensity of these courses was reduced after the other courses began.

Sand was rather critical of Soviet pedagogy. His female Russian teacher was described as formalistic and schematic, and the hurried pace also received a few critical remarks. The linguistic problems were eventually helped by setting up special classes. On the other hand, according to Sand, there were few problems in relation to the school's leadership, who were described as responsive towards these special problems and needs.[35] But in reality, this relationship was more complicated. Based on an undated evaluation report, it is possible to describe these special problems as well as the students' view of the courses and the course syllabuses.[36]

As for the lessons in Russian language, it was recommended that interpreters should be available to support the students during their initial lessons, which should facilitate a better understanding of basic Russian grammar. In addition, the students were lectured in six other fields and this was regularly supplemented by special lectures, an example of which was Nørlund's lecture in the spring of 1959.[37] The topic of the international labour movement was judged to be good and inspiring, while the topic of constitutional law was described as too broad and a reduction of hours was recommended. The same was the case for courses on the Soviet economy and the Seven-Year Plan, which it was recommended should be changed to tutorial classes. As for the ideological lectures on the history of the CPSU, more class lessons with homework were needed. Political economy was assessed as requiring too much rote learning and, here too, more class lectures and seminars were needed. The last major subject was philosophy, which was experienced as being too comprehensive, and both the structure and content were criticized.[38]

As such, the report was a detailed evaluation regarding the intellectual content and learning benefits and reflected the problems that the students encountered. A central criticism was the alleged insufficiency of the courses and their lack of consistency with Danish reality. This gap was widened by the lack of literature for the courses. It was recommended that children should not be allowed to follow their parents to Moscow – it was simply too problematic. In contrast, housing conditions were described as being satisfactory. Excursions and trips around the Soviet Union, which was a high priority in the effort to install the memory of a progressive and dynamic communist society, were mentioned in favourable terms only. The participants stated that:

> In conclusion, it is generally agreed that those who have had the opportunity to participate in this course feel both stronger and better qualified to return and retake our place in the daily political struggle in Denmark. Insofar as it is possible for us to assess, the teachers and leadership of the school have contributed to a significant strengthening of our ability to understand and apply our theoretical literature ... Given the fact that the group consisted solely of non-intellectual comrades, the completion of the studies must be said to have been quite satisfactory.[39]

The actual value was thus the strengthening of the student's ideological loyalty towards Soviet Marxism-Leninism. In general, the letters leave the impression that the first half of the stay was the best. In the second half, enthusiasm drops to something resembling doubt. The primary cause was personal problems, combined with an understanding of the depressing realities of Soviet life. This included observations of public drunkenness, Russian puritanism and general sloppiness or indifference, which collided culturally with the Danish students' values. Thus, in a personal letter, the relationship to the school's leadership was described in a less positive manner.[40] The recurrent internal clashes and arguments seem mostly to have been motivated by personal differences.[41] Tenacity and the ability to meddle in everything was a prerequisite for being a good Danish communist, but these traits were less appreciated by the Soviet regime, where personal initiative could trigger dire consequences. In a later letter to Nørlund, Sand wrote that the studies had progressed well. But simultaneously, he complained that the students were fatigued and weary because of the rapid pace of the programme.[42]

Among Red Factories and Model Institutions in Leningrad

Sand frequently expressed a strong belief in Khrushchev's reforms and their ability to turn communism into the dominant global ideology:

> When Khrushchev states that the whole world will be communist in 15 years' time, it is obviously not something he just blurts out because he would like it to be so. No, it is because he knows how fast the Soviet Union and other socialist countries are developing. More and more workers and other people are visiting these countries and are witnessing the progress for themselves. At the same time, the capitalists act more and more foolishly in their pursuit of

money. These two things will make all the people of the Earth embrace socialism in a few years' time.[43]

The belief in communist utopia was strong and the prior indoctrination played a central role in this. But just as importantly, this was reinforced by the travelling experiences, which in a symbolic sense became
time travel into the future. As mentioned before, the students were in
Leningrad in early 1959, where they visited factories and institutions.
Afterwards, Sand wrote a report that was heavily influenced by the official propaganda and in which Soviet statistical information regarding the
urban and industrial development was uncritically accepted. Here, the
Soviet authorities were clearly successful in staging a perfect Potemkin
village, which was fully accepted by the students, who saw a world consistent with their own ideological perceptions. The official purpose of
travelling was to visit the Soviet – that is, the local political leadership,
and to inspect a model shoe factory. A strong belief in the rationality of
the Soviet system was outspoken and was highly idealized as if the communist utopia had already occurred.

The visitor's picture of life conditions was uniformly optimistic and
leaves the reader with a highly idealized impression of reality in a major
Soviet city. The visit to the shoe factory, which employed around 10,000
workers, was characterized by the same kind of perceptions. A proud
display of the workers' decorations and awards was highlighted as proof
of the efficiency and capabilities of model factories and the superiority of

Illustration 13.1 Otto Sand in 1959. The picture was taken by his wife Lis Sand
close to Baku in Azerbaijan. Courtesy of Sand's family.

communism. Sand noted that everything seemed imbued with the party and its members, meaning that non-party members acted and spoke as if they were party members as well.[44] It never occurred to him that there hardly were any non-party members and that the visit had been carefully orchestrated in advance.

So why did the Soviet hosts send foreign students who were already well indoctrinated before their arrival on such costly visits, which required so much preparation? In short, they wished to convey and nurture a positive, progressive and caring image of Soviet communism, a projection that demanded loyalty – and here they seem to have succeeded in this endeavour. This is a significant observation, not least because the Scandinavians came straight from social democratic welfare states, with a comparatively high level of prosperity and democratic rights. Despite this, these travel letters portray the Soviet society as superior, a projection that was based on a juxtaposition of a refined Potemkin village and schooled observers who searched for something particular. Despite this being an illusion, it was this impression that the visitors brought back home.

Between Past and Future

During their visit to Leningrad, the Danes wondered aloud and questioned why the Russians placed flowers at the grave of Peter the Great. This conflict over what was communist behaviour was countered by the Russian guide, who responded with a long tirade about the Tsar's astonishing deeds. This only puzzled the Danes further, but eventually the visitors stopped asking questions and a looming political and cultural conflict was suppressed. On the whole, there seems to have been some kind of mental curtain, which could block out unwelcome impressions. Sand was aware of the discrepancy and seems to have considered the reasons for it, but again it was played down as being caused by a lack in understanding:

> To be fair, I must say that our friends are unusually open and straightforward, there is absolutely no secrecy present ... there are of course sides to the reality of this society that the Russians view as something obvious, but which to us can seem a little incomprehensible – until we get an explanation.[45]

Although Sand rarely questioned directly the contrasts between the past and the future, his more common descriptions of religious, ethnic or historical impressions are descriptive of the relationship between the

Russian past and the Soviet future. In the summer of 1959, the Danish students made a longer visit to the Soviet Republics of Georgia and Azerbaijan. Here they travelled around and visited the cities of Sukhumi and Baku plus an additional number of smaller villages. As for the official part of the programme, visits were made to oil refineries and other local model factories and institutions. After returning to Moscow, Sand reported his slightly critical impressions:

> Conversation with the leader of the city's Soviet. The conversation was long and boring and in no way productive ... The visit was an absolute disappointment.[46]

In contrast, a visit to a local Komsomol camp was given a much better review:

> We got an absolutely brilliant reception with brass music and a parade of banners. Everyone received flowers and a pioneer scarf ... the camp treated us with fine food in an absolutely lovely dining hall.[47]

This shows that a feeling of special attention from the hosts mattered a great deal and this could serve to remedy less fortunate experiences. The contrasts between rural life and the modern urban Soviet communities are also part of Sand's travel diaries. But again, these observations are projections of an edited reality in which the past merges with a vision of the future. A visit to a small Azeri village is described as characterized by donkey carts, a slow pace of life and exotic villagers wearing alien ethnic costumes. A conversation with an elderly man, who was described as cheerful and happy, was recounted as evidence of progress:

> In the past, I got whipped by the landowner who tormented all the peasants. But one day, when the workers drove their masters away from the factories, we killed the landowner and ever since then we have been well, because now we are in charge.[48]

A related description reflects upon the complex relationship between traditional gender roles and religious traditions in contrast to the idealized modern and formally egalitarian and atheistic Soviet society:

> Although forty years have passed since socialism was introduced and equal rights for women were achieved ... there are still some of the older women that don't want you to look them in the face. They all wear long veils and when encountering strangers they use them to cover their mouths. It seems difficult to eliminate all the old habits.[49]

Although this was an edited reality, it was not possible to cover up all the cracks. The students' perception of Soviet reality was not only filtered through an ideological communist lens, but was also conditioned by their own ethnicity and national identity. Furthermore, another intriguing prospect was whether the observant perceived this reality as Soviet or Russian. Sand took it for granted that a progressive future would triumph over a reactionary past, but at the same time he admitted that the present looked different from what the political ideals had promised.

Moscow – A Bird's Eye View of a Model Potemkin Village

Although it was expected of him, Sand did not always accept the idealized picture of the Soviet reality. Conflicts arose primarily when the hosts could or would not answer questions that fell outside the prepared framework. Although Sand was predisposed to a critical approach, it is unlikely that his reactions differed much from those of other Danish students, who all came from similar political and cultural backgrounds. Nevertheless, he remained dazzled by the grand display that the hosts put on. The participation in the grand May Day parades on Red Square, which was the prime Soviet projection of its capabilities, made a great impression and he subsequently described it in carefully selected religious terms.[50] Indeed, the visitors' awe at this grand spectacle was no coincidence. Since the early 1930s, the regime had worked to turn Moscow into the visual epiphany of Soviet cultural and spiritual dominance in the world: a 'Fourth Rome'.[51]

Nevertheless, it was not possible to maintain this illusion, since the students lived among ordinary Soviet citizens. It was especially in these encounters that the less fortunate sides to Soviet life surfaced. Systemic flaws such as housing shortage and social calamities made a strong impression on the students, who tried to convince themselves that this would all be solved.[52] Sometimes observations were caused by a special insight that could not be altered by the hosts' preparations. Sand was a worker and took a special pride in his knowledge of materials, trade and the quality of products and he also expected this to be the case for the Soviet workers, but he became enraged when he realized that most were indifferent.[53] On more than one level, this reflects the difficulty in maintaining a perfectly staged Potemkin village in the midst of a dysfunctional society. It thereby also illustrates the abyss that existed between the communist utopia and the harsh reality of Soviet everyday life.

Conclusion

Otto Sand's experiences illustrate a number of the paradoxes and problems that met Western students in their encounters with Soviet society. These students would not and could not openly criticize the general political and ideological root causes of the problems. Criticisms were still expressed on the basis of observations of Soviet everyday life, but these were never voiced in public and critique can primarily be found in letters to personal friends or family. Critique occurred as a result of the interaction with teachers, interpreters and ordinary citizens. Alongside everyday criticism, Sand continued to portray the Soviet society as the ideal future. Hence, the staged impressions had the intended effect, but since the students could not be effectively shielded from the realities of everyday life, they returned home with mixed impressions, which was not consistent with the host's intended purposes and investment. These schooling programmes were thus a double-edged sword for CPSU and the DKP, who could not expect the return of staunch comrades. Accordingly, the DKP had to ensure that the selected students were already stalwart communists who would ignore the Soviet reality. The holidays and excursions were mostly remembered positively.

But despite the fact that the 'hospitality techniques' in general functioned as intended, this conclusion also needs to be nuanced. The case of Otto Sand reveals a more diverse picture. He was not always fooled, but he did regularly choose not to see through the façade of the Potemkin village. He seems to have constructed two mental levels to deal with these impressions and this seems especially to have been the case when personal or cultural conflicts occurred. One level was ideological and public, which is predominant in the official letters to the party leadership back home. The other level, where most of the critique was anchored, was in the letters to close friends and family. Sand was neither an ideologue nor an intellectual, he was a worker and communist and as such he was representative of a relatively silent majority who came into contact with Soviet communism. For political ends, he never publicly spoke about his negative experiences, but he was capable of critique. In contrast to Hollander's description of an uncritical encounter, this paints a less decisive picture of a category of political traveller than previous studies have concluded.

Chris Holmsted Larsen gained his Ph.D. from Roskilde University, where he is an external lecturer at the Department of Communication and Arts, Roskilde University. He has been co-editor of *Arbejderhistorie* since 2007 and was a member of the board of Selskabet til Forskning

i Arbejderbevægelsens Historie (SFAH) 2010–2014. His primary research interests include biography, communism, the Cold War, radicalism and political extremism. He has published, among other work, *Tiden
arbejder for os: DKP og Vietnamkrigen 1963–1973* (2007); *Besetze deine
Stadt! - BZ din by!: Häuserkämpfe und Stadtentwicklung in Kopenhagen*
(2008); and *Datskie kadry Moskvy v stalinskoe vremia* (2013).

Notes

1. For the biographical approach in communist studies, see J. McIlroy, K. Morgan and A.
   Campbell (eds). 2001. *Party People, Communist Lives: Explorations in Biography*, London:
   Lawrence & Wishart, 5–7. See also K. Morgan, G. Cohen and A. Flinn (eds). 2005.
   *Agents of the Revolution: New Biographical Approaches to the History of International
   Communism in the Age of Lenin and Stalin*, Bern: Peter Lang, 13–18.
2. M. David-Fox. 2012. *Showcasing the Great Experiment: Cultural Diplomacy and Western
   Visitors to the Soviet Union 1921–1941*, Oxford: Oxford University Press, 101.
3. P. Hollander. 1997. *Political Pilgrims: Western Intellectuals in Search of the Good Society*,
   New Jersey: Transaction Publishers, 354. Hollander was not the first to study this phenomenon. Predating his study was David Caute's slightly less critical study from 1973, see
   D. Caute. 1973. *The Fellow-Travellers: Intellectual Friends of Communism*, New Haven
   and London: Yale University Press.
4. David-Fox, *Showcasing the Great Experiment*, 98–99.
5. David-Fox, *Showcasing the Great Experiment*, 175–284.
6. For a critique of Hollander's theories see I. Vyff. 2007. '*Øst, Vest – hvilken fremtid er bedst?*
   Danskere på rejse i USA og Sovjetunionen i 1950erne', Ph.D. dissertation, Roskilde:
   Roskilde University, 55–58.
7. Vyff, 'Øst, Vest', 122–218.
8. B. Jensen. 1984. *Stalinismens Fascination og Danske Venstreintellektuelle*, København:
   Lindhardt og Ringhof.
9. M. Thing. 1993. *Kommunismens Kultur: DKP og de intellektuelle 1918–1960*, Århus:
   Tiderne Skifter.
10. These few but important studies deserve to be mentioned, although most of these have
    a national framework and only few of them are available in English. See for example: J.
    Krekola. 1998. 'Praise for Learning: Finnish Communists in the Moscow Party School
    from 1950s to 1970s', in T. Saarela and K. Rentola (eds), *Communism National and
    International*, Helsinki: Finnish Literature Society, 315–28. In a Danish context, only one
    relevant contribution has been published so far, namely K.H. Nielsen. 2008. 'På skoling
    i Øst-blokken', *Arbejderhistorie* 1, 16–36. See also J. Krekola. 2006. *Stalinismin lyhyt
    kurssi: Suomalaiset Moskovan Lenin-koulussa 1926–1938*, Helsinki: University of Helsinki;
    for a summary in English see J. Krekola. 2007. 'A Short Course of Stalinism. Finns at the
    International Lenin School, Moscow 1926–1938', *Communist History Network Newsletter*
    20(XIII), 134–35; O.M. Rønning. 2010. 'Stalins elever: Komintern kadrerskoler og
    Norges Kommunistiske Parti 1926–1949', Ph.D. dissertation, Oslo: University of Oslo;
    J. Köstenberger. 2007. 'Die Internationale Lenin-Schule (1926–1938)', in M. Buckmiller
    and K. Meschkat (eds), *Biographisches Handbuch zur Geschichte der kommunistischen
    Internationale: Ein deutsch-russisches Forschungsprojekt*, Berlin: Akademie Verlag, 287–
    310; for the entire study, see J. Köstenberger. 2010. 'Die Geschichte der internationalen
    Leninschule in Moskau (1926–1938)', Ph.D. dissertation, Wien: Universität Wien. See
    also G. Cohen and K. Morgan. 2002. 'Stalin's Sausage Machine: British Students at the

International Lenin School 1926–37', *Twentieth Century British History* 13(4), 327–55; A. Campbell, J. McIlroy, B. McLouglin and J. Halstead. 2004. 'The International Lenin School: A Response to Cohen and Morgan', *Twentieth Century British History* 15(1), 51–76; G. Cohen and K. Morgan. 2004. 'British Students at the International Lenin School 1926–37: A Reaffirmation of Methods, Results, and Conclusions', *Twentieth Century British History* 15(1), 77–107; A. Campbell, J. McIlroy, B. McLouglin and J. Halstead. 2004. 'British Students at the International Lenin School: The Vindication of a Critique', *Twentieth Century British History* 16(4), 471–88.

11. K. Jacobsen. 1993. *Aksel Larsen: en politisk biografi*, København: Vindrose, 54, 67.
12. PET-Kommissionens beretning. 2009. 'PET's overvågning af Danmarks Kommunistiske Parti 6', 307. See: http://jm.schultzboghandel.dk/upload/microsites/jm/ebooks/pet/pet_bind6/index.html. Retrieved 1 November 2016.
13. According to K.H. Nielsen, the decision to expand the party school was taken in 1956, but according to Krekola the Finns were already invited in 1954. K.H. Nielsen. 2008. *Giv mig de rene og ranke*, København: SFAH, 254; Krekola, 'Praise for Learning', 316.
14. Köstenberger, 'Die Internationale Lenin-Schule', 287.
15. PET Kommissionens beretning 6, 300–308.
16. DIIS. 2005. 'Denmark During the Cold War 1963–1978', vol. 2, 331.
17. Ib Nørlund's personal file, Comintern-archive, RGASPI.
18. DIIS, 'Denmark During the Cold War 1963–1978', 332–33.
19. For a complete biography of Otto Sand see C.H. Larsen. 2009. 'Solidaritet, ikke almisser: Kommunisten og mennesket Otto Sand 1915–1984', *Arbejdermuseet & Arbejderbevægelsens Bibliotek og Arkivs Årbog*, 56–81; C.H. Larsen. 2011. 'Kursist på den Internationale Leninskole 1958–60', *Arbetarhistoria Arbejderhistorie* 137(1), 50–59.
20. K. Jacobsen, *Aksel Larsen*, 519–623.
21. These letters are today preserved by Otto Sand's daughter to whom I owe great gratitude for giving me access to this valuable material.
22. Quotes have been translated from Danish to English by the author.
23. V.M. Zubok. 2007. *A Failed Empire: The Soviet Union in the Cold War from Stalin to Gorbachev*, Chapel Hill: University of North Carolina Press, 179–91.
24. Letter to Kira Sand, 1 October 1959 and 9 November 1959.
25. Letter to the DKP, dated 16 December 1958.
26. Letter to the DKP, dated 16 December 1958.
27. Letter to the DKP, dated 16 December 1958.
28. Letter to Ib Nørlund, 27 April 1959.
29. Interview with Kira Sand, 11 June 2009.
30. Letter to Nørlund, dated 27 April 1959.
31. Letter to Helge Blicher Hansen, 20 March 1959.
32. Letter to Hansen, 15 March 1959.
33. Letter to Ingmar Wagner and Nørlund, 5 October 1959.
34. Letter to Ingmar Wagner and Nørlund, 5 October 1959.
35. Letter to the DKP, 6 December 1958.
36. Evaluation of schooling programme 1958–1960, DKP schooling committee, undated.
37. Until his death in 1991, Nørlund remained the most important person in the DKP and one of the most important persons in the West European communist parties. His sharp ideological skills, combined with a never faltering support for and ability to understand Soviet political and ideological developments, earned him high esteem in the Kremlin. Nørlund was from 1965 co-editor of the highly influential Soviet ideological journal *Problems of Peace and Socialism* (the English version was titled *World Marxist Review*).
38. Evaluation of schooling programme 1958–1960, DKPs schooling committee, undated.
39. Evaluation of schooling programme 1958–1960, DKPs schooling committee, undated.
40. Letter to Hansen, 20 March 1959.

41. Letter to Gudmund, 22 February 1959.
42. Letter to Wagner, dated 4 September 1959, and letter to Nørlund, 5 October 1959.
43. Letter to Kira, 14 September 1959.
44. Letter to Kira, 14 September 1959.
45. Letter to Kira, 14 September 1959.
46. Undated diary, summer 1959.
47. Undated diary, summer 1959.
48. Letter to Kira, 29 July 1959.
49. Letter to Kira, 29 July 1959.
50. Letter to Hansen, 9 May 1959.
51. K. Clark. 2011. *Moscow – The Fourth Rome: Stalinism, Cosmopolitanism, and the Evolution of Soviet Culture 1931–1941*, Harvard: Harvard University Press, 15–21.
52. Letter to Hansen, 9 May 1959.
53. Letter to Hansen, 9 May 1959.

References

Campbell, A., J. McIlroy, B., McLouglin and J. Halstead. 2004. 'British Students at the International Lenin School: The Vindication of a Critique', *Twentieth Century British History* 16(4), 471–88.

_____. 2004. 'The International Lenin School: A Response to Cohen and Morgan', *Twentieth Century British History* 15(1), 51–76.

Caute, D. 1973. *The Fellow-Travellers: Intellectual Friends of Communism*, New Haven and London: Yale University Press.

Clark, K. 2011. *Moscow – The Fourth Rome: Stalinism, Cosmopolitanism, and the Evolution of Soviet Culture 1931–1941*, Harvard: Harvard University Press.

Cohen, G. and K. Morgan. 2002. 'Stalin's Sausage Machine: British Students at the International Lenin School 1926–37', *Twentieth Century British History* 13(4), 327–55.

_____. 2004. 'British Students at the International Lenin School 1926–37: A Reaffirmation of Methods, Results, and Conclusions', *Twentieth Century British History* 15(1), 77–107.

David-Fox, M. 2012. *Showcasing the Great Experiment: Cultural Diplomacy and Western Visitors to the Soviet Union 1921–1941*, Oxford: Oxford University Press.

DIIS. 2005. 'Denmark During the Cold War 1963–1978', vol. 2, 331. Hollander, P. 1997. *Political Pilgrims: Western Intellectuals in Search of the Good Society*, New Jersey: Transaction Publishers.

Jacobsen, K. 1993. *Aksel Larsen: en politisk biografi*, København: Vindrose.

Jensen, B. 1984. *Stalinismens Fascination og Danske Venstreintellektuelle*, København: Lindhardt og Ringhof.

Krekola, J. 'Praise for Learning: Finnish Communists in the Moscow Party School from 1950s to 1970s', in T. Saarela and K. Rentola (eds), *Communism National and International*, Helsinki: Finnish Literature Society, 1998, 315–28.

_____. 2006. *Stalinismin lyhyt kurssi: Suomalaiset Moskovan Lenin-koulussa 1926–1938*, Helsinki: University of Helsinki.

———. 2007. 'A Short Course of Stalinism: Finns at the International Lenin School, Moscow 1926–1938', *Communist History Network Newsletter* 20(XIII), 134–35.

Köstenberger, J. 'Die Internationale Lenin-Schule (1926–1938)', in M. Buckmiller and K. Meschkat (eds), *Biographisches Handbuch zur Geschichte der kommunistischen Internationale: Ein deutsch-russisches Forschungsprojekt*, Berlin: Akademie Verlag, 2007, 287–310.

———. 2010. 'Die Geschichte der internationalen Leninschule in Moskau (1926–1938)', Ph.D. dissertation, Wien: Universität Wien.

Larsen, C.H. 2009. 'Solidaritet, ikke almisser: Kommunisten og mennesket Otto Sand 1915–1984', *Arbejdermuseet & Arbejderbevægelsens Bibliotek og Arkivs Årbog*, 56–81.

———. 2011. 'Kursist på den Internationale Leninskole 1958–60', *Arbetarhistoria Arbejderhistorie* 137(1), 50–59.

McIlroy, J., K. Morgan and A. Campbell (eds). 2001. *Party People, Communist Lives: Explorations in Biography*, London: Lawrence & Wishart.

Morgan, K., G. Cohen and A. Flinn (eds). 2005. *Agents of the Revolution: New Biographical Approaches to the History of International Communism in the Age of Lenin and Stalin*, Bern: Peter Lang.

Nielsen, K.H. 2008. *Giv mig de rene og ranke*, København: SFAH.

———. 2008. 'På skoling i Øst-blokken', *Arbejderhistorie* 1, 16–36.

PET-Kommissionens beretning. 2009. 'PET's overvågning af Danmarks Kommunistiske Parti 6', 307. See: http://jm.schultzboghandel.dk/upload/microsites/jm/ebooks/pet/pet_bind6/index.html. Retrieved 1 November 2016.

Rønning, O.M. 2010. 'Stalins elever: Kominterns kadrerskoler og Norges Kommunistiske Parti 1926–1949', Ph.D. dissertation, Oslo: University of Oslo.

Thing, M. 1993. *Kommunismens Kultur: DKP og de intellektuelle 1918–1960*, Århus: Tiderne Skifter.

Vyff, I. 2007. '*Øst, Vest – hvilken fremtid er bedst? Danskere på rejse i USA og Sovjetunionen i 1950erne*', Ph.D. dissertation, Roskilde: Roskilde University.

Zubok, V.M. 2007. *A Failed Empire: The Soviet Union in the Cold War from Stalin to Gorbachev*, Chapel Hill: University of North Carolina Press.

INDEX

International Studies in Social History

General Editor: Marcel van der Linden

Published under the auspices of the International Institute of Social History, Amsterdam, this series offers transnational perspectives on labor and working-class history. For a long time, labor historians have been working within national interpretive frameworks. But interest in studies contrasting different national and regional experiences and studying cross-border interactions has been increasing in recent years. This series is designed to act as a forum for these new approaches.

Lightning Source UK Ltd.
Milton Keynes UK
UKHW021203020220
358006UK00018B/531